CHILDREN
IN A VIOLENT SOCIETY

Children
in a Violent Society

Edited by

JOY D. OSOFSKY

Foreword by PETER SCHARF

THE GUILFORD PRESS
New York London

© 1997 The Guilford Press
A Division of Guilford Publications, Inc.
72 Spring Street, New York, NY 10012

Printed in the United States of America

This book is printed on acid-free paper.

Last digit is print number: 9 8 7 6 5 4 3

Library of Congress Cataloging-in-Publication Data

Children in a violent society / edited by Joy D. Osofsky : foreword by
    Peter Scharf.
        p.   cm.
    Includes bibliographical references and index.
    ISBN 1-57230-183-x —ISBN 1-57230-387-5 (pbk.)
    1. Children and violence—United States.   2. Children—United
States—Crimes against.   3. Children—United States—Crimes against—
Prevention.   4. City, children—United States.   5. Victims of
crimes—Services for—United States.   I. Osofsky, Joy D.
HQ784.V55C448   1997
303.6'083—dc21   97-1893
                                                                          CIP

Contributors

Anne Adelman, Ph.D., Child Study Center, School of Medicine, Yale University, New Haven, CT

Carl C. Bell, M.D., School of Medicine and School of Public Health, University of Illinois; Community Mental Health Council, Inc., Chicago, IL

Katherine Kaufer Christoffel, M.D., M.P.H., Children's Memorial Hospital, Chicago, IL

Ana C. Fick, Ph.D., Department of Psychiatry, School of Medicine, Louisiana State University, New Orleans, LA

Peter Fonagy, Ph.D., Department of Psychology, University College London; Anna Freud Centre, London, UK

James Garbarino, Ph.D., Family Life Development Center, Cornell University, Ithaca, NY

Betsy McAllister Groves, M.S.W., Boston Medical Center, School of Medicine, Boston University, Boston, MA

C. Boyd James, M.D., Department of Psychiatry and Human Development, Charles Drew University, Los Angeles, CA

Esther J. Jenkins, Ph.D., Department of Psychology, Chicago State University; Community Mental Health Council, Inc., Chicago, IL

Pamela Jenkins, Ph.D., Department of Sociology, University of New Orleans, New Orleans, LA

Kathleen Kostelny, Ph.D., Erikson Institute for Advanced Study in Child Development, Chicago, IL

Marva L. Lewis, Ph.D., School of Social Work, Tulane University, New Orleans, LA

Steven Marans, Ph.D., Child Study Center, School of Medicine, Yale University, New Haven, CT

Mary Sue Moore, Ph.D., Child and Family Department, Tavistock Clinic, London; Clinical Faculty, Psychology Department, University of Colorado, Boulder, CO

Lisa Murphy, Ph.D., Clinical Associate, Trauma Psychiatry Program, University of California, Los Angeles, Los Angeles, CA

John P. Murray, Ph.D., Department of Human Development and Family Studies, Kansas State University, Manhattan, KS

Joy D. Osofsky, Ph.D., Departments of Pediatrics and Psychiatry, School of Medicine, Louisiana State University, New Orleans, LA

Bruce D. Perry, M.D., Baylor College of Medicine, Houston, TX

Robert S. Pynoos, M.D., Director, Trauma Psychiatry Program, University of California, Los Angeles, Los Angeles, CA

Peter Scharf, Ph.D., Center for Society, Law, and Justice, University of New Orleans, Metairie, LA

Michael S. Scheeringa, M.D., Kennedy Krieger Institute, School of Medicine, Johns Hopkins University, Baltimore, MD

Ruth Seydlitz, Ph.D., Department of Sociology, University of New Orleans, New Orleans, LA

Howard Steele, Ph.D., Department of Psychology, University College London, London, UK

Miriam Steele, Ph.D., Department of Psychology, University College London; Anna Freud Centre, London, UK

Mary Target, Ph.D., Department of Psychology, University College London; Anna Freud Centre, London, UK

Charles H. Zeanah, M.D., Department of Psychiatry, School of Medicine, Louisiana State University, New Orleans, LA

Barry Zuckerman, M.D., Boston Medical Center, School of Medicine, Boston University, Boston, MA

Foreword

This very finely woven and crafted book alters the discussion of the many dimensions of violence toward children, its long-term impact, and some ways that police, social agencies, psychologists, and community helping institutions can ameliorate it. The book is unusual in that it will be useful to many different audiences.

First, it provides a broad description of the problem of children and violence for academic professional readers; it had a personal impact on me. Not many years ago, I had dinner with an African American police chief friend of mine and his wife. The police chief was late (it is a vocational consequence), and his wife and I chatted until he arrived. With tears in her eyes, she told me the story of how her son had sat (in a *good* city school) through a math class while another student (as a joke) poked him in the back with a loaded MAK 15 automatic weapon (which requires only the talent of a spray paint operator to kill). She spoke of her fear that her son would not reach adulthood. Support for her fear is evident in this book. African American males aged 1–19 are far more likely to die of gunshot wounds than any other group.

The reality of violence in the lives of inner-city children is an important fact the reader will confront in these pages. In winter 1993, I found myself on a ride-along with the police—with a vest, thank you—near the Barry Farms (one of the most violent housing projects in Washington, DC). I witnessed two violent incidents that evening. In the first, from the car I was in, I observed as Howard, a young drug dealer, was shot in the leg as a warning by another drug crew member, whose turf had been invaded by Howard's crew. He dragged himself up to his apartment and lying in trauma pants (dress du jour in this part of the city), was watched by his brothers and sisters, ages 4–16, as the medics attempted to save his life. It was the memory of the unforgettable silence of these children that returned to me as I read through the chapters of the first section in Joy Osofsky's book. It is a painful memory, but it provides a useful caution in attempting to empathize with how children interpret these events—the heart of the effort of this book.

In the second incident that evening, we responded to a call that there had been a cross fire of about 40 rounds. The comment of my escort was that this was about normal for the residents of Barry Farms (and the Taylor Homes in Chicago, and, until recently, the Desire project in New Orleans, etc.). Again, this memory returned when I read the chapters in this book. Statistical analysis at one point suggested that an adolescent male living in the Barry Farms had a greater mortality risk than a Vietnam soldier faced in a year of service in all but 2 years of the 15-year Vietnam conflict.

Another type of reader who will be fascinated by the information in this volume is anyone interested in criminology or criminal psychology. During the week I was reading the manuscript, I was visited by a friend, a commander of the Green River Task Force in Seattle, who was consulting with our team of criminologists at the University of New Orleans. He is a veteran of efforts to solve 60 murders in Seattle and also was part of the successful effort to identify Ted Bundy. He looked at this manuscript and commented, "The only way that someone could kill like this [as the serial killer he was investigating had] was if someone had shown him some terrible hurt as a child." For the killers he had investigated over the years, and the many more suspects, violence during childhood was a common theme: seeing a parent shot in a living room, child sexual abuse, the murder of a playmate. It is believed that Ted Bundy was sexually abused as a child and that he killed a Tacoma playmate while he was still in elementary school.

The theme of the first section, multiple impacts of violence, is a critical issue for any reader of this book to confront. Although the serial killer is an extreme case, the book suggests that the dreadful consequences of violence, experienced at an early age are difficult to determine, may lead to violence later, and are essential to understand in any serious effort at psychological explanation of criminal violence.

It should be noted that in these chapters there are many contributions that build on recent findings and interpretations of the rise in the rate of criminal violence. What, for example, is the impact of domestic abuse and sexual abuse on later criminal violence? What is the role of media violence, gun availability, fear of random violence?

Developmental psychologists will find much to appreciate in this book. The theme, in several chapters, that it is essential for us to understand the child's cognitive interpretation of violence is supported by almost all developmental psychologists interested in criminal outcomes. I found my own research on moral judgment and crime amplified by the contributions in Dr. Osofsky's book. Delinquents who have observed violent acts are often found to be of a lower moral stage and often have a gap between their highest cognitive level and their reasoning about moral or affective issues. A young man who had murdered a friend expressed *some* form of regret, but not much: "I felt badly, like you eat something bad at McDonald's." This is an example of a level of moral development that can become lethal (stage zero or 1 in Kohlberg's six-stage typology).

That violence experienced by children must be understood from the child's view of the world builds on earlier work by developmental psychologists on the etiology of violence. How kids' generalizations about events they perceive fit into their later constructions of reality is a powerful question posed by this volume. Also explored are the many ways that violence may be interpreted by children, and this is an important advance.

This book also belongs in the professional library of anyone concerned with preventing violence on the community level, as Joy Osofsky and others have done, to offer methods for prevention and postintervention to children who witness or are victims of violence.

The second section of the book, dealing with these prevention and postintervention strategies, offers important considerations for the police, those in social services, and psychologists. Most broadly, it is important to understand that different professional groups use different terms to describe approaches that are actually similar. For example, community mental health and public health concerns with primary, secondary, and tertiary prevention of violence are compatible with the longer term prevention strategies presented in this volume that embed sustained community violence prevention and postintervention in multiple time frames.

For those interested in community policing, this volume is a gold mine of information that extends many of community policing's core concepts. The notion of problem solving in community policing is one of these. Problem solving is an approach described by Herman Goldstein (1990) in which the police analyze the factors that cause crimes to occur and then act to reduce these conditions.

This volume's contributions to a conception of problem solving in community policing lie in four areas. First, community policing requires a 10- to 20-year perspective. Intervention with children who experience violence is probably essential to any longer-term solution to the crime epidemic. One police chief with whom I discussed this manuscript likened the process to the reduction in smoking. Fifteen years ago, it was "cool" to smoke on a date. Today, a date might end early if one took out a pack of Marlboro cigarettes, reflecting a slow but steady change in attitudes.

Second, community policing, as all smart beat cops know, is about children. We are playing for the "10-year-olds." "If they trust you, we win. If they don't, we lose," said one successful officer, who targeted his COP (community-oriented policing) efforts at school children.

Third, safe communities are developmentally productive communities as well. The New Orleans Desire Housing Project, a community policing effort commanded by Lt. Eddie Compass, offers an example of how the focus of the book can be used in practice. Two years ago, the project was a drug-dealing hell with 19 homicides in a year. Today, one sees children playing basketball in the evening with police officers, older males mentoring and protecting adolescents in positive ways, and a sense of safety that allows both community and psychological processes to begin to flourish.

Finally, community policing requires a psychological approach similar to the type presented in this volume. Preventing crime requires a broad understanding of the ways that criminal patterns are formed, and that is very effectively presented here.

PETER SCHARF, Ph.D.
Center for Society, Law, and Justice
University of New Orleans

REFERENCE

Goldstein, H. (1990). *Problem-oriented policing*. Philadelphia: Temple University Press.

Acknowledgments

This book evolved out of my experience in working with children and families who live with violence every day of their lives and my commitment to learning more about what can be done at many levels for children traumatized by violence. The colleagues who have contributed chapters for this book have provided inspiration for me and my team as we all continue with the often tedious and trying but needed efforts toward violence prevention. All agreed to contribute enthusiastically when I told them I was doing the book, and I am very grateful to the authors for the time and enormous effort that went into all of the excellent chapters. I want to recognize several people individually who played key roles in making this book a reality. First, I want to thank Emily Fenichel and Beverly Jackson of Zero to Three, the National Center for Infants, Toddlers, and Families, for their inspiration and belief in the work that we initiated in New Orleans for violence prevention, especially directed toward very young children, and their encouragement through the Violence Prevention Task Force of that organization. Second, Seymour Weingarten, Editor in Chief of The Guilford Press, has been available and interested in the work that I do. He was enthusiastic about this idea, offered helpful suggestions, and was patient and encouraging as it progressed. Third, I want to thank my team in New Orleans, Marva Lewis, Michael Rovaris, Ana Fick, and Bridget Scott, who have worked so diligently with the children, community residents, police, and schools since we initiated our project in 1992. Without their dedication to the difficult violence prevention, intervention, and treatment work that is part of the Violence Intervention Project for Children and Families, our program could not exist. A special thanks to Bridget Scott for her conscientious efforts with the tedious job of helping to finalize the chapters. Finally, I want to thank my family—my husband Howard, my daughter Hari, and my sons Justin and Michael—for their patience and understanding while I put this book together and for their support, help, and empathy related to the work that I do with children and families traumatized by violence. Funding for a portion of my time and for the VIP program was provided by the Entergy Corporation, Baptist Community Ministries of New Orleans, Institute of Mental Hygiene, Booth Bricker Fund, Greater New Orleans Foundation, Brown Foundation, Frost Foundation, Jones Family Foundation, Bell South Mobility, and other anonymous donors.

JOY D. OSOFSKY

Contents

II PREVENTION AND INTERVENTION PROGRAMS FOR CHILDREN AND FAMILIES EXPOSED TO VIOLENCE

I

SCOPE OF THE PROBLEM

IN THE FIRST PART OF the book, the authors present an overview of the incidence, scope, and impact of children and youth violence. After my brief overview of the issues, Esther J. Jenkins and Carl C. Bell introduce the volume with a comprehensive perspective on children's exposure to violence and the ways it can impact on them. James Garbarino and Kathleen Kostelny expand this view by discussing children exposed to violence during war, in addition to the violence that occurs in "urban war zones." Katherine Kaufer Christoffel presents a very important perspective on the extent of firearm injuries affecting children and adolescents in the United States, a topic too often overlooked by a large proportion of the general public that supports relatively free access to guns. Another important and until recently overlooked negative influence on children is media violence. John P. Murray has traced the history of reactions to violence in the media, what has been done in the past, and what might or should be done in this area in the future.

In understanding the scope of the problem, it is also important to focus on developmental issues related to violence exposure. Charles H. Zeanah and Michael S. Scheeringa present an important chapter on the effects of violence exposure in infancy, and Bruce D. Perry discusses in his chapter the important, but frequently overlooked, neurodevelopmental effects of children's exposure to violence. The final chapter in the first section by Peter Fonagy, Mary Target, Miriam Steele, and Howard Steele focuses on developmental factors, specifically the early attachment relationship between parent and child, that may influence the ability of the child to develop meaningful relationships in later life as well as contribute to later violent behaviors.

1

Children and Youth Violence: An Overview of the Issues

JOY D. OSOFSKY

> April 29, 1994
>
> Dear Mr. Clinton,
>
> *I want you to stop the killing in the city. People is dead and I think that somebody might kill me. Would you please stop the people from deading. I'm asking you nicely to stop it. I know you can do it. Do it now. I know you can.*
>
> Your friend,
>
> James

While walking home from a picnic with his family on Mother's Day, James Darby, 9 years old, was brutally and senselessly gunned down in a drive-by shooting 9 days after writing this letter to President Clinton.

PEOPLE MUST OPEN THEIR EYES. The United States is the most violent country in the industrialized world, with violence having reached epidemic proportions as we approach the end of the 20th century. Homicide is the second leading cause of death among all 15- to 24-year-olds, and is now the third leading cause of death among elementary school children, ages 5–14. The rate of known homicide offenders ages 14–17 has climbed from 16.2 per 100,000 youngsters in 1990 to 19.1 per 100,000 in 1994 (Herbert, 1996). A poll by Louis Harris and Associates of 2,000 teenagers from around the country (including suburban and rural areas) found that one in eight youths, and almost two in five from

3

high-violence neighborhoods, said they carried a weapon for protection. One in nine, and more than one in three in high-violence neighborhoods, said they had cut class or stayed away from school because of fear of crime (Appelbone, 1996).

And yet, most citizens of our country, while expressing fear and anger about the growing level of violence among juveniles (while adult violence has actually decreased), fail to either acknowledge or address the fact that witnessing violence and violence exposure can have a very negative impact on all people, and especially children, who are most vulnerable. Children learn what they see—and unfortunately, in our country through news reports, movies and television, and everyday life in many parts of our country, children see violence; and they do not learn that violence is bad. Too often, they learn that violence is an acceptable way to resolve conflict; furthermore, many children, because of their home and neighborhood environments, have little opportunity to learn about alternative ways to settle disputes. What can be done immediately and for the future? This issue is the topic of this book.

It is also time to acknowledge that prevention and intervention strategies represent crucial steps to stem this potentially overwhelming tide of violence in our country, even more so because of the demographic situation facing the United States. Despite the recent decrease in homicide levels in the past few years (1994–1995), overall there has been increase in homicides in the past decade, which has occurred with a teenage population that is smaller than it has been in recent years. Furthermore, the current generation of teenagers is only a fraction of the size of the much larger group of 5- to 15-year-olds who will soon be moving into the crime-prone teenage years. Thus, a consideration of prevention and intervention is not only crucial to address current soaring levels of violence, but also to curb the expected large increases as this younger age group reaches midadolescence. Some have concluded that we have lost a "generation of children." However, there is no need to assume that we must continue "losing generations" and turn our backs on issues of prevention and intervention.

What has been our society's focus regarding prevention and intervention? Unfortunately, too often it has been solely the criminal justice approach. By 1995, there were 1.5 million people incarcerated in state and federal prisons and in local jails around the country. Another 100,000 youths were confined in juvenile detention centers and institutions. The numbers of people who are in jail have tripled in the past two decades. And yet, with growing number of people in jail, do we see the level of crime decreasing? Unfortunately, the situation is just the opposite, with the numbers of jails increasing and the crime level also increasing. For our interests in children and youth violence, we see little evidence that prison deters crime, particularly for young people coming from poor neighborhoods with high levels of crime and violence. Furthermore, there is considerable evidence that the criminal justice solutions are very expensive, much more so than putting a sufficient portion of resources into providing quality education and early preventive intervention.

What is causing the increase in violence? Fox Butterfield (1995), in *All God's Children: The Bosket Family and the American Tradition of Violence*, a book about the American heritage of violence as shown through the tradition reflected in the experiences of one African American family, the Boskets, from the days of slavery to the present, emphasizes that we are confronted with a dilemma in trying to understand the current level of violence in the United States. He says:

> The very things that helped lower rates of violence in the past have become more difficult for us to reapply. . . . It is no coincidence that the centuries-long decline in murder rates was reversed during the 1960s, not only in the United States but also in Europe. Something fundamental changed. The sixties was the decade in which we cast off the long-accumulated rules of self-control for an exaltation of the individual, a "fatal liberty," as noted by de Toqueville many years ago. (p. 326)

There is little question that in the United States, instead of focusing on the needs of children for quality education, economic opportunities, safe and good homes, and loving families, all of which go a long way toward preventing violence, we more quickly opt for punishment after the fact. There is overwhelming evidence that many of the adolescents and young adults who first become delinquent and later develop into criminals were exposed earlier in their lives to much violence, disorganized families, poor education, and limited opportunities. What is needed is a shift in thinking and behaving within our society from people isolating themselves and not caring or taking the easy way out, to people working together, taking responsibility for others, and helping children develop the values and respect that comes from within families and community. In order to achieve such goals, the external society must be supportive and make a commitment to changing media values communicated to children, providing economic opportunities and other options for youth, applying stricter gun control and responsibility policies, and changing general attitudes to make violence unpopular, unappealing, and even unacceptable for the majority of people. I will return to proposals for public policy changes in the final chapter after we review research, prevention, and intervention programs, and treatment for children who are exposed to and witness violence.

A DEVELOPMENTAL PERSPECTIVE

In this volume, we will be taking a developmental perspective to understand the impact of violence exposure and witnessing violence on children and youth, as well as in searching for solutions. We know that early referral of a child who has witnessed violence and is showing symptoms makes an enormous difference in outcomes for the child and the family. We also know that early preventive intervention efforts that are community-based involving parents, schools, churches, and community centers help children, families, and communities deal with the traumas that they experience in their lives more effectively and build strength within communities and families.

The impact on children of exposure to violence depends on many factors, including the age of the child, frequency and type of violence exposure, characteristics of the neighborhood (including degree of community resources), amount and quality of support provided by caregivers and other significant adults, experience of previous trauma, proximity to the violent event, and familiarity with the victim or perpetrator. How much a child perceives or remembers a violent experience affects the presence or absence of symptoms and the circumstances under which they are likely to occur (Drell, Siegel, & Gaensbauer, 1993).

Adolescent problems, including delinquency and violence following an earlier history of witnessing violence, are most visible in both the literature and the media. Less well known are the problems that are seen frequently in younger children who witness violence; furthermore, little attention has been given to their traumatized parents. In fact, many people assume that very young children are not affected at all, erroneously believing that they are too young to know or remember what has happened. Although very young children may be partially protected and not fully appreciate the potential danger, it is important that we neither ignore nor deemphasize their reactions to violence. Numerous studies have documented that even young children are likely to exhibit emotional distress, more immature behavior, somatic complaints, and regressions in toileting and language (Drell et al., 1993; Pynoos, 1993; Osofsky, 1995). Recent reports have even noted the presence of symptoms very similar to posttraumatic stress disorder in adults, including repeated reexperiencing of the traumatic event, avoidance, numbing of responsiveness, and increased arousal (Pynoos, 1993; Zeanah, 1994; Scheeringa, Zeanah, Drell, & Larrieu, 1995). School-age children are likely to understand more about the intentionality of the violence. They may wonder what they could have done to prevent or stop it, and they may also exhibit symptoms akin to posttraumatic stress disorder. Several sources have reported that school-aged children who witness violence often show a greater frequency of externalizing (aggressive, delinquent) and internalizing (withdrawn, anxious) behavior problems in comparison to children who do not witness violence. Overall functioning, attitudes, social competence, and school performance are often affected negatively (Pynoos, 1993; Osofsky, 1995).

For adolescents, particularly those who have experienced violence exposure throughout their lives, high levels of aggression and acting out are common, accompanied by anxiety, behavior problems, school problems, truancy, and revenge seeking. Although some adolescents who witness violence may be able to overcome the experience, many others suffer considerable scars. Some report giving up hope, expecting that they may not live through adolescence or early adulthood. They may become deadened to feelings and pain, with resultant constrictions in emotional development. Or they may attach themselves to peer groups or gangs as substitute family and incorporate violence as a method of dealing with disputes or frustration (Pynoos, 1993; Bell & Jenkins, 1993).

It is important to note that since so much violence children witness takes place in their own homes, whatever protective influence a lack of understanding of violence or the support from parents or caregivers may afford the very young child appears to fail when severe trauma occurs, for example, when the child witnesses the murder of a parent. In our work, we have found that both parents and police perceive witnessing violence against a parent to have a much greater impact on a child than violence against a stranger. Our data indicate further that children are likely to show the strongest negative reactions when violence involves a parent or caregiver (Osofsky, Fick, Flowers, & Lewis, 1995). The child's vulnerability to violence exposure may be compounded by the parent's own response to violence—as witness or victim. Parents who realize they may not be able to protect their children from violence are likely to feel anxious, frustrated, and helpless (Osofsky & Fenichel, 1994). Such parents may fear for their own safety as well as that of their children, and may have difficulty being emotionally available and responsive to them. Individual and community support can be very helpful to such parents.

WHAT CAN BE DONE AND WHERE ARE THE SOLUTIONS?

In this volume, some of the best "solutions" to the violence problem are presented in terms of prevention and intervention efforts. Broader, more comprehensive "solutions" lie in the public policy arena and involve preventive efforts and resources being allocated for efforts and programs for much younger children and families than those who perpetrate the violence and contribute to the epidemic-level statistics. The book has been divided into two sections, with the first presenting information on the scope of the problem of children and youth violence, and the second describing several innovative prevention and intervention programs for children and families exposed to violence. It is important for the reader to be aware of the fact that important prevention and intervention work is going on in many major cities in the United States, as will be described in the second section of the book. Although the emphasis has been put on early preventive intervention, criminal justice perspectives are included in an effort for the two approaches to work together to search for solutions to the growing problem of children and youth violence. Neither our children nor our country can wait any longer.

REFERENCES

Appelbone, P. (1996, January 12). Crime fear is seen forcing changes in youth behavior. *New York Times*, p. A6.

Bell, C., & Jenkins, E. (1993). Community violence and children on Chicago's southside. *Psychiatry, 56,* 46–54

Butterfield, F. (1995). *All God's children: The Bosket family and the American tradition of violence.* New York: Knopf.

Drell, M., Siegel, C., & Gaensbauer, T. (1993). Post-traumatic stress disorder. In C. H. Zeanah (Ed.), *Handbook of infant mental health* (pp. 291–304). New York: Guilford Press.

Herbert, B. (1996, March 4). In trouble after school. *New York Times*, p. A15.

Osofsky, J. D. (1995). The effects of violence exposure on young children. *American Psychologist, 50,* 782–788.

Osofsky, J. D., & Fenichel, E. (1994). *Hurt, healing, and hope: Caring for infants and toddlers in violent environments.* Arlington, VA: Zero to Three/National Center for Clinical Infant Programs.

Osofsky, J. D., Fick, A. C., Flowers, A., & Lewis, M. (1995, March). *Trust in children living with violence.* Paper presented at the biennial meeting of the Society for Research in Child Development, Indianapolis, IN.

Pynoos, R. S. (1993). Traumatic stress and developmental psychopathology in children and adolescents. In J. M. Oldham, M. B. Riba, & A. Tasman (Eds.), *American Psychiatric Press review of psychiatry.* (Vol. 12, pp. 205–238). Washington, DC: American Psychiatric Press.

Scheeringa, M. S., Zeanah, C. H., Drell, M. J., & Larrieu, J. A. (1995). Two approaches to the diagnosis of post-traumatic stress disorder in infancy and early childhood. *Journal of the American Academy of Child and Adolescent Psychiatry, 34,* 191–200.

Zeanah, C. H. (1994). The assessment and treatment of infants and toddlers exposed to violence. In J. D. Osofsky & E. Fenichel (Eds.), *Hurt, healing and hope: Caring for infants and toddlers in violent environments* (pp. 29–37). Arlington, VA: Zero to Three/National Center for Clinical Infant Programs.

2

Exposure and Response to Community Violence among Children and Adolescents

ESTHER J. JENKINS
CARL C. BELL

A GROWING BODY OF EVIDENCE indicates that many children, particularly those in urban areas, are exposed to considerable amounts of life-threatening violence in their homes and communities. Such exposure may be a result of direct victimization or, more likely and more difficult to document, the witnessing of violence and having friends and family members victimized by violence. Often the violence is chronic, with children existing in milieus where violence and the threat of violence are constant. Although the exact response to the exposure will depend upon a number of variables related to the individual and the situation, the evidence indicates that these children are not unaffected by these experiences.

EXPOSURE TO VIOLENCE

Statistics

National and local statistics and self-report data indicate that youth have significant opportunities for violent encounters. Although recent reports indicate that after a 10-year surge, lethal and sublethal violence may be abating in the general population (Federal Bureau of Investigation, 1994), violence continues to occur at epidemic levels in many communities, particularly among the young. Nationally, homicide among 15- to 19-year-old males increased 153% between 1985 and 1991 (Centers for Disease Control and Prevention, 1994a) and was the second leading cause of death for this group. The increase for black adolescent males, who have a homicide rate approximately 10 times that of whites, and for whom homicide is the leading cause of death (Centers for Disease Control and Prevention, 1994b), was even more dramatic (Jenkins & Bell, 1992).

Data on nonlethal violence indicates that youth are also overrepresented as victims and perpetrators in assaults and other violent but nonfatal encounters. Youths aged 16–19 have the highest violent crime victimization rate (including attempted and completed rape, robbery, and simple and aggravated assault) of any age group, followed by 12- to 15-year-old youth (Christoffel, 1990; Bureau of Justice Statistics, 1994). As with lethal violence, the rate is higher among males than females, and among black youth.

Historically, just as with adult homicide, most youth homicides have occurred between acquaintances as a result of interpersonal altercations (Benedek & Cornell, 1989; Ewing, 1990). However, increasingly, youth violence is seen as resulting from gang and drug activities (Blumstein, 1995) in which the victim and perpetrator may not know each other. It is believed that this changing nature of homicide is responsible for the finding that in 1992, for the first time ever, the majority of murders (53%) were committed by strangers or unknown persons (Federal Bureau of Investigation, 1994).

These figures on adolescent homicide suggest that many young people will know of peers who have died violently. Newspaper reports and data on location of homicides suggest that they may also have the opportunity to personally witness these and other killings. For example, in Chicago in 1993, over half (56%) of the city's homicides occurred in a "public way" (e.g., street and alley; Chicago Police Department, 1994), bringing literal meaning to the term "community violence." This public nature of homicide not only makes it more likely that one will observe violence, but also increases one's risk of being a random or "accidental" victim.

Studies on Youth Violence Exposure

Although youth victimization, particularly in extreme cases, has been reasonably well documented with criminal justice and health statistics, youth witnessing of violence is much more difficult to determine. However, given the extraordinary levels of violence in many urban communities, it is not surprising that the handful of studies that do exist in the areas of witnessing violence and victimization have found extremely high rates of violence exposure. A summary of these studies, focusing on their findings regarding exposure to the most severe violence, is shown in Table 2.1. In particular, these studies, done over the last 10 years, report very high levels of witnessing of shootings, stabbings, and killings. The victimization rates in these samples, although much lower, paralleled those of witnessing.

In 1985, prior to the most dramatic surge in youth violence, the Community Mental Health Council (CMHC), a mental health center on the southside of Chicago, conducted a survey of over 500 youth at three elementary schools in its service area (Jenkins & Thompson, 1986; Bell & Jenkins, 1993). The purpose of that exploratory study was to examine the children's direct involvement in aggressive acts, that is, arguing and fighting, and factors affecting that involvement. The witnessing of specific acts of violence was asked about, almost as an aside, as one of many variables that would be examined as possible correlates of the children's aggression. Much to our surprise, these children's reports of witnessing extreme violence was quite high. As shown in Table 2.1, one in four had witnessed a shooting, and one-third reported that they had seen a stabbing (Jenkins & Thompson, 1986; Bell & Jenkins, 1993).

Consistent with the increase in violence in these communities over the years, additional surveys of youth in these Chicago neighborhoods have found increasing levels of violence exposure. A screening of 1,000 middle and high school students participating in violence prevention workshops during the 1987–1988 school year found that almost 40% of the students had witnessed a shooting, and close to one-fourth had seen someone killed (Shakoor & Chalmers, 1991; Uehara, Chalmers, Jenkins, & Shakoor, 1996; Bell & Jenkins, 1993). Among over 200 high school students surveyed in 1993, almost two-thirds (60.6%) had seen a shooting, and close to one-half (47%) had seen a stabbing. Three in five of those witnessing a shooting or stabbing (43% of the total sample) indicated that the incident ended in a death. Over one-fourth of these youth had personally experienced an act of severe violence: being shot, stabbed, raped, severely beaten, or being robbed with a weapon. Almost half of the sample reported that they had been shot at during their lifetime (Jenkins, 1995; Jenkins & Bell, 1994).

Other research on violent experiences of inner-city children has consistently found high levels of exposure. In a sample of youth and young adults in Detroit, Schubiner, Scott, and Tzelepis (1993) found that 42% had seen a shooting, and one in five had seen a killing. Fitzpatrick and Boldizar (1993) reported that almost 70% of a sample of youth in a public

TABLE 2.1. Survey Studies of Children's Exposure to Violence

Authors (year)	Location (date)	N	Age	Most severe acts witnessed			Victimization by severe violence		
				Shooting	Stabbing	Killing	Shot/ shot at	Knife attack	Beaten/ mugged
Jenkins & Thompson (1986); Bell & Jenkins (1993)	Chicago (1985)	536	7–15	26.3%	30.0%	—[a]	—	—	—
Shakoor & Chalmers (1991); Uehara et al. (1996); Bell & Jenkins (1993)	Chicago (1987–1988)	997	10–19	39.4%	34.6%	23.5%	10.9%	4.3%	—
Osofsky et al. (1993)	New Orleans (1990)	53	9–12	26.4%	18.9%	5.7%	0	1.9%	28.3%[b]
Richters & Martinez (1993)	Washington, DC (1990)	51	6–8	31.0%	17.0%	9.0%	11.0%	0	22.0%
		37	9–10	47.0%	31.0%	—	—	—	—
Fitzpatrick & Boldizar (1993)[c]	"Central City" (1991)	221	7–18	70.0[d]	53.0%	44.0%	15.0%	12.0%	15.0%
Jenkins & Bell (1994); Jenkins (1995)	Chicago (1992)	203	13–18	60.6%	45.0%	43.0%	46.8%	8.6%	8.5%
Singer et al. (1995)[e]	Denver	227	14–19	43.0%[d]	34.3%	—	20.1%	10.8%	7.9%
	Cleveland	228	14–19	55.5%	55.5%	—	21.8%	12.6%	15.6%
	Small town	862	14–19	30.4%	30.4%	—	11.4%	9.4%	7.8%
	Suburb (1992–1993)	379	14–19	5.0%	5.0%	—	1.6%	2.9%	1.9%
Schubiner et al. (1993)	Detroit	246	14–23	42.0%[f]	42.0%[f]	22.0%	—	—	—

[a] Not asked. [b] Beatings and chasings. [c] Approximations taken from graph. [d] Shot or shot at. [e] Within the past year. [f] Shooting or knifing.

12

housing development (N = 221) had witnessed someone get shot or shot at, and 43% had seen a murder.

In an important study in this field, which used a detailed questionnaire for examining the type and characteristics of violence exposure among youth, Richters and Martinez (1993a) studied 165 elementary school children in a moderately violent neighborhood in Washington, DC. Among the 37 fifth and sixth graders in the sample, 31% reported that they had seen a shooting, and 17% had seen a stabbing. In addition, many of these youth reported that they had experienced personal victimization (i.e., being physically threatened, chased by gangs, and mugged). In a collaborative, parallel study of 53 fifth graders in New Orleans, Osofsky, Wewers, Hann, and Fick (1993) found that over one-third of these children had witnessed a shooting, stabbing, or rape, with one in four reporting that they had seen a shooting.

In a study of adolescents using the largest sample to date (N = > 3,700), Singer, Anglin, Song, and Lunghofer (1995) examined regional and "size of city" differences in violence exposure. As shown in Table 2.1, the percentage of students witnessing a shooting ranged from less than 5% in a suburban community to over 50% in a large city. The victimization rates in these samples, although much lower, paralleled those of witnessing.

Indicative of the violent environments in which they live, repeated or chronic exposure to violence seems to be the norm for many of these children. In both the Richters and Martinez (1993a) sample of fifth and sixth graders and also among our high school sample (Jenkins & Bell, 1994), 70% of the youth witnessing a shooting had seen two or more. These children also witness many different types of violent acts, that is, rapes, drug use and trades, sexual assaults, beatings, and muggings, with greater exposure to less severe types of violence (Uehara et al., 1996; Richters & Martinez, 1993a; Fitzpatrick & Boldizar, 1993).

Furthermore, and with significant implications for its impact, these children are often close to the individuals whose victimization they witness. In our sample of over 200 inner-city high school students, 70% of those witnessing a shooting or stabbing reported that the closest victim was a friend or family member (Jenkins & Bell, 1994). Richters and Martinez (1993a) found similar results with their elementary school children, in which the majority of the victims of the witnessed violence (which ranged from severe to moderate) were friends, family, or acquaintances. Interestingly, the majority of perpetrators in that study, both against the youth and in acts that they witnessed, were also known to these youngsters.

In addition to exploring more direct encounters with violence, these same studies have also looked at hearing about and knowing of others who have been victimized. Predictably, in environments where children see and are personally victimized, knowledge of other's victimization is very high. Osofsky et al. (1993) found that four out of five of the 9- to 12-year-old youth in their sample had heard of someone being shot, stabbed, or raped. In research done at CMHC, the number of youth knowing about the severe victimization of friends and family members, whether they witnessed the incident or not, is over 70% (Shakoor & Chalmers, 1991; Uehara et al., 1996; Jenkins & Bell, 1994).

Factors Related to Exposure

Most research has found that exposure to violence varies by gender and type of exposure. Although girls are more likely to have been victims of sexual assault (Jenkins & Bell, 1994; Schubiner et al., 1993), boys report greater personal victimization in other areas (i.e., assault, shootings, stabbings; Richters & Martinez, 1993a; Jenkins & Bell, 1994; Shakoor & Chalmers, 1991; Fitzpatrick & Boldizar, 1993), particularly for those acts committed outside of the home (Singer et al., 1995). Gender differences in witnessing are less clear. Singer et al. found that boys were somewhat more likely to witness neighborhood violence, although not dramatically so, and girls were somewhat more likely to have witnessed violence in the home. Consistent with these findings, our research found that boys were more likely than girls to have witnessed the victimization of a stranger (Jenkins & Bell, 1994). Although further research in this area is needed, it seems that the gender differences in witnessing may be related to boys greater movement about their neighborhoods, outside of their homes.

Surprisingly, research that involves children in at least the first grade has not found very strong age differences, particularly in regard to witnessing. Richters and Martinez (1993a) found that more fifth and sixth graders reported victimization and witnessing of violence than first and second graders, but the differences were not statistically significant. In a sample of 7- to 15-year-old youth, reports of witnessing and age were not significantly related (Jenkins & Thompson, 1986; Bell & Jenkins, 1993). In an informal sample of 10 mothers in a Chicago public housing development, Dubrow and Garbarino (1989) found that all of their children had had a firsthand encounter with violence by the age of five. The absence of strong age differences in the incidence of witnessing among inner-city children suggest that children in these high-violence neighborhoods witness violence at a very early age. It also points to the pervasiveness of violence in these communities.

Other factors related to children's exposure to violence include living arrangements (Richters & Martinez, 1993a) and presence of the mother.

At least two studies have found that children from homes without a mother (Schubiner et al., 1993) or "primary female" (Fitzpatrick & Boldizar, 1993) are more likely to have witnessed violence and to have been victimized. Although the dynamics are not clear, perhaps this finding is related to a lack of adult supervision.

These studies, which together paint a portrait of youth experiencing violence and mayhem on a regular basis, have their limitations, particularly as indicators of prevalence. A frequent drawback is that the samples in the studies are taken from a few selected programs, agencies, or schools, and may not be representative of youth in their general area. Because these studies often are interested in the effects of the violence, they tend to focus on youth in moderate- or high-crime areas. As the Singer et al. (1995) study shows, youth exposure to violence varies considerably as a result of the area in which they reside.

Another possible limitation of these studies is that they typically involve self-report data that are difficult to verify. Research that found a poor match between students' reports of violence exposure and their parents' reports of the students' exposure (Richters & Martinez, 1993a) suggests that independent verification of events that occur outside of the home may be difficult. One would expect it to be even more problematic with older, more independent male youth. However, a comparison of students' self-reports of violence exposure with crime statistics in their communities shows that youths' reports were not out of line with what was expected, based on the level of violence in these communities (Richters & Martinez, 1993a; Jenkins, 1995).

EFFECTS OF EXPOSURE

Research, ranging from anecdotal, clinical case studies to large-scale surveys indicates that children who are exposed to violence are deeply affected by the experience. Most of the work in this area has focused on psychological disturbances associated with violence exposure, particularly posttraumatic stress disorder (PTSD).

PTSD, which was first included as a diagnosis in the third edition of the *Diagnostic and Statistical Manual of Mental Disorders* (DSM-III; American Psychiatric Association, 1980), occurs in response to some recognizable, extreme stressor. The disorder is characterized by specific behaviors that fall into the categories of reexperiencing the event, avoidance of reminders and psychic numbing, and increased arousal. The number of specific symptoms that an individual must display in each of the clusters varies, but the symptoms should exist for at least 1 month. PTSD may be acute, with symptoms lasting less than 3 months, or the symptoms may be much longer in duration; it may occur immediately after exposure to the stressor, or its onset may be delayed (American Psychiatric Association, 1994).

It is now clear that children display symptoms of PTSD. In his now-classic studies on children who witnessed homicide and other acts of violence, Pynoos (Pynoos & Eth, 1984; Pynoos & Nader, 1986, 1988) found that these children reexperienced the event in play, dreams, or intrusive images and sounds associated with the event; displayed avoidance behavior and psychic numbing, characterized by subdued behavior and inactivity, constricted affect, and diminished interest in previously enjoyed activities; and showed symptoms of increased arousal such as startle reactions and sleep disturbances. In addition, many of these children had fears of the reoccurrence of the event and guilt over their behavior during the incident (Pynoos & Nader, 1988).

Based on her clinical work with scores of children who had experienced trauma, Terr (1991) emphasizes four PTSD-specific symptoms that the children consistently display, regardless of the source of the trauma: repeatedly perceiving memories of the event through visualization or "reseeing" aspects of the trauma, engagement in behavioral reenactments and repetitive play related to some aspect of the trauma, and trauma-specific fears. The fourth change is pessimistic attitudes about people, life, and the future, manifesting as a sense of hopelessness and difficulty forming close personal relationships.

Terr also makes the useful distinction of traumas that result from "unanticipated single events" (Type-I Trauma) and those that result from long-standing or repeated exposure to an event or multiple events (Type-II Trauma). Whereas brief traumas may have only limited effects on the individual, repeated trauma may lead to anger, despair, profound psychic numbing, and dissociation resulting in major personality changes (Terr, 1991).

Surveys of youth exposed to community violence have found evidence of trauma symptoms in elementary school children (Martinez & Richters, 1993a; Osofsky et al., 1993) and adolescents (Jenkins & Bell, 1994; Schubiner et al., 1993). In their sample of 221 youth, 7 to 18 years of age from low-income housing developments, Fitzpatrick and Boldizar (1993) found that 27% of their sample met the criteria for PTSD, which included symptoms in the three clusters of reexperiencing, avoidance, and arousal. Using similar criteria, in a nonrandom sample of female adolescents visiting a medical clinic, Horowitz and Weine (1994) reported a PTSD rate twice as high. In a sample of more than 3,700 high school students, Singer et al. (1995) found that witnessing and victimization were significantly related to posttraumatic stress, anger, depression, anxiety, and dissociation.

As the first stress-related disorder given credibility by DSM-III as a result of the aftermath of the Vietnam War, most of the research and theorizing in this area has focused on PTSD. However, it is important to note that there are many other psychic and somatic reactions to trauma. Davidson (1993) and others (Marmar, Foy, Kagan, & Pynoos, 1993; Courtois, 1988; Herman, 1992) have proposed a "full panoply of trauma-associated disturbances," many of which can be experienced by children. These trauma-associated disturbances that can be experienced in children are shown in Table 2.2.

In addition to these DSM-IV disorders, Davidson (1993) proposes the existence of posttraumatic depression and disorders of extreme stress not otherwise specified. The latter are characterized by symptoms of somatization, dissociation, affective disturbance; personality changes characterized by pathological relationships and changes in identity; and harm-seeking and revictimization behaviors. There is also a host of adult psychiatric illnesses to which individuals are predisposed as a result of childhood trauma, such as borderline personality disorder, multiple personality disorder, antisocial personality disorder, sexual dysfunctions, and paraphillias.

In addition to recognizing that traumatic stress can cause stress-related disorders other than PTSD, it is also important to realize there are problems of comorbidity associated with PTSD. Such problems can occur when the traumatic experience is not therapeutically addressed, and can include an imbedding of the traumatic response into the personality and the development of additional problems such as substance abuse, eating disorders, depression, suicidal behavior, and vocational (school) impairment.

Trauma may occur immediately after the event, or symptoms may not occur until months or years later, resulting in the adult psychiatric

TABLE 2.2. DSM-IV, Trauma-Related Disorders Other Than PTSD in Children and Adolescents

Brief reactive psychosis	Conduct disorder
Dissociative fugue	Attachment disorders of infancy
Dissociative amnesia	Adjustment disorder
Conversion disorder	Depressive disorder not otherwise specified
Depersonalization disorder	Learning disorder not otherwise specified
Dream anxiety disorder	Communication disorder not otherwise specified
Somatization disorder	Disruptive behavior disorder not otherwise specified
Panic disorder	Impulse control disorder not otherwise specified
Generalized anxiety disorder	

disturbances just described. With delayed onset, repressed traumatic memories may be activated by a new trauma, hearing about a similar event, or some other reminder (Schwarz, Kowalski, & Hanus, 1993). For children, the full impact of a traumatic event may not occur until the child matures enough to fully comprehend and understand the incident (Pynoos, 1993).

In addition to the psychic sequelae of traumatic stress, researchers have found that there are neurochemical changes in those so exposed. Perry (1994) documented that children who have experienced trauma also have chronic changes in their brain and body chemistry, which are responsible for the symptoms observed in patients with stress-related disorders such as PTSD (i.e., exaggerated startle response, intrusive thoughts, and sleep disturbances). This theory is supported by the observation that treatment with medications (such as clonidine, which inhibits sympathetic and catecholaminergic systems) reduces the symptoms seen in stress-related disorders (Kolb, Burris, & Griffiths, 1984).

Developmental Issues

Children of any age may be affected by trauma; however, the impact of the event and the specific trauma symptoms are a result of the age and developmental level of the child (Pynoos & Eth, 1985; Pynoos & Nader, 1986, 1988). In addition, the trauma may interfere with the normal developmental process (Pynoos, 1993; Pynoos & Eth, 1985; Garbarino, 1993).

Although trauma reactions are observed in infants (Osofsky, 1995), most of the work in this area has addressed the categories of preschool, school-age, and adolescent youth. Preschool children are more likely to display passive reactions and regressive symptoms such as bed-wetting, decreased verbalization, dependence, and separation anxiety (clinging behavior), along with other manifestations of anxiety (i.e., nightmares, and sleep disturbances; Pynoos & Eth, 1985; Pynoos & Nader, 1988; Osofsky, 1995). They are also more likely to engage in traumatic reenactments in their play. School-age children are likely to report somatic complaints (stomachaches, headaches) and cognitive distortions and deficits that manifest as learning difficulties. They may be both passive and inhibited but also more aggressive, suffering impaired interpersonal relationships as a result of their belligerence and inconsistency (Pynoos & Eth, 1985; Eth & Pynoos, 1994).

Adolescent trauma reactions more closely resemble those of adults (Pynoos & Eth, 1985). Youth of this age who have witnessed or otherwise been exposed to violence may engage in acting-out and self-destructive behavior such as substance abuse, delinquent behavior, promiscuity, life-threatening reenactments, and other aggressive acts. These self-destructive behaviors may be interpreted as a defense mechanism used to distract them from anxiety and painful memories (Pynoos & Eth, 1985; Eth & Pynoos, 1994).

Not only are the observed symptoms in traumatized children a function of developmental level, but also exposure to violence impacts on and changes the developmental course. In other words, children who experience violence are often changed by that experience, which can affect the psychosocial, moral, cognitive, and general personality development of the child (Pynoos, 1993; Garbarino, 1993; Wallach, 1994). For example, adolescents, who have the greatest opportunities for violence exposure as victims and as witnesses, are coping with important developmental changes that can be negatively impacted by a traumatic experience. One of many significant tasks that they are facing is that of establishing their personal identities, which may be short-circuited by a traumatic experience. In fact, a major consequence of trauma for adolescents is a "premature entrance into adulthood or a premature closure of identity formation" (Pynoos & Eth, 1985, p. 47).

For younger children in violent environments, their major psychosocial tasks of establishing trust and autonomy can be compromised by the incident, as well as by frightened and stressed-out parents who are unable to provide consistent care (Wallach, 1994). In fact, there is a growing appreciation of the impact of violence on the parenting process, which has implications for children of all ages (Wallach, 1994; Osofsky, 1995; Pynoos, 1993). In high-violence neighborhoods, parents often place serious restrictions on their children's movements, keeping them indoors and away from windows in order to insure their safety. Such restrictions compromise the child's sense of autonomy by limiting opportunities for exploration and new relationships. Given the possible consequences, these parents may also engage in harsher discipline in order to keep their children "in line" and may be less emotionally accessible due to the stress of negotiating a violent and hostile environment.

Aggression and School Achievement

Two possible consequences of violence exposure that warrant special attention because of their implications for the community and the child's life chances are aggressive behavior and school performance deficits. Clinical evidence consistently points to violent behavior as a consequence of exposure to violence (Pynoos, 1993; Terr, 1991); recent survey data found that witnessing and victimization were the strongest predictors of self-reported involvement in fights and weapon-carrying behavior (Durant, Cadenhead, Pendergrast, Slavens, & Linder, 1994).

The aggressive reactions can come from several sources. Younger children may act out elements of the trauma in their play, whereas adolescents may engage in high-risk belligerent behavior in a counterphobic attempt to address their fears and deny their own vulnerability. Also, youth may seek revenge or retaliation (Pynoos & Nader, 1988) and engage in weapon carrying out of fear of victimization. In our study of high school students (Jenkins & Bell, 1994), for males, weapon carrying was more strongly correlated with violence exposure, particularly victimization, than was psychological distress. Ironically, weapon carrying, the original purpose of which may be to decrease victimization, is a contributor to the youth's involvement in violence as a perpetrator and a victim (Uehara et al., 1996).

Terr (1991) has noted that youth experiencing chronic abuse and exposure to violence often feel intense rage. This rage may manifest itself in aggressive behavior, or its intensity may frighten the child into a state of passivity leading to the passive–aggressive behavior sometimes observed in children exposed to violence (Dyson, 1990).

In addition to the psychoanalytically oriented explanations of aggression as a trauma reaction, a relationship between violence exposure and aggressive behavior is predicted by social learning theory (Bandura, 1973) and social information processing theory (Dodge, Bates, & Pettit, 1990; Dodge & Crick, 1990). A more comprehensive and integrated theory is supplied by Flay and Petraitis (1994).

Traumatized children often show a decline in academic performance (Pynoos & Eth, 1985; Dyson, 1990). The learning problems may result from the child being distracted by intrusive thoughts associated with the trauma and/or increased physiological arousal that can make it difficult to concentrate, a cognitive style of deliberate memory lapses in order to control the intrusive thoughts, or fatigue from lack of proper rest due to sleep disturbances (Pynoos & Nader, 1988; Nader, Pynoos, Fairbanks, & Frederick, 1990). It has also been suggested that exposure to chronic violence impairs learning by leading to an avoidance of the aggressive–assertive behavior necessary for problem solving (Gardner, 1971).

One would certainly not argue that all of the academic and behavioral problems that occur in—and are, unfortunately, considered the norm for—urban schools are reactions to trauma. However, an awareness that these are symptoms of violence exposure—in populations where chronic exposure is very high—is critical to accurately assessing and addressing the needs of these children.

Factors Mediating the Effects of Violence

Proximity

Many factors, including characteristics of the traumatic event and the personality of the child, affect the relationship between violence exposure and the appearance and severity of subsequent symptoms. A primary determinant of the impact of the event is the extent of the direct exposure (i.e., physical closeness) to the incident. In a 14-month follow-up with children attending the school where a sniper shot 14 students on the playground, Nader et al. (1990) found a linear relationship between level of exposure and symptoms, with children on the playground showing the most severe symptoms, followed by those in the school building, and then those not at school on that day.

Relationship with Victim

Another critical factor mediating the impact of the exposure is the child's relationship with the victim. Not surprisingly, children are most affected by incidents that involve individuals who are close to them. In the previously reported Martinez and Richter study (1993a), among the fifth and sixth graders, only those incidents involving known others, as victims or perpetrators, were significantly related to distress. In our survey of high school students in a high-crime area of Chicago, family victimization, whether it was witnessed or not, was as strongly correlated with psychological distress as personal victimization (Jenkins & Bell, 1994). There is evidence that violence in the family is particularly traumatic to youth (Osofsky et al., 1993; Jaffe, Wolfe, Wilson, & Zak, 1986), and the literature on the witnessing of a parents' victimization or death clearly indicates that this is one of the most life-altering events that a child can experience (Eth & Pynoos, 1994; Pynoos & Eth, 1985; Kaplan, Hendricks, Black, & Blizzard, 1994; Terr, 1991; Malmquist, 1986). The violent death of a loved one can be particularly problematic as trauma reactions clash with grief and mourning (Eth & Pynoos, 1994; Pynoos & Nader, 1986, 1988). The trauma–grief connection is most severe when the death is sudden or grisly (Rynearson, 1986). Whereas reminiscing about the person is important to grief resolution, survivors may avoid thinking about the person because of the anxiety that accompanies such memories.

Gender

Although some research has not found gender differences in responses to violence (Martinez & Richters, 1993), an increasing number of studies are finding quantitative or qualitative differences in the ways that boys and girls are affected by exposure to violence. Fitzpatrick and Boldizar (1993) found that victimized girls displayed more symptomatology than boys; Singer et al. (1995) found that girls had higher scores on anxiety, depression, anger, posttraumatic stress, and total trauma, and that female gender was the strongest demographic predictor of these symptoms. In a related study of responses to a natural disaster, Green et al. (1991) found that girls had higher levels of PTSD than boys.

Our study of high school students found a different pattern of results for boys and girls (Jenkins & Bell, 1994; Jenkins, 1995). First, results indicated that boys were much more affected by victimization, whereas girls were more affected by witnessing. Second, girls had much higher scores on psychological distress that was positively related to violence exposure; among boys, the strongest relationship was between exposure and risk behaviors, rather than exposure and psychological distress. In fact, for boys, the strongest relationship in the data was between victimization and weapon carrying (however, both boys and girls responded to violence with increased weapon carrying). Although it is difficult to explain the weakness of the victimization variable for girls (only 13 girls reported victimization), this finding of more externalizing behavior by boys and more internalizing behavior by girls is consistent with literature on children's responses to family violence (Jaffe et al., 1986) and with the psychiatric literature on gender differences in the manifestation of mental illness (American Psychiatric Association, 1980, 1994). Clearly, this is an area that needs more research. Our findings of a significant relationship between friends' victimization and psychological distress for girls and not for boys, and that girls feel significantly less safe than boys in their neighborhoods despite fewer instances of victimization, suggest that girls may be more vulnerable to the stressors of living in violent environments.

Other Stressors

Rarely is violence the only serious stressor to which these children are exposed. Students in our high school survey (Jenkins & Bell, 1994) reported an average of 3.5 stressful events in the previous year, not apparently related to violence (i.e., parent job loss, family illness and death, legal problems); Attar, Guerra, and Tolan (1994) found the same results in a sample of elementary school children. Inner cities, where violence is the greatest, are often characterized by poverty, itself a chronic stressor that produces other problems/stressors (crowding, poor medical attention and physical health, and family disruption). Because the impact of stressors appears cumulative, even multiplicative (Garmezy, 1993), for children who are already functioning in situations with multiple risks, exposure to violence may be even less well tolerated than by children who are not suffering the effects of additional stress (Garmezy, 1993; Masten, Best, & Garmezy, 1990).

Protective Factors

Although witnessing violence and being victimized can have serious negative consequences, clearly, not all children are equally affected by their experiences with violence. Just as there are risk factors that lead to increased negative outcomes, there are also protective factors that lessen the chances of maladaptive outcomes in the presence of the risk (Grossman et al., 1992; Rutter, 1987; Masten et al., 1990).

Very little of this research has looked specifically at protective factors or processes for violence exposure. The one process that has received some attention in this area and, in fact, dates to analyses of the impact of bombing raids on children in World War II (Freud & Burlingham, 1943) is that of parental or caregiver responses. When the adult caretaker appears appropriately calm and effective in the face of danger, while not minimizing its seriousness, the prognosis for the child is much better than if the parent is either not present (accessible) or is overwhelmed by the situation (Pynoos, 1993). Similarly, work by Richters and Martinez (1993b), which found that the adaptive success of children in violent environments was affected by the safety and stability of the children's homes (and not the level of community violence per se), also points to the importance of the integrity of the parenting process. Clearly, a future area of research should be an investigation of processes/circumstances that serve as protective factors for families that allow for effective parenting under conditions of high threat, stress, and neighborhood "disadvantage."

More general protective factors that have been shown to operate in other risk situations and may serve to buffer children exposed to a traumatic violent event include individual, familial, and social or external factors (Garmezy, 1993; Grossman et al., 1992). Individual factors include high self-esteem, internal locus of control (Grossman et al., 1992; Rutter, 1987), high IQ, personal efficacy or competency, good social skills, and good problem-solving skills (Masten et al., 1990; Garmezy, 1993). Familial factors include family cohesion (Garmezy, 1993; Grossman et al., 1992) and a good relationship with at least one parent or other adult in the family (Rutter, 1987). External factors include strong support outside of the home by another person or an institution (school, church; Garmezy, 1993; Masten et al., 1990). Among adolescent girls who witnessed violence or were victimized, Horowitz and Weine (1994) found that ties to communal institutions of family, school, and peers was negatively related to PTSD symptoms. Church attendance and religious faith (Garmezy, 1993) may operate in the same manner, particularly among people of color.

ADDRESSING THE NEEDS OF CHILDREN EXPOSED TO VIOLENCE

The obvious and long-range solution for children's exposure to community violence is to decrease the poverty, unemployment, and family disruption that has become disturbingly common in many urban communities. Such factors not only feed the violence epidemic in these areas, but also decrease families' abilities to protect and buffer their children from the violence and its deleterious effects. Unfortunately, however, given certain demographic trends and political realities, we are not optimistic about a quick reversal of the violence in these communities. In the meantime, we must address the issue of protecting children from the violence and treating the results of violence exposure.

As indicated in the previous discussion, critical work has been done in area of diagnoses and treatment of children exposed to violence (see Terr, 1991; Pynoos, 1993). We have been particularly impressed with the work of Robert Pynoos and his associates (Pynoos & Eth, 1984, 1985, 1986; Pynoos & Nader, 1986) which focused on identification of trauma symptoms by developmental level. Their crisis intervention model, or "psychological first aid" for children who have witnessed violence (Pynoos & Nader, 1988) has been especially useful. The model outlines symptoms and provides concrete responses for each developmental level, and can be used by caretakers as well as professionals and paraprofessionals in the aftermath of a traumatic incident.

Many factors determine the impact of witnessed violence on the child, and it is important to identify those factors that may promote or deter the resolution of the child's distress. Such factors relate to the incident (e.g., proximity, relationship to victim), as well as the child and his or her environment. Depending on these factors, including previous experiences with trauma, preexisting psychiatric problems, or developmental challenges, the child may have a need for long-term treatment. There are various approaches for treating traumatic stress, such as dynamic psychotherapy, cognitive-behavioral, and psychopharmacological treatment that can be used independently or in combination to achieve the best results (see Marmar et al., 1993).

Although the treatment of traumatic stress in children and adults, once recognized and diagnosed, is reasonably well established, much less attention has been given to the initial identification and referral of children traumatized by community violence. When violent acts occur, the most immediate attention is given to the victims and perpetrators, with the presence of others being of interest if it has a bearing on the legal outcome of the case. If the violence occurs in a public or quasi-public place, it may be difficult even to determine the number of witnesses. And, as Richters and Martinez (1993a) found, children, even relatively young ones, often see much more violence than their caretakers are aware of. Thus, one of the most pressing issues in this area, given the high numbers of children in these neighborhoods who may be suffering some negative effects of violence exposure (Fitzpatrick & Boldizar, 1993; Singer et al., 1995), is the identification and referral of these youth.

A promising approach to identifying children who have been exposed to violence is to screen children (and adults) as part of routine medical exams and treatment. Children (and adults) should be asked about personal victimization, witnessing of violence, and the death and injury of close others, along with other common questions about their medical history and condition. In addition, they can be asked about their personal involvement in acts of aggression and violence, weapon carrying, and anger management. Doctors and medical professionals can and should ask about experiences and behaviors that pose a risk to their patients' physical and mental well-being.

Children and adolescents who seek medical treatment for injuries caused by interpersonal violence must be considered at extreme risk for revictimization (Goins, Thompson, & Simpkins, 1992; Morrissey, Byrd, & Deitch, 1991; Urquiza & Goodlin-Jones, 1994) and/or perpetration, and their need for services provides an excellent opportunity for intervention. One such program at a Boston hospital does intensive social work with youth admitted for violence from intensive injury around issues of anger control, conflict resolution skills, and the simple logistics of staying safe upon release (De Vos, Stone, Goetz, & Dahlberg, 1996). A Harlem Hospital pediatric surgeon (using the logic that mildly injured child abuse victims are frequently admitted to the hospital to prevent their reinjury) admits that she uses an extremely liberal interpretation of injury in order to admit youth who appear to be at risk for serious injury in the future (Barlow, 1993). Once admitted, they receive intensive psychological and social services to alter their high-risk lifestyle and prevent revictimization.

As impressive as these programs may be, the reality is that few doctors and emergency rooms have procedures for intervening with youth victimized by nonfamilial violence, let alone for those who may have simply witnessed violence (Bell, Jenkins, Kpo, & Rhodes, 1994). Thus, it is quite significant that the American Academy of Pediatrics has developed a protocol for the identification, treatment, and referral of children who have witnessed or been victimized by violence, to be used in hospitals and private practices (American Academy of Pediatrics Task Force on Adolescent Assault Victim Needs, 1996; see also Educational Development Center, Inc., 1992). Such procedures and the participation and endorsement of major medical groups (e.g., the National Medical Association and the American Medical Association) are critical to the involvement of health care professionals who are often the first to see evidence of violence and trauma, but who, traditionally, have viewed their job as one of treating the patient's physical injury and not getting involved in "social work" issues.

In addition to medical professionals, teachers are in a good position to identify traumatized youth, as the symptoms may manifest themselves in learning difficulties or behavioral problems. Therefore, it is important for teachers, through inservices, to have a basic understanding of the symptoms of the traumatic stress that can result from witnessing and victimization, and for schools to have procedures for internal and external referrals.

Any discussion of identification, referral, and treatment assumes the existence of programs and services for those exposed to violence. Unfortunately, our experience is that this is not the case. Communities most in need are usually the least resourced in a number of areas, including the provision of adequate health care and mental health care. As a result, if there are services in these communities available for children exposed to violence, their level of sophistication is often lacking, and crucial issues may not be appreciated or addressed. For example, as previously mentioned, despite the fact that trauma may take on a different significance as the child matures, resulting in symptoms occurring long after the trauma has transpired, the needed follow-up may not be recognized (Bell & Davis, 1994).

The schools in these areas are often overcrowded and understaffed, making the job of developing relationships with schools to identify and refer children exposed to traumatic stress all the more difficult. The problem of referral is further compounded by the general lack of awareness that the absence of sustained overt symptoms in children, particularly preschoolers and school-age children, in no way indicates that they have been unaffected by their experience.

Despite these limitations, equipping health care professionals and school personnel with basic intervention skills is essential, given the paucity of services in these areas. Frequently these professionals are the only help available to underresourced communities and are viewed as legitimate caretakers in these areas.

In addition to using available resources to attempt to address the immediate needs of underresourced communities, we must also explore the development of an infrastructure for addressing this problem. We believe that programs for the identification and treatment of children exposed to violence can be modeled after those already in existence for the treatment of sexual assault. Advocacy (around policy, funds, service delivery, training), identification of victims in emergency rooms, referral for counseling and treatment, and referral to support groups are all elements of the sexual assault infrastructure that can be applied to problems involving physical assault and violence exposure. In fact, given the conceptual similarity of issues confronting these two groups and the fact that sexual assault counselors are trained in the treatment of traumatic stress, it is worth exploring attaching services for violence-exposed youth and adults to existing sexual assault programs, particularly where resources are limited.

CONCLUSION

The issue is not to treat all violence-exposed children as if they will be devastated by the experience, but rather to approach each exposed child as one at-risk and one for whom there must be some attempt to establish his or her level of potential morbidity. Thus, there must be procedures for identifying these youth, and there must be services for those who need them. The development (or identification) of an infrastructure for addressing these needs should be spearheaded by groups with sufficient expertise and investment in these issues, namely community-based groups, community psychiatry, and public health interests. Taking the responsibility for actualizing this solution cannot be stressed enough.

The issue is really quite simple: We have enough experience in treating traumatic stress to have a good idea of what is necessary to help a child exposed to violence who is experiencing stress-related disorders. The question is, will we make an investment in all of our children and start programs that will ameliorate their stress from being exposed to violence? Of course, this call to action is only a form of damage control; as indicated earlier, the ultimate solution for these children lies in strengthening families and reducing poverty and inequality, the underlying causes of the violence and other problems that plague these communities.

REFERENCES

American Academy of Pediatrics Task Force on Adolescent Assault Victim Needs. (1996). Adolescent assault victim needs: A review of issues and a model protocol. *Pediatrics, 98,* 991–1001.

American Academy of Pediatrics Work Group on Disasters. (1995, May). *Psychosocial issues for children and families in disasters: A guide for the primary care physician.* Washington, DC: U.S. Department of Health and Human Services, Public Health Service, Center for Mental Health Services.

American Psychiatric Association. (1980). *Diagnostic and statistical manual of mental disorders* (3rd ed.). Washington, DC: Author.

American Psychiatric Association. (1994). *Diagnostic and statistical manual of mental disorders* (4th ed.). Washington, DC: Author.

Attar, B. K., Guerra, N. G., & Tolan, P. H. (1994). Neighborhood disadvantage, stressful life events, and adjustment in urban elementary-school children. *Journal of Clinical and Child Psychology, 23,* 391–400.

Bandura, A. (1973). *Aggression: A social learning approach.* Englewood Cliffs, NJ: Prentice-Hall.

Barlow B. (1993). Penetrating gunshot and knife wounds. In F. D. Burg, J. Ingelfinger, & E. R. Wald (Eds.), *Gellis and Kagan: Current pediatric therapeutics 14.* Philadelphia: Saunders.

Bell, C. C., & Davis, K. E. (1994). Psychoanalytic therapy relevancy explored. *Psychiatric Times, 11*(11), 31–34.

Bell, C. C., & Jenkins, E. J. (1993). Community violence and children on Chicago's southside. *Psychiatry: Interpersonal and Biological Processes, 56,* 46–54.

Bell, C. C., Jenkins, E. J., Kpo, W., & Rhodes, H. (1994). Response of emergency rooms to victims of interpersonal violence. *Hospital and Community Psychiatry, 45* 142–146.

Benedek, F. P., & Cornell, D. G. (Eds.). (1989). *Juvenile homicide.* Washington, DC: American Psychiatric Press.

Blumstein, A. (1995). Youth violence, guns, and the illicit-drug industry. In R. Block & C. Block (Eds.), *Trends, risks, and interventions: Proceedings of the Third Annual Spring Symposium of the Homicide Research Working Group* (pp. 3–16). Washington, DC: U.S. Department of Justice.

Bureau of Justice Statistics. (1994). *National crime victimization survey.* Washington, DC: U.S. Department of Justice.

Centers for Disease Control and Prevention. (1994a). Homicide among 15–19 year old males: United States 1963–1991. *Morbidity and Mortality Weekly Report, 43,* 725–727.

Centers for Disease Control and Prevention. (1994b). Annual summary of births, deaths, marriages, divorces, and deaths: United States, 1993. *Morbidity and Mortality Weekly Report, 42*(13).

Chicago Police Department. (1994). *Murder analysis.* Chicago: Detective Division, Chicago Police Department.

Christoffel, K. K. (1990). Violent death and injury in U.S. children and adolescents. *American Journal of Diseases of Children, 144*(6), 697–706.

Courtois, C. (1988). *Healing the incest wound: Adult survivors in therapy.* New York: Norton.

Davidson, J. (1993). Issues in the diagnosis of posttraumatic stress disorder. In J. M. Oldham, M. B. Riba, & A. Tasman, (Eds.), *Review of psychiatry* (Vol. 12, pp. 141–155). Washington, DC: American Psychiatric Press.

De Vos, E., Stone, D. A., Goetz, M. A., & Dahlberg, L. L. (1996). Evaluation of a hospital-based youth violence intervention. *American Journal of Preventive Medicine 12*(Suppl. 2), 101–108.

Dodge, K. A., Bates, J. E., & Pettit, G. S. (1990). Mechanisms in the cycle of violence. *Science, 250,* 1678–1683.

Dodge, K. A., & Crick, N. R. (1990). Social information-processing of aggressive behavior in children. *Personality and Social Psychology Bulletin, 16,* 8–22.

Dubrow, N. F., & Garbarino, J. (1989). Living in the war zone: Mothers and young children in public housing development. *Journal of Child Welfare, 68,* 3–20.

Durant, R. H., Cadenhead, C., Pendergrast, R. A., Slavens, G., & Linder, C. W. (1994). Factors associated with the use of violence among urban black adolescents. *American Journal of Public Health, 84,* 612–617.

Dyson, J. (1990). The effects of family violence on children's academic performance and behavior. *Journal of the National Medical Association, 82,* 17–22.

Education Development Center, Inc. (1992). *Identification and prevention of youth violence: A protocol for health care providers.* Boston: Violence Prevention Project, Department of Health and Hospitals.

Eth, S., & Pynoos, R. S. (1994). Children who witness the homicide of a parent. *Psychiatry, 57,* 287–306.

Ewing, C. P. (1990). *When children kill: Dynamics of juvenile homicide.* Lexington, MA: Lexington Books.

Federal Bureau of Investigation. (1994). *Uniform crime reports: Crime in the United States, 1993.* Washington, DC: Department of Justice.

Fitzpatrick, K. M., & Boldizar, J. P. (1993). The prevalence and consequences of exposure to violence among African-American youth. *Journal of the American Academy of Child Adolescent Psychiatry, 32,* 424–430.

Flay, B. R., & Petraitis, J. (1994). The theory of triadic influence: A new theory of health behavior with implications for preventive interventions. *Advances in Medical Sociology, 4,* 19–44.

Freud, A., & Burlingham, D. (1943). *War and children.* New York: International Universities Press.

Garbarino, J. (1993). Children's response to war: What do we know? *Infant Mental Health Journal, 14,* 103–115.

Gardner, G. (1971). Aggression and violence—the enemies of precision learning in children. *American Journal of Psychiatry, 128,* 445–450.

Garmezy, N. (1993). Children in poverty: Resilience despite risk. *Psychiatry: Interpersonal and Biological Processes, 56,* 127–136.

Goins, W. A., Thompson, J., & Simpkins, C. (1992). Recurrent intentional injury. *Journal of the National Medical Association, 84,* 431–435.

Green, B. L., Korol, M., Grace, M. C., Vary, M. G., Leonard, A. C., Gleser, G. C., & Smitson-Cohen, S. (1991). Children and disaster: Age, gender, and parental effects on PTSD symptoms. *Journal of the American Academy of Child and Adolescent Psychiatry, 30*(6), 945–951.

Grossman, F. K., Beinashowitz, J., Anderson, L., Sakurai, M., Finnin, L., & Flaherty, M. (1992). Risk and resilience in young adolescents. *Journal of Youth and Adolescence, 21,* 529–549.

Herman, J. (1992). *Trauma and recovery.* New York: Basic Books.

Horowitz, K., & Weine, S. (1994, May). *Communal ties mediating violence and its effects.* Paper presented at the 147th annual conference of the American Psychiatric Association, Philadelphia, PA.

Jaffe, P., Wolfe, D., Wilson, S. K., & Zak, L. (1986). Family violence and child adjustment: A comparative analysis of girls' and boys' behavioral symptoms. *American Journal of Psychiatry, 143,* 74–76.

Jenkins, E. J. (1995). Violence exposure, psychological distress and risk behaviors in a sample of inner-city youth. In R. Block & C. Block (Eds.), *Trends, risks, and interventions: Proceedings of the Third Annual Spring Symposium of the Homicide Research Working Group* (pp 287–298). Washington, DC: U.S. Department of Justice.

Jenkins, E. J., & Bell, C. C. (1992). Adolescent violence: Can it be curbed? *Adolescent Medicine: State of the Art Reviews, 1,* 71–86.

Jenkins, E. J., & Bell, C. C. (1994). Violence exposure, psychological distress, and high risk behaviors among inner-city high school students. In S. Friedman (Ed.), *Anxiety disorders in African-Americans* (pp. 76–88). New York: Springer.

Jenkins, E. J., & Thompson, B. (1986, August). *Children talk about violence: Preliminary findings from a survey of black elementary school children.* Presented at the 19th annual convention of the Association of Black Psychologists, Oakland, CA.

Kaplan, T., Hendricks, J. H., Black, D., & Blizzard, B. (1994). Children who survive after one parent has killed the other: A research study. In C. Chiland & G. J. Young (Eds.), *Children and violence* (pp. 51–71). Northvale, NJ: Jason Aronson.

Kolb, L. C., Burris, B. C., & Griffiths, S. (1984). Propranolol and clonidine in the treatment of post-traumatic stress disorders of war. In B. A. van der Kolk (Ed.), *Post-traumatic stress disorders: Psychological and biological sequelae* (pp. 29–44). Washington, DC: American Psychiatric Press.

Malmquist, C. P. (1986). Children who witness parental murder: Posttraumatic aspects. *Journal of the American Academy of Child Psychiatry, 25,* 320–335.

Marmar, C. R., Foy, D., Kagan, B., & Pynoos, R. S. (1993). An integrated approach for treating posttraumatic stress. In J. M. Oldham, M. B. Riba, & A. Tasman (Eds.), *Review of psychiatry* (Vol. 12). Washington, DC: American Psychiatric Press.

Martinez, P., & Richters, J. (1993). The NIMH community violence project: II. Children's distress symptoms associated with violence exposure. *Psychiatry, 56,* 23–35.

Masten, A. S., Best, K. M., & Garmezy, N. (1990). Resilience and development: Contributions from the study of children who overcome adversity. *Development and Psychopathology, 2,* 425–444.

Morrissey, T. B., Byrd, C. R., & Deitch, E. (1991). The incidence of recurrent penetrating trauma in an urban trauma center. *Journal of Trauma, 31,* 1536–1538.

Nader, K., Pynoos, R. S., Fairbanks, L., & Frederick, C. (1990). Childhood PTSD reactions one year after a sniper attack. *Journal of the American Psychiatric Association, 147,* 1526–1530.

Osofsky, J. D. (1995). The effects of exposure to violence on young children. *American Psychologist, 50,* 782–788.

Osofsky, J. D., Wewers, S., Hann, D. M., & Fick, A. C. (1993). Chronic community violence: What is happening to our children? *Psychiatry, 56,* 7–21.

Perry, B. (1994). Neurobiologic sequelae of childhood trauma: PTSD in children. In M. Murberg (Ed.), *Catecholamine function in PTSD.* Washington, DC: American Psychiatric Press.

Pynoos, R. S. (1993). Traumatic stress and developmental psychopathology in children and adolescents. In J. M. Oldham, M. B. Riba, & A. Tasman (Eds.), *Review of psychiatry* (Vol. 12, pp. 205–237). Washington, DC: American Psychiatric Press.

Pynoos, R. S., & Eth, S. (1984). Child as a criminal witness to homicide. *Journal of Social Issues, 40,* 87–108.

Pynoos, R. S., & Eth, S. (1985). Developmental perspective on psychic trauma in childhood. In C. R. Figley (Ed.), *Trauma and its wake.* New York: Brunner/Mazel.

Pynoos, R. S., & Eth, S. (1986). Witness to violence: The child interview. *Journal of the American Academy of Child Psychiatry, 25*(3), 306–319.

Pynoos, R. S., & Nader, K. (1986). Children's exposure to violence and traumatic death. *Psychiatric Annals, 20,* 334–344.

Pynoos, R. S., & Nader, K. (1988). Psychological first aid: For children who witness community violence. *Journal of Traumatic Stress, 1,* 445–473.

Richters, J., & Martinez, P. (1993a). The NIMH community violence project: I. Children as victims of and witnesses to violence. *Psychiatry, 56,* 7–21.

Richters, J., & Martinez, P. (1993b). Violent communities family choices, and children's chances: An algorithm for improving the odds. *Development and Psychopathology, 5,* 609–627.

Rutter, M. (1987). Psychosocial resilience and protective mechanisms. *American Journal of Orthopsychiatry, 57,* 316–331.

Rynearson, E. K. (1986). Psychological effects of unnatural dying on bereavement. *Psychiatry Annals, 62,* 272–275.

Shakoor, B. & Chalmers, D. (1991). Co-victimization of African-American children who witness violence and the theoretical implications of its effects on their cognitive, emotional, and behavioral development. *Journal of National Medical Association, 83,* 233–238.

Schubiner, H., Scott, R., & Tzelepis, A. (1993). Exposure to violence among inner-city youth. *Journal of Adolescent Health, 14,* 214–219.

Schwarz, E., Kowalski, J., & Hanus, S. (1993). Malignant memories: Signatures of violence. In S. Leinstein (Ed.), *Adolescent psychiatry.* Chicago: University of Chicago Press.

Singer, M. I., Anglin, T. M., Song, L. Y., & Lunghofer, L. (1995). Adolescents' exposure to violence and associated symptoms of psychological trauma. *Journal of the American Medical Association, 273*(6), 477–482.

Terr, L. (1991) Childhood traumas: An outline and overview. *American Journal of Psychiatry, 48,* 10–20.

Uehara, E., Chalmers, D., Jenkins, E. J., & Shakoor, B. (1996). Youth encounters with violence: Results from the Chicago Community Mental Health Council violence screening project. *Journal of Black Studies, 26,* 768–781.

Urquiza, A. J., & Goodlin-Jones, B. L. (1994). Child sexual abuse and adult revictimization with women of color. *Violence and Victims, 9*(3), 223–232.

Wallach, L. B. (1994). *Violence and young children's development.* Urbana: University of Illinois. (ERIC Clearinghouse on Elementary and Early Childhood Education EDO-PS-94-7)

3

What Children Can Tell Us about Living in a War Zone

JAMES GARBARINO
KATHLEEN KOSTELNY

THE AMERICAN WAR ZONE

Violence is a fact of life for millions of American children. Television infuses images of violence into virtually every household; "real-life" violence on the streets, in the schools, or in the form of child or spousal abuse touches millions directly. What do we know about the impact of all this violence on children and their development? What can children tell us about the meaning of violence in their lives?

Homicide rates provide only an imprecise indicator of the overall problem of violence in the lives of American children and youth, for behind each murder stand many nonlethal assaults. The U.S. Surgeon General's report (Koop, 1985) estimated 100 assaults for each murder. This ratio varies as a function of both medical trauma technology (which prevents assaults from becoming homicides) and weapons technology (which can increase or decrease the lethality of assaults). An example from Chicago illustrates this. The city's homicide rates in 1973 and 1993 were approximately the same, yet the rate of serious assault increased approximately 400% during that period. Thus, the ratio of assaults to homicides increased substantially (from 100:1 in 1973 to 400:1 in 1993).

Data from Chicago's Cook County Hospital provide another perspective on the changing nature of violence facing children in America. In 1982, the hospital responded to approximately 500 gunshot cases. In 1992, the number was approximately 1,000. However, in 1982 almost all these cases involved injuries from a single bullet, whereas in 1992, 25% involved multiple bullets. Rates of permanent disability have thus increased substantially, although the homicide rate has shown only a modest increase.

Class, race, and gender exert important influences on exposure to community violence. The odds of being a homicide victim range from 1:21 for black males, to 1:369 for white females (with white males at 1:131, and black females at 1:104; Bell, 1991). Being an American is itself a risk factor. The United States far exceeds all other modern industrialized nations in its homicide rate (even for whites, where the rate of 11.2 per 100,000 is far more than the second place country, Scotland, with 5 per 100,000 (Richters & Martinez, 1993).

Whatever the exact constellation of causes, children growing up in the United States have particularly high levels of exposure to violence, particularly if they live in neighborhoods that constitute "war zones." A survey of sixth through 10th graders in New Haven, Connecticut, revealed that 40% had witnessed at least one incident of violent crime within the last 12 months (Marans & Cohen, 1993). In three high-risk neighborhoods in Chicago, 17% of the elementary school-age children had witnessed domestic violence, 31% had seen someone shot, and 84% had seen someone "beat up" (Bell, 1991). Some 30% of the children living in high-crime neighborhoods of cities such as Chicago have witnessed a homicide by the time they are 15 years old, and more than 70% have witnessed a serious assault. These figures are much more like the experience of children in the war zones we have visited in other countries (Garbarino, Kostelny, & Dubrow, 1991) than they are of what we should expect for our own children, living in "peace." Richters and Martinez (1993) have amplified these results. In their study, 43% of the fifth and sixth graders had witnessed a mugging in a "*moderately* violent" neighborhood in Washington, DC. Other researchers echo these findings (e.g., Groves, Zuckerman, Marans, & Cohen, 1993). In such settings, guns are a recurrent theme.

LISTENING TO CHILDREN: THE GUN CULTURE

In our interviews with families living in public housing projects in Chicago, we learned that virtually all the children had firsthand experiences with shooting by the time they were 5 years old (Dubrow & Garbarino, 1989). Interviews with school-age children confirm that the "gun culture" is a potent factor in the lives of children in diverse settings in the United States (Garbarino, 1995). The spread of the "gun culture" into the lives of school-children is associated with a clear and present danger to their mental health, social behavior, and educational success. We base this conclusion upon an analysis of the role of trauma, threat, and violence on the development of children (Garbarino, Dubrow, Kostelny, & Pardo, 1992).

A few examples will help illuminate the effects of this gun culture on the experience of childhood. In Detroit, a young boy whose idolized teenage brother was killed in a gang-related attack was asked, "If you could have anything in the whole world, what would it be?" His answer: "A gun so I could blow away the person that killed my brother" (Marin, 1989). In California, when we asked a 9-year-old boy living in a neighborhood characterized by declining security, "What would it take to make you feel safer here?" he replied simply, "If I had a gun of my own." In a middle-class suburb of Chicago, when we asked a classroom of 8-year-olds, "If you needed a gun, could you get one?" one-third of the children were able to describe in detail how they would get one. In a prison in North Carolina, when we asked three incarcerated teenagers about why they had done the shooting that had landed them in prison, all three replied, "What else was I supposed to do?" (Garbarino, 1995).

We must understand the gun culture infusing the minds and hearts of American children and youth. Whether this cultural infusion results in actual shooting depends upon the particular circumstances of those children and youth, specifically, whether they experience an accumulation of social and psychological risk factors in the absence of compensatory opportunity factors.

THE ACCUMULATION OF RISK

Risk accumulates. This is one of the conclusions we draw from our observations of children coping with chronic violence in the United States today. Children are capable of coping with one or two major risk factors in their lives. But when risk accumulates—the addition of a third, fourth, and fifth risk factor—we see a precipitation of developmental damage (Sameroff, Seifer, Barocas, Zax, & Greenspan, 1987). This developmental model is particularly relevant to understanding the impact of chronic community violence on inner-city children (Garbarino & Associates, 1992).

The experience of community violence takes place within a larger context of risk for most children. They often are poor, live in father-absent families, contend with parental incapacity due to depression or substance abuse, are raised by caretakers with little education or employment prospects, and are exposed to domestic violence (Kotlowitz, 1991).

This constellation of risk by itself creates enormous challenges for young children. For them, the trauma of community violence is often literally "the straw that breaks the camel's back." Bearing in mind that approximately 20% of American children live with this sort of accumulation of risk, the problem of violence is clearly a national problem with far-reaching implications for child development (Osofsky, 1995).

The task of dealing with the effects of this environmental conspiracy falls to the people who care for these children—their parents and other relatives, teachers, and counselors. But these adults who take on this task face enormous challenges of their own. We have found that human service professionals and educators working in the high-violence areas of our communities are themselves traumatized by their exposure to violence (Garbarino, Dubrow, Kostelny, & Pardo, 1992).

In one study we found that 60% of the Head Start staff members surveyed in Chicago had experienced traumatic events connected with violence (Garbarino et al., 1992). For these individuals, efforts to create a "safe zone" in the school are crucial to their ability to perform their important functions in the lives of high-risk children. For this safe zone to help children focus on their schoolwork, it must exist as part of their "social maps."

THE SOCIAL MAPS OF CHILDREN IN DANGER

Certainly one of the most important features of child development is the child's emerging capacity to form and maintain "social maps" (Garbarino, 1995; Garbarino & Associates, 1992). These representations of the world reflect the simple cognitive competence of the child (knowing the world in the scientific sense of objective, empirical fact). But they also indicate the child's moral and affective inclination.

We are concerned with the conclusions about the world contained in the child's social maps: "Adults are to be trusted because they know what they are doing"; "People will generally treat you well and meet your needs"; "Strangers are dangerous"; "School is a safe place." The forces shaping these maps include the child's experiences in counterpoint with the child's inner life—both the cognitive competence and the working of unconscious forces.

Young children must contend with dangers that derive from two sources not nearly so relevant to adults. First, their physical immaturity places them at risk for injury from trauma that would not hurt adults, because they are larger and more powerful. Second, young children tend to believe in the reality of threats from what most adults would define as "the fantasy" world. This increases their vulnerability to perceiving themselves as being "in danger." These dangers include monsters under the bed, wolves in the basement, and invisible creatures that lurk in the dark corners of bedrooms.

Trauma arises when the child cannot give meaning to dangerous experiences. This orientation is contained in the American Psychiatric Association's definition of posttraumatic stress disorder (PTSD), which refers to threatening experiences outside the realm of normal experience. Herman (1992) defined trauma thus: to come face to face with both human vulnerability in the natural world and with the capacity for evil in human nature.

This suggests experiences that are cognitively overwhelming, in which the process required to "understand" these experiences has pathogenic side effects; that is, in coping with traumatic events, the child is forced into patterns of behavior, thought, and feelings that are themselves "abnormal" when contrasted with that of the untraumatized, healthy child. Children are particularly vulnerable to the trauma caused by threat and fear—in one study, those exposed to trauma before age 10 were three times more likely to exhibit PTSD than those exposed after age 12 (Davidson & Smith, 1990).

Children and youth exposed to acute danger may require processing over a period of months (Pynoos & Nader, 1988). And, if the traumatic stress is intense enough, it may leave permanent "psychic scars" (Terr, 1990). This is particularly the case for children made vulnerable because of disruptions in their primary relationships (most notably with parents). These effects include excessive sensitivity to stimuli associated with the trauma and diminished expectations for the future.

But chronic danger imposes a requirement for *developmental* adjustment—accommodations. These are likely to include persistent PTSD, alterations of personality, and major changes in patterns of behavior or articulation of ideological interpretations of the world that provide a framework for making sense of ongoing danger (Garbarino et al., 1992). This is particularly true when that danger comes from the violent overthrow of day-to-day social reality, as is the case in war, communal violence, or chronic violent crime.

Beyond any individual strengths that come to a child with temperament and intellectual capacity at birth, the key lies in the balance of social supports from and for parents. It lies in parental capacity to buffer social stress in the lives of children and offer them a positive path to follow in dealing with that stress. The quality of life for young children—and their reservoirs of resilience—thus becomes a *social* indicator as well as a measure of personal worth. This hypothesis emerges from a wide range of research and clinical observation (Garbarino, 1995).

ADULTS AS TEACHERS

Adults are crucial resources for children attempting to cope with chronic danger and stress. Generations of studies focusing on the experience of children living in war zones testify to the importance of adult responses to danger as mediating factors in child response (Garbarino et al., 1991). So long as adults are in control of themselves and present children with a role model of calm, positive determination, most children can cope with a great deal of chronic stress associated with community violence. They may indeed be traumatized by their experiences, but the adults around them will be able to serve as a resource and support them in rehabilitative efforts.

However, once adults begin to deteriorate, to decompensate, to panic, children suffer. This is not surprising, given the importance of the images of adults contained in children's social maps. Traumatized children need help to recover from their experiences (Terr, 1990). Emotionally disabled or immobilized adults are unlikely to offer children what they need. Such adults are inclined to engage in denial, to be emotionally inaccessible, and are prone to misinterpret children's signals. Messages of safety are particularly important in establishing adults as sources of protection and authority for children living in conditions of threat and violence.

In Vygotsky's approach (1986), child development is fundamentally *social*: Cognitive development proceeds at its best through the process of interactive teaching. He focuses on the zone of proximal development: the difference between what the child can accomplish alone versus what the child can accomplish with the guidance of the teacher. How is this relevant to the child's ability to cope with trauma?

In the case of acute trauma (a single, horrible incident that violates the normal reality of the child's world), the child needs help believing that "things are back to normal." This is a relatively easy teaching task, this therapy of reassurance. But the child who lives with chronic trauma (e.g., the problem of community violence) needs something more. This child needs to be taught how to redefine the world in moral and structural terms.

The child needs assistance in "processing" the existing world if he or she is to avoid drawing social and/or psychologically pathogenic conclusions: "The world is a hostile and dangerous place"; "Adults have lost control of the world"; "Kill or be killed"; "Don't trust anyone"; "My enemies are less than human." Here, the role of the adult as teacher is crucial for the well-being of the child and for well-being of the community in which that child is to be a citizen.

CONSEQUENCES OF GROWING UP
IN A WAR ZONE

Many inner-city children are experiencing the symptoms of PTSD, symptoms that include sleep disturbances, intrusive thoughts, recreating trauma in play, extreme startle responses, emotional numbing, diminished expectations for the future, and even biochemical changes in their brains that impair social and academic behavior (Osofsky, 1995). This trauma can produce significant psychological problems that interfere with learning and appropriate social behavior in school, and that interfere with normal parent–child relationships.

Trauma and its consequences can also make children candidates for involvement in gangs. The violent economy of the illicit drug trade offers a sense of belonging and solidarity as well as cash income for kids who have few prosocial alternatives for either. The peer alliances offer some sense of security in a hostile world. If these children do not develop a sense of confidence that adults are committed to providing a safe zone, their willingness and ability to take advantage of developmental opportunities will decrease, and this will adversely affect their future.

Based upon our work in the field and our understanding of the research and clinical experience of our colleagues, we have reached the conclusion that there are many similarities between the experiences of children growing up in war zones around the world and children growing up amid chronic community violence in the United States (Garbarino et al., 1991). These similarities were particularly salient when we compared the situation of children in refugee camps we have visited in Thailand, Hong Kong, and the Middle East, and public housing projects in Chicago and other cities.

• In both the refugee camps and the public housing projects, there is a proliferation of weapons—a kind of "arms race"—that exacerbates the effects of conflict and violence. It is common for young people—particularly males—to be heavily armed and to be engaged in armed attacks and reprisals. Substantial numbers of "bystander" injuries occur.

• In both the refugee camps and the public housing projects, representatives of "mainstream" society have only partial control over what happens. The international relief workers leave the camps at the end of the working day, and so do the social workers and educators in the public housing projects. Both the camps and the projects are under the control of the local gangs at night. Therefore, no action during the day can succeed unless it is acceptable to the gangs that rule the community at night. For example, there have been cases in public housing projects in Chicago in which local gangs established curfews on their own initiative and made decisions about whether someone who commits a crime against residents will be identified and punished.

• In both the refugee camps and the public housing projects, women—particularly mothers—are in a desperate situation. They are under enormous stress, often are the target of domestic violence, and have few economic or educational resources and prospects. Men play a marginal role in the enduring life of families—being absent for reasons that include participating in the fighting, fleeing to escape enemies, being injured or killed, and (particularly in the case of public housing projects in the United States) being imprisoned. Largely as a result, there is a major problem of maternal depression. Studies in both settings have reported 50% of the women being seriously depressed. And this, in turn, is related to problems with early attachment relationships between mothers and children (Osofsky, 1995).

• In both the camps and the public housing projects, one consequence of maternal depression is neglect of children. This connection is well established in research. This neglect leads to elevated levels of "accidental injuries" to children as well as a more generalized parental lack of psychological availability.

• In both the refugee camps and the public housing projects, children and youth have diminished prospects for the future. This lack of a positive future orientation produces depression, rage, and disregard for human life—their own and others.

One focus of international initiatives (such as the U.N. Convention on the Rights of the Child) is to create "zones of peace" for children, and to encourage combatants to institute and respect protected areas for children. Violence-free zones in and around schools are a logical parallel in the United States. Underlying all such efforts is an attempt to communicate a message of safety to children, to stimulate a redrawing of their social maps (Osofsky, 1995).

International action does bring change for families living in refugee camps. For example, the signing of a peace accord has meant that repatriation has come to the Khmer, and they are returning to Cambodia to take up a more genuine community life. However, without some comparable national effort to achieve reconciliation, social justice, and a major peacekeeping force in our cities, most of the families in urban war zones in the United States will remain there, and another generation of children will experience the trauma of chronic community violence. Therein lies one major difference for children living in the world's refugee camps and children living in many public housing projects in the United States. In war zones, there is hope of peace, repatriation, and the renewal of community life. In the case of community violence in America, the war never ends, peace never comes.

Does this mean we are powerless in the face of community violence affecting children? No. We are never powerless if we choose not to be. What are our choices? Among them are the following.

1. *Support programmatic efforts to alter the "legitimization of aggression" among children and youth.* These efforts should include programs that start early—in the early childhood classroom and in the elementary school—to simultaneously stimulate cognitive restructuring and behavioral rehearsal of nonviolent responses to conflict, anger, frustration, injustice, and threat (e.g., Garbarino, 1993).

2. *Respond to trauma in early childhood.* These efforts should help train and support early childhood educators in recognizing and responding to traumatic experiences in the lives of young children in their care—and perhaps serve as a focal point for mental health services aimed at the parents of these children (Garbarino et al., 1992).

3. *Mobilize prosocial adult and youth members of the community to "take charge."* The greatest threat to young children comes when positive adults are defeated by the antisocial forces of community violence. Thus, efforts to mobilize adults and prosocial youth to have a visible presence and thus convey a clear message of strength and responsibility is crucial for redrawing the social maps of children living in violent communities (Garbarino, 1995).

Our efforts to understand the impact of chronic community violence on children and youth around the world and in our own cities highlight several concerns—unmet medical needs, the corrosive effects of coexperiencing poverty and violence on personality and on academic achievement, and so forth. But from our perspective, *the most important of these is that the experience of trauma distorts the values of children.* Unless we reach them with healing experiences and offer them a moral and political framework within which to process their experiences, *traumatized children are likely to be drawn to groups and ideologies that legitimatize and reward their rage, their fear, and their hateful cynicism.* This is an environment in which gangs flourish and community institutions deteriorate, a "socially toxic" environment (Garbarino, 1995).

At the heart of this downward spiral is declining trust in adults on the part of children and youth in high-violence communities. As one youth living in a small city experiencing a proliferation of gangs put it to us recently: "If I join a gang I will be 50% safe, but if I don't I will be 0% safe." He does not put his trust and faith in adults. That is what he is telling us, if we are prepared to listen. There are self-serving, antisocial individuals and groups in our society prepared to mobilize and exploit the anger, fear, alienation, and hostility that many kids feel. *They are listening. Are we?*

REFERENCES

Bell, C. (1991). Traumatic stress and children in danger. *Journal of Health Care for the Poor and Underserved, 2*, 175–188.

Davidson, J., & Smith, R. (1990). Traumatic experiences in psychiatric outpatients. *Journal of Traumatic Stress Studies, 3*(3), 459–475.

Dubrow, N., & Garbarino, J. (1989). Living in the war zone: Mothers and young children in a public housing development. *Child Welfare, 68*, 3–20.

Garbarino, J. (1993). *Let's talk about living in a world with violence.* Chicago: Erikson Institute.

Garbarino, J. (1995). *Raising children in a socially toxic environment: Childhood in the 1990's.* San Francisco: Jossey-Bass.

Garbarino, J., & Associates. (1992). *Children and families in the social environment.* New York: Aldine–de Gruyter.

Garbarino, J., Dubrow, N., Kostelny, K., & Pardo, C. (1992). *Children in danger: Coping with the consequences of community violence.* San Francisco: Jossey-Bass.

Garbarino, J., Kostelny, K., & Dubrow, N. (1991). *No place to be a child: Growing up in a war zone.* Lexington, MA: Lexington Books.

Groves, B., Zuckerman, B., Marans, S., & Cohen, D. (1993). Silent victims: Children who witness violence. *Journal of the American Medical Association, 269*, 262–264.

Herman, J. (1992). *Trauma and recovery.* New York: Basic Books.

Koop, C. E. (1985). *Toward a healthy America.* Washington, DC: U.S. Government Printing Office.

Kotlowitz, A. (1991). *There are no children here.* New York: Doubleday.

Marans, S., & Cohen, D. (1993). Children and inner-city violence: Strategies for intervention. In L. Leavitt & N. Fox (Eds.), *Psychological effects of war and violence on children* (pp. 281–302). Hillsdale, NJ: Erlbaum.

Marin, C. (1989, June 21). Grief's children. WMAQ TV Documentary, Chicago.

Osofsky, J. (1995). The effects of exposure to violence on young children. *American Psychologist, 50*, 782–788.

Pynoos, R., & Nader, K. (1988). Psychological first aid and treatment approach to children exposed to community violence: Research implications. *Journal of Traumatic Stress, 1*, 445–473.

Richters, J., & Martinez, P. (1993). The NIMH community violence project: Vol. 1. Children as victims of and as witnesses to violence. *Psychiatry, 56*, 7–21.

Sameroff, A., Seifer, R., Barocas, R., Zax, M., & Greenspan, S. (1987). Intelligence quotient scores of 4-year-old children: Socio-environmental risk factors. *Pediatrics, 79*, 343–350.

Terr, L. (1990). *Too scared to cry.* New York: Harper & Row.

Vygotsky, L. *Thought and language.* Cambridge, MA: MIT Press.

4

Firearm Injuries Affecting U.S. Children and Adolescents

KATHERINE KAUFER CHRISTOFFEL

I N THE FOUR DECADES after World War II, those who dedicated them-selves to saving the lives of U.S. children had goals that seemed increasingly realizable, because of the control of many infectious dis-eases. Although the scourges of poverty, racism, and other social ills continued to threaten and undermine the futures of too many children, certain goals for the children seemed feasible. These included survival through childhood, good health, successful attainment of critical devel-opmental milestones, a modicum of fun, and, after achievement of all of these, maturation into productive and nurturing adults.

In the last decade, these prospects have dimmed again. Those who care for children—as parents, teachers, day care workers, health care providers, child welfare workers, child advocates, or in any other capac-ity—now recognize that the prospects for children achieving these goals have been dramatically reduced by an epidemic of firearm injury.

EPIDEMIOLOGY

Many children today are distracted from the normal goals of childhood by an increasingly pervasive fear that they will be shot (Waldman, 1993). These fears reflect the facts.

In 1985, approximately 3,000 U.S. children and adolescents died from firearm fatalities. By 1989, this total was over 4,000; and by 1991, it was over 5,000. During this time, unintentional firearm injury counts (and rates) remained approximately stable. The firearm suicides increased about 20%. Pediatric firearm homicides have virtually tripled since 1985, increasing from 1,316 in 1985 to 3,351 in 1992.

Table 4.1 shows childhood firearm fatalities for American children aged 0–19 years by age, sex, and cause for 1988 and 1992. Table 4.2 shows a breakdown by age, race, and cause of firearm deaths for 1988 and 1992; Table 4.3 shows firearm death rates by age, race, sex, and cause for 1988 and 1992. Several salient points must be noted. First, although U.S. firearm suicides exceed homicides for all ages (Fingerhut, Jones, & Makuc, 1994), for children and adolescents, firearm homicides far exceed suicides: approximately 60% of deaths versus 30% for suicide. Second, no age is spared—some of the deaths even involve infants. Third, the vast majority of the child and adolescent deaths—approximately 90%—affect older adolescents, aged 15–19 years. Fourth, only about 10% of all pediatric firearm deaths involve unintentional injuries. Fifth, the majority of the child and adolescent firearm homicide victims are African Americans, whereas the majority of the victims of suicides and unintentional injury deaths are by whites.

The numbers and rates of firearm deaths tell only part of the story. The relative contribution of these deaths to all pediatric deaths is also important. In 1992, 13.6% of all deaths of 0- to 24-year-olds were due to firearm injuries, and 30.4% of all deaths of 15- to 24-year-olds were from these causes (Fingerhut et al., 1994). In 1990, for the first time, among deaths of 15- to 19-year-olds, deaths due to firearms outnumbered those due to natural causes: 1.4:1 for all teens, and 4.7:1 for black teens (Fingerhut, 1992). Firearm injury deaths are the leading cause of death for young black men (Fingerhut & Kleinman, 1991; Fingerhut, 1992).

When we compare the contemporary firearm epidemic to epidemics of the past, it becomes clear that this is a big one. In 1952, 3,145 Americans of all ages died from polio (Strebel et al., 1992). By contrast, over 37,000 Americans of all ages died from firearm injuries in 1992, including over 5,000 children and adolescents (Fingerhut et al., 1994). As best we can estimate, the number of cases of paraplegia due to handgun injuries in 1992 exceeded the number from polio in 1952 (Schmeck, 1995).

It is important to remember that those who die or are paralyzed are not the only victims of this epidemic. In 1994, a poll of high school students indicated that 30% of white students and 70% of black students knew someone who had been shot within the last 5 years; 19% of white students and 37% of black students identified violence as the biggest problem at school; and 5% of white students and 27% of black students

TABLE 4.1. Number of U.S. Firearm Deaths, Ages 1–19 Years, by Sex

Age (years)	Homicide		Suicide		Unintentional		All	
	1988	1992	1988	1992	1988	1992	1988	1992
1–4	50	69	0	0	41	35	91	104
Male	29	39			28	21	57	60
Female	19	29			11	14	30	43
Not specified	2	1				0	2	1
5–9	71	56	0	3	51	48	122	107
Male	36	38		2	43	38	79	78
Female	30	15		1	6	9	36	25
Not specified	5	3		0	2	1	7	4
10–14	183	348	125	172	185	132	493	652
Male	119	241	93	131	151	112	363	484
Female	57	89	28	36	30	16	115	141
Not specified	7	18	4	5	4	4	15	27
15–19	1,657	2,878	1,261	1,251	266	285	3,184	4,414
Male	1,424	2,518	1,049	1,069	242	258	2,715	3,845
Female	195	292	176	131	16	19	387	442
Not specified	38	68	36	51	8	8	82	127
1–19	1,961	3,351	1,386	1,426	543	500	3,890	5,277
Male	1,608	2,836	1,142	1,202	464	408	3,214	4,446
Female	301	425	204	168	63	44	568	637
Not specified	52	90	40	56	14	13	106	159

Sources: Fingerhut & Kleinman (1991); Fingerhut, Jones, & Makuc (1994).

TABLE 4.2. Number of U.S. Firearm Deaths, Ages 1–19 Years, by Race

Age (years)	Homicide		Suicide		Unintentional		All[a]	
	1988	1992	1988	1992	1988	1992	1988	1992
1–4								
White	29	27	0	0	28	21	57	48
Black	19	41	0	0	11	14	30	55
5–9								
White	40	31	0	2	36	27	76	60
Black	26	22	0	1	13	20	39	43
10–14								
White	83	164	107	148	145	102	335	414
Black	92	166	14	19	36	26	142	211
15–19								
White	558	1,072	1,117	1,015	205	180	1,880	2,267
Black	1,061	1,738	108	185	53	97	1,222	2,020
1–19								
White	710	1,294	1,124	1,165	414	330	2,348	2,789
Black	1,198	1,967	122	205	113	157	1,433	2,329

Sources: Fingerhut & Kleinman (1994); Fingerhut, Jones, & Makuc (1994).
[a] Includes intent unknown.

reported worrying about shootings (Chira, 1994). These survey results are consistent with a 1993 poll by Louis Harris, which reported that 59% of school children in grades 6 to 12 "could get a handgun if they wanted one"; 15% had carried a handgun for some purpose during the past 30 days; and 4% had carried a handgun to school. Nine percent reported having shot at somebody (Harris, 1993). Clearly, children whose childhoods are warped in these ways are also victims of this epidemic.

The price of the epidemic of child and adolescent firearm injuries is not only measured in terms of lives and spirits lost, but also in dollars. The National Association of Children's Hospitals and Related Institutions (NACHRI) did a survey in 1993 of 44 acute-care children's hospitals. It showed that the average cost of a hospitalization due to gun injury was over $14,000. The cost incurred by severely injured patients is much greater, as illustrated by an estimate of over $1 million in lifetime costs for a 12-year-old girl rendered paraplegic in a drive-by shooting (Sipchen, 1994).

When we look also at adult U.S. firearm deaths, the consequences for children and adolescents are even greater. In 1992, 37,776 Americans of all ages died from firearms. Their deaths affected hundreds of thousands of children, related or known to them. There are various estimates for the total cost of firearm injuries in the United States. One of the

TABLE 4.3. Rates of U.S. Firearm Deaths, Ages 1–19 Years, by Race and Sex

Age (years)	Homicide		Suicide		Unintentional		All[a]	
	1988	1992	1988	1992	1988	1992	1988	1992
1–4								
White males	0.3	—	0	0	0.3	—	0.6	0.4
Black males	1.1	1.8	0	0	0.7	—	1.8	2.7
White females	0.2	—	0	0	0.1	—	0.3	0.4
Black females	0.6	—	0	0	0.3	—	0.9	1.7
5–9								
White males	0.3	0.3	0	0	0.4	0.3	0.7	0.6
Black males	1.1	—	0	0	0.8	—	1.9	2.6
White females	0.3	—	0	0	0.1	—	0.4	—
Black females	0.7	—	0	0	0.1	—	0.9	—
10–14								
White males	0.8	1.6	1.2	1.5	1.8	1.2	4.2	4.5
Black males	4.5	8.4	0.7	—	2.1	1.6	7.8	11.6
White females	0.4	0.6	0.4	0.5	0.3	—	1.1	1.3
Black females	2.5	3.4	0.4	—	0.6	—	3.6	3.9
15–19								
White males	6.0	13.1	12.7	12.8	2.6	2.4	21.7	28.8
Black males	67.9	119.7	6.8	12.6	3.4	6.7	79.5	141.0
White females	1.3	2.3	2.3	1.7	0.2	—	3.8	4.3
Black females	7.1	10.5	0.9	—	0.4	—	8.4	12.4

Sources: Fingerhut & Kleinman (1991); Fingerhut, Jones, & Makuc (1994).
[a] Include intent unknown.

more conservative was that, in 1985, firearm injuries that occurred in that year cost the United States $14.4 billion. More than three-fourths of the costs of gunshot wounds are born by the public (General Accounting Office, 1991).

SURVEILLANCE

Disease surveillance is a critical component of all efforts to control epidemics. Consistent with this, there is routine surveillance in the United States for a wide variety of infectious diseases, as regularly reported in the Centers for Disease Control and Prevention's *Morbidity and Mortality Weekly Report*. Much of this is based on vestigial reporting systems, left over from epidemics of the past. For example, there was only one case of diphtheria and only one case of paralytic polio reported in 1994. The Centers for Disease Control and Prevention also issue periodic reports on surveillance for smoking-attributable mortality and years of life lost (Nelson et al., 1990).

Yet there is no national reporting system for (mild or disabling) nonfatal firearm injuries. Several locales are beginning to develop such systems in their regions (Handgun Epidemic Lowering Plan, 1994). One estimate is that, at least in the Los Angeles, California, area, the number of children and adolescents permanently disabled due to firearm injury equals the number who die from this cause (Montes, 1993). The same report indicated that 60% of Los Angeles victims under age 19 years with spinal cord injuries suffered their injuries as a result of firearms. A review of children with firearm injuries treated at Chicago's Children's Memorial Hospital over 9 years indicated that only 57% of the patients left the hospital normal, with the rest either dead (13%) or with permanent neurological (23%) or other (7%) abnormalities (Tanz & Barthel, 1989).

INTERNATIONAL COMPARISONS

The scale of the firearm epidemic in the United States is unique in the developed world (Figure 4.1). When international comparisons are made of homicide rates for 15- to 24-year-old males, U.S. rates are far, far above those of other countries (Rosenberg, 1994; Fingerhut & Kleinman,

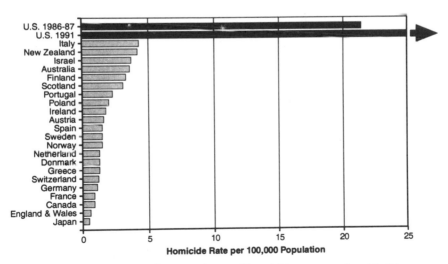

FIGURE 4.1. International comparisons of homicide rates, males, 15–24 years of age, 1988–1991. Age-specific rates were calculated using data for the most recent years available. *Source*: National Center for Injury Prevention and Control (1994).

1990). Although rates were under 5 per 100,000 for all the other countries studied, the United States white rate was between 15 and 20 per 100,000; the overall U.S. rate was between 35 and 40 per 100,000; and the U.S. black rate was close to 160 per 100,000. This represents an epidemic out of control, as surely as if the international comparison involved cancer, heart disease, AIDS, tuberculosis, or any other cause of death. The vast majority of U.S. homicides are due to firearms (Fingerhut, 1990).

A 1989 study of 14 countries surveyed the prevalence of powder guns in households and the relationship between this prevalence and reported rates of homicide and suicide (Killias, 1993). U.S. household gun-ownership rates were far above those of the other countries (48%, with the next highest rate 32%). Gun ownership was found to be highly statistically significantly correlated with homicides and suicides (with guns and overall). The correlation between household guns and suicide was .90; almost all of this was due to handguns (correlation of .79).

These data suggest that the handgun is the agent of this epidemic of violent death and injury. Other evidence supports this concept.

THE AGENT OF THE EPIDEMIC

Because identifying the cause of death and disability is a central goal of medical epidemiological research, there are well-established guidelines for assessing the role of the handgun in the current epidemic of violent death and disability. An outline of these was provided a generation ago by Sir Austin Bradford Hill, in his Presidential address to the Section of Occupational Medicine of the British Royal Society of Medicine, on January 14, 1965. He prefaced his remarks with this observation: "With the aims of occupational, and almost synonymously preventive, medicine in mind the decisive question is whether the frequency of the undesirable event B will be influenced by a change in the environmental feature A" (Hill, 1965). Sir Bradford Hill proceeded to outline nine "aspects of . . . association" that he suggested "we should especially consider before deciding that the most likely interpretation . . . is causation." He stressed that none of these

> can bring indisputable evidence for or against the cause-and-effect hypothesis and none can be required as a *sine qua non*. What they can do, with greater or less strength, is to help us to make up our minds on the fundamental question—is there any other way of explaining the set of facts before us, is there any other answer equally, or more, likely than cause and effect?

The nine aspects he discussed are the following:

- *Strength*, that is, the size of the risk associated with the environmental factor.
- *Consistency*, that is, an association that has been observed by different persons, in different places, circumstances, and times.
- *Specificity*, that is, an association between the environmental factor and a specific way of dying (this, he mentioned, was one of the weaker criteria, as some causes do affect more than one way of dying).
- *Temporality*, that is, exposure to the environmental factor precedes the development of increased risk.
- *Biological gradient*, that is, increasing risk with increasing exposure.
- *Plausibility*, that is, a connection between the environmental factor and the disease outcome.
- *Coherence*, that is, consistency across different fields of inquiry (e.g., bench research and epidemiology).
- *Experimental (or quasi-experimental) evidence*, that is, the effects of varying environmental feature A directly affects the frequency of undesirable outcome B.
- *Analogy*, that is, evidence from other types of health problems that is similar to the association under consideration.

To reach an understanding of what is and is not known about the role of handguns in the causation of violent death, it is useful to consider each of these aspects in turn. Tables 4.4–4.12 summarize the evidence from a 1995 literature review that handguns are, in these terms, the cause of violent death and injury. The tables suggest that numerous studies in the medical literature indicate that handguns meet these standard epidemiological criteria for a cause of environmental death.

Taken together, the studies cited suggest a particular causal sequence: Fear of crime leads to high and rising levels of handgun ownership and unsafe storage; these cause ready access to handguns; the access—at times of anger, sadness, intoxication, or fear—leads to a heightened risk of injury and death, which is highest when the accessible handguns are most lethal (e.g., currently popular semiautomatic pistols).

Only a few published studies fail to show that handguns are the predominant weapon in homicide and suicide; these studies are instructive as well. They suggest that access to handguns (or, perhaps, to loaded or unlocked handguns) has not been as high in rural as in urban areas. Thus rural ownership and storage patterns are important areas for study.

(An extended and refined version of this literature review is in progress.)

The role of the handgun is significant because handguns represent only a minority of the U.S. home arsenal. Widely accepted estimates are

TABLE 4.4. Association of Handguns with Violent Death and Injury: Strength

	Homicide	Suicide
No. of studies (Refs. 1–5)[a]	2	3
Years studied	1984–1992	1986–1990
Locations	Atlanta, GA; King Co., WA; Shelby Co., TN; Cuyahoga, Co., OH	W. PA; King Co., WA; Vancouver, BC
Ages	>12, all	<19, all
Findings	FA 12× more deadly than other weapons; HG in home at least doubled risk of homicide.	HG 6× more prevalent in homes of suicide victims of all ages; 9× more prevalent in homes of adolescent victims; firearms 9× more lethal than other means.

Note. In Tables 4.4–4.12, FA = firearm; HG = handgun.
[a] For references to Tables 4.4–4.12, see pages 68–71.

that there are approximately 200 million firearms in American homes, including approximately 60 million handguns. Handguns can thus be identified as high-risk weapons, just as we are accustomed to identifying high-risk individuals, families, and communities.

UNDERSTANDING THE AGENT OF THE EPIDEMIC

It is as important to understand how the hangun works as it is to understand the mechanisms of agents of other epidemics, including, for example, the measles and the AIDS viruses.

The key to understanding firearm injuries, including handgun injuries, is the equation $KE = MV^2$ (kinetic energy = mass × velocity^2). The reason for this is that injury, scientifically defined, is tissue damage that occurs when energy is transferred in an amount or at a rate that the tissues cannot sustain without damage (Haddon & Baker, 1981).

In many types of injury, including falls from great heights, car crashes, and firearm injuries, the energy involved is kinetic energy. In the case of a car crash, the mass is very large (measured in tons), the velocity is relatively modest (tens of miles per hour). In the case of a firearm injury, the mass is very small (the bullet), but the velocity is

TABLE 4.5. Association of Handguns with Violent Death and Injury: Consistency

	Homicide/assault	Suicide	Unintentional	All
No. of studies (Refs. 4, 6–34)	10	4	4	10
Years studied	1973–1994	1979–1991	1976–1988	1978–1992
Locations	IL, MD, MO, LA, OH cities; Philadelphia; VA; United States–Canadian border	Dallas Co., TX; Iowa; Sacramento Co., CA; W. PA; United States	NC; CA; NM; King Co., WA; VT; Cuyahoga Co., OH	MD; LA; Mobile Co., AL; Travis Co., TX; Chicago, IL; LaCrosse, WI; United States versus Canada
Ages	<20, ≥18, 15–24, all	<19, all, ≥65	<14, >10, all	<10, <11, all
Findings	73–94% of FA homicides due to HG. One study shows no association.	37–80% of FA suicides due to HG; HG 2× more prevalent among suicides than in homes; effect clearest in cities.	39–83% of unintentional FA deaths due to HG; 1.6× more prevalent among these than in homes.	20–89% of FA deaths involve HG; only one <48% is rural.

TABLE 4.6. Association of Handguns with Violent Death and Injury: Specificity

No. of studies (Refs. 2, 3, 5, 35–38)	7
Years studied	1959–1992
Locations	King Co., WA; Vancouver, BC; Cuyahoga Co., OH; W. PA; Shelby Co., TN; Washington, DC; 23 countries
Ages	>12, <19, all
Findings	In all but one study, FA, HG *not* associated with *non*-FA homicides, suicides. FA/HG associated with FA deaths, with OR as high as 75.

very high (measured in hundreds to thousands of feet per second). Thus, firearms—including handguns—are consumer products that are designed to muster deadly amounts of kinetic energy and to convey them on bullets to victims.

The bullets that are used in war are, by international convention, metal jacketed. This is because such jacketing reduces the chances of a bullet deforming after impact, and therefore increases the chances that the bullet will exit the body. In that eventuality, the velocity term in $KE = MV^2$ is [velocity of entry − velocity of exit]. In other words, if the bullet exits the body, the amount of energy transferred is minimized, and the damage is less. Therefore, if the bullet penetrates a vital organ, the victim is dead. However, if it does not, the victim can probably recover (Barach, Tomlanovich, & Nowack, 1986a, 1986b). Bullets that are sold for civilian use in the Unites States are not covered by that

TABLE 4.7. Association of Handguns with Violent Death and Injury: Temporality

No. of studies (Refs. 5, 38–41)	5
Years studied	1945–1991
Locations	Shelby Co., TN; King Co., WA; Washington, DC
Ages	All, >65
Findings	FA homicides and suicides rose as HG sales did ($R \geq .91$); fell with restrictive licensure of HG (23–25%). FA used in home suicides present in home > 2 weeks.

TABLE 4.8. Association of Handguns with Violent Death and Injury: Biological Gradient

	Suicide	Unintentional	>1 cause
No. of studies (Refs. 36, 37, 42–45)	2	1	3
Years studied	1959–1988	1962–1971	1920–1989
Locations	W. PA; United States	Wayne Co., MI	14 countries; United States
Ages	<19, all	All	All
Findings	69% of variance in suicide rates between states explained by crime rates, divorce rates, and handgun control laws affecting buyers and sellers; number of HG per home 2× higher in suicide victims than controls; gun ownership rates correlate with gun suicide rates (R = .68).	Rise in unintentional FA deaths with rise in new gun permits.	FA homicide and suicide rates rises paralleled FA sales after 1950. FA ownership related to suicide and homicide; most of effect on suicide due to HG (R = .79 for HG vs. .90 for FA).

53

TABLE 4.9. Association of Handguns with Violent Death and Injury: Plausibility

	Availability	Homicide	Suicide
No. of studies (Refs. 5, 7, 34, 46–54)	8	2	1
Year studies	1950–1991	1976–1985	1987–1990
Locations	United States; inner-city areas in CA, NJ, LA, IL	Cites in OH; United States–Canadian border	Shelby Co., TN; King Co., WA
Ages	High-school students, adults, families of children	≥18, all	All
Findings	HG acquisition rate is rising; adults and teens prefer HG for self-protection; HG owners twice as likely to keep guns loaded or unlocked, 13× as likely to keep loaded and unlocked.	44% of weapons used in homicides of families or friends involved guns stored loaded and unlocked; no consistent differences across border (but background rates low).	Suicides 2.8× more frequent in homes with loaded than unloaded guns; 2.3× more frequent in homes with unlocked than locked guns.

international convention. Indeed, manufacturers compete mightily to produce the most deformable bullets (with high "stopping power").

One such bullet, the Black Talon bullet, had a deformable tip that exploded into a rosette with razor-blade edges. It thus shredded the tissue along its path, and then came to rest, waiting for the trauma surgeon's (or emergency physician's) gloved hand. Protests by emergency and trauma physicians and pathologists ultimately have led the manufacturer of the bullet to withdraw it from the market. However, many similar bullets are still available for purchase.

CHILDREN'S EXPOSURE TO HANDGUNS

Senturia, Christoffel, and Donovan reported in 1994 on firearm ownership patterns in over 5,000 families attending pediatric practices in several states. Thirty-two percent reported owning powder guns, including 17% who reported owning handguns. Although recreation was the most common reason for ownership of both handguns (59%) and rifles (75%), self-protection was a far more common reason among handgun owners than rifle owners (48% vs. 21%), as was occupational use (12% vs. 5%). This probably explains why handguns were 13 times more likely to be kept both loaded and unlocked than rifles. (Senturia et al., 1994) The results of this survey were perhaps most surprising because the majority of the respondents were white and middle class; but this is not the only survey to show lower gun-ownership rates among minority families than among white families.

TAKING A PUBLIC HEALTH APPROACH

When we see firearm deaths and injuries as an epidemic phenomenon and the handgun as the agent of the epidemic, it makes sense to address

TABLE 4.10. Association of Handguns with Violent Death and Injury: Coherence

	Homicide/assault
No. of studies (Refs. 54–55)	2
Years studied	1983–1993
Locations	Washington, DC; Chicago, IL
Ages	>18, all
Findings	Increased death, number of gunshot wounds with increasing availability of semiautomatic pistols.

TABLE 4.11. Association of Handguns with Violent Death and Injury: Experimental/Quasi-experimental Evidence

	Homicide	Suicide	Homicide and Suicide
No. of studies (Refs. 4, 35, 37, 38, 56)	2	1	2
Year studies	1976–1986	1985–1987	1985–1987
Locations	Seattle and Vancouver; United States–Canadian border	Washington, DC	Seattle and Vancouver
Ages	All	All	All
Findings	Risk of homicide in Seattle 5× that in Vancouver, most due to HG; difference in homicides across border only in major cities.	FA homicide and suicide down ¼ after restrictive HG licensure.	HG suicide increased in Seattle: 5.7× for all ages, 9.6× for 15- to 24-year-olds.

TABLE 4.12. Association of Handguns with Violent Death and Injury: Analogy

	Suicide	Unintentional
No. of studies (Refs. 57–61)	3	2
Years studied	1940s–1987	NA, 1987
Locations	New York City; Germany; Surinam	Germany; Chicago area
Ages	All	All, children
Findings	New York City counties had similar suicide rates when methods equally accessible, different rates by methods that were differently available; suicides/attempts using paraquat (in Surinam) and cyanide (in Germany) were related to occupational access to these substances.	Occupational exposure to sodium azide (in Germany) and hazardous products (in Chicago) have been related to risk of poisoning and injury.

this as one would any other epidemic: efforts to reduce the spread of the agent. This requires a shift in approach, because the predominant themes in public discussions of firearm injuries until now have generally involved crime and criminal justice, rather than health and handgun regulation. When the focus is on crime, control approaches focus on law enforcement and incarceration of perpetrators, and public discussion tends to focus on issues of civil liberties. In contrast, when firearm injury is discussed in terms of public health, the focus is on prevention, and public discussion focuses on reducing death, disability, and suffering.

There is precedent for this kind of paradigm shift. Perhaps the best example concerns cigarette-related deaths. Prior to 1964, much of the public discussion about smoking focused on the civil liberties of smokers. But in 1964, the Surgeon General's report identified cigarette smoking as the leading cause of preventable death in the United States (U.S. Public Health Service, 1964). Since then, smoking rates among adult men have fallen by half, and those of adult women by one-third (Figure 4.2). This has saved many thousands of lives. Thus, the Surgeon General's report and its paradigm shift was a major public health intervention, which ultimately caused millions of people to reconsider their choices about smoking. It opened up a series of scientific investigations and public policy discussions that gradually led to a level of cigarette smoking restrictions in the 1990s that would have been unthinkable in the 1960s.

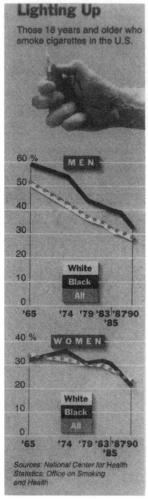

FIGURE 4.2. Effects of shift to a public health approach to cigarette smoking. *Source*: *The New York Times*, May 22, 1992, p. A12. Copyright 1992. Reprinted by permission.

Figure 4.3 shows the effects of a similar paradigm shift related to motor-vehicle injuries. In the late 1960s, motor-vehicle injuries were redefined as a public health problem. There followed a multidisciplinary approach to motor-vehicle injury control, including improvements in car construction; road construction; passenger restraints; changes in d .ving laws, particularly related to penalties for those intoxicated; and other such measures (Robertson, 1992). Figure 4.3

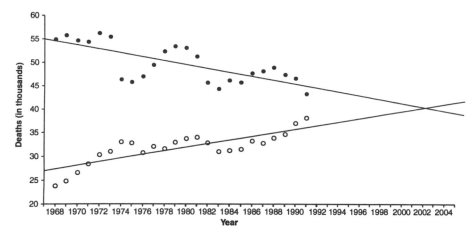

FIGURE 4.3. Recent observed and projected firearm- and motor-vehicle-related injury deaths, United States. *Source*: National Center for Injury Prevention and Control (1994).

shows the regression line that indicates a steep and steady decline in motor-vehicle crash injuries over the years (despite some year-to-year variation), with a fall from about 55,000 deaths per year in 1968 to about 45,000 deaths per year in 1990. This can be contrasted with the regression line for firearm injury deaths, which is just as steadily rising (also despite some year-to-year variation). The analysis shown projects that firearm injuries would replace motor-vehicle injuries as the leading cause of death in the United States by around the year 2000, as it already had in seven states (Fingerhut et al., 1994). A more recent analysis of preliminary 1994 data suggests that this may already have happened (Wintemute, 1995).

A public health approach to firearm injuries has a number of consequences for prevention planning. First, it defines an approach to policy that is based on science. Second, it focuses on protection of the many at risk, not just management of those who are hurt. Third, it defines measurable health outcomes to gauge success in addressing the epidemic. It focuses public attention and mobilizes support from the private sector.

Defining handgun death and injury as a public health problem also opens the history of public health as a textbook to study for approaches to other epidemics that may guide how we can deal with this one. One epidemic that seems particularly pertinent is the cholera epidemic of the early 1800s in London, made famous by the efforts of Dr. John Snow

(1855) to control it. Dr. Snow had the good idea to map the victims of the epidemic, and when he did so, he observed that they all resided in the area served by the Broad Street pump. He then went down and took the handle off, stopping the epidemic. (Then there was time to find out why this pump was polluted, and how it could be rendered safe, all of which was done.) If we view handguns as the agent of this epidemic, we can productively turn our attention to the "pumps" that bring handguns into our homes and communities, and see what we can do to "take the handles off."

There are approximately 2,000 firearm distributors in the United States, including about 1,000 manufacturers and about 1,000 importers (Sugarmann, 1992). The weapons that they produce bear little resemblance to those of the American Revolution, although gun use at that time is sometimes cited in defense of prevalent gun availability in our society.[1] A small group of companies in southern California is rapidly becoming the leading handgun source in the United States, replacing the traditional leading producers in Connecticut. The California companies have focused on an economic niche in handgun production that was created by the Gun Control Act of 1968, which banned *importation* of handguns that were very easy to conceal, very small, and failed certain design and performance criteria. It implicitly permitted the production of such handguns *domestically* (Wintemute, 1994). Many of these handguns cost under $100; they are particularly likely to be used in crime, and are quite unreliable. Until recently, manufacturers who profit from the spread of handguns have been left fairly untouched in the debate on how best to reduce firearm injuries.

The 2,000 distributors sell their handguns to over 150,000 federal firearm licensees. In 1990, the number of these outnumbered gas stations in the United States; there has been a marked reduction in the number of licensees following the passage of the Brady Bill (and an increase in the cost of licensure) that took effect in 1994 (Violence Policy Center, 1995). These licenses now cost $66 per year (up from about half that before the Brady Bill) and are quite easily obtained with a mail-in form. Local jurisdictions are now routinely advised of the licensees in their area, most of whom sell from their homes, garages, and cars (so-called "kitchen-table dealers"). Once licensed, federal firearm licensees can purchase any legal firearm (excluding fully automatic weapons and bazookas) by mail, across state lines, at a discount, and sell them, with little chance

---

[1] Visits to museums documenting weaponry in the late 18th century make it clear that there were no handguns as we now know them, nor were there bullets: The available weapons were individually loaded for every firing, under conditions that easily went awry, to the detriment of the loader.

that their adherence to regulations concerning proper sale will be checked (Sugarmann, 1992). This is a minimally regulated distribution system, which makes firearms quite unique among consumer products in the United States.

Another "pump" bringing guns into homes is manufacturer advertising. For example, an ad in the *Ladies' Home Journal* a few years ago, by Colt, showed a mother sitting next to her child, whom she was putting to bed, and bore the headline, "Self-protection is more than your right . . . it's your responsibility." It thus implied that a responsible mother would acquire a handgun to protect her family. Yet, data presented in Table 4.4 make it clear that handguns in the home actually increase the risk to household residents, a fact that the manufacturers surely know. This advertising campaign is a result of marketing research by the firearm industry in response to a slump in sales in the 1970s. As a result of that research, the industry came up with two strategies for improving sales: product diversification (particularly the introduction of the semiautomatic pistol), and targeting markets that were not saturated (particularly women and youth; Sugarmann, 1992).

Another "pump" fueling the distribution of handguns is a misunderstanding of the Second Amendment to the Constitution. It reads, in its entirety: "a well-regulated militia, being necessary to the security of a free state, the right of the people to keep and bear arms shall not be infringed." The Supreme Court has ruled, in decisions going back over a century, that this amendment prohibits Congressional interference with state militias. The rulings make it clear that the amendment has nothing to do with individual gun ownership; indeed, none of the tens of thousands of laws on the books in the United States at all jurisdictional levels concerning firearm ownership or use (national, state, local), has ever been declared unconstitutional because of the Second Amendment (Vernick & Teret, 1993). Nonetheless, there is a widespread belief that the Second Amendment protects individual gun ownership, and this misunderstanding appears in half of all high school textbooks (Bonderman, 1991).

If the effectiveness of the "pumps" were reduced, flow of the handgun—an agent of epidemic death and injury—into U.S. homes and communities would be likely to slow, and, many people might decide to dispose of those already in their possession. Based on the evidence that available handguns cause many deaths and injuries, the result should be lowered mortality and morbidity.

STRATEGIZING HOW TO PROTECT CHILDREN

It is crucial to keep in mind that handguns cause death and injury by adding lethality to other situations (Christoffel, 1994). For children and adolescents, these situations are frequently fairly ordinary parts of child-hood. Exploration of the environment can turn deadly if a young child happens upon a loaded and unlocked handgun. Preadolescent fantasy play can turn deadly if the gun used in an imaginary battle turns out to be real and loaded. Adolescent bravado can kill if the adolescent is armed not with a fist, but with a gun. The foolish squabbles that characterize adolescence (e.g., over transient relationships and clothing), can lead to death or paralysis when teens are armed with handguns. There is no way to take these behaviors out of childhood. It only makes sense, therefore, to try to take the guns—usually handguns—out of the same environ-ments of children.

Many efforts are under way to address the root causes of violence, which include poverty, drug use and trade, racism, unemployment, gang activity, mental illness, community decay, and so on. While these efforts proceed, it must be remembered that with those root causes still uncon-trolled, the last thing that children and adolescents need is an accessible handgun (Christoffel, 1995). Children who utilize drugs, who have men-tal health problems, or who come from broken and unsupportive fami-lies, have more than enough problems without the addition of a handgun to contribute disability or death. Thus, efforts must be undertaken to reduce the availability of the handgun, the agent of lethality, at the same time that efforts go on to reduce the contributing root causes of violence (see Table 4.13).

A number of years ago, the American Academy of Pediatrics (AAP, 1992a, 1992b) examined data like those reviewed in this chapter. It identi-fied as a critical goal a shifting of the debate on firearms from one that focuses on the Second Amendment and crime to one that focuses on the

TABLE 4.13. Strategies for Protecting Children and Adolescents from the Lethality of Handguns

Generally
- Shift the debate to a public health model.
- Develop handgun-free homes and havens.
- Legally restrict handgun sales and ownership.
- Develop alternative (safer) self- and home-protection devices.

Health professionals
- Identify and counsel high-risk families on the danger of handguns.
- Anticipatory guidance about handguns for all families.
- Work toward comprehensive tracking of handgun deaths and injuries at local, state, and national levels.
- Participate in coalitions to achieve public education and legal reforms.
- Join the HELP Network to keep abreast of current information and network with colleagues around the United States.

reduction of death, disability, and suffering due to handguns. In order to protect children from the direct and indirect effects of gun violence, the strategy adopted is to remove the guns from the environments of children. Because pediatricians deal with families, because so many families keep handguns, and because handguns in the home are a rich source of guns on the streets in the hands of adolescents (Sheley & Wright, 1993), a logical focus of that effort is removal of handguns from the home. The AAP has developed an office-based parent education program regarding firearms, particularly handguns. This includes materials to educate the provider and brochures for the family (Center to Prevent Handgun Violence, 1994).

The AAP calls for a ban on the manufacture, sale, and private ownership of handguns, because the risk–benefit ratio for handguns in the home is so disadvantageous. The AAP also calls for a ban on assault weapons and deadly airguns, although the focus is on handguns, because these are the main problems; and for a reduction in the romanticization of handgun use in movies and on television (American Academy of Pediatrics, 1992a, 1992b). These goals will not be achieved quickly. Along the way, every step that reduces the availability of handguns in the environments of children and adolescents (and the adults in their lives) is a step forward.

A variety of steps are possible. People acquire handguns for self-protection, and it is reasonable to want to protect oneself. However, handguns provide a feeling of protection but a fact of danger. Other technologies need to be explored that can provide a sense of safety (and, ideally, a fact of safety as well), but which do not kill tens of thousands of Americans each year. Efforts can be undertaken to make homes and neighborhoods handgun-free *safe havens*, where families do not need to worry that children will be shot, and the children can be worry-free for a time as well. Such safe havens can then expand and coalesce into larger handgun-free areas. *Education* must be undertaken in professional and community organizations, so that people can make intelligent and informed decisions about their own use of handguns and the policies that they wish to have undertaken in their communities.

Legislative efforts can be undertaken to reduce civilian access to handguns, and there are many options here (Christoffel, 1991; Teret & Wintemute, 1993; Dolins & Christoffel, 1994). It is important to remember that legislation and regulation regarding handguns are most likely to be effective when they come closest to the point of production, and least likely to be effective when they affect ownership and use long after distribution. At present, most laws and regulations pertain to ownership and use. In elections, *politicians* must be held accountable for policies that are in place (e.g., the lax regulatory system that applies to federal firearm licenses).

Because modification of the consumer product has been such a productive approach in reducing other types of injuries, modifications of handguns must be considered as one approach to reducing epidemic handgun injuries. These approaches can include the use of protective clothing (such as bulletproof vests that police use), reduction in barrel length and bore to reduce the kinetic energy of the bullet leaving the gun, reduction in magazine size (to reduce somewhat the possibility of multiple wounds), and banning particularly dangerous ammunition (National Center for Injury Prevention and Control, 1994). In addition, highly technological devices could be used to personalize handguns, so that one person's handgun cannot be used by somebody else (Teret & Wintemute, 1993). As research goes forward on these approaches, evaluations will be necessary to make sure that the modifications have the intended result. For example, it is conceivable that personalization of handguns would result in a larger number of handguns in the home, potentially increasing, rather than decreasing, risk. It is also possible that the product modification approach will work for some weapons, such as rifles, better than for other weapons such as handguns, because these differ from other successfully modified consumer products in key ways, including size and purpose (Christoffel, 1995).

THE ROLE OF HEALTH PROFESSIONALS

Health professionals and others who care for children undertake to protect them from leading dangers. Increasingly, these include handgun injury. The Handgun Epidemic Lowering Plan (HELP) Network of Concerned Professionals is a relatively new organization that unites professional organizations (in health, law, child welfare, advocacy, etc.) to address the handgun epidemic as a public health problem. The HELP Network facilitates the sharing of current information and strategies across organizations and regions. Member organizations use shared information to develop their own educational, clinical, and legislative agendas aimed at helping to control the handgun epidemic. Further information is available from the author or at 773–880–3826.

CONCLUSION

Figure 4.4 (*New York Times*, March 1, 1994) graphically portrays the dilemma that families and public policymakers must understand. As a nation, we have been holding our children in one hand and our handguns in the other. It has become clear how dangerous this is. Once it is

FIGURE 4.4. U.S. handgun policy dilemma. *Source: The New York Times*, March 1, 1994. Photo copyright 1994 by Evan Richman. Reprinted by permission.

understood that it is not possible to protect the children and the guns equally, more effort will be expended to protect the children, not the guns. When the children are protected in this way, the adults in their lives will be better off as well.

REFERENCES

American Academy of Pediatrics, Committee on Adolescence. (1992a). Firearms and adolescents. *Pediatrics, 894,* 784–787.

American Academy of Pediatrics, Committee on Injury and Poison Prevention. (1992b). Firearm injuries affecting the pediatric population. *Pediatrics, 894,* 788–790.

Barach, E., Tomlanovich, M., & Nowak, R. (1986a). Ballistics: A pathophysiologic examination of the wounding mechanisms of firearms: Part I. *Journal of Trauma, 26,* 225–235.

Barach, E., Tomlanovich, M., & Nowak, R. (1986b). Ballistics: A pathophysiologic examination of the wounding mechanisms of firearms: Part II. *Journal of Trauma, 26,* 374–383.

Bonderman, J. (1991). *Teaching the Bill of Rights—A case of the Second Amendment: A critique of existing educational materials and suggestions for change.* Washington, DC: Center to Prevent Handgun Violence.

Center to Prevent Handgun Violence (CPHV). (1994). *Steps to prevent (STOP) firearm injury.* Washington, DC: American Academy of Pediatrics and Center to Prevent Handgun Violence.

Centers for Disease Control and Prevention. (1994). *Morbidity and Mortality Weekly Report, 43*(51 & 52), 967.

Chira, S. (1994, July 10). Teenagers, in a poll, report worry and distrust of adults. *New York Times,* p. 1.

Christoffel, K. Kaufer. (1991). Toward reducing pediatric firearm injuries: Charting a legislative and regulatory course. *Pediatrics, 88,* 294–305.

Christoffel, K. Kaufer. (1994). Editorial: Reducing violence—How do we proceed? *American Journal of Public Health, 84*(4), 539–541.

Christoffel, K. Kaufer. (1995). Handguns in the environments of children. *Children's Environments Quarterly, 12*(1), 39–48.

Dolins, J. C., & Christoffel, K. Kaufer. (1994). Reducing violent injuries: Priorities for pediatrician advocacy. *Pediatrics,94*(4, Suppl.), 638–651.

Fingerhut, L. A. (1992). Firearm deaths and death rates; United States 1992. *NCHS, Data from the National Vital Statistics System.*

Fingerhut, L. A. (1993). Firearm mortality among children, youth, young adults 1–34 years of age, trends, and current status; United States, 1985–90. *NCHS, Advance Data from Vital and Health Statistics, 231.*

Fingerhut, L. A., Jones, C., & Makuc, D. (1994). Firearm and motor vehicle injury mortality—Variations by state, race, and ethnicity (1990–91): United States. *NCHS, Advance Data from Vital and Health Statistics, 242.*

Fingerhut, L. A., & Kleinman, J. C. (1990). International and interstate comparisons of homicide among young males. *Journal of the American Medical Association, 263,* 3292–3295.

Fingerhut, L. A., & Kleinman, J. C. (1991). Firearm mortality among children, youth, young adults 1–34 years of age, trends, and current status: United States, 1979–88. *NCHS, Monthly Vital Statistics Report, 39,* 11.

General Accounting Office. (1991) *Trauma care: Lifesaving system threatened by unreimbursed costs and other factors* (GAO/HRD-91-57). Washington, DC: General Accounting Office.

Haddon, W., & Baker, S. P. (1981). Injury control. In D. W. Clark & B. MacMahon (Eds.), *Preventive and Community Medicare.* Boston: Little, Brown.

Handgun Epidemic Lowering Plan (HELP). (1994, September 17). *Workshop on state and local surveillance of firearm injuries.* 2nd annual meeting, Chicago, IL.

Harris, L. (1993). *A survey of experiences, perceptions, apprehensions about guns among young people in America.* Cambridge, MA: LH Research, Inc., Harvard School of Public Health.

Hill, A. B. (1965). The environment and disease: Association or causation? *Proceedings of the Royal Society of Medicine, 58,* 295–300.

Killias, M. (1993). International correlations between gun ownership and rates of homicide and suicide. *Canadian Medical Association Journal, 148*(10), 1721–1725.

Lighting up. (1992, May 22). *New York Times,* p. A12.

Montes, L. (1993, October 17). *Physical morbidity.* Paper presented at the 1st Annual Handgun Epidemic Lowering Plan (HELP) Meeting, Chicago, IL.

National Association of Children's Hospitals and Related Institutions, Inc. (NACHRI). (1993). *Violence prevention focus '93: Reducing children's access to firearms.* Alexandria, VA: Author.

Nelson, D. E., Kirkendall, R. S., Lawton, R. L., Chrismon, J. H., Merritt, R. K., Arday, D. A., & Giovino, G. A. (1994). Surveillance for smoking-attributable mortality and years of potential life lost, by state—United States, 1990. *Morbidity and Mortality Weekly Report, 43*(1), 1–8.

Robertson, L. S. (1992). *Injury epidemiology.* New York: Oxford University Press.

Rosenberg, M. L. (1994, January 20). *Violence prevention: Integrating public health and criminal justice.* Presentation at the U.S. Attorneys' Conference, Washington, DC: National Center for Injury Prevention and Control.

Schmeck, H. M. (1995, June 24). Jonas Salk, whose polio drug altered life in the U.S. dies at age 80. *New York Times*, pp. 1, 10.

Senturia, Y. D., Christoffel, K. Kaufer, & Donovan, M. (1994). Children's household exposure to guns: A pediatric practice-based survey. *Pediatrics, 93*, 469–475.

Sheley, J. F., & Wright, J. D. (1993). *Gun acquisition and possession in selected juvenile samples.* Washington, DC: U.S. Department of Justice, Office of Justice Programs, National Institutes of Justice, Office of Juvenile Justice and Delinquency Prevention.

Sipchen, B. (1994, June 5). Putting a price on violence. *Los Angeles Times*, Part A, pp. 1–5.

Snow, J. (1855/1965). *On the mode of communication of cholera* (2nd ed.). Reprinted in *Proceedings of the Royal Society of Medicine, 58*, 295–300.

Strebel, P. M., Sutter, R. W., Cochi, S. L., Biellik, R. J., Brink, E. W., Kew, O. M., Pallansch, M. A., Orenstein, W. A., & Hinman, A. R. (1992). Epidemiology of poliomyelitis in the United States one decade after the last reported case of indigenous wild virus-associated disease. *Clinical Infectious Diseases, 14*, 568–579.

Sugarmann J. (1992) *National Rifle Association: Money, fire power, and fear.* Washington, DC: National Press Books.

Tanz, R. R., & Barthel, M. J. (1989). Bullets, BBs, and boys: Understanding gun injuries treated at a pediatric trauma center (Abstract). *American Journal of Diseases of Children, 143*, 426.

Teret, S. P., & Wintemute, G. J. (1993). Policies to prevent firearms injuries. *Health Affairs, 12*, 96–108.

U.S. Public Health Service. (1964). *Smoking and health report of the Advisory Committee to the Surgeon General of the Public Health Service.* Washington, DC: PHS Publication No. 1103, U.S. Department of Health, Education and Welfare, Centers for Disease Control.

Vernick, J. S., & Teret, S. P. (1993). Firearms and health: The right to be armed with accurate information about the Second Amendment. *American Journal of Public Health, 83*, 1773–1777.

Violence Policy Center. (1995, February 21). *In historic reversal, U.S. now has more gas stations than gun dealers, stricter ATF enforcement, new federal laws: State and local initiatives help weed out illegitimate "kitchen-table" gun dealers.* Press release.

Waldman, L. (1993). *My neighborhood: The words and pictures of inner-city children.* Chicago: Hyde Park Bank Foundation.

Wintemute, G. J. (1994). *Ring of fire: The handgun makers of southern California.* Sacramento, CA: Violence Prevention Research Program.

Wintemute, G. J. (1995). *Trauma in transition: Trends in deaths from firearm and motor-vehicle injuries.* Sacramento, CA: Violence Prevention Research Program.

TABLE REFERENCES
(for Tables 4.4–4.12)

1. Saltzman, L. E., Mercy, J. A., O'Carroll, P. W., Rosenberg, M. L., & Rhodes, P. H. (1992). Weapon involvement and injury outcomes in family and intimate assaults. *Journal of the Ameican Medical Association, 267,* 3043–3047.

2. Kellermann, A., Rivara, F. P., Rushforth, N. B., Banton, J. G., Reay, D. T., Francisco, J. T., Locci, A. B., Prodzinski, J., Hackman, B. B., & Somes, G. (1993). Gun ownership as a risk factor for homicide in the home. *New England Journal of Medicine, 329,* 1084–1091.

3. Brent, D. A., Perper, J. A., Allman, C. J., Moritz, G. M., Wartella, M. E., & Zelenak, J. P. (1991). The presence and accessibility of firearms in the homes of adolescent suicides: A case-control study. *Journal of the American Medical Association, 266,* 2989–2994.

4. Brent, D. A., Perper, J. A., Moritz, G., Baugher, M., Schweers, J., & Roth, C. (1993). Firearms and adolescent suicide: A community case-control study. *American Journal of Diseases of Children, 147,* 1066–1071.

5. Kellermann, A. L., Rivara, F. P., Somes, G., Reay, D. T., Francisco, J., Banton, J. G., Prodzinski, J., Fligner, C., & Hackman, B. (1992). Suicide in the home in relation to gun ownership. *New England Journal of Medicine, 327,* 467–472.

6. Christoffel, K. Kaufer, & Christoffel, T. (1986). Handguns as a pediatric problem. *Pediatric Emergency Care, 2,* 75–81.

7. Rowland et al. (1989). Firearm-associated homicides among family members, relatives, or friends. *Morbidity and Mortality Weekly Report, 38,* 253–256.

8. Fingerhut, L. A., & Kleinman, J. C. (1990). International and interstate comparisons of homicide among young males. *Journal of the American Medical Association, 263,* 3292–3295.

9. Hammett, M., Powell, K. E., O'Carroll, P. W., & Clanton, S. T. (1992). Homicide surveillance—United States, 1979–1988. *Morbidity and Mortality Weekly Report,* CDC–Surveillance Summaries, *41,* 1–33.

10. Wood, N. P., Amanfo, J., Rodgers, D., Dorsey, E. A., Rowe, R., Woods, E. V., Davis, S., Brown, L. T., & Simms, S. O. (1993). Intentional injury–homicide as a public health problem. *Maryland Medical Journal, 42,* 771–773.

11. McGonigal, M. D., Cole, J., Schwab, W., Kauder, D. R., Rotondo, M. F., & Angood, P. B. (1993). Urban firearm deaths: A five-year perspective. *Journal of Trauma, 35,* 532–537.

12. Hutson, H. R., Anglin, D., & Pratts, M. J. (1994). Adolescents and children injured or killed in drive-by shootings in Los Angeles. *New England Journal of Medicine, 330,* 324–327.

13. Weiss, B. (1994, November 1). Department of Health personal communication.

14. Frost, B. J., Neff-Smith, M., & Land, S. (1994, November). *Trends in intentional injury deaths for Virginia, 1990–92.* Papers presented at the American Public Health Association 122nd annual meeting, Washington, DC.

15. Wintemute, G. J., Teret, S. P., Kraus, J. F., & Wright, M. W. (1988). The choice of weapons in firearm suicides. *America Journal of Public Health, 78,* 824–826.

16. Stone, I. C. (1992). Characteristics of firearms and gunshot wounds as markers of suicide. *American Journal of Forensic Medicine and Pathology, 13,* 275–280.

17. Zwerling, C., Lynch, C. F., Burmeister, L. F., & Goertz, U. (1993). The choice of weapons in firearm suicides in Iowa. *American Journal of Public Health, 83,* 1630–1632.

18. Kaplan, M. S., & Adamek, M. E. (1994, October 31). *Firearm suicide among the young-old, old-old, and very old Americans.* Paper presented at the American Public Health Association 122nd annual meeting, Washington, DC.

19. Rushforth, N. B., Hirsch, C. S., Ford, A. B., & Adelson, L. (1974). Accidental firearm fatalities in a metropolitan county (1958–1973). *American Journal of Epidemiology, 100,* 499–505.

20. Waller, J. A., & Whorton, E. B. (1973). Unintentional shootings, highway crashes and acts of violence. *Accident Analysis and Prevention, 5,* 351–356.

21. Wintemute, G. J., Teret, S. P., Kraus, J. F., Wright, M. A., & Bradfield, G. (1987). When children shoot children: 88 unintended deaths in California. *Journal of the American Medical Association, 257,* 3107–3109.

22. Wintemute, G. J., Kraus, J. F., Teret, S. P., & Wright, M. A. (1989). Unintentional firearm deaths in California. *Journal of Trauma, 29,* 457–461.

23. Kellermann, A. L., & Reay, D. T. (1986). Protection or peril?: An analysis of firearm-related deaths in the home. *New England Journal of Medicine, 314,* 1557–1560.

24. Ordog, G. J., Wasserberger, J., Schatz, I., Owens-Collins, D., English, K., Balasubramanian, S., & Schlater, T. (1988). Gunshot wounds in children under 10 years of age: A new epidemic. *American Journal of Diseases Children, 142,* 618–622.

25. Beaver, B. L., Moore, V. L., Peclet, M., Haller, J. A., Smialek, J., & Hill, J. L. (1990). Characteristics of pediatric firearm fatalities. *Journal of Pediatric Surgery, 25,* 97–100.

26. Wintemute, G. J., & Wright, M. A. (1992). Initial and subsequent hospital costs of firearm injuries. *Journal of Trauma, 33,* 556–560.

27. Martin, J. R., Sklar, D. P., & McFeely, P. (1991). Accidental firearm fatalities among New Mexico children. *Annals of Emergency Medicine, 20,* 58–61.

28. Riddick, L., Wanger, G. P., Fackler, M. L., Carter, R. D., Hoff, C. J., Jinks, J. M., & Becker, J. A. (1993). Gunshot injuries in Mobile County, AL: 1985–1987. *American Journal of Forensic Medical Pathology, 14,* 215–225.

29. Choi, E., Donoghue, E. R., & Lifschultz, B. D. (1994). Deaths due to firearms injuries in children. *Journal of Forensic Science, 39,* 685–692.

30. Zane, D., Preece, M. J., Elerian, N., Svenkerud, E., Perrotta, D., Wilson, M., Schwertfeger, R., Retzlaff, C., & Carmack, N. (1994, October 27). *Gunfire in a Texas County: A multidisciplinary study of firearm-related deaths and hospitalizations.* Austin, TX: Injury Prevention and Control Program, Texas Department of Health.

31. Fingerhut, L. A., Ingram, D. D., & Feldman, J. J. (1992). Firearm and non-firearm homicide among persons 15–19 years of age; differences by level of urbanization, United States, 1979 through 1989. *Journal of the American Medical Association, 267,* 3048–3053.

32. Morrow, P. L., & Hudson, P. (1986). Accidental firearm fatalities in North Carolina, 1976–1980. *American Journal of Public Health, 76,* 1120–1123.

33. Dodge, G. C., Cogbill, T. H., Miller, G. J., Landercasper, J., & Strutt, P. J. (1994). Gunshot wounds: 10-year experience of a rural referral trauma center. *American Surgeon, 60,* 401–404.

34. Centerwall, B. S. (1991). Homicide and the prevalence of handguns: Canada and the United States, 1976 to 1980. *American Journal of Epidemiology, 134,* 1245–1260.

35. Sloan, J. H., Kellermann, A. L., Reay, D. T., Ferris, J. A., Koepsell, T., Rivara, F. P., Rice, C., Gray, L., & LoGerfo, J. (1988). Handgun regulations, crime, assaults, and homicide: A tale of two cities. *New England Journal of Medicine, 319,* 1256–1262.

36. Lester, D., & Clarke, R. V. (1991). Note on "suicide and increased availability of handguns in the United States": The influence of firearm ownership on accidental deaths. *Social Science and Medicine, 32,* 1311–1313.

37. Killias, M. (1993). International correlations between gun ownership and rates of homicide and suicide. *Canadian Medical Association Journal, 148,* 1721–1725.

38. Loftin, C., McDowall, D., Wiersema, B., & Cottey, T. G. (1991). Effects of restrictive licensing of handguns on homicide and suicide in the District of Columbia. *New England Journal of Medicine, 325,* 1615–1620.

39. Schwab, C. W. (1993). Violence: America's uncivil war—Presidential Address. Sixth Scientific Assembly of the Eastern Association for the Surgery of Trauma. *Journal of Trauma, 35,* 657–665.

40. Jones, M. A., & Krisberg, B. (1994). *Images and reality: Juvenile crime, youth violence, and public policy.* San Francisco.

41. Wintemute, G. J. (1987). Firearms as a cause of death in the United States, 1920–1982. *Journal of Trauma, 27,* 532–536.

42. Wintemute, G. J. (1988). Handgun availability and firearm mortality. *Lancet, 2,* 1136–1137.

43. Clarke, R. V., & Jones, P. R. (1989). Suicide and increased availability of handguns in the United States. *Social Science Medicine, 8,* 805–809.

44. Boor, M., & Bair, J. H. (1990). Suicide rates, handgun control laws, and sociodemographic variables. *Psychological Reports, 66,* 923–930.

45. Newton, G. D., & Zimring, F. E. (1969). *Firearms and violence in American life: A staff report to the National Commission on the causes and prevention of violence.* Washington, DC: U.S. Government Printing Office.

46. Eckholm, E. (1992, March 8). Ailing gun industry confronts outrage over glut of violence. *New York Times*, p. 1ff.

47. Division of Injury Control, National Center for Environmental Health and Injury Control and Division of Adolescent and School Health, National Center for Chronic Disease Prevention and Health Promotion, Centers for Disease Control. (1991). Weapon-carrying among high school students— United States, 1990. *Morbidity and Mortality Weekly Report, 40*, 681–684.

48. Sheley, J. F., & Wright, J. D. (1993, December). *Gun acquisition and possession in selected juvenile samples.* U.S. Department of Justice, National Institute of Justice, Office of Juvenile Justice and Delinquency Prevention, Research in Brief, p. 11.

49. Wintemute, G. J. (1994). *Ring of fire: The handgun makers of southern California.* Sacramento, CA: Violence Prevention Research Program.

50. Weil, D. S., & Hemenway, D. (1992). Loaded guns in the home: Analysis of a national random survey of gun owners. *Journal of the American Medicine Association, 267*, 3033–3037.

51. Senturia, Y. D., Christoffel, K. Kaufer, & Donovan, M. (1994). Children's household exposure to guns: A practice-based survey. *Pediatrics, 93*, 469–475.

52. Hemenway, D., Solnick, S. J., & Azrael, D. R. (1995). Firearm training and storage. *Journal of the American Medical Association, 273*, 46–50.

53. Haught, K., Grossman, D., & Connell, F. (1995). Parents' attitudes to firearm injury prevention counseling in urban pediatric clinics. *Pediatrics, 96*, 649–653.

54. Webster, D. W., Champion, H. R., Gainer, P. S., & Sykes, L. (1992). Epidemiologic changes in gunshot wounds in Washington, D.C., 1983–1990. *Archives of Surgery, 127*, 694–698.

55. Block, C. R., & Block, R. (1993, December). *Street gang crime in Chicago.* U.S. Department of Justice, National Institute of Justice, Office of Justice Programs, Research in Brief, p. 7.

56. Sloan, J. H., Rivara, F. P., Reay, D. T., Ferris, J. A., & Kellermann, A. L. (1990). Firearm regulations and rates of suicide. *New England Journal of Medicine, 322*, 369–373.

57. Marzuk, P. M., Leon, A. C., Tardiff, K., Morgan, E. B., Stajic, M., & Mann, J. J. (1992). The effect of access to lethal methods of injury on suicide rates. *Archives of General Psychiatry, 49*, 451–458.

58. Perriens, J., Vander Stuy, P., Chee, H., & Benimadlio, S. (1989). The epidemiology of paraquat intoxication in Surinam. *Tropical and Geographical Medicine, 41*(3), 266–269.

59. Morath, M., & Hartmann, H. (1985). Cyanide poisoning: Forensic toxicology observations in the study of 54 cases of fatal poisoning. *Zeitschrift für Rechtsmedizin, 95*, 35–43. [English Medline abstract]

60. Wollenek, G. (1989). Acute poisoning caused by sodium azide. *Wiener Klinische Wochenschrift, 101*, 314–317. [English Medline abstract]

61. Senturia, Y. D., Binns, J. H., Christoffel, K. Kaufer, Tanz, R. R., & the Pediatric Practice Research Group. (1993). In-office survey of children's hazard exposure in the Chicago area: Age-specific exposure information and methodological lessons. *Journal of Developmental and Behavioral Pediatrics, 14*(3), 169–175.

5

Media Violence and Youth

JOHN P. MURRAY

THE IMPACT OF MEDIA violence on youth has been a topic of intense discussion and debate in the United States for the better part of this century. Beginning in the 1920s and '30s, there were questions raised about the influence of crime and violence portrayed in comic books, movies, radio serials, and, by the 1950s, television. For example, the initial studies and concerns about movies were outlined as early as Charters's (1933) monograph *Motion Pictures and Youth: A Summary*. In each instance, the concerns about violence are similar: Does media violence influence the attitudes and behavior of the youngest members of our society? Of course, similar questions could be asked about the influence of media violence on adults, but most of the social concern and much of the scientific research has been focused on children and youth.

Despite almost 70 years of research on media violence, it is still possible to spark a lively discussion of this issue. Moreover, each new form of media—such as video games or the Internet—inspires renewed discussion of the issue of media violence. If the hypothetical "Martian" were to scan the 20th-century discussions of media violence, he/she/it would be appalled by the circularity and indecisiveness of professionals and public policy pundits.

And yet, part of the compelling nature of the media violence discussions is the seemingly transparent relationship between what we see and hear and the way we think and act. Some have argued that this transparent relationship is truly gossamer, whereas others contend that the relationship of media violence and societal violence is substantial and profoundly disturbing. The reason that these two viewpoints can coexist—and have done so for many decades—is the fact that media violence and societal violence are not related in any direct and simple manner, and there are multiple causes for both phenomena.

This chapter will explore the relationships between media violence and violence in youth with a focused examination of the issue of television violence. Although there are differences in the intensity, interest, and interpretation of violence found across various media, there are great similarities in the process of effects. On the one hand, the intensity of violence in films is often greater (in terms of the graphic nature and frequency of violent acts) than that found in prime-time television programs. On the other hand, the frequency of contact with film violence is usually less than the frequency of contact with television violence. This is one example of a "trade-off" of frequency of viewing versus intensity of portrayal. So too, adolescents are more likely to encounter graphic film violence than would be the case for very young children. However, young children, who are still in the early stages of learning social roles and standards of acceptable behavior, may be more affected by the frequent depictions of violence on television than the adolescent who is watching a "slasher" film. Of course, the complicating feature in this analysis is the fact that the adolescent sitting in the movie theater was once a child sitting in front of a television set and, therefore, has a long history of exposure to media violence.

VIOLENCE IN THE 'HOOD AND IN HOLLYWOOD

In New York, in the fall of 1995, youths set fire to a subway token booth by spraying a flammable substance through the opening for the change and token slot. The booth exploded and burned the subway attendant. The attendant died in December 1995 as a result of extensive burns. This was one of the more dramatic episodes in a series of attacks that seemed to be related to a recently released movie, *Money Train*, in which a similar act occurred.

A few years earlier in Los Angeles, a filmmaker interviewed a young man who was being held in the Los Angeles County Juvenile Detention Center on a charge of attempted murder. The 16-year-old was asked how it happened, and he replied, "The guy came after me and I had a gun. So, I shot him. I shot him twice. It's easy to get a gun in the 'hood." When asked about his favorite television programs, he said, "I like to watch that show, the *Cops*, or *America's Most Wanted*; I might see some of my friends out there, messin up" (Mediascope, 1993).

In the late 1970s, when the movie *The Deerhunter* was released, it contained a very graphic portrayal of Russian roulette. While the film was playing in theaters and in video release, there were numerous reports of adolescents, usually males, imitating the Russian roulette scene, often with tragic results. Of course, there were many additional factors that influenced this result, such as watching the video with a group of young males who were drunk, or a history of depression or suicide attempts. Nevertheless, some incidents of death from this film were simply accidents of imitation gone awry.

In the early 1970s, a made-for-television movie called *The Doomsday Flight* contained an easily imitated bomb threat/hostage plot. When the movie was broadcast in the United States, there were numerous bomb threats directed to various airlines. When the movie was sold to an Australian commercial television network, the result was a ransom of one million dollars paid by Qantas Airlines to save a jetliner en route from Sydney to Hong Kong. (The plot involved a bomb that was activated on takeoff and would detonate when the plane dropped to an altitude of 4,000 feet. In the United States, the bomb threats to the airlines were handled by diverting aircraft to Denver or Mexico City—high-altitude airports. However, Qantas lacked a high-altitude airport for diversion between Sydney and Hong Kong.)

Are these reports of tragic events merely the isolated outcomes of unfortunate circumstances, or are these events simply the more dramatic examples of a subtle and pervasive influence of media violence? What do we know about the nature of the violence on television?

The most extensive analyses of the incidence of violence on television are the studies conducted by a research team at the University of Pennsylvania, directed by George Gerbner. The results of these yearly analyses of the level of violence on American television for the 22-year period 1967–1989 (Gerbner & Signorielli, 1990) indicate a consistently high level of violence. There were some minor fluctuations in the early 1970s, followed by a steady increase to 1976, a sharp decline in 1977, and then a steady climb to an all-time high in 1982–1983. According to Gerbner's initial analysis (Gerbner, 1972), eight out of every 10 plays broadcast during the survey period in 1969 contained some form of violence, and eight episodes of violence occurred during each hour of broadcast time. Furthermore, programs especially designed for children, such as cartoons, were the most violent of all programming. Later analyses by Gerbner and Gross (1974, 1976a, 1976b) indicated that there was some decline in violence levels from 1969 to 1975, at least in terms of the prominence of killing. However, the level of violence dramatically increased in 1976 (Gerbner et al., 1977) and was followed by a decline to one of the lowest levels in the 1977 season (Gerbner et al., 1978). This decline was quite dramatic. From the "bumper-crop violence harvest" of 1976 to the relatively placid 1977, the percentage of programs containing violence fell from 90% to 75.5%; the rate of violent episodes per hour fell from 9.5 to 6.7; and the rate of violence per program fell from 6.2 to 5.0 episodes. However, this downward trend was reversed in 1978 and through the early 1980s, and violence in weekend children's programs reached 30.3 violence episodes per hour in the 1982–1983 season (Gerbner & Signorielli, 1990). Overall, the levels of violence in prime-time programming have averaged about five acts per hour, and children's Saturday morning programs have averaged about 20 to 25 violent acts per hour. Although the 1992–1993 season manifested a sharp decline from those levels, it is not clear whether this will be a permanent change (Gerbner, Morgan, & Signorielli, 1994).

In addition to broadcast television, cable television adds to the level of violence through new, more violent programs, and by recycling older violent broadcasts. A recent survey by the Center for Media and Public Affairs (Lichter & Amundson, 1992) identified 1,846 violent scenes broadcast and cablecast between 6:00 A.M. to midnight on one day in Washington, DC. The most violent periods were between 6:00 to 9:00 A.M., with 497 violent scenes (165.7 per hour) and between 2:00 to 5:00 P.M. with 609 violent scenes (203 per hour). Most of this violence is presented without context or judgment as to its acceptability. And, most of this violence in the early morning and afternoon is viewed by children and youth. A follow-up study conducted in 1994 found a 41% increase in violence: 2,605 violent acts during one day on the television screens of Washington, DC (Lichter & Amundson, 1994).

In a more recent *qualitative* study of television violence, funded by the commercial television networks (UCLA Center for Communication Policy, 1995), the research team concluded: "The world of television, from broadcast networks, to syndication, to cable, to home videos, is not as violent as we had feared and not as wholesome as we might have hoped. There is room for substantial improvement" (p. 151). However, it is difficult to compare the results of this study with the results of previous research, because its analysis is discursive rather than quantitative as was the evidence found in the reports from the University of Pennsylvania (Gerbner & Signorielli, 1990; Gerbner et al., 1994) or the Center for Media and Public Affairs (Lichter & Amundson, 1992, 1994).

In February 1996, a new report financed by the National Cable Television Association provided a comprehensive review of the nature and extent of violence on commercial and public broadcast television and cable television. The *National Television Violence Study* (Mediascope, 1996) reviewed about 2,500 hours of television involving 2,693 programs by randomly selecting 20 composite weeks of programming on 23 channels, monitoring programs between 6:00 A.M. and 11:00 P.M. The investigators found that the typical perpetrator of violence is adult (76%), male (78%), and Caucasian (76%). Movies are the most likely form of programming to contain violence (90%), although children's programs (67%) frequently portray violence in a humorous context. Also, only 5% of the violent acts on children's programs show any long-term, negative consequences to the violence. Overall, 44% of programs on the broadcast networks contain violence: independent broadcast stations (55%), basic cable (59%), premium cable subscription (85%), and public television (18%).

POTENTIAL EFFECTS OF TELEVISION VIOLENCE

What can be said about violence in society and the relationship to media violence? Is there a rational pattern of relationships; a reasonable level of concern about media violence; a systematic body of evidence from research conducted in various settings? The answer is "yes" to all of these questions. Although there are many causes of violence in society, there are scientifically sound studies from diverse perspectives that link media violence to violent attitudes, values, and behaviors.

One of the suggestions about the way in which media violence affects audiences of all ages is that such depictions transmit a sense of acceptance or normativeness about violence in our lives—a confirmation that violence is an acceptable and usual way to resolve conflicts. This is the sense that Berkowitz (1984) uses when he describes the effects of "thoughts" on the manifestation of antisocial behavior, and it is the sense that is captured in his popular article on gun control entitled "When the Trigger Pulls the Finger" (Berkowitz, 1985).

It is important to note that psychologists and psychiatrists involved in media studies (Donnerstein, Slaby, & Eron, 1994; Menninger, 1995; Murray, 1994, 1995; Murray, Menninger, & Grimes, 1993) do not suggest that violent media are the only cause of violence in society. Rather there are many wellsprings of violent behavior, such as growing up in an abusive home or a violent neighborhood (Osofsky, 1995). However, media are one component of a potentially toxic environment for youth, and it is important to understand the roles that media play in youth violence and ways to mitigate these harmful influences. So, what do we know, and what can we do about media violence? In particular, since it is the most pervasive form of media violence in the lives of children and youth, what can be done about television violence?

Concern about television violence made its official debut in 1952 with a congressional hearing in the House of Representatives before the Commerce Committee (United States Congress, 1952). The following year, in 1953, the first major Senate hearing was held before the Senate Subcommittee on Juvenile Delinquency, headed by Senator Estes Kefauver (United States Congress, 1955a, 1955b).

One of the first major reports on media violence was the National Commission on the Causes and Prevention of Violence (Baker & Ball, 1969). The next landmark event occurred when the Surgeon General of the United States released a report in 1972 that concluded that violence on television does influence children who view that programming and does increase the likelihood that viewers will become more aggressive. Not all children are affected, not all children are affected in the same way, but there is evidence that television violence can be harmful to young viewers (Surgeon General's Scientific Advisory Committee on Television and Social Behavior, 1972; Murray, 1973). Ten years later, the National Institute of Mental Health (1982) concluded that violence on television does affect the aggressive behavior of children and there are many more reasons for concern about violence on television. "The research question has moved from asking whether or not there is an effect to seeking explanations for that effect" (p. 6).

In 1992, the American Psychological Association Task Force on Television and Society (Huston et al., 1992) concluded that 30 years of research confirms the harmful effects of television violence. And, these conclusions were reaffirmed by the American Psychological Association Commission on Violence and Youth (1993; Eron, Gentry, & Schlegel, 1994).

How are we affected by television violence? There seem to be three major avenues: direct effects, desensitization, and the Mean World Syndrome:

1. The *direct effects* process suggests that children and adults who watch a lot of violence on television may become more aggressive and/ or they may develop favorable attitudes and values about the use of aggression to resolve conflicts.

2. The second effect, *desensitization*, suggests that children who watch a lot of violence on television may become less sensitive to violence in the real world around them, less sensitive to the pain and suffering of others, and more willing to tolerate ever-increasing levels of violence in our society.

3. The third effect, the *Mean World Syndrome*, suggests that children or adults who watch a lot of violence on television may begin to believe that the world is as mean and dangerous in real life as it appears on

television, and hence, they begin to view the world as a much more mean and dangerous place.

What is the net result of this exposure to televised violence? What do we know about the influence of television violence from systematic research?

SYSTEMATIC RESEARCH ON TELEVISION VIOLENCE

The broad dimensions of research on television violence over the past 40 years can be described under three categories of research strategies: correlational studies, experimental studies, and field studies. These three rather different approaches to studying the "effects" of violent portrayals in television or film converge on the common conclusion that viewing violence can lead to changes in attitudes, values, and behavior concerning the acceptance and expression of violence. The following sections include examples of research in each of these three areas.

Correlational Studies

The weight of evidence from correlational studies is fairly consistent: Viewing and/or preference for violent television is related to aggressive attitudes, values, and behaviors. This result was true for the studies conducted when television was new, and the measures of children's aggression were teachers' ratings. It is still true for more recent studies in which the measures of aggressiveness have become more sophisticated.

To choose several early studies as examples, Robinson and Bachman (1972) found a relationship between the number of hours of television viewed and adolescent self-reports of involvement in aggressive or antisocial behavior. Atkin, Greenberg, Korzenny, and McDermott (1979) used a different measure of aggressive behavior. They gave 9- to 13-year-old boys and girls situations such as the following: Suppose that you are riding your bicycle down the street and some other child comes up and pushes you off your bicycle. What would you do? The response options included physical or verbal aggression, along with options to reduce or avoid conflict. These investigators found that physical or verbal aggressive responses were selected by 45% of heavy-television-violence viewers compared to only 21% of the light-violence viewers. In a further study, Sheehan (1983) followed two groups of Australian children, first and third graders, for a 3-year period. He found that for the older group, now third through fifth graders, both the overall amount of violence viewing and the intensity of viewing were significantly related to the children's level of aggressive behavior as rated by their classmates. In a more recent study of adolescent attitudes concerning television violence (Walker & Morley, 1991), the authors interviewed both adolescents and their parents concerning television viewing patterns, perceptions of violent portrayals, and aggressive tendencies. They found that adolescents who reported liking television violence held more aggressive attitudes. The amount of television violence viewing and parental patterns did have some influence on teens' willingness to behave aggressively, but their liking television violence was the strongest predictor of aggression. Finally, in a study focused on adults, Phillips (1983) investigated the effects of the portrayal of suicides in television soap operas on the suicide rate in the United States using death records compiled by the National Center for Health Statistics. He found, over a 6-year period, that whenever a major soap opera personality committed suicide on television, within 3 days there was a significant increase in the number of female suicides across the nation.

Experimental Studies

The initial experimental studies of the cause-and-effect relation between television/film violence and aggressive behavior were conducted by Bandura and his colleagues (Bandura, Ross, & Ross, 1961, 1963) working with young children, and by Berkowitz and his associates (Berkowitz, 1962; Berkowitz & Rawlings, 1963; Berkowitz, Corwin, & Heironimus, 1963) who studied adolescents. In a typical early study conducted by Bandura (Bandura et al., 1963), a young child was presented with a film, back-projected on a television screen, of a model who kicked and punished an inflated plastic doll. The child was then placed in a playroom setting and the incidence of aggressive behavior was recorded. The results of these early studies indicated that children who had viewed the aggressive film were more aggressive in the playroom than those children who had not observed the aggressive model. These early studies were criticized on the grounds that the aggressive behavior was not meaningful within the social context and that the stimulus materials were not representative of available television programming. Subsequent studies have used more typical television programs and more realistic measures of aggression, but basically Bandura's early findings still stand.

Another early study (Liebert & Baron, 1972) investigated young children's willingness to hurt another child after viewing videotaped sections of aggressive or neutral television programs. The boys and girls were in two age groups, 5 to 6 and 8 to 9 years old. The aggressive program consisted of segments of *The Untouchables*, whereas the neutral program featured a track race. Following viewing, the children were placed in a setting in which they could either facilitate or disrupt the game-playing performance of an ostensible child playing in an adjoining room. The main findings were that the children who viewed the aggressive program demonstrated a greater willingness to hurt another child. One could ask, does the same effect hold for cartoons? The answer seems to be "yes." Several studies have demonstrated that one exposure to a violent cartoon leads to increased aggression (Ellis & Sekyra, 1972; Lovaas, 1961; Mussen & Rutherford, 1961; Ross, 1972). Moreover, Hapkiewitz and Roden (1971) found that boys who had seen violent cartoons were less likely to share their toys than those who had not seen the aggressive cartoon.

More recent experimental studies focused on children with emotional disorders (Gadow & Sprafkin, 1993; Grimes, Cathers, & Vernberg, 1996), have demonstrated that these youngsters are particularly vulnerable to the influence of television violence. For example, Grimes et al. (1996) found that 8- to 12-year-olds who were diagnosed as having either attention-deficit/hyperactivity disorder, oppositional defiant disorder, or conduct disorder manifested less emotional concern for victims and were more willing to accept violence as justified than a matched group of children who did not have these disorders.

It seems clear from experimental studies that one can produce increased aggressive behavior as a result of either extended or brief exposure to televised violence, but questions remain about whether this heightened aggressiveness observed in the experimental setting spills over into daily life.

Field Studies

In the typical field experiment, the investigator presents television programs in the normal-viewing setting and observes behavior where it naturally occurs. The investigator controls the television diet either by arranging a special series of programs or by choosing towns that in the natural course of events receive different television programs.

One early field experiment was a study conducted by Stein and Friedrich (1972) for the Surgeon General's project. These investigators presented 97 preschool children with a diet of either "antisocial," "prosocial," or "neutral" television programs during a 4-week viewing period. The antisocial diet consisted of 12 half-hour episodes of "Batman" and "Superman" cartoons. The prosocial diet was composed of 12 episodes of *Mister Rogers' Neighborhood* (a program that stresses such themes as sharing and cooperative play). The neutral diet consisted of children's programming that was neither violent nor prosocial. The children were observed through a 9-week period, which consisted of 3 weeks of pre-viewing baseline, 4 weeks of television exposure, and 2 weeks of post-viewing follow-up. All observations were conducted in a naturalistic setting while the children were engaged in daily school activities. The observers recorded various forms of behavior that could be regarded as prosocial (i.e., helping, sharing, cooperative play) or antisocial (i.e., pushing, arguing, breaking toys). The overall results indicated that children who were judged to be initially somewhat aggressive became significantly more so as a result of viewing the "Batman" and "Superman" cartoons. Moreover, the children who had viewed the prosocial diet of *Mister Rogers' Neighborhood* were less aggressive, more cooperative, and more willing to share with other children.

One might ask whether such results are found when the variation in television diets occurs naturally rather than by special arrangement. Williams and her colleagues (Joy, Kimball, & Zabrack, 1986; Williams, 1986) had the opportunity to evaluate the impact of televised violence on the behavior of children before and after the introduction of television in a Canadian community. They compared children living in the before–after television town with their peers in two other towns where television was well established. The three towns were called Notel (no television reception), Unitel (receiving only the government-owned commercial channel—CBC), and Multitel (receiving the CBC and three American commercial networks—ABC, CBS, and NBC). Children in all three towns were evaluated at Time 1, when Notel did not receive a television signal, and again at Time 2, when Notel had had television for 2 years (it had received the government channel—CBC). Results indicated that there were no differences across the three towns at Time 1, but at Time 2, the children from the former Notel town were significantly more aggressive, both physically and verbally, than the children in the Unitel or Multitel towns. Moreover, only children in the Notel town manifested any significant increase in physical and verbal aggression from Time 1 to Time 2.

FACTORS INFLUENCING THE EXTENT OF EFFECTS

We get a clearer picture about the extent of television violence effects when we know more about the way children watch televised violence. For example, Ekman and his associates (1972) found that those children whose facial expressions, while viewing televised violence, depicted the positive emotions of happiness, pleasure, interest, or involvement were more likely to hurt another child than were those children whose facial expressions indicated disinterest or displeasure.

The long-term influence of television has not been extensively investigated, but we do have indications from several major studies. In an initial longitudinal study, Lefkowitz, Eron, Walder, and Huesmann (1972) were able to demonstrate long-term effects in a group of children followed up over a 10-year period. In this instance, Eron (1963) had previously demonstrated a relationship between preference for violent media and the aggressive behavior of these children at the age of 8. One question now posed was, would this relationship hold at later ages? To answer this question, the investigators obtained peer-rated measures of aggressive behavior and preferences for various kinds of television, radio, and comic books when the children were 8 years old. Ten years later, when the members of the group were 18 years old, the investigators again obtained measures of aggressive behavior and television program preferences. The results for boys indicated that preference for television violence at age 8 was significantly related to aggression at age 8 ($r = .21$), but that preference for television violence at age 18 was not related to aggression at age 18 ($r = .05$). A second question posed was, could this adolescent aggressiveness be predicted from our knowledge of their viewing habits in early childhood? And, the answer seems to be "yes." The important finding here is the significant relationship, for boys, between preference for violent media at age 8 and aggressive behavior at age 18 ($r = .31$). Equally important is the lack of relationship in the reverse direction; that is, preference for violent television programs at age 18 was not produced by aggressive behavior in early childhood ($r = .01$). The most plausible interpretation of this pattern of correlations is that early preference for violent television programming and other media is one factor in the production of aggressive and antisocial behavior when the young boy becomes a young man.

In more recent, short-term, longitudinal studies conducted by Lefkowitz and Eron and by their colleagues (Eron, 1982; Huesmann, Langerspetz, & Eron, 1984; Sheehan, 1983), significant effects of viewing violence on aggressive behavior of children were found in the United States, Australia, and Finland. Finally, the 22-year longitudinal study (Huesmann & Eron, 1986; Huesmann, Eron, Lefkowitz, & Walder, 1984)—a follow-up to the earlier Lefkowitz et al. (1972) study—has found significant causal correlations ($r = .41$) between violence viewing at age 8 and serious interpersonal criminal behavior at age 30.

In summarizing the extent of the effects, Comstock and Paik (1991) suggest that there are four factors that affect the likelihood that media violence will influence viewers: efficacy, normativeness, pertinence, and suggestibility. *Efficacy* relates to whether the violence on the screen is rewarded or punished: *normativeness* refers to whether the screen violence is justified or lacks any consequences; *pertinence* describes the extent to which the screen violence has some similarity to the viewer's social context; and *suggestibility* concerns the predisposing factors of arousal or frustration. Drawing on these four dimensions, Comstock and Paik (1991, pp. 254–255) enumerate 15 situations for which we have experimental evidence of the effects of film or television violence:

1. There are rewards or lack of punishment for those who act aggressively (e.g., Bandura et al., 1963).
2. The aggressive behavior is seen as justified (e.g., Berkowitz & Rawlings, 1963).
3. There are cues in the portrayed violence that are similar to those in real life (e.g., Donnerstein & Berkowitz, 1981).
4. There is similarity between the aggressor and the viewer (e.g., Rosekrans, 1967).
5. There is strong identification with the aggressor, such as imagining being in his or her place (e.g., Turner & Berkowitz, 1972).
6. There is behavior motivated to inflict harm or injury (e.g., Geen & Stonner, 1972).
7. There is depiction of violence in which the consequences are lowered, such as no pain, sorrow, or remorse (e.g., Berkowitz & Rawlings, 1963).
8. There is violence that is portrayed more realistically or seen as a real event (e.g., Atkin, 1983).
9. There is violence that is not subjected to critical commentary (e.g., Lefcourt, Barnes, Parke, & Schwartz, 1966).
10. Portrayals of violence seem to please the viewer (e.g., Ekman et al., 1972).
11. Portrayals of violence are unrelieved by other events (Lieberman Research, 1975).
12. Violence portrayed includes physical abuse in addition to or compared to verbal aggression (e.g., Lieberman Research, 1975).
13. Violence leaves the viewer in a state or arousal (e.g., Zillmann, 1971).
14. Violence predisposes viewers to act aggressively (e.g., Donnerstein & Berkowitz, 1981).
15. Viewers are in a state of frustration after they view violence, either from an external source or from the viewing itself (e.g., Worchel, Hardy, & Hurley, 1976).

CHANGES IN POLICY AND PRACTICE

The broad area of children's television has been a very sensitive issue for Congress and the FCC (Kunkel & Watkins, 1987) because there is extensive and intensive public concern. And, within this broad area of concern, television violence is the most explosive.

What can we do about television violence? I would contend that we know enough about television violence to warrant action. We know that there is a relationship between television violence and changes in attitudes and behavior. As noted earlier, the three main types of effects are (1) direct effects—increased aggressive behavior or willingness to use violence, (2) desensitization—increased acceptance of violence as normal, and (3) Mean World syndrome—increased fearfulness and a belief that the real world is as dangerous as the television world.

The Chairman of the FCC, Reed Hunt, has said on several occasions that he is concerned about the amount of violence on television and has called for a "New Social Compact" to change children's television. He noted in a speech to the American Psychological Association in August 1994:

> I am joined in my deep concern about TV violence by many members of Congress. I have discussed the topic with Senators Hollings, Inouye, Simon, Dorgan, Congressman Markey, and many other Members of the House and Senate. In fact, it is one of the issues most frequently raised in my discussions with Congress, and it was the topic of the first question that was addressed to me at my confirmation hearing before the Senate Commerce Committee. . . . Television has a significant impact on children's lives. That impact is only going to increase as our technology matures and true, interactive video replaces simple television viewing. Social science has documented that television can be an effective educational tool, especially for young children, and our public policies must ensure that this positive potential does not escape us. (Hundt, 1994, pp. 10–13)

It is too early to assess the impact of this "New Social Compact" viewpoint on public policy, but Reed Hundt has been outspoken in his concern about children's television (Hundt, 1995a, 1995b; Hundt & Minow, 1995). Moreover, in April 1995, the FCC promulgated a rule-making procedure (Federal Communications Commission, 1995) that would enhance the implementation of the Children's Television Act of 1990. In the proposed rules, broadcasters would be required to air 3 hours of educational programming for children each week.

Although the debate about the future of children's television continues—as it has for the past 45 years (Berry & Asamen, 1993; Huston et al., 1992; Keeshan, 1994; Murray, 1980; Murray & Kippax, 1979; Murray

& Salomon, 1984)—there are signs that we can expect to see changes in policy at the national level. Certainly, the passage of the Children's Television Act of 1990 was an expression of the will of Congress to change the nature of children's television-viewing opportunities. Also, the Federal Communications Commission has demonstrated renewed interest in children's television. Both the FCC, as an agency, and each of the five Commissioners have expressed concerns about the nature of programming available to children and specific worries about television violence (Federal Communications Commission, 1995; Barrett, 1995; Chong, 1995; Hundt, 1995a, 1995b; Ness, 1994; Quello, 1995a, 1995b). Although the FCC Commissioners are not in full agreement on ways to resolve the issue of television violence, they do agree that this is an important concern. As Commissioner Rachelle Chong (1995) has noted, "Television does have the potential to influence our children, so public awareness is necessary so that we may assume a shared responsibility for managing this impact."

Can we change the nature of children's television? I believe the answer is "yes," and it would seem that there are three areas or levels in which we can bring about some changes: home, school, and industry.

At the *home level*, we can encourage greater awareness of the influence of television on children and enhance understanding of ways that parents and teachers can help children use television effectively. For example, the U.S. Department of Agriculture Cooperative Extension Service at Kansas State University (Murray & Lonnborg, 1995) has produced a parent-guide publication on this topic. This guide, available on the Internet (http://www.ksu.edu/humec/fshs/c&t.htm), is a review of some concerns about television and children, and provides suggestions for parents in using television in a constructive manner. One of the straight-forward techniques for use at home that is very effective is viewing along with your children and talking about what they see on television. With very young children, talking about how violence is faked and what would happen if they actually did some of those things that they see on television is a very basic intervention. Such interventions, at the personal or family level, can lead to enhanced understanding of television's influence and more effective use of this medium. As Milton Chen (1994) points out in his recent book, *The Smart Parent's Guide to Kids' TV*, "Once parents start talking about their kids' TV, we have a lot to say and learn from each other. The hard part is getting started" (p. 9)

At the *school level*, interventions such as advocating for the inclusion of media literacy courses in school systems can be very effective. These "critical viewing" programs help children understand how television works and the process of effects. There are many very effective programs, but, in the case of media literacy addressed to the violence issue, one interesting new program has been developed by the Center for Media Literacy (1995). Called "Beyond Blame: Challenging Violence in the Media—A Multimedia Literacy Program for Community Empowerment," this program is one that a school system or a community agency might use as a general educational intervention. Another approach to enhancing public awareness is working with parents and communities to address television violence as a public health issue. There has been a long history of public advocacy concerning television violence (Kunkel & Murray, 1991; Montgomery, 1989), and there are several major organizations—Center for Media Education, Center for Media Literacy (1995), Mediascope (Federman, 1993), National Alliance for Nonviolent Programming (1995), and the National Telemedia Council (1995)—that are producing materials for parents and community organizations. One such videotape, *The Kids Are Watching*, from Mediascope (1993) is very effective in stimulating discussion of the impact of television violence.

Finally, there are *industry* and government activities that might be undertaken to change children's television. The Children's Television Act of 1990 did set some limits on the amount of advertising in children's programming, and did set some expectations that stations applying for license renewal will have to explain how they have served the educational needs of children in their broadcast area. And, the FCC is now thinking about elaborating that by including quantitative guidelines (Federal Communications Commission, 1995), such as 3 hours per week of children's educational television. These changes would ensure that some educational programming would be available on commercial broadcast television, rather than the standard entertainment programs (Kunkel & Canepa, 1994; Kunkel, 1995a).

Another approach, which is more voluntary than regulatory, involves working with the industry to introduce changes in the role that advertising plays in supporting children's programming. One might encourage advertisers to shift their support of children's programming from advertising to underwriting. Sponsorship of children's television would then shift from *advertising* to enhance corporate *income* to *underwriting* to enhance corporate *image*.

Why recommend a shift from "income" to "image"? The rationale for this change begins with the observation that Saturday morning children's television is currently a mass-audience format and there are few age-specific, targeted educational programs. One of the reasons for this absence of age-specific programming is the need to generate programming that will fit advertisers' needs for a large audience of 2- to 12-year-old children. One result is the large number of violent cartoons. For example, we have noted that there are about 25 violent acts per hour in Saturday morning programming directed at children. And, one might ask, why does Saturday morning programming look the way it does? Why is it as violent as it is, and what is the relationship to advertising? One of the reasons for cartoon programs on Saturday morning is the fact that advertisers want to get a maximum return on their investment, and they need to have the largest possible audience. The only way this can be done is to accumulate the audience from among 2- to 12-year-old children. When advertisers talk about the child audience, they are not talking about 6-year-olds or 4-year-olds, they are talking about that entire range of childhood from age 2 to 12 years. The only format that will hold the attention span of the large, heterogeneous audience is fast-action, fast-paced programming—animated programming. And so, Saturday morning programming contains fast-action, fast-paced cartoons that tend to be violent. You can create fast-paced, fast-moving, *nonviolent* programming—"Sesame Street" is an example—but, it is difficult to create such programming for a broad age range. Therefore, we are likely to have fast-action, fast-paced, highly violent cartoons because they hold the attention of a broad age range of 2- to 12-year-olds. However, if we moved from advertising supporting corporate "income" to sponsorship supporting corporate "image," there would be no need to assemble a huge audience, and the nature of programming might change. For example, one might find advertisers underwriting specialized, age-specific programming that is targeted to particular interest areas of a highly differentiated child audience.

Other industry-level initiatives might include further development of the parental advisory that the television networks began implementing in 1987. The "viewer discretion" warnings that have been attached to prime-time movies since September 1987 have been shown to have some influence in *reducing* viewership among the 2- to 11-year-old audiences. Hamilton (1994) conducted an analysis of audience rating data for network movies carrying viewer discretion advisories broadcast during the period from September 17, 1987, to September 26, 1993. He found that movies carrying the warnings lost .59 ratings points among children aged 2 to 11. This translates into 222,000 fewer children—or a 14% drop in average audience rating for this age group—for movies that contained viewer discretion warnings. There were no changes in viewership for teens or adults. These findings suggest that parents are sensitive to the warnings and will act on the information provided concerning program content.

A related development being considered by the industry is the possible rating of violence levels on television programs and the potential coordination with electronic screening devices known as "V-chip" technology. Although there is no clear agreement on the implementation of ratings and screening technology, some members of Congress have suggested legislation that would require the FCC to mandate the inclusion of an electronic circuit, or V-chip, in all new television sets. This technology is rather similar to the circuitry required for decoding "closed-caption" program signals. In this instance, the industry would transmit a signal concerning the violent content, and parents could program their television set to block programs containing the identified signal. The successful implementation of this type of intervention would require the participation of the industry in rating and coding programs, and the involvement of parents in responding to these ratings (Kleeman, 1995). A different approach is being taken by the OKTV Foundation (1995), a nonprofit institution that is planning to provide a service combining a convenient means of parental control with program appraisals developed by a panel of child development experts who are independent of industry or commercial ratings. OKTV (Our Kids' TV) enables parents to use their remote control to change their television set to function as a set for children, whether parents are at work or at home. The system would operate through cable television set-top units to allow parents to avoid harmful material such as horror, violence, sexual, or other content unsuitable for several age groups. Parents can select programming for three age groups: toddlers (up to 36 months), early childhood (3–7 years), and midchildhood (8–12 years). Parents can also choose programming recommended for coviewing with their children. Although there are questions about the impact of the V-chip approach or the use of the OKTV system, there is evidence from the Hamilton (1994) study that parents may be responsive to viewer warnings in relation to young children.

CONCLUSIONS

Clearly, the issue of media violence and youth has been the topic of extensive research and public discussion throughout the 20th century and, doubtless, these discussions will extend into the 21st century. Given this history, there is the tendency to become dispirited about the possibility of change in the way our society approaches the merchandizing of entertainment violence. And yet, there are reasons to hope that concerted efforts on the part of the creative community in the television and film industries—working with parents, social scientists and mental health professionals, and policy specialists in both the public and private sectors—can bring about significant changes in portrayal of violence and its impact on young viewers.

Why should we be hopeful about change? Some would argue that more than 40 years of research and discussion of television violence has only led to increased levels of violence on the small screen. However, I would argue that the pattern of media violence has not been as homogeneous and consistently incremental as it might appear at first glance. True, the levels of television violence charted by the University of Pennsylvania studies conducted from 1967 to 1993 (Gerbner et al., 1994) show persistent increases up to the 1992 season, but they also show great variation in levels of violence in response to public concern. For example, the 1973–1974 seasons contained far less violence than earlier or later time periods, because there was intense scrutiny of the television violence issue following the Surgeon General's report in 1972. Also, the 1993 season showed a marked decline in violence because of the intense Congressional debate on this issue and legislation that encouraged the commercial television networks and cable television systems to begin monitoring violence levels. Moreover, the recent reports on television violence that were funded by the commercial television networks (UCLA Center for Communication Policy, 1995) and the National Cable Television Association (Mediascope, 1996) show that violence is still a major component of television entertainment, but the industry—both broadcast and cable—has begun to recognize television violence as a serious issue confronting American society.

As the mid-1990s mergers and realignments of major information and entertainment corporations develop into long-term production and distribution relationships, there needs to be an increased sensitivity to the social impact of communication. It is no longer acceptable for media production and distribution companies to assert that they are merely providing what the public wants, and that they are in the entertainment business not education. That view, popular in the 1960s and 1970s, began to change in the 1980s and has been transformed into what FCC Commissioner Chong (1995) has identified as a "shared responsibility" between broadcasters and consumers. The fact that FCC Chairman Hundt (a Democrat) has been joined by Commissioner Chong (a Republican), and both have been joined by members of Congress from both political parties in expressing this need for enhanced awareness of the impact of entertainment programming, suggests that we may see a new sensitivity to media violence.

Only in hindsight in the next decade will we know whether the 1990s served as a turning point in the difficult struggle over media violence, but the signs are encouraging: New corporations, such as Walt Disney/ABC, that are willing to rethink the nature of children's television programming; the revisiting of procedures designed to develop entertaining *and* educational programs, such as those produced by CBS in the 1970s (Columbia Broadcasting System, 1977); a renewed interest in expanding the Children's Television Act of 1990 to provide enhanced educational

1995); new technologies that will empower parents to play an active role in selecting programming for young viewers (Kleeman, 1995; OKTV, 1995); a renewed commitment to the need to involve parents, the educational system, and children in developing a better understanding of the role that the media play in the lives of all viewers (Center for Media Literacy, 1995; Charren, 1994; Hundt & Minow, 1995; Keeshan, 1994; Minow, 1995); and the possibilities of new respect for the concerns about media violence and the development of a new partnership between media and mental health professionals to address these concerns (Eron & Slaby, 1994; Livingstone, 1994; Murray et al., 1993). Yes, there is reason to hope that we will soon see the tide turn on media violence.

ACKNOWLEDGMENT

This chapter was prepared with a fellowship grant from the Mind Science Foundation, San Antonio, Texas.

REFERENCES

American Psychological Association. (1993). *Violence and youth: Psychology's response: Vol. I. Summary report of the American Psychological Association Commission on Violence and Youth.* Washington, DC: Author.

Atkin, C. K. (1983). Effects of realistic TV violence vs. fictional violence on aggression. *Journalism Quarterly, 60,* 615–621.

Atkin, C. K., Greenberg, B. S., Korzenny, F., & McDermott, S. (1979). Selective exposure to televised violence. *Journal of Broadcasting, 23*(1), 5–13.

Baker, R. K., & Ball, S. J. (1969). *Mass media and violence: A staff report to the National Commission on the Causes and Prevention of Violence.* Washington, DC: U.S. Government Printing Office.

Bandura, A., Ross, D., & Ross, S. H. (1961). Transmission of aggression through imitation of aggressive models. *Journal of Abnormal and Social Psychology, 63*(3), 575–582.

Bandura, A., Ross, D., & Ross, S. H. (1963). Imitation of film-mediated aggressive models. *Journal of Abnormal and Social Psychology, 66*(1), 3–11.

Barrett, A. C. (1995). Reflections on television violence and regulating new technologies. *Kansas Journal of Law and Public Policy, 4*(3), 105–108.

Berkowitz, L. (1962). *Aggression: A social psychological analysis.* New York: McGraw-Hill.

Berkowitz, L. (1984). Some effects of thoughts on anti- and prosocial influences of media events: A cognitive–neoassociation analysis. *Psychological Bulletin, 95,* 410–427.

Berkowitz, L. (1985). *When the trigger pulls the finger.* Washington, DC: American Psychological Association, Board on Social and Ethical Responsibility.

Berkowitz, L., Corwin, R., & Heironimus, M. (1963). Film violence and subsequent aggressive tendencies. *Public Opinion Quarterly, 2,* 217–229.

Berkowitz, L., & Rawlings, E. (1963). Effects of film violence on inhibitions against subsequent aggression. *Journal of Abnormal and Social Psychology, 66*(5), 405–412.

Berry, G. L., & Asamen, J. K. (1993). *Children and television: Images in a changing sociocultural world.* Newbury Park, CA: Sage.

Center for Media Literacy. (1995). *Beyond blame: Challenging violence in the media—A multi-media literacy program for community empowerment.* Los Angeles, CA: Center for Media Literacy. (Available from the Center for Media Literacy, 1962 S. Shenandoah Street, Los Angeles, CA 90034)

Charren, P. (1994). Government censorship is not the solution, education is. *Hofstra Law Review, 22*(4), 863–869.

Charters, W. W. (1933). *Motion pictures and youth: A summary.* New York: Macmillan.

Chen, M. (1994). *The smart parent's guide to kids' TV.* San Francisco: KQED Books.

Chong, R. B. (1995, March 14). *Regulation: Alternative national models.* Presentation at the World Summit on Television and Children, Melbourne, Australia.

Columbia Broadcasting System. (1977). *Learning while they laugh.* New York: CBS Office of Social Research

Comstock, G., & Paik, H. (1991). *Television and the American child.* San Diego: Academic Press.

Donnerstein, E., & Berkowitz, L. (1981). Victim reactions in aggressive erotic films as a factor in violence against women. *Journal of Personality and Social Psychology, 41,* 710–724.

Donnerstein, E., Slaby, R., & Eron, L. D. (1994). The mass media and youth aggression. In L. D. Eron, J. H. Gentry, & P. Schlegel (Eds.), *Reason to hope: A psychosocial perspective on violence and youth* (pp. 219–250). Washington, DC: American Psychological Association Press.

Ekman, P., Liebert, R. M., Friesen, W., Harrison, R., Zlatchin, C., Malmstrom, E. V., & Baron, R. A. (1972). Facial expressions of emotion as predictors of subsequent aggression. In G. A. Comstock, E. A. Rubinstein, & J. P. Murray (Eds.), *Television and social behavior: Vol. 5. Television's effects: Further explorations* (pp. 22–58). Washington, DC: U.S. Government Printing Office.

Ellis, G. T., & Sekyra, F. (1972). The effect of aggressive cartoons on behavior of first grade children. *Journal of Psychology, 81,* 37–43.

Eron, L. D. (1963). Relationship of TV viewing habits and aggressive behavior in children. *Journal of Abnormal and Social Psychology, 67,* 193–196.

Eron, L. D. (1982). Parent–child interaction: Television violence and aggression of children. *American Psychologist, 27,* 197–211.

Eron, L. D., Gentry, J. H., & Schlegel, P. (1994). *Reason to hope: A psychosocial perspective on violence and youth.* Washington, DC: American Psychological Association Press.

Eron, L. D., & Slaby, R. G. (1994). Introduction. In L. D. Eron, J. H. Gentry, & P. Schlegel (Eds.), *Reason to hope: A psychosocial perspective on violence and youth* (pp. 1–22). Washington, DC: American Psychological Association Press.

Federal Communications Commission. (1995, April 5). Notice of proposed rule making: In the matter of policies and rules concerning children's television programming—Revision of programming policies for television broadcast stations, *FCC 95-143*, MM Docket No. 93-48.

Federman, J. (1993). *Film and television ratings: An international assessment*. Studio City, CA: Mediascope.

Gadow, K. D., & Sprafkin, J. (1993). Television "violence" and children with emotional and behavioral disorders. *Journal of Emotional and Behavioral Disorders, 1*(1), 54–63.

Geen, R. G., & Stonner, D. (1972). Context effects in observed violence. *Journal of Personality and Social Psychology, 25*, 145–150.

Gerbner, G. (1972). Violence in television drama: Trends and symbolic functions. In G. A. Comstock & E. A. Rubenstein (Eds.), *Television and social behavior: Vol. 1. Media content and control*. Washington, DC: U.S. Government Printing Office.

Gerbner, G., & Gross, L. (1974). *Violence profile No. 6: Trends in network television drama and viewer conceptions of social reality 1967–1973*. Unpublished manuscript, University of Pennsylvania.

Gerbner, G., & Gross, L. (1976a). Living with television: The violence profile. *Journal of Communication, 26*, 173–199.

Gerbner, G., & Gross, L. (1976b, April). The scary world of TV's heavy viewer. *Psychology Today*, pp. 41–45, 89.

Gerbner, G., Gross, L., Eleey, M. F., Jackson-Beeck, M., Jeffries-Fox, S., & Signorielli, N. (1977). TV violence profile no. 8: The highlights. *Journal of Communication, 27*, 171–180.

Gerbner, G., Gross, L., Eleey, M. F., Jackson-Beeck, M., Jeffries-Fox, S., & Signorielli, N. (1978). Cultural indicators: Violence profile no. 9. *Journal of Communication, 28*, 176–207.

Gerbner, G., Morgan, M., & Signorielli, N. (1994). *Television violence profile no. 16: The turning point—from research to action*. Unpublished manuscript, Annenberg School of Communications, University of Pennsylvania.

Gerbner, G., & Signorielli, N. (1990). *Violence profile, 1967 through 1988–89: Enduring patterns*. Unpublished manuscript. Annenberg School of Communications, University of Pennsylvania.

Grimes, T., Cathers, T., & Vernberg, E. (1996). *Emotionally disturbed children's reaction to violent media segments*. Unpublished manuscript, School of Journalism and Mass Communication, Kansas State University.

Hamilton, J. T. (1994). *Marketing violence: The impact of labeling violent television content*. Unpublished manuscript, Sanford Institute of Public Policy, Duke University.

Hapkiewitz, W. G., & Roden, A. H. (1971). The effect of aggressive cartoons on children's interpersonal play. *Child Development, 42*, 1583–1585.

Huesmann, L. R., & Eron, L. D. (Eds.). (1986). *Television and the aggressive child: A cross-national comparison*. Hillsdale, NJ: Erlbaum.

Huesmann, L. R., Eron, L. D., Lefkowitz, M. M., & Walder, L. O. (1984). Stability of aggression over time and generations. *Developmental Psychology, 20*, 1120–1134.

Huesmann, L. R., Langerspetz, K., & Eron, L. D. (1984). Intervening variables in the television violence–viewing–aggression relation: Evidence from two countries. *Developmental Psychology, 20,* 746–775.

Hundt, R. E. (1994, August 13). *A role for psychologists in the communication revolution.* Paper presented at the 101st annual meeting of the American Psychological Association, Los Angeles, CA.

Hundt, R. E. (1995a, October 25). Letter to Ann Landers: "Block out objectionable shows." *The Manhattan Mercury,* p. A-7.

Hundt, R. E. (1995b, July 27). *Remarks on television broadcasting.* Presentation at the National Press Club, Washington, DC. (http://www.fcc.gov/Speeches/Hundt/spreh517.txt)

Hundt, R. E., & Minow, N. N. (1995, October 19). A cure for kids' TV. *New York Times,* p. 12.

Huston, A. C., Donnerstein, E., Fairchild, H., Feshbach, N. D., Katz, P. A., Murray, J. P., Rubinstein, E. A., Wilcox, B., & Zuckerman, D. (1992). *Big world, small screen: The role of television in American society.* Lincoln: University of Nebraska Press.

Joy, L. A., Kimball, M., & Zabrack, M. L. (1986). Television exposure and children's aggressive behavior. In T. M. Williams (Ed.), *The impact of television: A natural experiment involving three towns* (pp. 303–360). New York: Academic Press.

Keeshan, B. (1994, August 14). *Media culture and the American family.* Presentation at the 101st annual meeting of the American Psychological Association, Los Angeles, CA.

Kleeman, D. W. (1995). *The V-chip: "V" as in versatile.* Unpublished manuscript, American Center for Children's Television, Des Plaines, IL.

Kunkel, D. (1995a). What Is educational programming?—Comments of Dale Kunkel, Ph.D. Submission to the Federal Communications Commission Inquiry on Policies and Rules Concerning Children's Television Programming, *FCC 95-143,* MM Docket No. 93-48.

Kunkel, D. (1995b, November 20). Reply comments of Dale Kunkel, Ph.D. Submission to the Federal Communications Commission Inquiry on Policies and Rules Concerning Children's Television Programming, *FCC 95-143,* MM Docket No. 93–48.

Kunkel, D., & Canepa, J. (1994). Broadcaster's license renewal claims regarding children's educational programming. *Journal of Broadcasting and Electronic Media, 38,* 397–416.

Kunkel, D., & Murray, J. P. (1991). Television, children, and social policy: Issues and resources for child advocates. *Journal of Clinical Child Psychology, 20*(1), 88–93.

Kunkel, D., & Watkins, B. A. (1987). Evolution of children's television regulatory policy. *Journal of Broadcasting and Electronic Media, 31,* 367–389.

Lefcourt, H. M., Barnes, K., Parke, R., & Schwartz, F. (1966). Anticipated social censure and aggression-conflict as mediators of response to aggression induction. *Journal of Social Psychology, 70,* 251–263.

Lefkowitz, M., Eron, L., Walder, L., & Huesmann, L. R. (1972). Television violence and child aggression: A follow-up study. In G. A. Comstock &

E. A. Rubinstein (Eds.), *Television and social behavior: Vol. 3. Television and adolescent aggressiveness* (pp. 35–135). Washington, DC: U.S. Government Printing Office.

Lichter, R. S., & Amundson, D. (1992). *A day of television violence.* Washington, DC: Center for Media and Public Affairs.

Lichter, R. S., & Amundson, D. (1994). *A day of TV violence: 1992 vs. 1994.* Washington, DC: Center for Media and Public Affairs.

Lieberman Research. (1975). *Children's reactions to violent material on television: Report to the American Broadcasting Company.* New York: Lieberman Research.

Liebert, R. M., & Baron, R. A. (1972). Short-term effects of television aggression on children's aggressive behavior. In J. P. Murray, E. A. Rubinstein, & G. A. Comstock (Eds.), *Television and social behavior: Vol. 2. Television and social learning* (pp. 181–201). Washington, DC: U.S. Government Printing Office.

Livingstone, J. B. (1994). *The violence framework: Guidelines for understanding, reporting, and portraying violence.* Washington, DC: Institute for Mental Health Initiatives.

Lovaas, O. I. (1961). Effect of exposure to symbolic aggression on aggressive behavior. *Child Development, 32,* 37–44.

Mediascope. (1993). *The kids are watching: A 13-minute video for teachers, parents, and community organizations.* Studio City, CA: Author. (Available from Mediascope, 12711 Ventura Boulevard, Studio City, CA 91604)

Mediascope. (1996). *National television violence study: Executive summary, 1994–1995.* Los Angeles: Author.

Menninger, R. W. (1995). Reducing TV violence may curb antisocial behavior. *Menninger Letter, 3*(10), 4–5.

Minow, N. N. (1995, March 2). *Television's values and the values of our children.* Presentation to the Annenberg Washington Program, Washington, DC.

Montgomery, K. C. (1989). *Target: Prime time—Advocacy groups and the struggle over entertainment television.* New York: Oxford University Press.

Murray, J. P. (1973). Television and violence: Implications of the Surgeon General's research program. *American Psychologist, 28*(6), 472–478.

Murray, J. P. (1980). *Television and youth: 25 years of research and controversy.* Boys Town, NE: Boys Town Center for the Study of Youth Development.

Murray, J. P. (1994). The impact of televised violence. *Hofstra Law Review, 22*(4), 809–825.

Murray, J. P. (1995). Children and television violence. *Kansas Journal of Law and Public Policy, 4*(3), 7–15.

Murray, J. P., & Kippax, S. (1979). From the early window to the late night show: International trends in the study of television's impact on children and adults. In L. Berkowitz (Ed.), *Advances in experimental social psychology* (Vol. 12, pp. 253–320). New York: Academic Press.

Murray, J. P., & Lonnborg, B. (1995). *Children and television: Using TV sensibly* (Bulletin LB-790). Manhattan: Kansas State University, Cooperative Extension Service. (Available on the worldwide web at http://www.ksu.edu/humec/fshs/c&t.htm)

Murray, J. P., Menninger, R. W., & Grimes, T. (1993, August 2). TV violence: Yes, mayhem does echo in our lives. *USA Today,* p. 9A.

Murray, J. P., & Salomon, G. (1984). *The future of children's television: Results of the Markle Foundation/Boys Town Conference.* Boys Town, NE: Boys Town Center.

Mussen, P., & Rutherford, E. (1961). Effects of aggressive cartoons on children's aggressive play. *Journal of Abnormal and Social Psychology, 62*(2), 461–464.

National Alliance for Nonviolent Programming. (1993). Media and violence: Creating an agenda for change. *Wingspread Journal, 15*(4), 8–9.

National Institute of Mental Health. (1982). *Television and behavior: Ten years of scientific progress and implications for the eighties: Vol. 1. Summary report.* Washington, DC: U.S. Government Printing Office.

National Telemedia Council. (1995). National media literacy conference: Special report. *Telemedium, 41*(3), 1–17.

Ness, S. (1994, December 9). *Creating critical viewers and the Children's Television Act.* Presentation at the National Academy of Television Arts and Sciences, Washington, DC.

OKTV Foundation. (1995). Comments of the OKTV Foundation Submission to the Federal Communications Commission Inquiry on Policies and Rules Concerning Children's Television Programming, *FCC 95-143*, MM Docket No. 93-48.

Osofsky, J. D. (1995). The effects of exposure to violence on young children. *American Psychologist, 50*(9), 782–788.

Phillips, D. P. (1983). The impact of mass media violence on U.S. homicides. *American Sociological Review, 48*, 560–568.

Quello, J. H. (1995a, September 21). *Enough already!* Presentation at the National Association of Broadcasters Children's Television Symposium, Washington, DC.

Quello, J. H. (1995b, November 1). Quello's column: Parents, broadcasters and the First Amendment. *FCC Homepage Web Site* (http://www.fcc.gov/Quello.html).

Robinson, J. P., & Bachman, J. G. (1972). Television viewing habits and aggression. In G. A. Comstock & E. A. Rubinstein (Eds.), *Television and social behavior: Vol. 3. Television and adolescent aggressiveness.* Washington, DC: U.S. Government Printing Office.

Rosekrans, M. A. (1967). Imitation in children as a function of perceived similarities to a social model of vicarious reinforcement. *Journal of Personality and Social Psychology, 7*(3), 305–317.

Ross, L. B. (1972). The effect of aggressive cartoons on the group play of children. Doctoral dissertation, Miami University, Miami, FL.

Sheehan, P. W. (1983). Age trends and the correlates of children's television viewing. *Australian Journal of Psychology, 35*, 417–431.

Stein, A. H., & Friedrich, L. K. (1972). Television content and young children's behavior. In J. P. Murray, E. A. Rubinstein, & G. A. Comstock (Eds.), *Television and social behavior: Vol. 2. Television and social learning* (pp. 202–317). Washington, DC: U.S. Government Printing Office.

Surgeon General's Scientific Advisory Committee on Television and Social Behavior. (1972). *Television and growing up: The impact of televised violence.* Washington, DC: U.S. Government Printing Office.

Turner, C. W., & Berkowitz, L. (1972). Identification with film aggressor (covert role taking) and reactions to film violence. *Journal of Personality and Social Psychology, 21*(2), 256–264.

UCLA Center for Communication Policy. (1995). *The UCLA Television Violence Monitoring Report.* Los Angeles: UCLA Center for Communication Policy.

United States Congress House Committee on Interstate and Foreign Commerce. (1952). *Investigation of radio and television programs, hearings and report, 82nd Congress, 2nd session, June 3–December 5, 1952.* Washington, DC: U.S. Government Printing Office.

United States Congress, Senate Committee of the Judiciary, Subcommittee to Investigate Juvenile Delinquency. (1955a). *Juvenile delinquency (television programs), hearings, 83rd Congress, 2nd session, June 5–October 20, 1954.* Washington, DC: U.S. Government Printing Office.

United States Congress, Senate Committee of the Judiciary, Subcommittee to Investigate Juvenile Delinquency (1955b). *Juvenile Delinquency (Television Programs), Hearings, 84th Congress, 1st session, April 6–7, 1955.* Washington, DC: U.S. Government Printing Office.

Walker, K. B., & Morley, D. D. (1991). Attitudes and parental factors as intervening variables in the television violence–aggression relation. *Communication Research Reports, 8*(2), 41–47.

Williams, T. M. (1986). *The impact of television: A natural experiment in three communities.* New York: Academic Press.

Worchel, S., Hardy, T. W., & Hurley, R. (1976). The effects of commercial interruption of violent and nonviolent films on viewer's subsequent aggressiveness. *Journal of Experimental Social Psychology, 12*(2), 220–232.

Zillmann, D. (1971). Excitation transfer in communication-mediated aggressive behavior. *Journal of Experimental Social Psychology, 7,* 419–434.

6

The Experience and Effects of Violence in Infancy

CHARLES H. ZEANAH
MICHAEL S. SCHEERINGA

THERE IS SOMETHING DEEPLY disturbing about the juxtaposition of violence and infancy. Infancy is a period of development that we associate with innocence, with hope, and with promise for the future. Babies' very appearance has been noted to have profound effects on adults (Stern, 1977). Physical attributes of the young throughout mammalian species are designed to be appealing, to elicit interest and caregiving responses from adults (Hofer, 1981). As a result, adult attributions and perceptions of their infants in the first year of life are overwhelmingly positive (Zeanah, Zeanah, & Stewart, 1990). Infants also stimulate protective urges in adults, who are motivated to shelter them from the danger that violence entails.

Under ordinary circumstances, of course, infants return the adoration of their caregivers. They attach themselves to their caregivers with unquestioning loyalty and devotion. They develop a hierarchy of a small number of preferred caregivers to whom they turn for comfort when upset, for protection when afraid, for nurturance when needing affection (Bowlby, 1969). With the primary caregiver, infants know delight that they cannot know alone, and they experience the profound power of empathy, the sense of being noticed, valued, and understood. As a result, infants make their caregivers the center of their world.

Unfortunately, sometimes the world of infants involves exactly the experiences of violence that we are inclined to resist associating with them. Instead of acknowledging these experiences, we attempt to minimize, dismiss, or deny the effects of violence on infants and young children. Despite our reluctance to consider violence and infancy, the topic is important to consider from both clinical and developmental perspectives.

We will advance two major theses in this chapter. The first is that violence is a major and too often underappreciated context for infant development. Infants have not been spared in the epidemic of violence that is currently sweeping America. In the initial part of the chapter, we will consider what is known about the experience of violence in infancy. Although convincing epidemiological data regarding infants' exposure to violence are lacking, we draw upon indirect and anecdotal data to call attention to infants' exposure to community, media, and family violence.

The second thesis of this chapter is that the violence that infants experience has profound developmental and clinical effects, some of which may be lasting. In response to their experiences of community and family violence, many infants exhibit various kinds of developmental compromises and clinical symptomatology. We review what is known about these effects, drawing upon developmental and clinical research. Relatively more data are available documenting the effects of family violence on infant development, especially physical abuse. After reviewing these data, we suggest associations between certain forms of family violence and specific clinical disorders of infancy. We illustrate these disorders with clinical vignettes.

Finally, throughout the chapter we attempt to highlight areas in which there are significant gaps in our understanding. Having suggested that infants do experience violence and are at times profoundly affected by it, we conclude by suggesting possible directions for future research.

THE EXPERIENCE OF VIOLENCE

There are several contexts in which to consider the degree to which infants are exposed to violence. Direct effects include those experiences in which infants witness or are physically injured by violent events.

Indirect effects include those created by the effects of violence on infants' caregiving context, especially the primary caregiving relationship.

Community Violence

The initial context in which to consider the effects of violence on infants is the community. Recent research has documented that large numbers of urban school children in the United States are exposed to community violence, in the form of witnessing armed robberies, shootings, and stabbings (Garbarino & Kostelny, Chapter 3, this volume; Jenkins & Bell, Chapter 2, this volume; Marans & Adelman, Chapter 10, this volume; Osofsky, Wewers, Hann, & Fick, 1993; Osofsky, 1995; Richters & Martinez, 1993). Although little research has addressed the numbers of infants who may have witnessed or experienced community violence, it seems safe to assume that children under 3 years of age are living in many of the same neighborhoods as the school-age children in the studies. For example, in a study at Boston City Hospital, 10% of children less than 6 years old reported having witnessed a stabbing or a shooting (Taylor, Zuckerman, Harik, & Groves, 1994).

Indirect effects of community violence are likely to be more common than direct effects for two related reasons. First, if violent events are not within infants' immediate proximal environment, their ability to focus on and process those events will be limited by their cognitive and perceptual immaturity. For this reason, many events of community violence that might be terrifying to older children and adults will not be registered by infants. Second, the caregiving relationship is so crucial for infant development that events that impinge upon it are likely to have profound effects (Lyons-Ruth & Zeanah, 1993). The same community violence that infants do not notice may affect profoundly the infants' caregivers and compromise their caregiving.

Media Violence

Research on the effects of exposure of media violence on children's development over the past 25 years points to some disturbing conclusions (reviewed in Huesmann & Miller, 1994; Murray, Chapter 5, this volume) that may or may not be applicable to children in the early years. Research suggests that media violence is robustly and perhaps even causally related to subsequent aggressive behavior (Comstock & Paik, 1991; Huesmann & Miller, 1994) when the exposure occurs in middle childhood or early adolescence.

Although none of these investigations have included young children, it would seem unlikely that they are spared the exposure, if not the effects. Murray (Chapter 5, this volume) points out that Saturday morning cartoons contain more violent acts per hour than any other programming. In our experience, mothers of young children living in violent neighborhoods are often afraid to let their children play outside. Instead, they often have the children watching television for long hours, beginning as early as a few months of age. It is likely that these very young children watch a large number of violent programs, since many of these programs are targeted specifically to them.

With regard to infants, the crucial questions are at what point in development do children begin to watch significant amounts of violent television, and at what point do they become vulnerable to the harmful effects of watching violence on television? Other important questions regarding young children are whether realistic depiction of violence is perceived differently than cartoon violence, and whether exposure to these two types of violence have different effects. Furthermore, it is important to explore how watching violent television interacts with other family risk variables in promoting or inhibiting aggressive behavior and violence.

Family Violence

Because of the importance of context for infant development (Sameroff, 1992), the most important form of violence for infants is within the family. Infants are likely to experience violence directly through witnessing parental conflict and violence, and through experiencing physical abuse themselves.

Partner Violence

Increasingly recognized as a major public health problem, partner violence is another important context for infant development. Strauss and Gelles (1988) estimated that 1.8 million women in the United States were physically assaulted by their husbands during the year of their national survey. A large although undocumented number of abused women are mothers caring for very young children who are witnesses not only to marital conflict but also to extremes of physical violence.

According to the National Family Violence Survey in 1985, over 3.3 million children witnessed physical assaults between their parents. In a Pediatric Primary Care Clinic in Boston, parents reported that 5% of the children less than 6 years old had witnessed a stabbing or shooting in their homes (Taylor et al., 1994). Since clinicians suspect significant underreporting by parents (Zuckerman, Augustin, Groves, & Parker, 1995), especially about violence witnessed by very young children, these data are even more alarming. Pynoos and Eth (1984) reported that in 1981 children witnessed 10% of the homicides in Los Angeles County—the majority of these homicides were parent murdering parent, and many of the child witnesses were 5 years old or younger. All of these indirect data converge to suggest that a major experience of violence for very young children is witnessing serious interparental violence, although no studies of witnessing violence have broken down age sufficiently to know in particular about children in the first 3 years of life. Further-more, in our clinical experiences, battered women frequently overlook or fail to recognize the potentially traumatic effects of infants' wit-nessing violence.

Physical Abuse

Based on what is known about validated reports of maltreatment, conser-vative estimates are that over 1,000,000 children are abused and neglected each year in the United States (National Center on Child Abuse and Neglect, 1995). A recent Gallup Poll asked parents if they engaged in a variety of disciplinary techniques that included abusive acts. Results of this survey, in which parents reported on their own behavior, suggested a rate 12 to 20 times the rate detected by the child welfare system (Gallup Organization, 1995). Many physically abused children are very young, and in fact, more abuse and more fatal abuse occurs to children in the first year of life than in any other 1-year period in their development (National Center on Child Abuse and Neglect, 1995).

Determining an exact incidence of abuse is difficult because of the problems in determining exactly which types of maltreatment actually occurred (Cicchetti & Toth, 1995). As an example, infants who sustain fractures while in the care of their parents may be validated for lack of supervision, a form of neglect, because it is too difficult to prove which adult perpetrated the abuse. Many types of maltreatment commonly co-occur, and it is not always possible to know which maltreated infants have experienced only physical abuse, which have experienced some combination of physical abuse with other forms of maltreatment, and which have experienced unrecognized physical abuse in the midst of other types of maltreatment. Clinically, it is wise to suspect abuse in any case involving another form of maltreatment or family violence.

The limited data available point to large numbers of infants being exposed to serious family violence. Since this is the type of violence likely to have the most profound effects on infant development, relation-ships, and health, we turn next to what is known about the effects of family violence on infants.

EFFECTS OF VIOLENCE IN INFANCY

The risks of exposure to severe domestic or community violence are not, of course, randomly distributed in the population. Some infants are substantially more likely to have such experiences associated with where and with whom they live. Infants who have other risk factors in their lives, such as emotionally abusive relationships, parental substance abuse, and/or poverty, are at increased risk for exposure to violence as well. Although we know that violence and trauma exposure *can* have severely debilitating effects, we do not yet know how to link specific risk conditions with specific outcomes. An important question is whether exposure to specific types of violence is related to specific outcomes, or whether risks for adverse outcomes are better predicted by the number of risk factors rather than by the type of violence exposure.

In this section, we begin by reviewing what is known about the effects of maltreatment on the developmental domains of social relatedness and emotion regulation, attachment, communication, and self-organization. We propose an attachment theory framework for understanding these results, as well as considering their implications for the intergenerational transmission of maltreatment, one of the most serious effects of violence in infancy. Next, we review data suggesting that merely witnessing violence may have profound effects. This includes highlighting some suggestive evidence for neurobiological effects of witnessing violence, even when there is no physical brain injury, as well as evidence of developmental compromise related to witnessing parental conflict and partner violence. Finally, we also review several clinical disorders of infancy that are believed to be associated with violence. Throughout, we emphasize that more serious effects are more likely with family violence because of its proximity to infants' direct experience, and because of the importance of the primary caregiving context for infant development.

Maltreatment and Infant Development

The most important concern about maltreatment in infancy is fatality. Abuse is the leading cause of death in the first year of life after the perinatal period (National Center for Child Abuse and Neglect, 1995), and more infants die from abuse in the first year of life than in any other 1-year period. If they survive physical abuse, infants' vulnerability to serious injury is partially compensated for by the plasticity of the central nervous system at this age. Nevertheless, a number of profound developmental sequelae have been demonstrated following physical abuse, most of which are not directly related to the physical injury that the infant sustained. We will focus on findings that implicate maltreatment and the development of interpersonal relationships.

Social Relatedness and Emotional Regulation

A number of studies have documented abnormalities in the emotional and social development of maltreated infants as early as the first year of life. Infants who are failing to thrive and abused infants have been documented to exhibit abnormalities in social signaling and emotional responsiveness, such as expressionless faces, avoidant gaze, lack of smiling, undirected vocalizations, and frozen watchfulness (Powell & Low, 1983; Steele, 1970, 1983).

Based on her observations of maltreated infants in clinic and naturalistic settings, Fraiberg (1982) described three defensive patterns of *avoidance*, *freezing*, and *fighting*. Avoidance, as she observed it during mother–infant interactions, is an aberration of the usual pattern of comfort seeking. In situations in which babies ordinarily seek their caregivers, maltreated infants avoid their caregivers through failure to approach, failure to make eye contact, or failure to direct vocalizations to the caregiver. This is not merely a separation-specific avoidance, as in the Strange Situation Procedure, but a more pervasive (although sometimes subtle) avoidance of the caregiver during social interchanges. Freezing refers to prolonged episodes of immobilization that resemble typical responses to extreme danger but which in the maltreated infants observed by Fraiberg were triggered often by mild stressors. The pattern of fighting, including episodes of extreme and disintegrative anger and tantrums, describes breakdowns in emotional regulation of negative affect in maltreated infants. Fraiberg considered these patterns to reflect defensive distortions of normal developmental processes and pointed out that they could be observed as early as the first 6 months of life.

The second year of life ushers in developmental advances resulting initially from capacities for intersubjectivity and intentionality that develop toward the end of the first year. These changes lead to changes in the social and emotional regulation problems apparent in maltreated infants. Fraiberg (1982), for example, noted other patterns of defensive behavior in maltreated infants that appear in the second year, which she described as *turning aggression against the self* and sadomasochistic *transformation of pain into pleasure*. These defensive patterns also represents distortions in the development of healthy aggressive responses in infants in the second year, much as avoidance, freezing, and flight represent pathological markers the first year.

Abnormal emotional responses and social signals in maltreated infants should affect how these infants relate to caregivers and peers in the second and third years of life. In fact, Erickson, Egeland, and Pianta (1989) documented that maltreated toddlers are significantly angrier, more frustrated, and noncompliant with their caregivers during an experimental interactive paradigm than were nonmaltreated toddlers. Both clinicians (Steele, 1983) and investigators (Crittenden & DiLalla, 1988) have noted wariness and hypercompliance in some maltreated infants interacting with their mothers.

In an uncontrolled, descriptive study, Gaensbauer, Mrazek, and Harmon (1981) videotaped laboratory sessions of interactions between maltreated infants and their biological or foster caregivers. Based on consensual ratings of videotapes of these sessions, the investigators suggested that maltreated infants and toddlers demonstrate a variety of abnormalities in social and emotional development. They described 40% of a sample of 30 maltreated toddlers to be *developmentally and affectively retarded*, 20% to be *depressed*, 25% to be *ambivalent/affectively labile*, and 15% to be *angry* during interactions with their caregivers.

Other studies have documented increased aggression toward peers and caregivers and abnormal responses to peer distress, including less concern, more physical attacks, and more fear and anger (George & Main, 1979; Main & George, 1985). These results converge with findings from studies of older maltreated children, indicating patterns of peer social relatedness characterized by increased aggression and increased withdrawal (Mueller & Silverman, 1989).

Attachment

Findings of abnormal relatedness with caregivers raise the question of attachment relationships between infants and their caregivers. One of the important findings of developmental research on attachment was a demonstration that infants do become attached to parents who abuse them (Egeland & Sroufe, 1981; Cicchetti & Toth, 1995). Attachment in these studies generally has been assessed using the Strange Situation Procedure (Ainsworth, Blehar, Waters, & Wall, 1978). Some of the maltreated infants studied by Crittenden (1988) exhibited mixtures of high levels of avoidance and high levels of resistance in reunions with their caregivers, leading to the designation of an atypical classification, "A/C." An even more curious finding in this literature, however, was that an unexpectedly large number of infants in these studies were classified in the Strange Situation as securely attached, which is asserted to be associated with sensitive and responsive caregiving (Ainsworth et al., 1978). Main and Solomon (1986) sought to resolve this when they described the disorganized attachment pattern, or "D" pattern, in which infants exhibited various anomalous behaviors with their attachment figures that were believed to represent breakdowns in their strategies for attaining a feeling of security from their caregivers. Many of the infants formerly classified "securely" attached to their maltreating caregivers actually had "disorganized" attachments according to this reasoning.

Two studies have examined attachment in samples of maltreated infants using the new classification of disorganized attachment. In the first investigation, Carlson, Cicchetti, Barnett, and Braunwald (1989) found that 82% of maltreated 12-month-old infants compared to only 19% of infants in a demographically comparable control group were classified disorganized. In the second investigation (Cicchetti & Barnett, 1991), 36% of maltreated 30-month-olds, compared to 15% of controls and 28% of maltreated 36-month-olds, compared to 17% of controls, were classified disorganized. These results support the association of maltreatment and disorganized attachment hypothesized by Main and Solomon (1986). Further research is needed to determine whether the hypothesized interactive patterns do in fact link the two.

An increase in disorganized attachment classifications in maltreated infants and toddlers is important for at least two reasons. First, the disorganized classification in infants and toddlers has been related to disruptive behavior disorders in preschoolers (Lyons-Ruth, Alpern, & Repacholi, 1993; Greenberg, Speltz, & DeKlyen, 1993) and to role-inappropriate interactions with caregivers in school-age children (Main & Cassidy, 1988; Solomon, George, & DeJong, 1995). Second, attachment classifications are believed to reflect different types of internal representations of self and other, which may generalize subsequently to other relationships. In fact, this is the hypothesized mechanism that explains intergenerational transmission of maltreatment.

Communicative Development

Cicchetti and Beeghly (1987) examined communicative development in maltreated toddlers. On the one hand, they found no differences in expressive language development in maltreated and comparison infants. On the other hand, the investigators did find that the maltreated toddlers used significantly fewer words to describe their internal states than non-maltreated toddlers. The investigators recently replicated these findings in another sample (Beeghly & Cicchetti, 1994). These findings suggest possible impairments in self-perception, which also have been investigated in toddlers.

Development of the Sense of Self

Observations of the social and emotional behaviors of maltreated infants described earlier raise questions about the effects of maltreatment on the development of the sense of self. Clinical reports have called attention to a number of distortions of the sense of self in maltreated children (Galdston, 1981; Osofsky, Cohen, & Drell, 1995; Steele, 1983; Stern, 1985), although to date, developmental researchers have approached the problem more narrowly from the standpoint of self-recognition.

Ordinarily, at about the age of 18 months, when infants experience significant gains in representational processes, they also develop the capacity to recognize themselves physically and to distinguish their appearance from that of others (Lewis & Brooks-Gunn, 1979). This is usually demonstrated by placing an infant in front of a mirror and having an experimenter surreptitiously place a small spot of rouge on the infant's nose. Prior to 18 months of age, infants typically point to the image of the red spot on the nose in the mirror. After 18 months, infants point to their own noses, as if they recognize that the image in the mirror belongs to them.

Schneider-Rosen and Cicchetti (1984) demonstrated that maltreated 19-month-olds exhibited self-recognition as expected when examined in this paradigm. Interestingly, what distinguished them from a comparison group was that the maltreated infants were significantly more likely to exhibit neutral or negative emotional responses to their image. These results provide preliminary evidence of more negative perceptions of the self in maltreated infants.

Implications of Developmental Sequelae of Maltreatment

Bowlby's (1969, 1973, 1980) theoretical perspective makes these differences in attachment, internal language, and emotional responses to self-recognition in maltreated infants especially disturbing. He suggested that based on the quality of their caregiving experiences, infants develop representational models of self and other by the end of the first year of life. He believed that because infants have a limited cognitive capacity to consider themselves apart from their own experiences, models of self and other are likely to be constructed similarly at this point in development. The high proportion of disorganized attachment classifications and the deficient internal state language and negative emotional responses to self-recognition all are compatible with significant abnormalities in representational models of maltreated infants as early as the second year of life. Given evidence for the stability (Lyons-Ruth, Repacholi, McLeod, & Silva, 1991; Main & Cassidy, 1988) and predictive validity (Lyons-Ruth, Alpern, & Repacholi, 1993; Lyons-Ruth, Easterbrook, & Davidson Cibelli, in press) of disorganized attachment classifications, maltreated infants may well carry forward maladaptive representational models of self and other into the preschool and school years.

Witnessing Violence and Infant Development

There has been increasing recognition, especially in studies of older children, that even when abuse does not occur, children may be affected by witnessing violence between others, especially when the violence involves their caregivers. Although it is important to recall that infants who witness violence between others often also experience it directly themselves, nevertheless, there is value in attempting to understand the effects of witnessing violence apart from abuse. In this section, we consider possible neurobiological effects of being traumatized by violence in the earliest years, and then consider other developmental compromises that may be associated with witnessing violence.

Neurobiological Effects of Violence

Even when there is no physical injury to the brain, as in abuse, there may be neurobiological effects of experiencing violence and trauma. Although there are no known psychophysiological studies of infants following exposure to violence and trauma, Perry and colleagues (Perry, Pollard, Blakley, Baker, & Vigilante, 1995; Perry, Chapter 7, this volume) have suggested that profound and perhaps permanent brain changes can result following violent trauma in the first 3 years of life. Based on nonhuman research and on their extensive clinical experience with infants and young children, they reasoned that the organization and maturation of neural systems of the developing brain are susceptible to influence by life experiences, such as exposure to violence. The activation of a neural network involves "use-dependent" internalization of new information. Once a neural response is sensitized by some experience, the same neural activation can be activated subsequently by a lower threshold stimulus. In the developing brain of a youngster, "states" that have been internalized by use-dependence—such as a fear response—could serve also to organize neural systems, thereby resulting in "traits."

According to this reasoning, human infant brains are more susceptible to influence in response to experiences (including traumatic ones) than brains of mature individuals. The same plasticity that makes infant brains more likely to recover from biological insults may render them more vulnerable to psychologically traumatic experiences.

Perry et al. (1995) postulated two major response patterns for the traumatized child: the hyperarousal continuum (the classic fight-or-flight response), and the dissociative continuum (the freeze-or-surrender response). In addition to behavioral differences, there are also neurobiological differences between the patterns. The dissociative pattern involves an increase in vagal tone, decreased blood pressure and heart rate. On the one hand, the endogenous opioid systems may be important for mediating pain and altering the senses of time and reality in this response pattern. The hyperarousal response, on the other hand, involves an increase in the sympathetic nervous system, resulting in increased blood pressure, heart rate, respiration, release of stored sugar, muscle tone, and hypervigilance. Because they are not well suited for fight or flight, it is much more likely infants will use the freeze response (see Fraiberg, 1982 and Main & Solomon, 1986, for behavioral descriptions). The challenge for future research is to determine whether these hypothesized psychophysiological findings apply to traumatized infants.

Other Developmental Effects of Witnessing Violence

Whatever effects of witnessing violence on infants' central nervous system ultimately can be demonstrated, it is already clear that infants need not experience violence directly to be affected by it profoundly. In this section, we review what is known about the effects of witnessing violence on infant behavior and development.

Adult Verbal Conflict. A wealth of research has demonstrated that marital conflict is profoundly harmful to child development. Since marriages are more likely to be discordant during the infancy and toddlerhood of the couple's children (Belsky & Rovine, 1990), marital conflict is a potent risk factor for infant mental health. For some time, it was assumed that the effects of such conflict were transmitted through the effect of conflict on parenting behaviors. For example, in home observations, anger, distress, and involvement in conflict with their toddlers were related to mothers' reports of the number of marital conflicts they experienced (Cummings, Zahn-Waxler, & Radke-Yarrow, 1981).

Recently, it has become clearer that another pathway is that marital conflict contributes directly to infant maladaptation, over and above what is contributed by parenting behaviors (Davies & Cummings, 1994). This suggests that infants are affected by witnessing conflict, even when parenting behaviors are relatively unaffected by the conflict.

Davies and Cummings's (1994) extensive review of research on marital conflict suggests that marital conflict has stronger effects on infant maladaptation than conflict between other adults, and that witnessing physical violence has stronger effects than witnessing verbal anger. In one study with older, high-risk children (aged 3 to 6 years), for example, verbal interparental conflict only was associated with a moderate level of conduct problems, but verbal plus physical conflict was associated with clinical levels of conduct problems and moderate levels of emotional problems (Fantuzzo et al., 1991). With these findings in mind, it is worth examining the effects of witnessing partner violence on infant development.

Partner Violence. With increasing documentation of the importance of partner violence as a public health problem in the United States, more attention has focused on children as witnesses of this violence (Zuckerman et al., 1995). Research on partner violence with older children has generally examined behavior problems, but the most important questions regarding partner violence and infancy concern infant development. One recent investigation examined two domains of infant development in relation to the mother's experience of partner violence. In a longitudinal investigation of infant development in a sample of impoverished families, Zeanah and colleagues (Zeanah et al., 1995) explored infant–mother attachment and infant mastery motivation as they related to mothers' reports of violent experiences with current and ex-partners.

In this investigation, infant–mother attachment patterns, derived from Strange Situation classifications (Ainsworth et al., 1978), were related strongly to mothers' reports of partner violence. Specifically, on the one hand, mothers of infants with secure attachment classifications (52% of sample) reported significantly lower levels of violence with their current partners than mothers of infants with insecure attachments, most of whom had disorganized attachments (39% of sample). Reports of violence with ex-partners, on the other hand, did not distinguish infants classified secure and disorganized. Although mastery motivation itself was unrelated to partner violence, infants whose mothers reported higher levels of partner violence displayed significantly more negative affect during the mastery motivation assessment procedure.

How do we interpret these findings? A closer examination of the attachment data in this study revealed that 63% of mothers of securely attached infants, but only 25% of the mothers of insecurely attached infants, reported no violence with current partners. In contrast, all of the infants whose mothers reported the highest levels of violence had disorganized attachment organizations. Since the probability of disorganized attachment is believed to increase when infants are afraid of or for their mothers (Main & Hesse, 1990), as might be expected if mothers are engaged in significantly violent relationships, the finding of a high proportion of disorganized infants is not surprising.

Obviously, the direction of effects cannot be ascertained in a study in which infant and maternal variables were obtained concurrently, and the possibility of a third factor must always be considered. Nevertheless, these data strongly suggest that relationship-specific quality of caregiving between mother and infant may be related to the mother's experiences of partner violence.

In addition to raising questions about the effects of infants witnessing partner violence, these results are in keeping with hypotheses suggesting that violence interferes with the emotional availability and sensitivity of the primary caregiver for infants (Osofsky, 1995). More attention needs to be directed to processes through which violence exposure interferes with or disrupts caregiving of very young children.

A final caveat is that there is convincing evidence that parents who are involved in violent relationships with their partners are more likely to abuse their children (Strauss & Gelles, 1988). This suggests that clinicians who encounter families of infants in which partner violence occurs ought to be alert for the additional possibility of infant maltreatment and vice versa.

Results from studies of domains of infant development and family violence all point to profound effects. Nevertheless, they do not convey the clinical picture of what profoundly affected infants look and feel like. For that, we next consider the association between family violence and clinical disorders of infancy.

Violence and Clinical Disorders of Infancy

Although data from systematic investigations are limited, our clinical experiences suggest that violence also is associated with several different clinical disorders of infancy. In our experience, two of the most common and severe disorders are posttraumatic stress disorder (PTSD) and attachment disorders.

Posttraumatic Stress Disorder

Increasingly, it is recognized that infants traumatized by violence develop posttraumatic symptomatology. Although little research has been conducted on posttraumatic reactions in infants and young children, the research that exists indicates that posttraumatic reactions in children under 48 months of age can be profound, long-lasting, and appear similar to reactions in older children and adults (Drell, Siegel, & Gaensbauer, 1993; Zeanah, 1994).

The classic triad of symptoms of reexperiencing the traumatic event, avoidance and numbing of responsiveness, and hyperarousal all are apparent in infants and young children, although there are important differences in the appearance and detection of symptoms in this age group. The fourth edition of the *Diagnostic and Statistical Manual of Mental Disorders* (DSM-IV; American Psychiatric Association, 1994) diagnostic criteria for PTSD were developed from adult patients reporting on their symptomatology and subjective experiences. Since this is impossible for infants and toddlers, it is worth asking how useful these criteria are for very young children.

In order to address this question, Scheeringa and colleagues (Scheeringa, Zeanah, Drell, & Larrieu, 1995) compared DSM-IV criteria to an alternative set of criteria (Zero to Three, 1994) for PTSD in children younger than 48 months. The alternative criteria were developed from clinical experiences with traumatized infants, and from modifications of the DSM-IV diagnostic criteria. They were designed to be (1) less dependent on verbalizations and more behaviorally anchored and (2) more geared to the developmental issues of this age group. Also, fewer items were required than in the DSM-IV (four compared to six) to reach the threshold for diagnosis. The investigators found higher interrater reliabilities and better construct validity for the alternative criteria. In addition to the classic triad of reexperiencing, avoidance/numbing of responsiveness, and hyperarousal, the investigators also found that new fears and new aggression were present in infants after the traumatic event that had not been present before.

This study illustrates that infants may be severely traumatized by violent events, and that when the expression of symptomatology is considered from a developmentally appropriate vantage point, it is possible to identify posttraumatic disorders in the first 4 years of life. The following case vignette illustrates the typical clinical picture of an infant traumatized by witnessing severe violence.

CASE VIGNETTE

Jasmine was 19 months old when she witnessed her mother being assaulted and raped by an acquaintance. After Jasmine's mother fought with the man for several minutes, he grabbed Jasmine and held a gun to her head in order to get her mother to do what he said. Jasmine was not physically injured during the attack.

Immediately after the rape, mother and daughter moved a short distance away to live with a relative. Several weeks later, they moved back into the apartment where the rape had occurred, and Jasmine became obviously symptomatic. Immediately, she exhibited great distress on returning to the apartment and remained quite fearful until her mother rearranged the furniture. Afterward, she was somewhat calmer, but she displayed a number of other persistent symptoms.

Her sleep was quite disturbed. Although falling asleep without protest, she cried out three to four times per night, unresponsive and inconsolable until she fell back asleep again. She also woke up screaming for her mother or for her mother's assailant to leave her alone. At these times, she could be comforted. On occasions following the rape, she slept throughout the entire day without awakening, although, in general, she did not seem to her mother to be more tired than usual.

Aggressive behavior, which had not been apparent prior to the rape, dominated her interactions with younger children afterwards. At the same time, she tended to avoid interacting with older children. She was not only noted to be more stubborn and defiant with her mother, but also to be more sensitive and to cry more readily than before. She became "more attached" to her pacifier after the trauma.

Following the rape, Jasmine tended to avoid contact with men, except for her mother's boyfriend. Nevertheless, once when Jasmine's mother and this man playfully wrestled together, Jasmine came over to him and hit him and cursed him.

Jasmine also developed staring spells that lasted for 2–3 minutes and occurred about two or three times per week. Her mother was unaware of any obvious precipitant for these episodes. During the spells, Jasmine was mute, unresponsive, and tended to "stare" without any seeming focus or recognition.

With regard to play, Jasmine developed a repetitive sequence in which she threw dolls down on the floor and hit them. She tended to repeat this over and over, without elaboration and without obvious affect, according to her mother. She did not demonstrate this play in the examining office but only at home with her mother.

Jasmine illustrates symptoms of reexperiencing the traumatic event (becoming fearful on returning to the apartment where the rape occurred, nightmares in which she wakes screaming for the assailant to leave her alone, and becoming angry and distressed by her mother's playful wrestling with a man), of numbing of responsiveness (avoiding playing with friends and affective constriction), hyperarousal (sleep disturbance), and new fears (separation protest) and aggression (more oppositional behavior and more overt aggression than had been present before the rape).

Beyond simply classifying severely traumatized youngsters as disordered or not, it is important to consider individual differences in how infants react to different violent and traumatic events. The factors likely to influence such reactions include within-the-child characteristics, the nature of the traumatic events themselves, and parental/family factors that affect the infant–caregiver relationship.

Few within-the-child characteristics have been studied so far. In 41 children less than 4 years of age, Scheeringa and Zeanah (1995) found no gender differences in the rates of diagnosis of the disorder of PTSD or in differential expression of the PTSD symptom clusters (reexperiencing, avoidance/numbing, hyperarousal, or new fears/aggression). Children 18–48 months of age expressed more reexperiencing symptoms than children under 18 months of age, believed to be due to greater capacities for symbolic representation and verbalizations in the older group.

Infants and young children who witnessed violence or a threat of violence *against* their caregivers met the diagnosis of PTSD significantly more often than children whose trauma did not involve witnessing threats against the caregivers. Additionally, infants and young children who witnessed threats to their caregivers showed significantly fewer numbing/avoidance symptoms, more hyperarousal symptoms, and more new fears and aggression than children whose trauma did not involve a threat to caregivers. The question that is unclear from this finding is whether the threat to caregiver is important because the baby perceives the caregiver to be threatened or injured and is more affected as a result, or if the caregiver is merely more affected, leading to powerful indirect effects on the baby.

Obviously, these findings should be considered preliminary until they are replicated. Many other factors deserve study in this regard, including the severity, controllability, and predictability of the traumas.

Unpublished data by the authors on 16 clinic-referred children younger than 48 months of age, assessed in a standardized laboratory paradigm for diagnosing PTSD in the children and their caregivers, demonstrated a high concordance between PTSD infants and caregivers. Of the 6 infants who met diagnostic criteria for PTSD, and who were living with their natural mothers (2 others with PTSD were in foster care), four of their mothers (67%) had current PTSD. The traumas causing the mothers' PTSD symptoms sometimes were the same traumas the children experienced, but often were events from the mothers' own childhoods.

The suspected direction of effects in this association is that caregiver symptomatology has adverse effects on young children. One possibility is that traumatized caregivers are not able to provide the emotional availability, affect attunement, or supportive presence to allow the therapeutic expression of anxieties by the children. Another possibility is that caregivers may be so visibly overwhelmed by reminders of their traumas that children are drawn from their normal, developmentally appropriate activities and into imitative/social-learning patterns that promote symptoms or emotionally role-reversed relationships. The following case vignette illustrates some of the complexities of relational effects of traumatized caregivers on infants' symptomatology following exposure to violence.

CASE VIGNETTE

Emerald was 18 months old and her mother, Ida, was 18 years old at the time that they were first seen together. They were residing in a homeless shelter, but they were referred to an infant mental health clinic for evaluation when Ida described some of her experiences to a psychiatrist at the shelter.

According to Ida, Emerald had grown up in a world of violence. Both her father and her maternal grandparents had active problems with substance abuse, and her mother had episodes of depression. Emerald's father was physically and verbally abusive to her mother during much of Emerald's first year of life, including one especially dramatic incident when the father attacked Ida as they were driving in the car.

When Emerald was 17 months old, Ida was hospitalized for suicidal ideation, and Emerald was cared for by Ida's mother for several weeks. Ida believed that her mother physically abused Emerald during that time because of scars she found on Emerald's buttocks. Ida's mother admitted that Emerald had witnessed two fights between the grandparents that included at least one knife attack. Ida's conflicted relationship with her parent's and her concern about what had happened to Emerald led her to the homeless shelter after her discharge from the psychiatric hospital.

At the time of evaluation, Ida exhibited aggressive play, fearful reactions at any reminders of her father, and hyperarousal when her parents argued, including accelerated heart rate, tremulousness, and labored respiration. She also played less than usual, fearfully avoided certain toys, and tried to avoid all males. She was vigilant, especially around strangers, when Ida mentioned her father's name.

Ida had a long history of punitive treatment and physical abuse herself, and she was raped by a relative when she was 6 years old. She had also witnessed a gruesome fire in her apartment building when she was 8 years old. As a result of these multiple traumas, she met diagnostic criteria for PTSD herself.

What was deeply disturbing about their interaction at the time of the evaluation was a pattern of Ida teasing Emerald, repeatedly provoking her to tears. Ida enacted a variety of violent scenes with Emerald in the play, including handcuffing her and shooting her multiple times with a toy gun. Her only obvious reaction to Ida's tears about this play was impatience that she wasn't playing along. The pressure with which Ida seemed to be enacting scenes of violence and her obliviousness to the effects of such play in Emerald were chilling.

It was clear to all who watched a videotape of this dyad's evaluation that Ida's symptomatology not only rendered her insensitive to Emerald's needs, but also that her unconscious identification with the aggressor was further traumatizing Emerald. We have come to think of such cases of two (or more) generations of violence and trauma as relational post-traumatic stress disorder, and we believe that they are more common than has been recognized in infants and young children. A discussion of the effects of violence on infant–caregiver relationships leads us next to consider disorders of attachment.

Attachment Disorders

Clinical experience suggests that attachment disorders in infancy are associated with family violence. This is not surprising, given that DSM-IV (American Psychiatric Association, 1994) and ICD-10 (World Health Organization, 1992) criteria for attachment disorders rely heavily on the literature on social characteristics of maltreated children (Zeanah & Emde, 1994).

Lieberman and Zeanah (1995) have proposed an alternative classification of disorders of attachment that includes several types of attachment disorders other than those specified in DSM-IV and ICD-10. In the alternative system, disorders of attachment also include attachment relationships between infants and caregivers in which emotions and behaviors displayed in attachment relationships are significantly disturbed. Infant–caregiver attachment relationships that are disordered are more profoundly and pervasively disturbed than insecure attachment classifications in the Strange Situation Procedure (Zeanah, Mammen, & Lieberman, 1993).

Although a number of different types of disorders of attachment may be associated with maltreatment or witnessing family violence, we describe and illustrate two of these types in the following sections.

Attachment Disorder with Vigilance/Hypercompliance. The infant's attachment behavioral system motivates the infant to seek comfort and protection from a discriminated attachment figure, especially at times when the infant feels frightened. The pattern of insecure attachment designated disorganized describes anomalous attachment behaviors believed to indicate conflict behaviors in the child for whom the source of comfort is also the source of fear (Main & Hesse, 1990). Attachment disorder with vigilance/hypercompliance describes even more extreme cases in which the child is consistently overtly afraid of the attachment figure and immediately complies with the caregiver's dictates. This pattern has been shown to be increased in abusive and punitive treatment by caregivers, and it is speculated that the infant's vigilance and hypercompliance serve to minimize the likelihood of abuse (Crittenden & DiLalla, 1988; Steele, 1983). What differentiates this disorder from infants and toddlers who are disposed to be pervasively inhibited is the relationship specificity of the behavior; that is, the vigilance, subdued but wary affect, and lack of spontaneity are exhibited during interactions only with the abusive/punitive attachment figure rather than with other caregivers.

A 30-month-old girl in foster care following severe abuse in infancy was referred for evaluation by social services. She had documented cognitive and language delays secondary to brain damage suffered from "shaken infant syndrome" in the first year of life. The referral question was about the possibility of reuniting her with her biological mother, who had visited with her regularly since removal and had completed parenting classes.

An intensive evaluation that included home and clinic-based observations and interviews revealed a distinctive and disturbing pattern of interaction between this girl and her mother. In her mother's presence, this girl sat or stood with virtually no spontaneous movements, and with a bland but wary emotional display. This behavior contrasted sharply with the boisterous behavior of the girl's two brothers who lived with their mother and had not been removed. Her mother was aware of the behavior and reported it to be a consistent pattern, but she believed it was the result of inadequate care in the foster home in which the little girl resided. The evaluation made clear, however, that the behavior was relationship specific, and that the girl was capable of spontaneous and even oppositional behavior with each of her foster parents, both at home and in the clinic.

Attachment Disorder with Role Reversal. Another type of disordered attachment that we believe is often associated with family violence is role reversal. The essence of this type of attachment disorder is that the emotional burden of the relationship has shifted from the adult caregiver to the child. The child becomes precocious in monitoring the caregiver's emotional well-being and in self-care, presumably in order not to burden the caregiver. Controlling behavior, which varies from bossiness to solicitousness to sexualized interactions, characterizes the pattern of relatedness of infant and caregiver. In a number of case reports of this disorder, mothers who were in violent relationships with their partners developed role-reversed relationships with their toddlers.

An interaction observed between a mother with a long history of a violent partner relationship and her 39-month-old daughter illustrates the pattern of role reversal. The mother and daughter were being observed in a playroom by a clinical team through a one-way mirror. The mother and daughter were playing with a doctor kit when the following dialogue occurred:

DAUGHTER: We have to check . . . take . . . I have to . . . check you.
MOTHER: You're going to check me? OK.

DAUGHTER: Let me check your blood pressure. In that arm. Where's your boo boo? (*pointing to an imaginary injury on the mother's arm*) Right there? OK. Who did it?

MOTHER: Daddy. [With this comment the mother introduces a harsh reminder of reality into the play.]

DAUGHTER: Your husband? OK, I never saw your husband. [Here, the little girl reminds her mother that they are playing and that she is the doctor rather than the daughter.] OK, your blood pressure is . . . 600 pounds.

MOTHER: 600 pounds! Oh no, oh no, I'm going to die! [The clinical team believed that this was intended to be a normal blood pressure reading from the perspective of a 3-year-old "doctor," although the mother responded as if it were a reading that was actually life threatening. This play has become deadly serious. Following this, the team observed the little girl visibly shaken by the dilemma of a "medical emergency" and struggling with how to resolve it.]

DAUGHTER: Mmmmm . . . mmmm. . . . But Daddy's not going to do it . . . to be doing it . . . no more, OK? 'Cause you got to tell them that you weighed 1,300 pounds, OK? [The clinical team understood this response as an attempt to resolve the emergency by reassuring her mother about not being hurt again and also by normalizing the blood pressure reading. It is interesting that the little girl relates not only the boo boo but also her mother's blood pressure reading as having been caused by "Daddy."]

What follows this part of the interaction is that the mother announces that she is hungry, and the daughter begins an elaborate and methodical preparation of a meal for her mother. At the conclusion of the meal, the mother "drinks" some juice she has requested that her daughter prepare for her. Mother then collapses on the floor, announcing, "I'm dead." What made this development especially disturbing was that the mother had made a suicide attempt about 6 months previously.

To the degree that this observed interaction was part of a pattern, it reflected a relationship in which the emotional well-being of the mother was paramount over that of the 3-year-old daughter. Although this relationship had many positive aspects, and the mother did have some capacity to respond to needs in her daughter, nevertheless, this little girl experienced developmentally inappropriate pressure from worrying about her mother's safety and well-being.

Of course, not all role-reversed relationships between infants and caregiver's are associated with a mother's experience of violence, but it is clear that women engaged in battering relationships could be motivated to seek care and comfort from a child that they cannot obtain from their partners.

CONCLUSIONS

Infants experience violence in a number of different contexts, but what we know suggests that the family, and especially infants' intimate relationships with caregivers, are the most important of these contexts. Some profound and lasting effects have been demonstrated already, from both witnessing and directly experiencing violence, although many questions remain unanswered.

A number of pressing concerns deserve attention at present. First, it is vital to obtain longitudinal data about risk and protective factors and the range of outcomes likely in infants exposed to violence. Outcome of infants in a number of developmental domains, as well as the course and outcome of specific disorders of infancy related to violence, are important to delineate. Posttraumatic symptomatology and attachment disturbances seem to be especially important areas to track over time based upon results to date. Second, the efficacy of prevention and/or treatment approaches to the problems that plague violent families must be assessed. Given the high levels of co-occurence of child abuse and partner violence, integrative treatment efforts directed at families known to be violent or at high risk for violence should be explored. Third, the interrelationships between development and psychopathology in infants exposed to violence ought to be explored. One example of this line of investigation would be to examine salient developmental issues in infants who develop clinical disorders. The question is the degree to which violence is associated with compromise in specific domains of infant functioning. Fourth, more research is needed to define the mechanisms by which experiences of violence in infancy are transformed into the effects of violence on infants. Mediating and moderating variables are important to identify in order to design effective interventions. Finally, given that a range of outcomes is likely to be demonstrated, it is important to attend to protective factors that enable infants to overcome early adversity and to avoid intergenerational cycles of violence for which they are at risk.

It is easy to feel impatient with the plodding pace of gains in scientific knowledge in the face of the horrifying experiences of violence with which infants so clearly must grapple. Nevertheless, given the complexities of the factors contributing to these problems, there will always be a place for detailed clinical observations and careful research efforts helping us to delineate and to understand the links between the experience and the effects of violence in infancy.

REFERENCES

Ainsworth, M. D., Blehar, M. C., Waters, E., & Wall, S. (1978). *Patterns of attachment.* Hillsdale, NJ: Erlbaum.

American Psychiatric Association. (1994). *Diagnostic and statistical manual of mental disorders* (4th ed.). Washington, DC: Author.

Beeghly, M., & Cicchetti, D. (1994). Child maltreatment, attachment and the self-system: Emergence of an internal state lexicon in toddler at high social risk. *Development and Psychopathology, 6,* 5–30.

Belsky, J., & Rovine, M. (1990). Patterns of marital change across the transition to parenthood. *Journal of Marriage and the Family, 52,* 5–19.

Bowlby, J. (1969). *Attachment.* New York: Basic Books.

Bowlby, J. (1973). *Separation, anxiety and anger.* New York: Basic Books.

Bowlby J. (1980). *Loss.* New York: Basic Books.

Carlson, V., Cicchetti, D., Barnett, D., & Braunwald, K. (1989). Disorganized/disoriented attachment relationships in maltreated infants. *Developmental Psychology, 25,* 525–531.

Cicchetti, D., & Barnett, D. (1991). Attachment organization in maltreated preschoolers. *Development and Psychopathology, 3,* 397–412.

Cicchetti, D., & Beeghly, M. (1987). Symbolic development in maltreated youngsters: An organizational perspective. *New Directions in Child Development, 36,* 47–68.

Cicchetti, D., & Toth, S. L. (1995). A developmental psychopathology perspective on child abuse and neglect. *Journal of the American Academy of Child and Adolescent Psychiatry, 34,* 541–565.

Comstock, G. A., & Paik, H. (1991). The effects of television violence on aggressive behavior: A meta-analysis. In *A preliminary report to the National Research Council on the understanding and controlling of violent behavior.* Washington, DC: National Research Council.

Crittenden, P. M. (1988). Relationships at risk. In J. Belsky & T. Nezworski (Eds.), *Clinical implications of attachment theory* (pp. 136–174). Hillsdale, NJ: Erlbaum.

Crittenden, P. M., & DiLalla, D. L. (1988). Compulsive compliance: The development of an inhibitory coping strategy in infancy. *Journal of Abnormal Child Psychology, 16,* 585–599.

Cummings, E. M., Zahn-Waxler, C., & Radke-Yarrow, M. (1981). Young children's responses to expressions of anger and affection by others in the family. *Child Development, 52,* 1274–1282.

Davies, P. T., & Cummings, E. M. (1994). Marital conflict and child adjustment: An emotional security hypothesis. *Psychological Bulletin, 116,* 387–411.

Drell, M., Siegel, C., & Gaensbauer, T. (1993). Post-traumatic stress disorder. In C. H. Zeanah (Ed.), *Handbook of infant mental health* (pp. 291–304). New York: Guilford Press.

Egeland B., & Sroufe L. A. (1981). Attachment and early maltreatment. *Child Development, 52*, 44–52.

Erickson, M. F., Egeland, B., & Pianta, R. (1989). The effects of maltreatment on the development of young children. In D. Cicchetti & V. Carlson (Eds.), *Child maltreatment: Theory and research on the causes and consequences of child abuse and neglect* (pp. 647–684). New York, Cambridge University Press.

Fantuzzo, J. W., DePaolo, L. M., Lambert, L., Martino, T., Anderson, G., & Sutton, S. (1991). Effects of interparental violence on the psychological adjustment and competencies of young children. *Journal of Consulting and Clinical Psychology, 59*, 258–265.

Fraiberg, S. (1982). Pathological defenses in infancy. *Psychoanalytic Quarterly, 51*, 612–635.

Gaensbauer, T., Mrazek, D., & Harmon, R. (1981). Affective behavior pattern in abused and/or neglected infants. In N. Freud (Ed.), *The understanding and prevention of child abuse: Psychological approaches* (pp. 120–135). London: Concord Press.

Galdston, R. (1981). The domestic dimensions of violence: Child abuse. *Psychoanalytic Study of the Child, 36*, 391–414.

Gallup Organization. (1995). *Disciplining children in America: A Gallup Poll report.* Princeton, NJ: Gallup Organization.

George, C., & Main, M. (1979). Social interactions in young abused children: Approach, avoidance, and aggression. *Child Development, 50*, 306–318.

Greenberg, M. T., Speltz, M. L., & DeKlyen, M. (1993). The role of attachment in the early development of disruptive behavior problems. *Development and Psychopathology, 5*, 191–213.

Hofer, M. (1981). *The roots of human behavior.* San Francisco: W. H. Freeman.

Huesmann, L. R., & Miller, L. S. (1994). Long-term effects of repeated exposure to media violence in childhood. In L. R. Huesmann (Ed.), *Aggressive behavior: Current perspectives* (pp. 153–187). New York: Plenum Press.

Lewis, M., & Brooks-Gunn, J. (1979). *Social cognition and the acquisition of self.* New York: International Universities Press.

Lieberman, A., & Zeanah, C. H. (1995). Disorders of attachment in infancy. In K. Minde (Ed.), *Infant psychiatry: Child psychiatric clinics of North America* (pp. 571–588). Philadelphia: Saunders.

Lyons-Ruth, K., Alpern, L., & Repacholi, B. (1993). Disorganized infant attachment classification and maternal psychosocial problem as predictors of hostile–aggressive behavior in the preschool classroom. *Child Development, 64*, 572–585.

Lyons-Ruth, Easterbrooks, M. A., & Davidson Cibelli, C. (in press). Disorganized attachment strategies and mental lag in infancy: Prediction of externalizing problems at age seven. *Child Development.*

Lyons-Ruth, K., Repacholi, B., McLeod, S., & Silva, E. (1991). Disorganized attachment behavior in infancy: Short-term stability, maternal correlates, and risk-related subtypes. *Development and Psychopathology, 3*, 377–396.

Lyons-Ruth, K., & Zeanah, C. H. (1993). The family context of infant mental health: I. Affective development in the primary caregiving relationship. In

C. H. Zeanah (Ed.), *Handbook of infant mental health* (pp. 14–37). New York: Guilford Press.

Main, M., & Cassidy, J. (1988). Categories of response to reunion with the parent at age 6: Predictable from infant attachment classifications and stable over a 1-month period. *Developmental Psychology, 24,* 415–426.

Main, M., & George, C. (1985). Responses of abused and disadvantaged toddlers to distress inagemates: A study in the day care setting. *Developmental Psychology, 21,* 407–412.

Main, M., & Hesse, E. (1990). Parents' unresolved traumatic experiences are related to infant disorganized attachment status: Is frightened and/or frightening behavior the linking mechanism? In M. T. Greenberg, D. Cicchetti, & E. M. Cummings (Eds.), *Attachment in the preschool years* (pp. 161–182). Chicago: University of Chicago Press.

Main, M., & Solomon, J. (1986). Discovery of an insecure disorganized/disoriented attachment pattern: Procedures, findings and implications for the classification of behavior. In M. Yogman & T. B. Brazelton (Eds.), *Affective development in infanty* (pp. 95–124). Norwood, NJ: Ablex.

Main, M., & Solomon, J. (1990). Procedures for identifying infants as disorganized/disoriented during the Ainsworth Strange Situation. In M. T. Greenberg, D. Cicchetti, & E. M. Cummings (Eds.), *Attachment in the preschool years* (pp. 121–160). Chicago: University of Chicago Press.

Mueller, E., & Silverman, N. (1989). Peer relations in maltreated children. In D. Cicchetti & V. Carlson (Eds.), *Child maltreatment: Theory and research on the causes and consequences of child abuse and neglect.* New York: Cambridge University Press.

National Center on Child Abuse and Neglect, U.S. Department of Health and Human Services, (1995). *Child maltreatment 1993: Reports from the states to the national center on child abuse and neglect.* Washington, DC: U.S. Government Printing Office.

Osofsky, J. D. (1995). The effects of exposure to violence on young children. *American Psychologist, 50,* 782–788.

Osofsky, J. D., Cohen, G., & Drell, M. (1995). The effects of trauma on young children: A case of two-year-old twins. *International Journal of Psycho-Analysis, 76,* 595–607.

Osofsky, J. D., Wewers, S., Hann, D. M., & Fick, A. (1993). Chronic community violence: What is happening to our children? *Psychiatry, 56,* 36–45.

Perry, B. D., Polland R., Blakley, T., Baker, W., & Vigilante, D. (1995). Childhood trauma, theneurobiology of adaptation and "use-dependent" development of the brain: How "states" become "traits." *Infant Mental Health Journal, 16,* 271–291.

Powell, G. F., & Low, J. F. (1983). Behavior in nonorganic failure to thrive. *Journal of Developmental and Behavioral Pediatrics, 8,* 18–24.

Pynoos, R. S., & Eth, S. (1984). The child as criminal witness to homicide. *Journal of Social Issues, 40,* 87–108.

Richters, J. E., & Martinez, P. (1993). The NIMH community violence project: Vol. 1. Children as victims of and witnesses to violence. *Psychiatry, 56,* 7–21.

Sameroff, A. J. (1992). Systems, development and early intervention: A commentary. In J. Shonkoff, P. Hauser-Cram, M. W. Krauss, & C. C. Upshur (Eds.), *Development of infant with disabilities and their families. Monographs of the Society for Research in Child Development, 57*(6, Serial No. 230), pp. 154–163.

Scheeringa, M. S., & Zeanah, C. H. (1995). Symptom differences in traumatized infants and young children. *Infant Mental Health Journal, 16*, 259–270.

Scheeringa, M. S., Zeanah, C. H., Drell, M. J., & Larrieu, J. A. (1995). Two approaches to the diagnosis of post-traumatic stress disorder in infancy and early childhood. *Journal of the American Academy of Child and Adolescent Psychiatry, 34*, 191–200.

Schneider-Rosen, K., & Cicchetti, D. (1984). The relationship between affect and cognition inmaltreated infants: Quality of attachment and the development of visual self-recognition. *Child Development, 55*, 648–658.

Schneider-Rosen, K., & Cicchetti, D. (1991). Early self-knowledge and emotional development: Visual self-recognition and affective reactions to mirror self-image in maltreated and nonmaltreated toddlers. *Developmental Psychology, 27*, 481–488.

Solomon, J., George, C., & De Jong, A. (1995). Children classified as controlling at age six: Evidence of disorganized representational strategies and aggression at home and at school. *Development and Psychopathology, 7*, 447–464.

Steele, B. (1970). Parental abuse of infants and small children. In E. J. Anthony & T. Benedek (Eds.), *Parenthood, its psychology and psychopathology*. Boston: Little, Brown.

Steele, B. (1983). Psychological effects of child abuse and neglect. In J. D. Call, E. Galenson, & R. L. Tyson (Eds.), *Frontiers of infant psychiatry* (pp. 235–244). New York: Basic Books.

Stern, D. N. (1977). *The first relationship, infant and mother*. Cambridge, MA: Harvard University Press.

Stern, D. N. (1985). *The interpersonal world of the infant*. New York: Basic Books.

Strauss, M. A., & Gelles, R. J. (1988). How violent are American families? Estimates from the National Family Violence Resurvey and other studies. In C. T. Hotaling, D. Finkelhor, J. T. Kirkpatrick, & M. A. Strauss (Eds.), *Family abuse and its consequences: New directions in research* (pp. 14–36). Beverly Hills, CA: Sage.

Taylor, L., Zuckerman, B., Harik, V., & Groves, B. (1994). Witnessing violence by young children and their mothers. *Journal of Developmental and Behavioral Pediatrics, 15*, 120–123.

World Health Organization. (1992). *The ICD-10 classification of mental and behavioral disorders: Clinical descriptions and diagnostic guidelines*. Geneva: Author.

Zeanah, C. H. (1994). Assessment and treatment of infants exposed to violence. In J. Osofsky & E. Fenichel (Eds.), *Hurt, healing and hope* (pp. 29–37). Arlington, VA: Zero to Three.

Zeanah, C. H., & Emde, R. N. (1994). Attachment disorders in infancy. In M. Rutter, L. Hersov, & E. Taylor (Eds.), *Child and adolescent psychiatry: Modern approaches* (pp. 490–504). Oxford: Blackwell.

Zeanah, C. H., Hirshberg, L., Danis, B., Brennan, M., Miller, D., & Davis, A. (1995, March 30). *On the specificity of the Adult Attachment Interview in a high-risk sample*. Paper presented at the biennial meeting of the Society for Research in Child Development, Indianapolis, IN.

Zeanah, C. H., Zeanah, P. D., & Stewart, L. (1990). Parents' constructions of their infants personalities before and after birth. *Child Psychiatry and Human Development, 20,* 191–206.

Zeanah, C. H., Mammen, O., & Lieberman, A. (1993). Disorders of attachment. In C. H. Zeanah (Ed.), *Handbook of infant mental health* (pp. 332–349). New York: Guilford Press.

Zero to Three. (1994). *Diagnostic classification of mental health and developmental disorders of infancy and early childhood.* Arlington, VA: Author.

Zuckerman, B., Augustin, M., Groves, B. M., & Parker, S. (1995). Silent victims revisited: The special case of domestic violence. *Pediatrics, 96,* 511–513.

7

Incubated in Terror: Neurodevelopmental Factors in the "Cycle of Violence"

BRUCE D. PERRY

C HILDREN ARE NOT RESILIENT, children are malleable.

> **Resilient**: 1. Marked by the ability to recover readily, as from misfortune. 2. Capable of *returning to an original shape or position*, as after having been compressed.
> **Malleable**: 1. *Capable of being shaped or formed*, as by hammering or pressure: a malleable metal. 2. Easily controlled or influenced; tractable. 3. *Able to adjust to changing circumstances; adaptable*. (*Random House Dictionary*, *Electronic Version*, Microsoft Bookshelf, 1994, emphasis added)

Approximately 250,000 years ago, a few thousand *Homo sapiens* (our first genetically equivalent ancestors) migrated out of Africa, beginning the long transgenerational process of inhabiting and, ultimately, dominating the rest of the natural world (Leakey, 1994). This fragile process was aided by a great deal of luck and the remarkable potential of the human brain to allow nongenetic, transgenerational transmission of information (sociocultural evolution). For thousands of generations, life was characterized by danger—omnipresent threat and pervasive intra- and interspecies violence. Humankind and our current sociocultural practices evolved in, and therefore reflect, a brutal, violent, and unpredictable world. The evolution of complex cultures and "civilization" have not protected millions from the brutality that characterized the "ascent" of humankind. Although "civilization" has decreased our vulnerability to nonhuman predators, it has done little to decrease intraspecies violence (Keegan, 1993). Indeed, modern history is characterized by increasingly efficient, systematic, and institutionalized violence (e.g., the Inquisition, slavery, the Holocaust, the Trail of Tears). Men were, and men remain, the major predators of vulnerable humans (typically women and children). The profound impact of domestic violence, community violence, physical and sexual abuse, and other forms of predatory or impulsive assault cannot be overestimated. Violence impacts the victims, the witnesses, and, ultimately, us all. Understanding and modifying our violent nature will determine, in large part, the degree to which we will successfully "adapt" to the challenges of the future—the degree to which future generations of human beings can actually experience humanity.

In order to understand the origins and impact of interpersonal violence, it is essential to appreciate how violence alters the developing child. The child and the adult reflect the world in which they are raised. And, sadly, in today's world, millions of children are raised in unstable and violent settings. Literally, incubated in terror.

In the United States alone, at least 5 million children are victims of and/or witnesses to physical abuse and domestic or community violence, all while they are bathed in the powerful images on television that overrepresent violent acts and overvalue the viability of violence as a solution to conflict (Perry, 1994; Prothrow-Stith, 1991; Dodge, Bates, & Pettit, 1991; Osofsky, 1995). What is the impact of these pervasive experiences with violence on the developing child? How does violence change the child? What is the impact of being repeatedly assaulted by a parent? How is that different from being targeted in a drive-by shooting or watching a loved one being assaulted, or watching a "pretend," but graphic, murder on television? How do these childhood experiences contribute to the much-discussed but little-understood "cycle of violence"?

This chapter will examine these questions in context of neurodevelopment—how these experiences influence brain development and subsequent emotional, behavioral, cognitive, and social functioning of children. The amazing capacity of the human brain to develop in a "use-dependent" fashion, growing, organizing, and functioning in response to developmental experience, means that the major modifier of all human behavior is *experience*. Experience, not genetics, results in the critical neurobiological factors associated with violence. A common error in examining the "neurobiology" of violence is to presume a neurobiological trait, a biochemical marker (e.g., whole blood serotonin, or cerebrospinal fluid 5-hydroxyindoleacetic acid), which may be altered in "violent" populations suggests a genetic difference. Nothing could be further from the truth.

There is no more specific "biological" determinant than a relationship. Human beings evolved as social animals, and the majority of the biology of the brain is dedicated to mediating the complex interactions required to keep small, naked, weak, individual humans alive by being part of a larger *biological* whole—the family, the clan. Indeed, it is the primary caretaking relationships of infancy and childhood that determine the core neurobiological organization of the human individual, thereby allowing this incredible social specialization. Early life experience determines core neurobiology. The experiences that will be the focus of this chapter include those that predispose people to violent behavior, and those that result from exposure to violent behavior. The two are inextricably intertwined.

VIOLENCE AND THE DEVELOPING BRAIN

Violence is heterogeneous—in etiology, quality, quantity, and impact on its victims. Physical violence can be the result of impulsive, reactive behavior or predatory, remorseless aggression. Physical violence can be related to intoxication from alcohol or derived from psychosis or other neuropsychiatric conditions (e.g., dementia, traumatic head injury). Physical violence may be the result of a personal (Oklahoma City bombing) or a cultural (political terrorism) belief system. Physical violence can be sexualized (rape) or directed at a specific victim (domestic violence) or at a specific group (e.g., African Americans, homosexuals, Jews). Violence may be physical or emotional. Indeed, some of the most destructive violence does not break bones, it breaks minds (Vachss, 1994). Emotional violence does not result in the death of the body, it results in death of the soul.

The major setting for violence in America is the home (Straus, 1974). Intrafamilial abuse, neglect, and domestic battery account for the majority of physical and emotional violence suffered by children in this country (see Koop & Lundberg, 1992; Horowitz, Weine, & Jekel, 1995; Carnegie Council on Adolescent Development, 1995). Despite this, a majority of our entertainment, media, and public policy efforts focus on community or predatory violence. Understanding the roots of community and predatory violence is impossible unless the effects of intrafamilial violence, abuse, and neglect on the development of the child are examined. Indeed, the adolescents and adults responsible for community and predatory violence likely developed the emotional, behavioral, cognitive, and physiological characteristics that mediate these violent behaviors as a result of intrafamilial violence during childhood (O'Keefe, 1995; Myers, Scott, Burgess, & Burgess, 1995; Mones, 1991; Hickey, 1991; Loeber et al., 1993; Lewis, Mallouh, & Webb, 1989).

What are the pathways from terrorized infant to terrorizing adolescent? How can someone develop the capacity to stalk, torture, murder, and mutilate another human being and feel no remorse—even feel pleasure? How can a 14-year-old kill someone over a jacket? How can someone load a truck with explosives and blow up a building full of anonymous and innocent people? How can a man beat senseless the woman he "loves" and, if she leaves, taking the children, track them down and kill them all? Why are men so much more violent than women? What happens to people to make them act like "animals"?

All violent behavior impacts the children in its wake, but there is heterogeneity of impact. Important factors in the differential impact on the developing child include the type of violence, the pattern of violence, the presence (or absence) of supportive adult caretakers and other support systems, and, of key importance, the age of the child (for review see Pynoos, 1990; Schwarz & Perry, 1994). Under all circumstances, however, the organ that allows the child victim to adapt to any violent trauma is the brain, just as the brain is the organ that is the origin for the violent behaviors of the victimizer. How is it that the very neurobiological adaptations that allow the child to survive violence may, as the child grows older, result in an increased tendency to be violent? It is not the finger pulling the trigger that kills; it is not the penis that rapes—it is the brain. In order to understand violence, we need to understand the organization and functioning of its birthplace—the brain.

BRAIN ORGANIZATION AND FUNCTION

The human brain is an amazing organ that acts to sense, process, perceive, store, and act on information from outside and inside the body, all solely to promote survival. In order to carry out these functions, the human brain has evolved a highly functional hierarchical organization, from the lower, more simple portions to the more complex, higher cortical regions (Figure 7.1). Various functions are mediated by various brain areas, with more simple, regulatory functions (e.g., regulation of respiration, heart rate, blood pressure, body temperature) mediated by the "lower" parts of the brain (brainstem and midbrain) and the most complex functions (e.g., language and abstract thinking) by its most complex cortical structures. The hierarchy of increasingly complex functions is mediated by the hierarchy of increasingly complex brain areas (Figure 7.1).

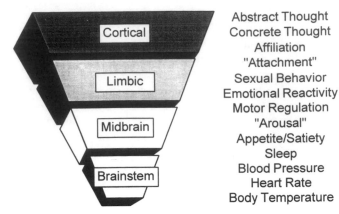

FIGURE 7.1. Hierarchy of brain function. The human brain is organized from the most simple (e.g., fewest cells: brainstem) to most complex (e.g., most cells and most synapses: frontal cortex). The various functions of the brain, from most simple and reflexive (e.g., regulation of body temperature) to most complex (e.g., abstract thought), are mediated in parallel with these various areas. These areas organize during development and change in the mature brain in a "use-dependent" fashion. The more a certain neural system is activated, the more it will "build in" this neural state, creating an internal representation of the experience corresponding to this neural activation. This use–dependent capacity to make internal representations of the external or internal world is the basis for learning and memory.

The structural organization and functional capabilities of the mature brain develop throughout life, with the vast majority of the critical structural organization taking place in childhood. Brain development is characterized by (1) sequential development and "sensitivity," from the brainstem to the cortex and (2) "use-dependent" organization of these various brain areas (to be discussed). As the brain develops in this sequential and hierarchical fashion, as the more complex limbic, subcortical and cortical areas organize, they begin to modulate, moderate, and "control" the more primitive and "reactive" lower portions of the brain (Figure 7.2). These various brain areas develop, organize, and become fully functional at different stages during childhood (Singer, 1995). At birth, for example, the brainstem areas responsible for regulating cardiovascular and respiratory function must be intact, whereas the cortical areas responsible for abstract cognition have years before they are required to be fully functional. Frustrated 3-year-olds (with a relatively unorganized cortex) will have a difficult time modulating the reactive, brainstem-mediated state of arousal—they will scream, kick, bite, throw, and hit. However, older children when frustrated may *feel* like kicking, biting, and spitting, but

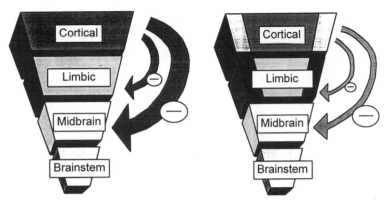

FIGURE 7.2. Cortical modulation. The capacity to moderate frustration, impulsivity, aggression, and violent behavior is age-related. With a set of sufficient motor, sensory, emotional, cognitive, and social experiences during infancy and childhood, the mature brain develops, in a use-dependent fashion, a mature, humane capacity to tolerate frustration, contain impulsivity, and channel aggressive urges.

have "built in" the capacity to modulate and inhibit those urges. All theoretical frameworks in developmental psychology describe this sequential development of ego functions and superego that are, simply, cortically mediated, inhibitory capabilities that modulate the more primitive, less mature, reactive impulses of the human brain. Loss of cortical function through any variety of pathological process (e.g., stroke, dementia) results in "regression"—simply, a loss of cortical modulation of arousal, impulsivity, motor hyperactivity, and aggressivity, all mediated by lower portions of the central nervous system (brainstem, midbrain). Conversely, any deprivation of optimal developmental experiences (which leads to underdevelopment of cortical, subcortical, and limbic areas) will necessarily result in persistence of primitive, immature behavioral reactivity. And, thereby, predispose to violent behavior (see Figures 7.5 and 7.7 below).

Essential to understanding the neurobiology of violence is this: The brain's impulse-mediating capacity is related to the ratio between the excitatory activity of the lower, more primitive portions of the brain and the modulating activity of higher, subcortical and cortical areas (Figure 7.3). Any factors that increase the activity or reactivity of the brainstem (e.g., chronic traumatic stress) or decrease the moderating capacity of the limbic or cortical areas (e.g., neglect, alcohol) will increase an individual's aggressivity, impulsivity, and capacity to display violence (Halperin et al., 1995; see below). A key neurodevelopmental factor that

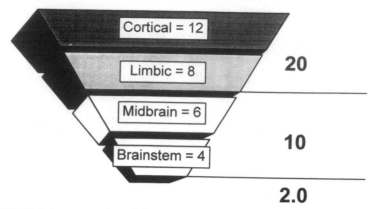

FIGURE 7.3. Ratio of modulation: Optimal development. A healthy cortical modulation ratio (cortical and limbic/midbrain and brainstem) develops when the child experiences a variety of optimal emotional, behavioral, cognitive, and social experiences at key times during development. This ratio indicates the relative "power" of the maturing and mature brain to modulate the more primitive, reactive, reflexive output of the brainstem and midbrain. During infancy and childhood, sequential development of the brain necessitates that the lower, more primitive portions of the brain develop first and, over time, the output of these areas is shaped, modulated, and modified in more mature fashion as the higher brain areas develop. Any disruption of development that either "overdevelops" the midbrain and brainstem or "underdevelops" the limbic and cortical areas will result in an imbalance in the cortical modulation ratio, predisposing to aggressive and violent behavior.

plays a major role in determining this moderating capacity is the brain's amazing capacity to organize and change in a "use-dependent" fashion.

In the developing brain, undifferentiated neural systems are critically dependent upon sets of environmental and microenvironmental cues (e.g., neurotransmitters, cellular adhesion molecules, neurohormones, amino acids, ions) in order for them to appropriately organize from their undifferentiated, immature forms (see Perry, 1994; Perry & Pate, 1994; Lauder, 1988). Lack (or disruption) of these critical cues can result in abnormal neuronal division, migration, differentiation, synaptogenesis—all of which contribute to malorganization and diminished functional capabilities related to that portion of the brain (Perry, 1988, 1994; Perry, Pollard, Baker, et al., 1995). These molecular cues, in turn, are dependent upon the experiences of the developing child. The quantity, pattern of activity, and nature of these neurochemical and neurotrophic factors depend upon the presence and the nature of the child's total sensory experience (e.g., Kandel, 1989; Goelet & Kandel, 1986; Thoenen, 1995).

Different areas of the central nervous system are in the process of organization at different times. During these critical periods of primary neural system organization, the brain requires and is most sensitive to organizing experiences (and the neurotrophic cues related to these experiences). Disruptions of experience–dependent neurochemical signals during these periods may lead to major abnormalities or deficits in neurodevelopment, some of which may not be reversible (see below). Disruption of critical cues can result from (1) lack of sensory experience during critical periods or (2) atypical or abnormal patterns of necessary cues due to extremes of experience. Due to the sequential development of the brain, disruptions of normal developmental processes early in life (e.g., during the perinatal period) that alter development of the brainstem or midbrain will necessarily alter the development of limbic and cortical areas because critical signals these area depend on for normal organization originate in these lower brain areas (see Figure 7.4). The clear implication of this immutable neurophysiological chain of development is that, again, early life experiences have disproportionate importance in organizing the mature brain. Experiences that could be tolerated by a 12-year-old child can literally destroy an infant (e.g., being untouched for 2 weeks). Both lack of critical nurturing experience and excess exposure to traumatic violence will alter the developing central nervous system, predisposing to a more impulsive, reactive, and violent individual.

EMOTIONAL NEGLECT

A 15-year-old boy sees some fancy sneakers he wants. Another child is wearing them, so he pulls out a gun and demands them. The younger

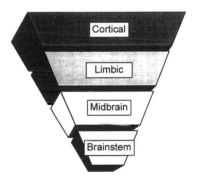

FIGURE 7.4. Sequential development of the brain. The simple and unavoidable result of this sequential neurodevelopment is that the organizing, "sensitive" brain of an infant or young child is more malleable to experience than a mature brain. Whereas experience may alter and change the functioning of an adult, experience literally provides the organizing framework for an infant and child. The brain is most plastic (receptive to environmental input) in early childhood; therefore, the child is more vulnerable to variance of experience during this time.

child, at gunpoint, takes off his shoes and surrenders them. The 15-year-old puts the gun to the child's head, smiles, and pulls the trigger. When he is arrested, the officers are chilled by his apparent lack of remorse. Asked later whether, if he could turn back the clock, he would do anything differently, he thinks and replies, "I would have cleaned my shoes." His bloody shoes led to his arrest. He exhibits regret for being caught—an intellectual, cognitive response. But remorse—an affect—is absent. He feels no connection to the pain of his victim. Neglected and humiliated by his primary caretakers when he was young, this 15-year-old murderer is, literally, emotionally retarded. The part of his brain that would have allowed him to feel connected to other human beings—empathy—simply did not develop. He has affective blindness. Just as the retarded child lacks the capacity to understand abstract cognitive concepts, this young murderer lacks the capacity to be connected to other human beings in a healthy way. Experience, or rather lack of critical experiences, resulted in this affective blindness, this emotional retardation.

Very narrow windows, critical periods, exist during which specific sensory experience is required for optimal organization and development of any brain area (e.g., Singer, 1995; Thoenen, 1995). Absent such experience and development, dysfunction is inevitable (e.g., Carlson, Cicchetti, Barnett, & Braunwald, 1989). When critical periods have been examined in great detail in nonhuman animals for the primary sensory modalities, similar use-dependent differentiation in development of the brain occurs for the rest of the central nervous system (Diamond, Krech, & Rosenzweig, 1964; Altman & Das, 1964; Cragg, 1967, 1969; Cummins & Livesey, 1979). Abnormal microenvironmental cues and atypical patterns of neural activity during critical and sensitive periods can result in malorganization and compromised function in other brain-mediated functions such as empathy, attachment, and affect regulation (e.g., Green, 1983). Some of the most powerful clinical examples of this are related to lack of "attachment" experiences early in life. The child who has been emotionally neglected or abandoned early in life will exhibit attachment problems that are persistently resistant to any "replacement" experiences, including therapy (Carlson et al., 1989; Ebinger, 1974). Examples of this include feral children, Spitz's orphans (Spitz & Wolf, 1946), the Romanian orphans (Chisholm, Carter, Ames, & Morison, 1995) and, sadly, the remorseless, violent child (Ressler, Burgess, & Douglas, 1988; Myers et al., 1995; Mones, 1991; Hickey, 1991; Greenberg, Speltz, & DeKlyen, 1993).

Lack of appropriate affective experience early in life and the resulting malorganization of attachment capabilities plays a major role in the current epidemic of senseless violence in the United States today (Lewis et al., 1989). So often, these acts are inhuman—throwing a 6-year-old boy out of a window because he refused to steal candy for you; planning, stalking, kidnapping, and torturing someone who "disrespected" you; hunting *any* homeless man to set on fire. *Senseless*—or are they senseless acts? The abilities to feel remorse, to be empathetic, to be sympathetic are all experience-based capabilities. If a child feels no emotional attachment to any human being, then one cannot expect any more remorse from him or her after killing a human than one would expect from someone who ran over a squirrel. These behaviors are not senseless; they are not beyond our understanding. They arise from children reflecting the world in which they have been raised (Taylor, Zuckerman, Harik, & Groves, 1992; Perry, Pollard, Blakley, Baker, & Vigilante, 1995).

It is important to emphasize that the majority of individuals who are emotionally neglected in childhood do not grow into violent individuals. These victims carry their scars in other ways, usually in a profound emptiness, or in emotionally destructive relationships, moving through life disconnected from others and robbed of some of their humanity. The effects of emotional neglect in childhood *predispose* to violence by decreasing the strength of the subcortical and cortical impulse-modulating capacity, and by decreasing the value of other humans due to an incapacity to empathize or sympathize with them. This decreased value of humans means that there is a much lower threshold for unattached persons to act in an antisocial fashion to gratify their impulses.

COGNITIVE NEGLECT

There are other deprivations of experience that play a major role in impulsive and reactive violence. These are experiences that, in effect, "feed" and grow the human cortex (Singer, 1995; Thoenen, 1995; Brown, 1994). As the cortex plays a major role in inhibiting, modulating, and regulating the functioning of the lower parts of the central nervous system, any experiences that increase this cortical capacity would be expected to decrease violent behavior (Moffitt & Silva, 1988; MacEwen, 1994). The human cortex grows in size, develops complexity, makes synaptic connections, and modifies as a function of the quality and quantity of sensory experience (Chisholm et al., 1995; Singer, 1995; Courchesne, Chisum, & Townsend, 1994). Lack of type and quantity of sensory–motor and cognitive experiences leads to underdevelopment of the cortex (see Figure 7.5). The cortical and subcortical areas are smaller in individuals who have suffered global environmental neglect. In our preliminary studies, we have demonstrated "cortical atrophy" (as read independently by neuroradiologists) in 7 of 12 severely neglected children

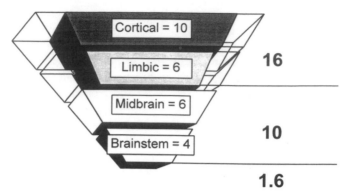

FIGURE 7.5. Developmental neglect: Emotional or experiential deprivation. The ability of the brain to develop a healthy cortical modulation ratio (cortical and limbic/midbrain and brainstem) is impaired when key experiences are minimal or absent. This results in poor modulation of impulsivity, persisting "primitive" or immature emotional and behavioral functioning and, in combination with other developmental experiences, a predisposition to violence. The ability of the maturing brain then, to modify impulsive and reactive responses in the face of stress or frustration is decreased in individuals deprived of specific developmental experiences.

(Pollard & Perry, submitted). These children (average age 8) did not develop cortical and subcortical structures that subsequently atrophied. These areas, which develop in a use-dependent fashion, were underused, resulting in profound underdevelopment of these areas. There are multiple examples of the negative impact of environmental deprivation on the developing brain in animal studies. Rats raised in environmentally enriched setting have a 30% higher synaptic density in cortex than rats raised in an environmentally deprived setting (Bennett, Diamond, Krech, & Rosenzweig, 1964; Altman & Das, 1964). Animals raised in the wild have from 15% to 30% larger brain mass than their offspring who are domestically reared (Darwin, 1868; Rehkamper, Haase, & Frahm, 1988; Rohrs, 1955).

A striking example of the role of cognitive development (development of a literate population) on impulsive violence comes from historical accounts of violence. In the year 1340 in Amsterdam, the murder rate was in excess of 150 murders per 100,000 people. Two hundred years later, the murder rate was below 5 per 100,000 people. Clearly this is not a "genetic" phenomenon. The genetics of the population of Amsterdam likely did not change much in 200 years. This marked decrease in the incidence of murderous violence likely was due to the development of a higher percentage of individuals in that society having better developed cortices—more capable of abstract cognition, and, thus, more capable of modulation of aggressive and violent impulses. The sociocultural phenomenon underlying the development of healthier and more capable cortices was, without question, literacy. The introduction of the printing press allowed the percentage of literate (i.e., cortically enriched, cognitively capable individuals) to dramatically increase. Over a few generations, the impact of a number of bright, abstract individuals transformed the society.

The introduction of television has had a similar revolutionary impact on the organization and functional capacity of the human brain (remember, the organization and functional capacity of the brain reflects the pattern and nature of sensory input during development). The implications of this major sociocultural and environmental phenomenon on development have yet to be fully realized. Ominous clues abound, however (Donnerstein, Slaby, & Eron, 1995). American children raised on "Sesame Street" and MTV are impatient with even moderately slow presentations of any stimuli, written, spoken, or visual (Carnegie Council on Adolescent Development, 1995). The brain of a human infant born in 20,000 B.C. had the same potential as an infant born in 1995. Despite the fact that 22,000 years ago there was essentially no written language, no science, and no understanding of "computers," if this prehistoric infant were raised today, he or she would be playing Nintendo, watching MTV, reading, writing, and "thinking" in as abstract a fashion as any child born today. The brains of our children are organized differently from ours. The increase in youth violence is related to the world we have provided for our children to grow up in (Wright, Sheley, & Smith, 1992; Taylor et al., 1992; Richters, 1993; Osofsky, 1995), a world markedly different from the one in which our brains developed.

TRAUMATIC VIOLENCE: THE PERSISTING STATE OF FEAR

Children exposed to chronic violence are more likely to be violent (e.g., Loeber et al., 1993; Lewis et al., 1989; Koop & Lundberg, 1992; Hickey, 1991; Halperin et al., 1995). This is related to many factors, including modeling and learning that violent aggression is an acceptable, even a preferable and honorable, solution to problems. Analysis of much of the violent behavior by children and adolescents today reveals a troubling degree of impulsive, reactive violence. This violence is often interpreted by the perpetrators as defensive. "If I didn't shoot him, he would have shot me." "I could tell that he was going to jump me—he looked me in the eyes." "Listen, man, I just did him before he did me. So." These verbalizations reflect the persistence of a state of fear, literally, a persisting "fight or flight" state that these adolescents are unable to escape. The persistence of this originally adaptive internal state is due to growing up in a persistently threatening environment (Perry, 1994, 1996).

If, during development, this stress–response apparatus is required to be persistently active, a commensurate stress–response apparatus in the central nervous system will develop in response to constant threat. These stress–response neural systems (and all functions they mediate) will be overactive and hypersensitive. It is highly adaptive for a child growing up in a violent, chaotic environment to be hypersensitive to external stimuli, to be hypervigilant, and to be in a persistent stress–response state (see Figure 7.6). In most cases, however, these "survival tactics" ill serve the child when the environment changes.

Clinically, this is very easily observed in children who are exposed to chronic neurodevelopmental trauma (Perry, 1994; Perry, Pollard, Baker, et al., 1995). These children are frequently diagnosed as having attention deficit disorder with hyperactivity (ADD-H) (Haddad & Gorralda, 1992). This is somewhat misleading, however. It is not that they have a core abnormality of their capacity to attend to a given task, it is that they are hypervigilant. These children have behavioral impulsivity and cognitive distortions (Pynoos & Eth, 1985; Pynoos, 1990) that result from a use-dependent organization of the brain (Perry, Pollard, Blakley,

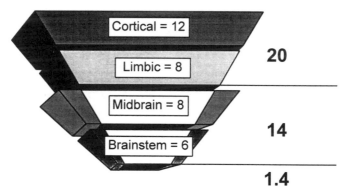

FIGURE 7.6. The persisting fear response: Developmental trauma. A child raised in an environment characterized by persisting trauma (e.g., domestic violence, physical abuse, community violence) will develop an excessively active and reactive stress-response apparatus. The majority of the stress-response systems reside in the brainstem and midbrain (e.g., locus coeruleus). Overdevelopment of these areas, even in the presence of optimal emotional or cognitive experience will result in an altered cortical modulation ratio and a predisposition to act in an aggressive, impulsive, behavioral reactive fashion.

et al., 1995). During development, these children spent so much time in a low-level state of fear (mediated by brainstem and midbrain areas) that they were focusing consistently on nonverbal cues. In our clinical population, children raised in chronically traumatic environments reveal a prominent V-P split on IQ testing ($n = 108$; Wechsler Intelligence Scale for Children (WISC) Verbal = 8.2; WISC Performance = 10.4, Perry, Arvinte, Marcellus, & Pollard, submitted). This is consistent with the clinical observations of teachers that these children are often "smart" but cannot learn easily. Often these children are labeled as learning disabled. These difficulties with cognitive organization contribute to a more primitive, less mature style of problem solving, with violence often being employed as a "tool." All of these symptoms are the result of a use-dependent organization of the brainstem nuclei involved in the stress response apparatus (Perry, 1988; Perry et al., 1994).

These children are also characterized by persistent physiological hyperarousal and hyperactivity (Perry, Pollard, Baker, et al., 1995; Perry, Pollard, Blakley, et al., 1995). They are observed to have increased muscle tone, frequently a low-grade increase in temperature, an increased startle response, profound sleep disturbances, affect regulation problems, and generalized (or specific) anxiety (Kaufman, 1991; Ornitz & Pynoos, 1989; Perry, 1994). In addition, our studies indicate that a significant portion of these children have abnormalities in cardiovascular regulation (Perry, 1994; Perry, Pollard, Baker, et al., 1995). Using continuous heart-rate monitoring during clinical interviews, male, preadolescent children exposed to violence exhibited a mild tachycardia during nonintrusive interviews and a marked tachycardia during interviews about specific exposure to trauma ($n = 83$; resting heart rate = 104; interview heart rate = 122). In comparison, females exposed to traumatic events tended to have normal or mild tachycardia that decreased during interviews about the traumatic event ($n = 24$; resting heart rate = 98; interview heart rate = 82). This gender difference was associated with differences in emotional and behavioral symptoms, with males exhibiting more "externalizing" and females more "internalizing" symptoms (Perry, Pollard, Baker, et al., 1995; Perry, Pollard, Blakley, et al., 1995; Perry et al., submitted).

In our work with another population of boys exposed to severe, prolonged domestic violence ($n = 65$) at a residential treatment center, a subset of the hyperaroused, reactive boys ($n = 65$ total; predatory subset = 12) developed predatory, aggressive behaviors. In early adolescence, this subset of boys actually had a normalization of the tacycardia noted when they were younger. Indeed, they began exhibiting decreases in heart rate when asked to discuss specific violent events in which they had been involved. Some of these youth described a soothing, calming feeling when they began "stalking" a potential victim. The detached, calm, dissociated (and reinforcing) feeling these boys felt is reminicent of the feelings described by borderline adolesent girls who cut themselves and may be related to an endogenous opioid release similar to that seen in various dissociative states (Perry et al., submitted). These preliminary observations are consistent with recent reports of the physiological differences between a cohort of 15-year-old antisocial youth followed to age 29. In the group that by age 29 had become criminal, resting heart rates were much lower than controls and the comparison antisocial cohort (Raine, Venables, & Williams, 1995).

The implications of this for the violent youth are profound (Figure 7.7). First, any child exposed to chronic intrafamilial violence will develop a persisting fear response. Because there are marked gender differences in this response (Perry, Pollard, Baker, et al., 1995; Perry, Pollard, Blakley, et al., 1995), with females more likely to dissociate and males more likely to display a classic "fight or flight" response, more males will develop the aggressive, impulsive, reactive, and hyperactive symptom presentation. Males will more likely be violent (George & Main, 1979). This can be explained, in part, by the persistence of this "fight or flight" state, and by the profound cognitive distortions that accompany this

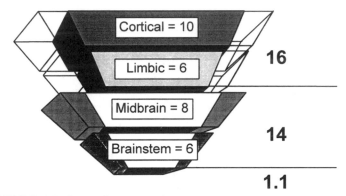

FIGURE 7.7. Neglect and trauma: The malignant combination. Developmental neglect or traumatic stress during childhood can profoundly alter development. Unfortunately, emotional and cognitive neglect usually occur in combination with traumatic stress. The combination of a lack of critical emotional experiences and persisting traumatic stress leads to a dramatic alteration in the brain's modulation and regulation capacity. This is characterized by an overdevelopment of brainstem and midbrain neurophysiology and functions (e.g., anxiety, impulsivity, poor affect regulation, motor hyperactivity) and an underdevelopment of limbic and cortical neurophysiology and functions (e.g., empathy, problem-solving skills). This experience-based imbalance predisposes to a host of neuropsychiatric problems—and violent behavior.

neurodevelopmental state. A young man with these characteristics, then, will very easily misinterpret a behavior as threatening and will, being more reactive, respond in a more impulsive and violent fashion, literally using the original (childhood) adaptive "fight or flight" response in a new context but, now, later in life, in a maladaptive fashion.

Finally, this reactivity of response is profoundly exaggerated by the influence of alcohol or other drugs (Shupe, 1954; Lindqvist, 1986; Cordilla, 1985). Unfortunately, the emotional emptiness resulting from neglect can only be filled by the temporary pleasure that an exogenous euphoriant (e.g., heroin, cocaine) can provide. Similarly, a young man may find the only escape from the distress and pain caused by the anxiety of a persisting fear response is with alcohol. It is often the intoxicating agents that allow expression of the neurodevelopmentally determined predisposition for violence (Figure 7.8).

IDEOLOGY OF AGGRESSION

There are multiple pathways to engaging in violent behavior (Wolfgang & Ferracuti, 1967). Some are defensive, some are predatory, some are impulsive. All of these pathways, however, are facilitated by the individual practitioner's belief system (MacEwen, 1994; Burton, Foy, Bwanausi, & Johnson, 1994). The majority of neglected children never become violent. The majority of traumatized children never become violent (e.g., Belmore & Quinsey, 1994). Even the majority of traumatized and neglected children do not become remorselessly violent. Belief systems, in the final analysis, are the major contributors to violence. Racism, sexism, misogyny, children as property, idealization of violent "heroes," cultural tolerance of child maltreatment, tribalism, jingoism, and nationalism all unleash, facilitate, encourage, and nurture violent individuals. Without these facilitating belief systems and modeling, neglected and abused children would carry their pain forward in less violent ways, as silent, scarred, adult members of the vast army one commentator has termed the "Children of the Secret" (Vachss, 1991).

Extreme violence of the most heinous sort (organized, systematic, and remorseless) is conducted by individuals, groups of individuals, and by governments with the blessing of various belief systems (for God and Country). Indeed, the current "Violence Prevention" initiatives are really not interested in preventing *all* violence. These programs are focused on random, unpredictable physical violence against "us." The pervasive community violence of the inner cities was of little concern to the public policymakers in government until it metastasized to other parts of our society. Widespread ignorance of the intimate relationships between cul-

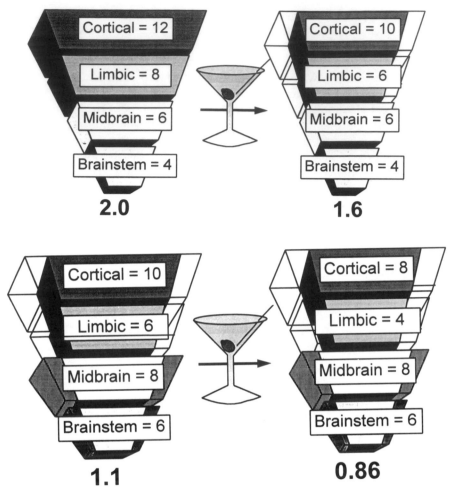

FIGURE 7.8. Alcohol decreases the cortical modulation ratio. Upper panel: Alcohol has a well-documented relationship to violent behavior. Under optimal circumstances, drinking can decrease judgment, impair capacity to modulate impulsivity, and predispose to aggressive and violent behaviors. Alcohol does this, in part, because of mass action effects of the nonspecific actions on neurons, decreasing functional capacity in all cells. Because the cortex has the most cells, however, it is relatively more sensitive to the nonspecific effects of alcohol, resulting in the general phenomenon of "getting" drunk from the top down. The sequence of loss of function under the influence of alcohol match the hierarchical sequence as illustrated in Figure 7.1. The temporary decrease of cortical modulation ratio under the influence of alcohol leads to many violent actions. Lower panel: The capacity of alcohol to impair functioning and decrease cortical modulation ratio is even more dramatic in the poorly organized brain. The combination of alcohol (or other drugs) and a neglected, abused adolescent often leads to deadly and chilling violence.

tural belief systems, childrearing practices, and the development of violent behaviors will doom any attempts to truly understand, and prevent, violence (Dodge et al., 1991; Richters, 1993).

A MALIGNANT COMBINATION
OF EXPERIENCES

The most dangerous among us have come to be this way because of a malignant combination of experiences—lack of critical early life nurturing (Radke-Yarrow et al., 1995), chaotic and cognitively impoverished environments (Carlson et al., 1989), pervasive physical threat (O'Keefe, 1995), persisting fear (Schwab-Stone et al., 1995) and, finally, watching the strongest, most violent in the home get what he wants, and seeing the same aggressive, violent use of power idealized on television (Miedzian, 1991) and at the movies (Figure 7.9). These violent offenders have

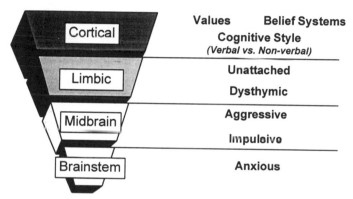

FIGURE 7.9. Malignant combination of experiences. Neurodevelopmental experiences of trauma or neglect alter a variety of brain areas and functions important in predisposing to violence. Depending upon the time in development, the nature (trauma, neglect, or both) and extent of the abuse, and the presence of attentuating factors, the developing brain will be impacted differentially. These experiences may occur *in utero* or in the perinatal period, impacting the brainstem and resulting in symptoms of anxiety. Experiences in the perinatal and first few years of life can impact the midbrain, resulting in impulsive and aggressive symptoms. Trauma and neglect during infancy and childhood can impact the subcortical and limbic areas, resulting in dysthymic, depressed, or unattached individuals. Finally, experiences throughout childhood can impact the development of cognitive capabilities resulting in processing and problem-solving styles that predispose to violent solutions. Ultimately, however, being anxious or impulsive or depressed or unattached or cognitively impaired does not compel violence by individuals. It is a malignant combination of one or more of these vulnerabilities in concert with a facilitating or encouraging belief system that leads to violent behaviors.

been incubated in terror, waiting to be old enough to get "one of those guns," waiting to be the one who controls, the one who takes, the one who hits, the one who can "make the fear, not take the fear." Nowhere is this predatory food chain more evident than in juvenile justice settings where, too often, the youth is either victim or predator, with no third option. Due to clear sociocultural devolution in some segments of our communities, there are more and more undersocialized, traumatized children (Horowitz et al., 1995; Carnegie Council on Adolescent Development, 1995). These children get little cognitive stimulation. The public schools are falling apart; their lives are devoid of emotional contact. Mom is a child herself and pregnant again; no predictability, structure, or nurturing can be found out of the home—the community has dissolved.

CLINICAL IMPLICATIONS

There are a variety of important clinical considerations when examining the interplay between developmental trauma and brain development. One of the most obvious is the developmental stage at which it occurs. What may be partially "absorbable" at age 15 may be devastating at age 5. The younger someone is, the fewer defensive capabilities he or she has. As we get older, reasoning and cognitive capabilities facilitate adaptation.

The intensity and frequency of the trauma determines how, in a use-dependent fashion, the brain will internalize the traumatic event. The proximity to (and reality of) threat, the degree to which body integrity and life-threatening experiences take place, and the presence of protective factors all play some role in this. The presence of a strong supportive family network or a strong, stable adult figure is critically important. Children exposed to violence benefit from the presence of a stable adult, even outside the home (for review see Pynoos, 1990; Schwarz & Perry, 1994).

Predictability of threat is important in determining the impact of a trauma. Stress is much more tolerable when it is relatively predictable. Indeed, there are a number of behavioral features of traumatized children that initially appear to be very maladaptive but are in fact very highly adaptive. This is seen with behaviors that solicit or promote either physical or sexual abuse. A child who has been a victim of unpredictable sexual or physical abuse learns (consciously or unconsciously) that if this abuse *is* going to happen, it is far preferable to control *when* it happens. As a result, children who have been violently physically assaulted will frequently engage in provocative, aggressive behavior in an attempt to elicit a predictable response from their "environment." This behavior is often misinterpreted, and the school or foster placement will punish them severely (often following a restraint situation), thereby reinforcing the child's view of the world—adults are aggressive and solve problems using force. Our ineffective child protective, mental health, and juvenile justice systems teach this lesson to children again and again, until they are big enough, smart enough, or violent enough to turn the tables.

Intervention strategies with the emotionally empty violent youth must be different from those designed for purely impulsive, reactively violent youth. Heterogeneity of violence dictates heterogeneity of intervention. Effective implementation of intervention and prevention strategies, therefore, requires effective assessment of the emotional, behavioral, cognitive, social, and physiological functioning of the individual child (Vachss & Bakal, 1979). A "boot camp" model may be very effective for some and dreadfully ineffective for others. Therapeutic intervention based upon interpersonal relationships may be critical for rehabilitation of some, whereas they are a waste of resources for others.

State-dependent storage and state-dependent recall are critical issues to consider when focusing on the violent youth (Ungerleider, 1995; Maunsell, 1995). These powerful principles of neurophysiological functioning relate back to the way in which the brain internalizes new information—in a use-dependent fashion. The only parts of the brain that can change are those parts that are on, those that are being used, so that when asleep, storage of information, or recall of previously stored information from parts of the brain that are active only during waking hours, is impossible. This state-dependence is very important in the clinical approach to the traumatized child. When a child is in a state of hyperarousal—a persisting fear state—the child will not easily be taught complex cognitive information (i.e., if the cortex is not active, it will not store information). The child will be focusing on nonverbal cues—body movements, facial expressions, tone of voice—and searching for threat. The child is processing *that* information, not the accompanying words. Only when significantly "calmed" will these children benefit from "words." What we can expect children to have access to during these states of arousal is their "catalogue" of previous experiences, their nonverbal memories, many of which are characterized by unpredictability, threat, pain, and assault. They will (re)act accordingly. It is the task of therapeutic interventions to begin to provide a set of consistent alternative memories based upon trial after trial of neutral or positive interaction. Unfortunately, our interventions frequently mistarget the needs of a given child.

Interventions that are based simply upon a cognitive, problem-solving approach to conflict resolution cannot be easily generalized to a perceived-threat situation. When a child or adolescent sits quietly in a room with peers and can think through a situation, nonviolent resolution comes more easily. This same child, however, when threatened, will be in a different internal state. The fearful child's cognition and behavior is being mediated by more primitive parts of the brain; he or she will be more reactive, reflexive, and will have a very difficult time pulling cognitive solutions from the cortex. Experience-based conflict resolution models offer advantages over simple cognitive, classroom-based programs. Imagine a soldier trying to effectively learn how to act in combat by sitting in class. The soldier could learn, on a cognitive level, what to do. In combat, however, finding and applying this "book-learning" would be virtually impossible. And any mistakes could be fatal.

PUBLIC POLICY IMPLICATIONS

The ultimate solution to the problems of violence, whether from the remorseless predator or the reactive, impulsive youth, is primary prevention. Our society is creating violent children and youth at a rate far faster than we could ever treat, rehabilitate, or even lock them away (Groves, Zuckerman, Marans, & Cohen, 1993; Garbarino, 1993; Sturrock, Smart, & Tricklebank, 1983; Richters, 1993). No single intervention strategy will solve these heterogeneous problems. No set of intervention strategies will solve these transgenerational problems. In order to solve the problems of violence, *we need to transform our culture.*

We need to change our childrearing practices. We need to change the malignant and destructive view that children are the property of their biological parents. Human beings evolved not as individuals, but as communities. Despite Western conceptualizations, the smallest functional biological unit of humankind is not the individual—it is the clan. No individual, no single parent–child dyad, no nuclear family could survive alone. We survived and evolved as clans—interdependent socially, emotionally, and biologically. Children *belong* to the community; they are *entrusted* to parents. American society, and its communities, have failed parents and children alike. We have not provided parents with the information and resources to optimize their children's potential and, when parents fail, we act too late and with impotence to protect and care for maltreated children (Kendall, Dale, & Plakitsis, 1995; Urquiza, Wirtz, Peterson, & Singer, 1994; Klee & Halton, 1987; McIntyre & Kessler, 1986; Carnegie Council on Adolescent Development, 1995).

The true potential of the human brain is rarely, if ever, realized. The major expressor of that potential is experience. The most critical and formative experiences are those provided to the developing child in the incubator of the family and, optimally, by a vital, invested community. Past and present, our society dramatically undervalues its young, despite the claims that "we love children."

It is *in* the nature of humankind to be violent, but it may not be *the* nature of humankind. Without major transformation of our culture, without putting action behind our "love" of children, we may never learn the truth.

ACKNOWLEDGMENTS

This work was supported in part by grants from the CIVITAS Initiative, the CIVITAS ChildTrauma Programs, Mr. Alan Grant, and Anonymous-X. I would like to thank the many violent children and adults, victims all, who shared their experiences in an attempt to teach "us," and Andrew Vachss, who provided special editorial assistance on earlier versions of this chapter.

REFERENCES

Altman, J., & Das, G. D. (1964). Autoradiographic examination of the effects of enriched environment on the rate of glial multipication in the adult rat brain. *Nature, 204,* 1161–1165.

Belmore, M. F., & Quinsey, V. L. (1994). Correlates of psychopathy in a noninstitutional sample. *Journal of Interpersonal Violence, 9*(3), 339–349.

Bennett, E. L., Diamond, M. L., Krech, D., & Rosenzweig, M. R. (1964). Chemical and anatomical plasticity of the brain. *Science, 146,* 610–619.

Brown, J W (1994) Morphogenesis and mental process. *Development and Psychopathology, 6,* 551–563.

Burton, J., Foy, D., Bwanausi, C., & Johnson, J. (1994). The relationship between the traumatic exposure, family dysfunction and post-traumatic stress symptoms in male juvenile offenders. *Journal of Traumatic Stress, 7,* 83–93.

Carlson, V., Cicchetti, D., Barnett, D., & Braunwald, K. (1989). Disorganized/disoriented attachment relationships in maltreated infants. *Developmental Psychology, 25,* 525–531.

Carnegie Council on Adolescent Development. (1995). *Great transitions: Preparing adolescents for a new century.* New York: Carnegie Corporation of New York.

Chisholm, K., Carter, M. C., Ames, E. W., & Morison, S. J. (1995). Attachment security and indiscriminately friendly behavior in children adopted from Romanian orphanages. *Development and Psychopathology, 7,* 283–294.

Cordilla, A. (1985). Alcohol and property crime: Exploring the causal nexus. *Journal of Studies on Alcohol, 46*(2), 161–171.

Courchesne, E., Chisum, H., & Townsend, J. (1994). Neural activity–dependent brain changes in development: Implications for psychopathology. *Development and Psychopathology, 6*(4), 697–722.

Cragg, B. G. (1967). The density of synapses and neurons in the motor and visual areas of the cerebral cortex. *Journal of Anatomy (London), 101,* 639–654.

Cragg, B. G. (1969). The effects of vision and dark-rearing on the size and density of synapses in the lateral geniculate nucleus measured by electron microscopy. *Brain Research, 13,* 53–67.

Cummins, R. A., & Livesey, P. (1979). Enrichment-isolation, cortex length, and the rank order effect. *Brain Research, 178,* 88–98.

Darwin, C. (1868). *The variations of animals and plants under domestication.* London: John Murray.

Diamond, M. C., Krech, D., & Rosenzweig, M. R. (1964). The effects of an enriched environment on the histology of the rat cerebral cortex. *Comparative Neurology, 123,* 111–119.

Dodge, K. A., Bates, J. E., & Pettit, G. S. (1991). Mechanisms in the cycle of violence. *Science, 250,* 1678–1683.

Donnerstein, E., Slaby, R., & Eron, L. (1995). The mass media and youth aggression. In L. Eron, J. Gentry, & P. Schlegel (Eds.), *Reason to hope: A psychosocial perspective on violence and youth* (pp. 219–250). Washington, DC: American Psychological Association Press.

Ebinger, P. (1974). A cytoarchitectonic volumetric comparison of brains in wild and domestic sheep. *Zeitschrift fuer Anatomie und Entwicklungsgeschichte, 144,* 267–302.

Garbarino, J. (1993). Children's response to community violence: What do we know? *Infant Mental Health Journal, 14,* 103–115.

George, C., & Main, M. (1979). Social interactions of young abused children: Approach, avoidance and aggression. *Child Development, 50,* 306–318.

Goelet, P., & Kandel, E. R. (1986). Tracking the flow of learned information from membrane receptors to genome. *Trends in Neuroscience, 9,* 492–499.

Green, A. H. (1983). Dimensions of psychological trauma in abused children. *Journal of the American Academy of Child and Adolescent Psychiatry, 22,* 231–237.

Greenberg, M. T., Speltz, M. L., & DeKlyen, M. (1993). The role of attachment in the early development of disruptive behavior problems. *Development and Psychopathology, 5,* 191–213.

Groves, B., Zuckerman, B., Marans, S., & Cohen, D. (1993). Silent victims: Children who witness violence. *Journal of the American Medical Association, 269,* 262–264.

Haddad, P., & Garralda, M. (1992). Hyperkinetic syndrome and disruptive early experiences. *British Journal of Psychiatry, 161,* 700–703.

Halperin, J. M., Newcorn, J. H., Matier, K., Bedi, G., Hall, S., & Sharma, V. (1995). Impulsivity and the initiation of fights in children with disruptive behavioral disorders. *Journal of Child Psychology and Psychiatry, 36*(7), 1199–1211.

Hickey, E. (1991). *Serial murderers and their victims.* Belmont, CA: Wadsworth.

Horowitz, K., Weine, S., & Jekel, J. (1995). PTSD symptoms in urban adolescent girls: Compounded community trauma. *Journal of the American Academy of Child and Adolescent Psychiatry, 34*(10), 1353–1361.

Kandel, E. R. (1989). Genes, nerve cells and remembrance of things past. *Journal of Neuropsychiatry and Clinical Neurosciences, 1,* 103–125.

Kaufman, J. (1991). Depressive disorders in maltreated children. *Journal of the American Academy of Child and Adolescent Psychiatry, 30*(2), 257–265.

Keegan, J. (1993). *A history of warfare.* New York: Knopf.

Kendall, J., Dale, G., & Plakitsis, S. (1995). The mental health needs of children entering the child welfare system: A guide for case workers. *The APSAC Advisor, 8*(3), 10–13.

Klee, L., & Halfon, N. (1987). Mental health care for foster children in California. *Child Abuse and Neglect, 11,* 63–74.

Koop, C. E., & Lundberg, G. (1992). Violence in America: A public health emergency. *Journal of the American Medical Association, 22,* 3075–3076.

Lauder, J. M. (1988). Neurotransmitters as morphogens. *Progress in Brain Research, 73,* 365–388.

Leakey, R. (1994). *The origins of humankind.* New York: Basic Books.

Lewis, D. O., Mallouh, C., & Webb, V. (1989). Child abuse, delinquency, and violent criminality. In D. Chiccetti & V. Carlson (Eds.), *Child maltreatment: Theory and research on the causes and consequences of child abuse and neglect.* Cambridge, UK: Cambridge University Press.

Lindqvist, P. (1986). Criminal homicide in northern Sweden 1970–1981: Alcohol intoxication, alcohol abuse and mental disease. *International Journal of Law and Psychiatry, 8,* 19–37.

Loeber, R., Wung, P., Keenan, K., Giroux, B., Stouthamer-Loeber, M., Van Kammen, W. B., & Maughan, B. (1993). Developmental pathways in disruptive child behavior. *Development and Psychopathology, 5,* 103–133.

MacEwen, K. E. (1994). Refining the intergenerational transmission hypothesis. *Journal of Interpersonal Violence, 9*(3), 350–365.

Maunsell, J. H. R. (1995). The brain's visual world: Representation of visual targets in cerebral cortex. *Science, 270,* 764–769.

McIntyre, A., & Kessler, T. (1986). Psychological disorders among foster children. *Journal of Child and Clinical Psychology, 15,* 297–303.

Miedzian, M. (1991). *Boys will be boys.* New York: Doubleday.

Mones, P. (1991). *When a child kills: Abused children who kill their parents.* New York: Pocket Books.

Myers, W. C., Scott, K., Burgess, A. W., & Burgess, A. G. (1995). Psychopathology, biopsychosocial factors, crime characteristics and classification of 25 homicidal youths. *Journal of the American Academy of Child and Adolescent Psychiatry, 34*(11), 1483–1489.

O'Keefe, M. (1995). Predictors of child abuse in maritally violent families. *Journal of Interpersonal Violence, 10*(1), 3–25.

Ornitz, E. M., & Pynoos, R. S. (1989). Startle modulation in children with post-traumatic stress disorder. *American Journal of Psychiatry, 147,* 866–870.

Osofsky, J. (1995). The effects of exposure to violence on young children. *American Psychologist, 50,* 782–788.

Perry, B. D. (1988). Placental and blood element neurotransmitter receptor regulation in humans: Potential models for studying neurochemical mechanisms underlying behavioral teratology. *Progress in Brain Research, 73,* 189–206.

Perry, B. D. (1994). Neurobiological sequelae of childhood trauma: Post-traumatic stress disorders in children. In M. Murberg (Ed.), *Catecholamines in post-traumatic stress disorder: Emerging concepts* (pp. 253–276). Washington, DC: American Psychiatric Association Press.

Perry, B. D. (1997). *Maltreated children: Experience, brain development and the next generation.* New York and London: Norton.

Perry, B. D., Arvinte, A., Marcellus, J., & Pollard, R. (submitted). Syncope, bradycardia, cataplexy and paralysis: Sensitization of an opioid-mediated dissociative response following childhood trauma. *Journal of the American Academy of Child and Adolescent Psychiatry.*

Perry, B. D., & Pate, J. E. (1994). Neurodevelopment and the psychobiological roots of post-traumatic stress disorders. In L. F. Koziol & C. E. Stout (Eds.), *The neuropsychology of mental illness: A practical guide* (pp. 129–147). Springfield, IL: Charles C. Thomas.

Perry, B. D., Pollard, R. A., Baker, W. L., Sturges, C., Vigilante, D., & Blakley, T. L. (1995). Continuous heartrate monitoring in maltreated children [Abstract]. In *Proceedings, Annual Meeting of the American Academy of Child and Adolescent Psychiatry, New Research* (Vol. 21, p. 69).

Perry, B. D., Pollard, R. A., Blakley, T. L., Baker, W. L., & Vigilante, D. (1995). Childhood trauma, the neurobiology of adaptation and use-dependent development of the brain: How states become traits. *Infant Mental Health Journal, 16*(4), 271–291.

Pollard, R., & Perry, B. D. (submitted). Evidence of altered brain development following global environmental neglect in childhood. *Journal of Neuropsychiatry and Clinical Neurosciences.*

Prothrow-Stith, D. (1991). *Deadly consequences.* New York: HarperCollins.

Pynoos, R. S. (1990). Post-traumatic stress disorder in children and adolescents. In B. Garfinkel, G. Carlson, & E. Weller (Eds.), *Psychiatric disorders in children and adolescents* (pp. 48–63). Philadelphia: W. B. Saunders.

Pynoos, R. S., & Eth, S. (1985). Developmental perspectives on psychic trauma in childhood. In C. R. Figley (Ed.), *Trauma and its wake* (pp. 36–52). New York: Brunner/Mazel.

Radke-Yarrow, M., McCann, K., DeMulder, E., Belmont, B., Martinez, P., & Richardson, D. T. (1995). Attachment in the context of high-risk conditions. *Development and Psychopathology, 7,* 247–265.

Raine, A., Venables, P. H., & Williams, M. (1995). High autonomic arousal and electrodermal orienting at age 15 years as protective factors against criminal behavior at age 29 years. *American Journal of Psychiatry, 152*(11), 1595–1600.

Rehkamper, G., Haase, E., & Frahm, H. D. (1988). Allometric comparison of brain weight and brain structure volumes in different breeds of the domestic pigeon, *Columbia livia f. d. Brain, Behavior and Evolution, 31,* 141–149.

Ressler, R., Burgess, A., & Douglas, J. (1988). *Sexual homicide.* Lexington, MA: Lexington Books.

Richters, J. E. (1993). Community violence and children's development: Toward a research agenda for the 1990's. *Psychiatry, 56,* 3–6.

Rohrs, M. (1955). Vergleichende untersuchungen an wild- und hauskatzen. *Zoologischer Anzeiger, 155,* 53–69.

Schwab-Stone, M. E., Ayers, T. S., Kasprow, W., Voyce, C., Barone, C., Shriver, T., & Weissberg, R. P. (1995). No safe haven: A study of violence exposure in an urban community. *Journal of the American Academy of Child and Adolescent Psychiatry, 34*(10), 1343–1352.

Schwarz, E. D., & Perry, B. D. (1994). The post-traumatic response in children and adolescents. *Psychiatric Clinics of North America, 17*(2), 311–326.

Shupe, L. M. (1954). Alcohol and crime. *Journal of Criminal Law, Criminology and Police Science, 44*, 661–664.

Singer, W. (1995). Development and plasticity of cortical processing architectures. *Science, 270*, 758–764.

Spitz, R. A., & Wolf, K. M. (1946). Anaclitic depression: An inquiry into the genesis of psychiatric conditions in early childhood. II. *Psychoanalytic Study of the Child, 2*, 313–342.

Straus, M. (1974). Cultural and organizational influences on violence between family members. In R. Prince & D. Barried (Eds.), *Configurations: Biological and cultural factors in sexuality and family life* (pp. 121–132). Washington, DC: Heath.

Sturrock, R. R., Smart, J. L., & Tricklebank, M. D. (1983). A quantitative neurohistological study of the long-term effects in the rat brain of stimulation in infancy. *Journal of Anatomy (London), 136*, 129–144.

Taylor, L., Zuckerman, B., Harik, V., & Groves, B. (1992). Exposure to violence among inner-city parents and young children. *American Journal of Diseases of Children, 146*, 487.

Thoenen, H. (1995). Neurotrophins and neuronal plasticity. *Science, 270*, 593–598.

Ungerleider, L. G. (1995). Functional brain imaging studies for cortical mechanisms for memory. *Science, 270*, 769–775.

Urquiza, A., Wirtz, S., Peterson, M., & Singer, V. (1994). Screening and evaluating abused and neglected children entering protective custody. *Child Welfare League of America, 73*, 155–171.

Vachss, A. (1994, August 28). Emotional abuse: A plea for the wounded. *Parade.*

Vachss, A. H., & Bakal, Y. (1979). *The life-style violent juvenile: The secure treatment approach.* Lexington, MA: Lexington Books/D. C. Heath.

Vachss, A. H. (1991) *Sacrifice.* New York: Knopf.

Wolfgang, M. E., & Ferracuti, F. (1967). *The subculture of violence.* London: Tavistock.

Wright, J., Sheley, J., & Smith, M. D. (1992). Kids, guns and killing fields. *Society, 30*, 84–89.

8

The Development of Violence and Crime as It Relates to Security of Attachment

PETER FONAGY
MARY TARGET
MIRIAM STEELE
HOWARD STEELE

BACKGROUND

Social Trends

Almost all developed, industrialized countries have experienced large increases in the level of recorded crime since World War II (Smith, 1995). Statistics of recorded crimes, victim surveys, and surveys of self-reported conduct disorders consistently demonstrate that there has been a substantial rise in all forms of criminal behavior, whatever definition is taken. Evidence suggests high rates of crime in the early 19th century, especially in large cities, followed by falling rates in the second half of the century and the early part of the current century, with a large increase after 1945 (Archer & Garner, 1984; Gurr, 1977a, 1977b, 1981; Monkkonen, 1981; Wilson & Herrnstein, 1985). Farrington and Langan (1992) report decreases in the United States in some violent offenses over the late 1980s based on victim surveys, although police records show a 20% increase in assaults over the same period. It is generally accepted that the current drop in serious crime in big cities is due to demographic trends, there simply being fewer young men to commit crimes (Easterlin, 1968; Field,

1990). As there are currently in excess of 40 million children under age 10, by the 21st century, there will be 500,000 more male youths in U.S. cities. If the rate of offending fails to change, there will be 30,000 young villains committing crimes.

Thus, crime is a developmental issue. Crimes are mainly committed by teenagers and young adults. Based on median ages of arrest, criminality appears to peak in late adolescence, decreasing gradually after age 18. The peak does not represent a changing disposition toward crime, but rather the proportion of people offending within a given period (prevalence), which peaks reliably across cultures, settings, and crimes in the teenage years. Changes in the structure and functioning of families is suggestively linked to the rise in crime rates since World War II. The family remains the social institution that exerts the most control over the psychosocial development of humans across the life span (Amato & Keith, 1991; Lerner & Spanier, 1978; Maccoby & Martin, 1983). Most sociologists agree that since the 1960s and '70s, most industrialized countries have experienced a major transition of family structures brought about by increasing differentiation and individualization (Durkheim, 1893/1933). There has been an increase in extramarital births (Kiernan & Estaugh, 1993) and single-parent and stepfamily households (Cseh-Szombathy, 1990; Popenoe, 1987; Roll, 1992). Family size is decreasing (Chesnais, 1985). Divorce rates are increasing (Burns, 1992; Haskey, 1983; Kiernan, 1988), and children are increasingly likely to experience multiple transitions in the structure and functioning of families (Festy, 1985; Kiernan, 1988; White & Booth, 1985).

Concurrent with the changes to the structure of the "postmodern" family has been the increasing and widespread recognition of the high prevalence of physical and sexual abuse of children (Hess, 1995). Importantly, this increased recognition has been linked to increased awareness of the psychological sequelae of maltreatment (Cicchetti & Toth, 1995; Skuse & Bentovim, 1994). Arguably, the rise in crime rates could be linked to a similar upturn in the prevalence of maltreatment. There is suggestive evidence of an increase in abuse based on registers of at-risk children (Creighton, 1992; Pieterse & Van Urk, 1989). However, this information is confounded by changes of definition of abuse and a growing recognition of the problem. There has been no increase in infant homicide rates between the 1950s and the 1980s (Marks & Kumar, 1993). Contemporary surveys of sexual abuse in the United States yield comparable figures to Kinsey's survey in the 1940s (Feldman et al., 1991). Retrospective studies with adult women show no evidence of younger women reporting more abusive childhood sexual experiences than older ones (Anderson, Martin, Mullen, Romans, & Herbison, 1993; Wyatt,

1985; Wyatt & Peters, 1986). Thus, increase in child maltreatment is only likely to have had a minor contributory role in the increased general levels of crime and violence over the past decades.

It is widely recognized that family relationships characterized by emotional warmth, positive parental involvement and a fostering of individual strivings for independence, particularly in adolescence, are associated with healthy psychosocial adjustment, good peer relationships, superior academic performance, and higher self-esteem (Bell, Cornwell, & Bell, 1988; Cooper, Grotevant, & Condon, 1983; Hirsch, 1985; Hunter & Youniss, 1982). Could the changing trends in family structure (smaller families, disappearance of larger family units, weaker ties with traditional families, consensual unions as opposed to marriages, children born outside of marriages, frequent family dissolutions, remarriages, frequent family relocations, etc.) then be an important part of an explanation for the increased rates of violence and crime? The impact of divorce on children's psychosocial development has been extensively investigated over recent years (see Amato & Keith, 1991; Barber & Eccles, 1992; Cherlin et al., 1991; Emery, 1982; Hetherington, 1988; Wallerstein, 1991). It appears that divorce has an important negative financial implication for families (Duncan & Hoffman, 1985; Weitzman, 1985; Weiss, 1984) with consequent elevation of emotional difficulties in both parents and children (Elder, Conger, Foster, & Ardelt, 1992) and entrance into deviant subcultures during adolescence (Voydanoff & Majka, 1988). Amato and Keith (1991), in their meta-analysis of 92 studies of the impact of divorce on children, found small but significant effects on psychological adjustment, self-concept, and social adjustment, as well as academic achievement. The effects were smaller in the United States than in European studies, probably because of the greater social acceptability of divorce. It is nevertheless unlikely that increased divorce rates are in themselves to blame for increased conduct problems in children. In a number of longitudinal investigations, conduct problems were shown to be linked to parental conflict prior to the divorce (Block, Block, & Gjerde, 1986; Buchanan, Maccoby, & Dornbusch, 1991; Cherlin et al., 1991; Kline, Johnston, & Tschann, 1991). Thus, it is high levels of parental conflict, rather than divorce or family structural changes per se, that place children at risk of conduct problems.

Attachment and Other Theories of Crime

In 1969, Bowlby (1969/1982) identified three psychological states associated with the disruption of early attachment in the first 3 years of life. Following on from the acute distress of the protest state, the despair state is characterized by preoccupation, withdrawal, and hopelessness. Most pertinent, from our viewpoint, is Bowlby's third state, which is thought to follow prolonged separation, that of detachment. Detachment represents an apparent recovery from protest and despair, but there is no resumption of normal attachment behavior following the refinding of the object. The infant is apathetic and may totally inhibit bonding. There is an intensification of interest in physical objects and a self-absorption that is only thinly disguised by superficial sociability.

In 1946, Bowlby linked affectionless psychopathy to the absence of a maternal object and a biological predisposition. The term "affectionless" is perhaps unfortunate in light of the common clinical experience that emotional detachment from others in the past and present does not stop psychopathic characters from repeatedly and aggressively engaging with objects (Meloy, 1992). In primary psychopathy (Hare & Cox, 1987; Meloy, 1988b), the violence is predatory; it is planned, purposeful, and only apparently emotionless. By contrast, affective violence is not predatory; rather, it is a reaction to a perceived threat and is accompanied by heightened emotional (autonomic) arousal (Meloy, 1988a). The attachment system may be involved in both predatory and affective acts of violence; whereas in the former case the individual seeks the object, and the purpose of such proximity seeking is primarily destructive, in the latter case, proximity triggers an intense defensive reaction of a violent kind. Violence and crime are, for Bowlby, disorders of the attachment system. They are permitted by lack of concern for others (consequent on the inhibition of bonding) and motivated by distorted desires to engage the other in emotionally significant interchange. In this section we shall attempt to place attachment theory of crime in the context of other theories of violent and criminal behavior.

Data are not yet available to answer many important questions considering the potential role of attachment. For example, although there is evidence of a specific link between cognitive capacity and delinquency (Moffitt, 1993), and some data linking attachment security and cognitive development (Carlson & Sroufe, 1995), in most studies of crime the causes of intellectual impairment are not considered.

Some theories relating to crime provide relatively obvious points of contact with attachment theory. However, most current formulations are both developmental and multifactorial, and attachment-related formulations have yet to find an appropriate place within such conceptual frameworks. For example, Loeber and Hay (1994) have proposed a compelling model for the integration of genetic (constitutional) and environmental factors, proposing that peer group relationships serve to consolidate the relationship of aggression and criminality. Children manifesting early conduct problems are rejected by their nondeviant peer groups that attribute aggressive motives to them even when they are behaving normally; in their turn, these children see others' behavior as aggressive in intent, even when the latter's motivation is neutral (Dodge, 1991). Peer groups are not the causes of delinquent behavior (as Sutherland & Cressey, 1978, suggested); rather, they help to reinforce the individual's existing predispositions (Sampson & Laub, 1993; Rowe, Woulbroun, & Gulley, 1994). Attachment may be a further factor that influences an individual's peer-group behavior and acceptance (Grossman & Grossman, 1990) and in addition to or in combination with attribution bias may influence final outcome.

In summary, attachment as a construct may be highly pertinent to current formulations of crime, but a full integration of attachment theory with current formulations is made problematic by a series of practical and conceptual difficulties: (1) lack of availability of data concerning the etiology of risk factors for crime; (2) difficulties in identifying the role of attachment within complex multifactorial models; (3) controversies between rival formulations, even within the same theoretical domain; (4) lack of an unequivocal causal sequence that might permit placing attachment within current models; (5) problems of terminology as a consequence of the need to combine social with individual levels of analysis, particularly in cases in which the same term is used to denote social and individual phenomenology. In the light of these difficulties, we must be cautious in using existing theories to elaborate an attachment theory of violence and crime. Although an adequate theory must integrate known facts (both risk and protective factors), placing these within a single conceptual framework may be beyond our current state of knowledge.

In this chapter, we shall advance the view that attachment may protect the individual from criminal behavior by reducing vulnerability to high-risk environments. We shall attempt to demonstrate that secure attachment facilitates the development of mental capacities that both reduce the motivation for criminal behavior and inhibit the individual's potential to commit acts of aggression.

DETERMINANTS OF INFANT ATTACHMENT SECURITY

There are many excellent reviews of the determinants of infant security (e.g., Belsky, Rosenberger, & Crnic, 1995) that will not be reiterated here. The influence of temperament on attachment security is controversial, but the balance of the evidence is now against the appropriateness of a temperamental account (Fox, Kimmerly, & Schafer, 1991; Kagan, 1982; Lamb, Thompson, Gardner, Charnov, & Estes, 1984). There is little evidence that distress-prone infants become anxious–resistant babies (van den Boom, 1990). Temperament changes in the first year of life (Belsky, Fish, & Isabella, 1991) and the attachment pattern of a child to his or her two parents appear to be dependent on the internal working model of each parent (Steele, Steele, & Fonagy, 1996).

The quality of maternal care has been repeatedly shown to predict infant security. The parameters assessed include ratings of maternal sensitivity (e.g., Cox, Owen, Henderson, & Margand, 1992; Isabella, 1993); prompt responsiveness to distress (Del Carmen, Pedersen, Huffman, & Bryan, 1993); moderate stimulation (Belsky, Rovine, & Taylor, 1984); nonintrusiveness (Malatesta, Grigoryev, Lamb, Albin, & Culver, 1986); interactional synchrony (Isabella, Belsky, & von Eye, 1989); warmth, involvement, and responsiveness (O'Connor, Sigman, & Kasasi, 1992). These associations have been strengthened by findings from experimental studies in which the enhancement of maternal sensitivity has been shown to increase the proportion of secure infants in high-risk populations (van den Boom, 1990). Similar parameters have been predictive for fathers (Cox et al., 1992) and for professional caregivers (Goosens & van IJzendoorn, 1990).

Negative parental personality traits are associated with insecurity in many studies, although by no means all (Zeanah et al., 1993). This has been shown for anxiety (Del Carmen et al., 1993), aggression (Maslin & Bates, 1983) and suspicion (Egeland & Farber, 1984). Parental psychopathology is also found to be a risk factor in some studies (Campbell, Cohn, Meyers, Ross, & Flanagan, 1993). Of the contextual factors, support from the partner (Goldberg & Easterbrooks, 1984) and from others in the mother's environment (Crnic, Greenberg, Ragozin, Robinson, & Basham, 1983) appears important. The strength of these associations is reinforced by experimental studies in which social support was systematically manipulated (Jacobson & Frye, 1991; Lieberman, Weston, & Pawl, 1991; Lyons-Ruth, Connell, & Grunebaum, 1990).

A recent discovery is the remarkable predictive power of qualities of the parents' narrative of their own childhoods, as assessed by the Adult Attachment Interview (Main & Goldwyn, in press; van IJzendoorn, 1995). Across over 800 infant–mother pairs, interviewees coded as secure appear to predict secure attachment behavior in the infant. The findings from our own lab suggest that parental attachment patterns predict variance, in addition to temperament measures or contextual factors such as experience, social support, marital relationship, psychopathology, or personality (Steele et al., 1996). If attachment is linked to criminality, we might predict a substantial overlap between long-term predictors of criminal behavior and determinants of infant security. The aim of this review is to explore the extent of this overlap. Although we cannot claim to have been exhaustive in our coverage of the literature, the trends we have identified do support the assumption of a link, even if the pattern of associations is perhaps somewhat more complex than classical attachment theory had assumed. We will cover three areas that relate to attachment: (1) disruptive behavior, (2) delinquent or criminal behavior, and (3) parenting in attachment and disruptive behaviors.

ATTACHMENT AND EARLY DISRUPTIVE BEHAVIOR PROBLEMS

Crime Is Rooted in Early Experience

Criminology is often said to neglect early childhood characteristics and consequently has not come to grips with the link between early childhood characteristics and later adult outcomes (Caspi, Darryl, & Glen, 1989; Farrington, 1989; Gottfredson & Hirschi, 1990; Sampson & Laub, 1990). Criminal behavior peaks in the teenage years, but longitudinal studies offer good evidence of both early delinquency and the continuation of criminal behavior over the life course (Wilson & Hernstein, 1985). High-rate offenders begin deviant behavior very early in their lives, well before traditional sociological variables (e.g., labor markets, community, peer groups, marriage) "could play much of a role" (p. 311). Acknowledging the importance of early childhood experience does not automatically involve a corresponding reduction of concern with later adult factors (Sampson & Laub, 1990; Wilson & Hernstein, 1985) but creates conceptual space for the consideration of the importance of attachment processes.

Reviewing over 16 studies on aggressive behavior, Daniel Olweus (1979) found substantial stability between early aggression and later criminality ($r = .68$). Heusman, Eron, Lefkowitz, and Walder (1984) studied aggressiveness in 600 subjects, their children, and their parents over a 22-year period and found that aggressiveness predicted later antisocial behavior consistently across a number of situations: criminality, spousal abuse, traffic violations, self-reported physical aggression. Sampson and Laub's (1990) reanalysis of the Gluecks' data (Glueck & Glueck, 1950) from 500 delinquent boys and 500 individually matched controls for age, ethnicity, IQ, and neighborhood socioeconomic status showed that delinquency and childhood temper tantrums at 10–17 years (mean = 14 years) predicted adult criminality, alcohol and drug abuse, and general deviance, (gambling, illicit sexual behavior, involvement with prostitution) for up to 18 years. The Dunedin multidisciplinary health developmental study (White, Moffitt, Earls, Robins, & Silva, 1990) found that motor problems and parent-rated behavioral problems at ages 3 and 5 years predicted delinquency at age 11 in boys (and emotional problems in girls). Robins (1991), in overviewing the study, points out that 84% of children found to be "uncontrolled" at age 11 met the criteria for antisocial disorder at age 13. In turn, antisocial disorder at 13 was predicted by "externalizing behavior" at age 3 and behavior problems at age 5. Loeber and Stouthamer-Loeber's (1987) review of prospective, longitudinal studies underscored the continuity of criminal behavior: The best predictors of delinquency turned out to be early conduct problems such as aggression, stealing, truancy, lying, and drug use. Many of those working in the field accept that childhood conduct problems and delinquency are expressions of the same underlying continuum (Gottfredson & Hirschi, 1990; Reiss & Roth, 1993; Rowe, 1990). The majority of studies reviewed by the Loebers showed continuity from early teens. The study of the relationship of preschool behavior and the early onset of delinquent behavior is just beginning (Farrington et al., 1990; Tonry et al., 1991).

This is clearly only part of the picture, as the majority of antisocial children do not become antisocial adults (Gove, 1985), and many adult criminals have no history of juvenile delinquency (McCord, 1980). The White et al. (1990) analysis of the Dunedin data reveals that although behavioral problems at age 5 predicted persistent antisocial behavior at age 11, and those manifesting such behaviors were more likely to have committed criminal offenses by age 15, behavioral problems in early childhood were more weakly predictive of criminality at the age of 15. Thus, although there is a considerable degree of continuity from one stage to the next, the predictive power of behavioral problems in early childhood can become diluted, hinting at a variety of possible environmental (protective or vulnerability) influences along the way. It should be noted that in the Epidemiologic Catchment Area Study (Robins & Regier, 1991), only 26% of individuals who met the childhood criteria for antisocial personality also met the adult criteria. However, the severity (number of symptoms) of the childhood disorder was predictive of the likelihood of an adult diagnosis of this condition.

Disruptive Behavior and Adolescent Delinquency

Linking disruptive behavior in 6-year-olds to criminality may seem at first glance far-fetched. Nevertheless, longitudinal studies are now available that substantiate the existence of a developmental pathway between disruptive behaviors in preschool and early school years, and delinquency, substance abuse, and diagnosis of conduct disorder in adolescence and adult antisocial personality disorder (Campbell, 1990; McGee, Partridge, Williams, & Silva, 1991; Richman, Stevenson, & Graham,

1982). Children on this developmental trajectory may be differentiated from those whose delinquency and other conduct problems develop in adolescence (Loeber, 1991). They are characterized by frequent and severe disruptive behaviors in multiple settings and a co-occurrence of hyperactivity (Campbell, 1991; Kelso & Stewart, 1986; Moffitt, 1990, 1993).

Recent studies have attempted to identify more specific pathways from early childhood to antisocial behavior in adulthood. It appears that, for boys in particular, early manifestation of behavioral problems is strongly linked to later problems (Loeber & Hay, 1994). The Pittsburgh Youth Study has demonstrated at least three pathways from early problems to conduct disorder: (1) *Authority conflict* starts with stubborn, oppositional behavior that leads to defiance and later total avoidance of authority (e.g., running away); (2) *covert acts* similarly can escalate, with development taking on increasingly serious implications and ending in confrontation with the law; (3) *aggression* can also increase in severity with development, with quite serious ultimate implications (Loeber, Keenan, Green, Lahey, & Thomas, 1993). It is important to note that any one boy may follow more than one of these pathways to offending simultaneously, although some combinations of these pathways entail greater risks of later offending than others. In particular, early aggression has been shown to be a common precursor to violence in adolescence and young adulthood (Farrington, 1978; Magnusson, 1987; Magnusson, Stattin, & Duner, 1983).

Such findings raise questions about the steep increase in antisocial behavior in adolescence. Although the relabeling of childhood antisocial behavior as criminal behavior in adolescents may be part of an explanation, we cannot consider this a full account, since the nature of the actual behavior changes and a wide variety of criminal behaviors show the same pattern of increase (Smith, 1995). More important, and consistent with an attachment theory perspective, we must assume that the nature of bonds change at this time and the parent–child links that predominate in early childhood are transferred to bonds to social institutions and the adult figures that represent them (teachers, employers, etc.). The need to reconfigure internal representations of relationships in this way may make all adolescents prone to antisocial behavior for brief periods. The situation is, however, far more serious for those whose early attachments and consequent internal organizations (working models) of social relationships are compromised or distorted by adverse early experience. Although the absence of appropriate parent–child bonding may express itself as oppositional, avoidant, secretive, and aggressive behaviors in childhood (see below) we assume that the failure to transfer these attachments to social institutions in adolescence and young adulthood would bring with it quite different consequences (see Sampson & Laub, 1993).

The absence of a strong attachment to the parent in the early years may be masked by the adults' physical capacity to control the child, and the absence of parental control through emotional ties may not become fully manifest until the individual's behavior requires internal controls through morality, empathy, caring, and commitment. The weakening of parental influence thus creates a control vacuum in adolescence in these children. They stay unattached to the structures provided by society and remain so for substantial periods, because the psychological structures that normally underpin such bonds are inadequately developed.

Parenting in Attachment and Disruptive Behavior

Factors that interfere with the development of secure attachment have also been shown to be associated with the development of disruptive behavior problems; these include life stress and family adversity (Spieker & Booth, 1988), parental psychopathology (Lyons-Ruth, Zoll, Connell, & Grunebaum, 1989), and social support satisfaction (Crnic, Greenberg, & Slough, 1986). Forehand, Lautenschlager, Faust, and Graziano (1986) reported a direct link between parental depression, ineffective management techniques, and the development of childhood noncompliance. Qualities of parenting that are associated with secure attachment (warmth, sensitive and responsive mothering) appear to be the negative of the behavior of parents of disruptive children (Isabella & Belsky, 1991).

In an important study, Martin (1981) showed that the somewhat dissociated interactions of uninvolved, unresponsive mothers with aversively demanding 10-month-old infants foreshadowed noncompliance and coercive cycles of power-assertive interactions in the third and fourth years of life. Lack of maternal responsiveness and infant demandingness were predictive of disruptive child behavior in interaction.

The relationship between inconsistent power-assertive and somewhat neglectful parental monitoring and antisocial behaviors in children (Dishion, 1990; Loeber & Dishion, 1984; Olweus, 1984; Patterson & Stouthamer-Loeber, 1984) may go beyond the creation of an insecure attachment relationship. However, there is a growing recognition in the literature that in addition to inconsistency of parenting and severity of punishment (Loeber & Dishion, 1983; McMahon & Forehand, 1988; Sampson & Laub, 1993), and the coerciveness of parent–child interaction (Patterson, 1982, 1986), the absence of a positive warm bond between parent and child may have an important role to play in the etiology of disruptive behaviors (Loeber & Stouthamer-Loeber, 1986; Pettit & Bates, 1989; Robinson, 1985; Rutter, 1985a). Encouraging positive parent–child relations seems to have a beneficial effect in the treatment of early non-compliance (Speltz, Greenberg, & DeKlyen, 1990; Strayhorn & Weidman, 1991) and in resilience to childhood adversity (Crockenberg & Litman, 1990; Werner & Smith, 1982).

Attachment theory shifts the focus from the observation of parent–child interaction to the representation of the parent–child relationship in the child's mind (Main, Kaplan, & Cassidy, 1985). There is good evidence that secure attachment with a caregiver is not only related to greater compliance and reciprocity (Richters & Walters, 1991) but also to better peer relations, self-control, and sociability in the preschool years (Greenberg & Speltz, 1988).

Longitudinal Studies of Attachment and Disruptive Behavior

A number of longitudinal studies have attempted to identify a simple relationship between attachment status in the second year of life and disruptive behavior problems in 4- to 6-year-olds (Bates, Bayles, Bennett, Ridge, & Brown, 1991; Fagot & Kavanagh, 1990; Lewis, Feiring, McGuffog, & Jaskir, 1984). None of these studies reported a simple relationship between attachment and externalizing problems, although in one study (Lewis et al., 1984), insecure boys appeared to have more externalizing problems.

The Minnesota Mother–Child Project followed a high social risk sample whose attachment classification was determined in the second year of life. Follow-up assessments show that early insecure relations foreshadowed moodiness, depression, and aggression in the preschool years (Troy & Sroufe, 1987), in early elementary school (Renken, Egeland, Marvinney, Mangelsdorf, & Sroufe, 1989; Sroufe, Egeland, & Kreutzer, 1990), and in the preadolescent period (Urban, Carlson, Egeland, & Sroufe, 1991). For example, Renken and colleagues (1989) used a combination of variables, including quality of parental care, life stress, as well as Strange Situation classification at 12 and 18 months to predict teacher ratings of aggressiveness at 8 years. Aggressive boys were more likely than others to have been avoidant, although it should be noted that the modal classification of aggressive boys was secure at both 12 and 18 months. Harsh parental treatment and stressful life events were related to later aggression for boys and girls, but avoidant attachment was a significant predictor only for boys.

The Minnesota Mother–Child Project was particularly important because, although early assessments of attachment were predictive, the study shows that even securely attached infants develop behavioral problems if the transactional patterns between mother and child are less than optimal (unsupportive, inconsistent, uninvolved, confused). Conversely, insecure children are less likely to develop problems if their mother is warm, supportive, and appropriate at limit setting at 3½ years. Thus, the subsequent variation in the parent–child relationship and family circumstances appears to be critical in determining whether the developmental pathway set by early mother–infant relationship is continued or abandoned.

The development of a method for assessing attachment between 3 to 6 years of age (Cassidy & Marvin, 1989; Main & Cassidy, 1985) has given an additional boost to the study of the relationship of attachment and disruptive disorders. Two studies have shown insecurely attached boys to be more aggressive, disruptive, and attention seeking (Cohn, 1990; Turner, 1991). Two substantial clinic-based investigations show that boys meeting the criteria for oppositional defiant disorder manifested insecure attachment in over 80% of cases, compared to an age, social class, and family composition matched group in which the prevalence of insecurity was less that 30% (Greenberg, Kusche, & Speltz, 1991; Speltz et al., 1990).

There is both a conceptual and a methodological problem associated with these investigations, in that the assessment of attachment security in the modified Strange Situation may be strongly influenced by disruptive behavior, and thus the attachment assessment cannot be considered to be independent of the diagnosis. At a conceptual level, studies are not yet available to conclusively demonstrate a link between child attachment at age 5 and infant attachment in the second year.

Models of Attachment and Disruptive Behavior

There are a number of ways to understand relationships that have been found between attachment and disruptive behaviors. Sroufe (1983) suggested that avoidant children may develop hostile, aggressive responses as a reaction to an unavailable and rejecting caregiver, whereas a resistant child may become externalizing in response to overstimulation and a lack of adequate, age-appropriate affect regulation (Lyons-Ruth et al., 1989). Rubin and colleagues (Rubin, Hymel, Mills, & Rose-Krasnor, 1991) suggest that the unresponsive, rejecting mother of the avoidant infant may respond to the child's attachment strategy in a hostile manner, leading to aggressive behavior in the child.

Greenberg, Speltz, and DeKlyen (1993) propose that insecurely attached children might develop internal working models "in which relationships are generally viewed as characterized by anger, mistrust, chaos and insecurity" (p. 201). This would account for the attributional biases that have been noted in aggressive children (Dodge, 1991). In fact, Suess (1987), cited in Renken et al. (1989), found evidence that anxious, avoidant infant attachment is a predictor of a later tendency to attribute hostile intent in an ambiguous social situation. The avoidant child may have learned to expect hostility from early experience, and the persistence of the internal working model leads to preemptive aggression in later situations.

Disruptive behaviors may also be viewed as strategies initially adopted by children who receive nonoptimal care in order to maximize parental attention (Greenberg & Speltz, 1988), eventually ending up in the coercive interaction pattern noted in such families. Insecure attachment may also reduce the child's predisposition to socialization (Richters & Walters, 1991), thus reducing the child's prosocial orientation. The insecurity of parental representations of attachment may have an independent impact upon the child apart from its influence on the child's own attachment system. For example, parents with unresolved experiences of loss or abuse may at times act in ways that are frightening for the child (Main & Hesse, 1990), as such lack of resolution is assumed to be linked to states of dissociation (Main & Hesse, 1992) that may well play a role in violent behavior.

Shaw and Bell (1993) have proposed a developmental model of antisocial behavior making extensive use of the attachment concept. They suggest that temperamentally difficult infants of nonresponsive mothers may be at particular risk, in that nonresponsive parenting exacerbates the irritability or demandingness of the infant, which exacerbates the mother's difficulty in parenting. Avoidance of the mother develops as a strategy to avoid being blocked from access to her, and such approaches decline in frequency toward the middle of the second year. Increased mobility, together with more frequent episodes of undirected anger and negative reactions, may provoke mothers of avoidant infants to view their child's behavior as demanding and difficult. By 24 months, the avoidant dyad may be predisposed to a coercive style of interaction. It must be harder to control a child whose bond to the caregiver is insecure, as a major means of control (threat of loss of love) has a significantly reduced potency. In the fourth year, the characteristics of the dyadic process will be generalized to other family members. For example, the child may extend his or her expectations of interaction to the school situation. Coercive intervention strategies become more extreme and, therefore, almost by necessity less consistent; harsh or threatening punishments cannot be employed to address every instance of rule violation. The avoidant child's motivational system is extrinsic, aiming to maximize rewards and minimize punishment. Enhanced feelings of self-control associated with intrinsic motivation fail to emerge.

There are important challenges to the attachment theory models of disruptive disorders. Insecure attachment is unlikely to be a direct cause, as the vast majority of children with this pattern of relationships do not manifest any kind of psychological disorder, and it is overrepresented in childhood disorders different in etiology, presentation, course, and outcome from disorders of conduct (e.g., depression, generalized anxiety state, borderline personality disorder). There are a large number of secure attachments observed in conduct disordered groups.

It may be more consistent with the literature to suggest that insecure attachment is a risk factor, whereas secure attachment may be a protective one against the kind of biological and experiential factors that may be operative in early conduct problems (see Rutter, 1985b, 1987, 1988). Elsewhere we have suggested that the capacity to develop a singular and coherent model of attachment relationships, rather than the nature of the relationship per se, may be the best predictor of delinquency behavior (Fonagy et al., 1997).

For a thorough attachment theory account of violence, we still require substantial data from infancy linking attachment status to ecological variables in a developmental context (Robins, 1991). Few studies bridge the two traditions of attachment theory: the clinical approach rooted in psychoanalytic observation at the microlevel (Bowlby, 1969/1982) and the ecological approach to attachment focused on social factors (Bronfenbrenner, 1979). Finally, there is a striking absence of studies in the literature that address the impact of the child's attachment to the father and the role of paternal representations of attachment.

THE LINK BETWEEN ATTACHMENT AND CRIMINALITY

Adult Attachment Interview Study of Prison Populations

There are a number of research teams working with prison populations using the Adult Attachment Interview (AAI). We have almost completed a small study of prison hospital patients with a matched group of psychiatric controls (Levinson & Fonagy, submitted). There were 22 male patients in the prison sample, mean age 27.6 years. Eleven had been sentenced by the end of the study, and the remainder were on remand. Another 5 patients were subsequently convicted. Their crimes included attempted burglary, theft, damage to property, car theft, handling stolen goods, obtaining property and services by deception, gross indecency, possession and intent to supply heroin, importation of drugs, grievous bodily harm, malicious wounding, multiple armed robbery, kidnapping, rape, and murder. They were interviewed using the Structured Clinical Interview for DSM-III-R Disorders (SCID-I and II). They all had at least one

Axis I disorder (80% had three or more diagnoses), and 91% had at least one Axis II diagnosis. Fifty percent had a DSM diagnosis of borderline personality disorder. The average Global Assessment of Functioning (GAF) score for the group was 47. These patients were individually matched with patients from a sample of nonpsychotic inpatients.

A number of striking correspondences have emerged between a subgroup of these 22 criminals and the borderline patients in our hospital sample. In this subgroup, entangled classifications were also the most common; extreme deprivations in childhood were commonly and convincingly reported; these mostly involved severe physical abuse at the hands of borderline or psychotic parents. The interviews were marked by incoherence and a notable lack of an "intentional stance" toward both attachment objects and the self.

The offenders could be divided into two groups on the basis of the patterns of AAI ratings: those in Group 1 were predominantly dismissing, preoccupied (passive), and autonomous, had reflective function (RF) ratings higher than the median and were unlikely to be classified unresolved (U) or cannot classify (CC). Group 2 subjects tended to be preoccupied (angry/conflicted or fearfully preoccupied), or manifesting simultaneously more than one insecure category (cannot classify), there were no F's (secure/free autonomous), and all but two scored above the cutpoint on the lack of resolution scale; they scored below the median on coherence of mind and reflective function, and all had histories of abuse. The groups could also be differentiated in terms of the crimes they committed. The index offenses of prisoners in Group 1 were predominantly crimes against property, whereas those of prisoners in Group 2 were largely serious, violent assaults, including rape and a murder associated with pathological jealousy.

This is only a pilot investigation, but the results are promising to the extent that they link the AAI narratives to type of crime. Naturally, an important alternative account to the one proposed here is that it was these crimes that caused the disorganization of the attachment system, and this permeated the interviews of Group 2. The less serious offenses may have made less impact on the representation of relationships.

A Model of Violence and Criminal Behavior

We propose that crimes, at least in adolescence, are often committed by individuals with inadequate mentalizing capacities, as part of their pathological attempt at adaptation to a social environment in which mentalization is essential. We assume that these individuals did not have access to meaningful attachment relationships that would have provided them with the intersubjective basis for developing a metacognitive capacity capable of organizing and coordinating their internal working models of relationships. The disavowal of the capacity to represent mental states (momentary or permanent) may be a key component of crime against the person. Thus, violence against another may not be possible unless the mental state of the other is insufficiently clearly represented for this to block the violent act. Violence is a solution to psychological conflict because of the inadequacy of the mental representation of the mental world in the minds of these individuals. Their metacognitive capacity is limited, and they experience ideas and feelings in physical, often bodily, terms.

Thus, the current implementation of an attachment theory of crime is in essence a social control theory (Sampson & Laub, 1993). It starts from the need to explain why most people do not normally commit crime rather than why some people commit crimes and violent acts. We assume that crimes against people are normally inhibited by the painful psychic consequences of identifying with the victim's mental state and the equally uncomfortable awareness of the beliefs and feelings of important others. Without this level of social awareness, it is hard to see how informal sanctions by family, peers, neighbors, school, or employer could be exercised. Mentalizing capacity is also essential for some of these social agencies (particularly school and family) to exercise their socializing function. Tomasselo, Kruger, and Ratner (1993) demonstrated that mentalizing capacity was essential to culture-based learning, in which knowledge transmitted was available only through active understanding of the mental state of those transmitting it. Thus, mentalizing ability is seen here as a prerequisite to socialization: the internalization of rules and values and their integration into a coherent system of self-evaluation (Bandura, 1991).

There are at least four ways in which a failure of mentalization can lead to a moral disengagement:

1. If we accept that mentalizing capacity lies at the core of self-awareness, those with reduced ability to envision the mental states of others will also have a less well-established sense of their own identity. Although this may be a source of substantial discomfort, it may also serve to reduce an individual's sense of responsibility for their own actions. Such individuals may more readily feel that they are not responsible for their actions, because they genuinely lack a sense of agency (of intentionality) within which an experience of personal responsibility may be located. By the same token, thinking about others may impinge on individuals with fragile self-representations in a far more threatening way than most of us normally experience.

2. We have already noted the importance of mentalizing capacity to anticipating the consequences of an action on the mind of both victim

and observer. Limitations upon mentalizing might permit the individual to disregard or at least misrepresent the psychological consequences of an act on others.

3. A further related process may entail the devaluing or dehumanizing of the victim, which permits treating other people like physical objects.

4. The limitations of metacognitive capacity may result in a fluidity of the entire mental representational system within which ideas may be readily reconstructed and actions reinterpreted. Thus, unacceptable conduct may be reconstrued as acceptable in a selective and self-serving manner.

There is a second aspect that concerns the changed significance and meaning of behaviors and mental states for the individual with limited mentalizing capacity, which may, speculatively, be linked to acts of criminality and violence. This highlights the adaptive value of violent acts within the internal world of such individuals. For example, the concrete nature of mental representations may create a situation in which unpalatable ideas may be felt to be removed by destroying the physical object that embodies that idea (Fonagy & Target, 1995). Aggression may serve as a defense to safeguard the self from thoughts and fantasies which it cannot protect itself against through mental manipulation (Fonagy, Moran, & Target, 1993). Similarly, aggression in disruptive children may be an adaptation to the activation of discordant internal working models by a caregiver, through disruption of the relationship. In more severe disorders, this defense might come to be integrated within the working model of relationships of self with others; thus, aggression may become a part of self-assertion. The violent act can then be seen to be aimed at destroying symbolic representation. The assault on the perpetrator's fragile sense of self has to be removed. As one murderer put it: "Either he or I must die, something has to give" (Meloy, 1992, p. 58).

To summarize our model: We assume that certain psychosocial environments, particularly those characterized by high conflict and negativity, and low warmth and support, threaten (perhaps constitutionally) vulnerable children. Their internal working models of their caregivers will be limited because of the lack of the critical component, the capacity to see the other's behavior as motivated by mental states, particularly in the context of intense, affectively charged interactions. In the context of such emotionally charged situations, these individuals might revert to mental models of self–other interaction in which both are depicted as essentially physical rather than psychological, mentalizing entities. This state of affairs is most likely to arise for individuals whose core self-structure includes a relatively fragile mentalizing component. We assume that in early childhood, and subsequently, these individuals did not have access to relationships in which they could see themselves as intentional beings motivated by mental states in the eyes of their caregiver. Thus they were deprived of a relationship in which they could have felt sufficiently safe to explore the mind of the other, to find within it an image of themselves as thinking and feeling beings. Their limited and hostile internal working models are therefore overwhelmingly powerful, unchecked by the attenuating influence of a metacognitive capacity. Physical experience has a motivational immediacy because there is no insight into the merely representational basis of human interaction. The failure of mentalizing, however, offers them concrete solutions to intrapsychic and social problems. They are limited in their ability to form bonds with the social world and its institutions, as these are based in a multitude of ways upon the assumption of human intentionality. But in its place, they can control, distance, or indeed bring into proximity subjective states through physical, principally bodily experiences. As self-cohesion is limited by the deficit in the core psychological self, by the inhibition of their capacity to reflect on and integrate mental experiences, these individuals avail themselves of the opportunity to use bodily experiences (alcohol, drugs, physical violence, and crime) to provide them with a sense of consolidation and a coherent identity. In many instances, following the turmoil of adolescence, when working models of self–other relationships are transferred from the primary caregivers to the social world, some of these individuals encounter situations and persons within them that enable them to rebuild their limited reflective capacity. These are the lucky ones, perhaps the ones without a genetic predisposition that undermines close interpersonal ties. In the context of these attachment relationships, many may be able to undo the damage created by their early deprivation and form reflective models of themselves and others, which both reduce the motivation for violent acts and arguably create a powerful block against these. However, for those who, through social happenstance or genetic predisposition, are deprived of such critical interpersonal relations in their young adulthood, the life of violence and crime may be perpetuated beyond the adolescent years. To these individuals, society has surprisingly little to offer.

REFERENCES

Amato, P. R., & Keith, B. (1991). Parental divorce and the well-being of children: A meta-analysis. *Psychological Bulletin, 110,* 26–46.

Anderson, J. C., Martin, J. L., Mullen, P. E., Romans, S. E., & Herbison, G. P. (1993). The prevalence of sexual abuse experiences in a community sample of women. *Journal of the American Academy of Child and Adolescent Psychiatry, 32,* 911–919.

Archer, D., & Gartner, R. (1984). *Violence and crime in cross-national perspective.* New Haven, CT: Yale University Press.

Bandura, A. (1991). Social cognitive theory of moral thought and action. In W. M. Kurtines & J. L. Gewirtz (Eds.), *Handbook of moral behavior and development: Vol. 1. Theory* (pp. 45–103). Hillsdale, NJ: Erlbaum.

Barber, B. L., & Eccles, J. S. (1992). Long-term influence of divorce and single parenting on adolescent family- and work-related values, behaviors and aspirations. *Psychological Bulletin, 111,* 108–126.

Bell, L. G., Cornwell, C. S., & Bell, L. G. (1988). Peer relationships of adolescent daughters: A reflection of family relationship patterns. *Family Relations, 37,* 171–174.

Belsky, J., Fish, M., & Isabella, R. (1991). Continuity and discontinuity in infant negative and positive emotionality: Family antecedent and attachment consequences. *Developmental Psychology, 27,* 421–431.

Belsky, J., Rosenberger, K., & Crnic, C. (1995). The origins of attachment security: "Classical" and contextual determinants. In S. Goldberg, R. Muir, & J. Kerr (Eds.), *Attachment theory: Social, developmental, and clinical perspectives* (pp. 153–184). Hillsdale, NJ: Analytic Press.

Belsky, J., Rovine, M., & Taylor, D. G. (1984). The Pennsylvania Infant and Family Development Project, III: The origins of individual differences in infant–mother attachment: Maternal and infant contributions. *Child Development, 55,* 718–728.

Block, J. H., Block, J., & Gjerde, P. F. (1986). The personality of children prior to divorce: A prospective study. *Child Development, 57,* 827–840.

Bowlby, J. (1946). *Forty-four juvenile thieves: Their character and homelife.* London: Balliere, Tyndall & Cox.

Bowlby, J. (1982). *Attachment and loss: Vol. 1. Attachment.* New York: Basic Books. (Original work published 1969)

Bronfenbrenner, U. (1979). *The ecology of human development.* Cambridge, MA: Harvard University Press

Buchanan, C. M., Maccoby, E. E., & Dornbusch, S. M. (1991). Caught between parents: Adolescents' experience in divorced homes. *Child Development, 62,* 1008–1029.

Burns, A. (1992). Mother-headed families: An international perspective and the case of Australia. *Social Policy Report, 6,* 1–22.

Campbell, S. B. (1990). *Behavior problems in preschool children: Clinical and developmental issues.* New York: Guilford Press.

Campbell, S. B. (1991). Longitudinal studies of active and aggressive preschoolers: Individual differences in early behavior and outcome. In D. Cicchetti & S. L. Toth (Eds.), *Rochester Symposium on Developmental Psychopathology: Vol. 2. Internalizing and externalizing expressions of dysfunction* (pp. 57–90). Hillsdale, NJ: Erlbaum.

Campbell, S. B., Cohn, J. F., Meyers, T. A., Ross, S., & Flanagan, C. (1993). *Chronicity of maternal depression and mother–infant interaction.* Paper presented to "Depressed Mothers and Their Children: Individual Differences in Mother–Child Outcome," Symposium at the meeting of the Society for Research in Child Development, New Orleans, LA.

Carlson, E. A., & Sroufe, L. A. (1995). Contribution of attachment theory to developmental psychopathology. Pp 581–617. In D. Cicchetti & D. J. Cohen (Eds.), *Developmental psychopathology: Vol 1. Theory and methods* (pp. 581–617). New York: Wiley.

Caspi, A., Darryl, J. B., & Glen, J. E. (1989). Continuities and consequences of international styles across the life course. *Journal of Personality, 57,* 375–406.

Cassidy, J., & Marvin, R. S. (1989). *Attachment organization in three and four year olds: Coding guidelines.* Unpublished scoring manual, MacArthur Working Group on Attachment.

Cherlin, A. J., Furstenberg Jr., F. F., Chase-Lansdale, P. L., Kiernan, K. E., Robins, P. K., Morrison, D. R., & Teitler, J. O. (1991). Longitudinal studies of effects of divorce on children in Great Britain and the United States. *Science, 252,* 1386–1389.

Chesnais, J. C. (1985). The consequences of modern fertility trends in the member states of the Council of Europe. *Population Studies 16.* Strasbourg: Council of Europe.

Cicchetti, D., & Toth, S. L. (1995). Child maltreatment and attachment organization. In S. Goldberg, R. Muir, & J. Kerr (Eds.), *Attachment theory: Social, developmental, and clinical perspectives.* (pp. 279–308). Hillsdale, NJ: Analytic Press.

Cohn, D. A. (1990). Child–mother attachment of six-year-olds and social competence at school. *Child Development, 61,* 152–162.

Cooper, C. R., Grotevant, H. D., & Condon, S. M. (1983). Individuality and connectedness in the family as a context for adolescent identity formation and role taking skill. *New Directions for Child Development, 22,* 43–59.

Cox, M., Owen, M., Henderson, V., & Margand, N. (1992). Prediction of infant–father and infant–mother attachment. *Developmental Psychology, 28,* 474–483.

Creighton, S. J. (1992). *Child abuse trends in England and Wales 1988–1990; and an Overview from 1973–1990.* London: National Society for the Prevention of Cruelty to Children (NSPCC).

Crnic, K. A., Greenberg, M. T., Ragozin, A. S., Robinson, N. M., & Basham, R. B. (1983). Effects of stress and social support on mothers and premature and full-term infants. *Child Development, 54,* 209–217.

Crnic, K. A., Greenberg, M. T., & Slough, N. M. (1986). Early stress and social support influence on mothers' and high-risk infants' functioning in late infancy. *Infant Mental Health Journal, 7,* 19–33.

Crockenberg, S., & Litman, C. (1990). Autonomy as competence in 2-year olds: Maternal correlates of child defiance, compliance, and self assertion. *Developmental Psychology, 26,* 961–971.

Cseh-Szombathy, L. (1990). Modelling the interrelation between macro-society and the family. *International Social Science Journal, 126,* 441–449.

Del Carmen, R., Pedersen, F., Huffman, L., & Bryan, Y. (1993). Dyadic distress management predicts security of attachment. *Infant Behavior and Development, 16,* 131–147.

Dishion, T. J. (1990). The family ecology of boys' peer relations in middle childhood. *Child Development, 61,* 874–892.

Dodge, K. A. (1991). The structure and function of reactive and proactive aggression. In D. J. Pepler & K. H. Rubin (Eds.), *The development and treatment of childhood aggression* (pp. 201–218). Hillsdale, NJ: Erlbaum.

Duncan, G. J., & Hoffman, S. D. (1985). A reconsideration of the economic consequences of marital disruption. *Demography, 22,* 485–498.

Durkheim, E. (1933). *The division of labor.* New York: Free Press. (Original work published 1893)

Easterlin, R. A. (1968). *Population, labor force and long swings in economic growth: The American experience.* New York: National Bureau of Economic Research.

Egeland, B., & Farber, E. A. (1984). Infant–mother attachment: Factors related to its development and changes over time. *Child Development, 55,* 753–771.

Elder, Jr., G. H. Conger, R. D., Foster, E. M., & Ardelt, M. (1992). Families under economic pressure. *Journal of Family Issues, 13,* 5–37.

Emery, R. E. (1982). Interparental conflict and the children of discord and divorce. *Psychological Bulletin, 92,* 310–330.

Farrington, D. P. (1978). The family backgrounds of aggressive youths. In L. A. Hersov, M. Berger, & D. Shaffer (Eds.), *Aggression and antisocial behaviour in childhood and adolescence* (pp. 73–93). Oxford: Pergamon Press.

Farrington, D. P. (1989). Later adult life outcomes of offenders and nonoffenders. In M. Brambring, F. Losel, & H. Skowronek (Eds.), *Children at risk: Assessment, longitudinal research, and intervention* (pp. 220–244). New York: de Gruyter.

Farrington, D. P., & Langan, P. A. (1992). Changes in crime and punishment in England and America in the 1980s. *Justice Quarterly, 9,* 5–46.

Farrington, D. P., Loeber, R., Elliott, D. S., Hawkins, D., Kandel, D. B., Klein, M. W., McCord, J., Rowe, D. C., & Tremblay, R. E. (1990). Advancing knowledge about the onset of delinquency and crime. In B. B. Lahey & A. E. Kazdin (Eds.), *Advances in clinical child psychology* (pp. 283–342). New York: Plenum Press.

Feldman, W., Feldman, E., Goodman, J. T., McGrath, P. J., Pless, R. P., Corsini, L., & Bennett, S. (1991). Is childhood sexual abuse really increasing in prevalence? An analysis of the evidence. *Pediatrics, 88,* 29–33.

Festy, P. (1985). Divorce, judicial separation and remarriage. *Population Studies 17.* Strasbourg: Council of Europe.

Field, S. (1990). Trends in crime and their interpretation: A study of recorded crime in postwar England and Wales. *Home Office Research Study 119.* London: Her Majesty's Stationery Office.

Fonagy, P., Moran, G. S., & Target, M. (1993). Aggression and the psychological self. *International Journal of Psychoanalysis, 74,* 471–485.

Fonagy, P., Steele, H., & Steele, M. (1991). Maternal representations of attachment during pregancy predict the organization of infant–mother attachment at one year of age. *Child Development, 62,* 891–905.

Fonagy, P., & Target, M. (1995). Understanding the violent patient: The use of the body and the role of the father. *International Journal of Psycho-Analysis, 76,* 487–502.

Fonagy, P., Target, M., Steele, M., Steele, H., Leigh, T., Levinson, A., & Kennedy, R. (1997). Crime and attachment: Morality, disruptive behavior, borderline personality disorder, crime, and their relationship to security of attachment. In L. Atkinson & K. J. Zucker (Eds.), *Attachment and psychopathology* (pp. 223–274). New York: Guilford Press.

Forehand, R., Lautenschlager, G. J., Faust, J., & Graziano, W. G. (1986). Parent perceptions and parent–child interactions in clinic-referred children: A preliminary investigation of the effects of maternal depressive moods. *Behaviour Research and Therapy, 24,* 73–75.

Fox, N. A., Kimmerly, N. L., & Schafer, W. D. (1991). Attachment to mother/ attachment to father: A meta-analysis. *Child Development, 62,* 210–225.

Glueck, S., & Glueck, E. T. (1950). *Unraveling juvenile delinquency.* Cambridge, MA: Harvard University Press.

Goldberg, W. A., & Easterbrooks, M. A. (1984). The role of marital quality in toddler development. *Developmental Psychology, 20,* 504–514.

Goosens, F., & van IJzendoorn, M. (1990). Quality of infants' attachment to professional caregivers. *Child Development, 61,* 832–837.

Gottfredson, M., & Hirschi, T. (1990). *A general theory of crime.* Stanford, CA: Stanford University Press.

Gove, W. R. (1985). The effect of age and gender on deviant behavior: A biopsychosocial perspective. In A. S. Rossi (Ed.), *Gender and the life course* (pp. 115–144). New York: Aldine.

Greenberg, M. T., Kusche, C. A., & Speltz, M. (1991). Emotional regulation, self-control, and psychopathology: The role of relationships in early childhood. In D. Cicchetti & S. L. Toth (Eds.), *Rochester Symposium on Developmental Psychology: Vol. 2. Internalizing and externalizing expressions of dysfunction* (pp. 21–36). Hillsdale, NJ: Erlbaum.

Greenberg, M. T., & Speltz, M. L. (1988). Contributions of attachment theory to the understanding of conduct problems during the preschool years. In J. Belsky & T. Nezworski (Eds.), *Clinical implications of attachment* (pp. 177–218). Hillsdale, NJ: Erlbaum.

Greenberg, M. T., Speltz, M. L., & DeKlyen, M. (1993). The role of attachment in the early development of disruptive behavior problems. *Development and Psychopathology, 5,* 191–213.

Grossmann, K. E., & Grossmann K. (1990). The wider concept of attachment in cross-cultural research. *Human Development, 33,* 31–47.

Gurr, T. R. (1977a). Contemporary crime in historical perspective: A comparative study of London, Stockhold and Sydney. *Annals, 434,* 114–136.

Gurr, T. R. (1977b). Crime trends in modern democracies since 1945. *International Annals of Criminology, 16,* 41–85.

Gurr, T. R. (1981). Historical trends in crime: A review of the evidence. In N. Morris & M. Tonry (Eds.), *Crime and justice: An annual review of research* (Vol. 3, pp. 295–353). Chicago: University of Chicago Press.

Hare, R. D., & Cox, D. N. (1987). Clinical and empirical conceptions of psychopathy, and the selection of subjects for research. In R. D. Hare & D. Schalling (Eds.), *Psychopathic behavior: Approaches to research* (pp. 1–21). Toronto: Wiley.

Haskey, J. (1983). Remarriage of the divorced in England and Wales—A contemporary phenomenon. *Journal of Biosocial Science, 15,* 253–271.

Hess, L. E. (1995). Changing family patterns in Western Europe. In M. Rutter & D. J. Smith (Eds.), *Psychosocial disorders in young people: Time trends and their causes.* Chichester, UK: Academia Europea, Wiley.

Hetherington, E. M. (1988). Parents, children, and siblings: Six years after divorce. In R. A. Hinde & J. Stevenson-Hind (Eds.), *Relationships within families* (pp. 311–331). Oxford: Clarendon Press.

Hirsch, B. J. (1985). Adolescent coping and support across multiple social environments. *American Journal of Community Psychology, 13,* 381–392.

Huesmann, L. R., Eron, L. D., Lefkowitz, M. M., & Walder, L. O. (1984). Stability of aggression over time and generations. *Developmental Psychology, 20* 1120–1134.

Hunter, F. T., & Youniss, J. (1982). Changes in functions of three relations duirng adolescence. *Developmental Psychology, 18,* 806–811.

Isabella, R. A. (1993). Origins of attachment: Maternal interactive behavior across the first year. *Child Development, 64,* 605–621.

Isabella, R. A., & Belsky, J. (1991). Interactional synchrony and the origins of infant–mother attachment: A replication study. *Child Development, 62,* 373–384.

Isabella, R. A., Belsky, J., & von Eye, A. (1989). Origins of infant–mother attachment: An examination of interactional synchrony during the infant's first year. *Developmental Psychology, 25,* 12–21.

Jacobson, S. W., & Frye, K. F. (1991). Effect of maternal social support on attachment: Experimental evidence. *Child Development, 62,* 572–582.

Kagan, J. (1982). *Psychological research on the human infant: An evaluative summary.* New York: W. T. Grant Foundation.

Kelso, J., & Stewart, M. A. (1986). Factors which predict the persistence of aggressive conduct disorder. *Journal of Child Psychology and Psychiatry, 27,* 77-86.

Kiernan, K. E. (1988). The British family: Contemporary trends and issues. *Journal of Family Issues, 9,* 298–316.

Kiernan, K. E., & Estaugh, V. (1993). *Cohabitation: Extra-marital childbearing and social policy.* London: Family Policy Studies Centre.

Kline, M., Johnston, J. R., & Tschann, J. M. (1991). The long shadow of marital conflict: A model of children's postdivorce adjustment. *Journal of Marriage and the Family, 53,* 297–309.

Lamb, M. E., Thompson, R. A., Gardner, W. P., Charnov, E. L., & Estes, D. (1984). Security of infantile attachment as assessed in the "strange situation": Its study and biological interpretation. *Behavioral and Brain Sciences, 7,* 127–172.

Lerner, R. M., & Spanier, G. B. (Eds.). (1978). *Child influence on marital and family interactionl a life-span perspective.* New York: Academic Press.

Levinson, A., & Fonagy, P. (submitted). *Adult attainment patterns in forensic nonpsychiatric patients.*

Lewis, M., Feiring, C., McGuffog, C., & Jaskir, J. (1984). Predicting psychopathology in six-year-olds from early social relations. *Child Development, 55,* 123–136.

Lieberman, A. F., Weston, D. R., & Pawl, J. H. (1991). Preventive intervention and outcome with anxiously attached dyads. *Child Development, 62*, 199–209.

Loeber, R. (1991). Antisocial behavior: More enduring than changeable? *Journal of the American Academy of Child and Adolescent Psychiatry, 30*, 393–397.

Loeber, R., & Dishion, T. (1983). Early predictors of male delinquency: A review. *Psychological Bulletin, 93*, 68–99.

Loeber, R., & Dishion, T. (1984). Boys who fight at home and school: Family conditions influencing cross-setting consistency. *Journal of Consulting and Clinical Psychology, 52*, 759–768.

Loeber, R., & Hay, D. F. (1994). Developmental approaches to aggression and conduct problems. In M. Rutter & D. H. Hay (Eds.), *Development through life: A handbook for clinicians* (pp. 488–516). Oxford: Blackwell Scientific.

Loeber, R., Keenan, K., Green, S. M., Lahey, B. B., & Thomas, C. (1993). Evidence for developmentally based diagnoses of oppositional defiant disorder and conduct disorder. *Journal of Abnormal Child Psychology, 21*, 377–410.

Loeber, R., & Stouthamer-Loeber, M. (1986). Family factors as correlates and predictors of juvenile conduct problems and delinquency. In M. Tonry & N. Morris (Eds.), *Crime and justice: An annual review of research* (Vol. 7, pp. 29–149). Chicago: University of Chicago Press.

Loeber, R., & Stouthamer-Loeber, M. (1987). Prediction. In H. C. Quay (Eds.), *Handbook of juvenile delinquency* (pp. 325–382). New York: Wiley.

Lyons-Ruth, K., Connell, D. B., & Grunebaum, H. U. (1990). Infants at social risk: Maternal depression and family support services as mediators of infant development and security of attachment. *Child Development, 61*, 85–98.

Lyons-Ruth, K., Zoll, D., Connell, D., & Grunebaum, H. V. (1989). Family deviance and family disruption in childhood: Associations with maternal behavior and infant maltreatment during the first years of life. *Development and Psychopathology, 1*, 219–236.

Maccoby, E., & Martin, J. (1983). Socialization in the context of the family: Parent–child interaction. In E. M. Hetherington (Eds.), *Handbook of child psychology* (pp. 1–101). New York: Wiley.

Magnusson, D. (1987). Adult delinquency in the light of conduct and physiology at an early age: A longitudinal study. In D. Magnusson & A. Ohman (Eds.), *Psychopathology* (pp. 221–234). Orlando, FL: Academic Press.

Main, M., & Cassidy, J. (1985) *Assessments of child–parent attachment at six years of age*. Unpublished scoring manual, Department of Psychology, University of California, Berkeley.

Main, M., & Goldwyn, R. (in press). Adult attachment scoring and classification system. In M. Main (Ed.), *Systems for assessing attachment organization through discourse, behavior and drawings* (Working title). Cambridge, UK: Cambridge University Press.

Main M., & Hesse, E. (1990). Adult lack of resolution of attachment-related trauma related to infant disorganized/disoriented behavior in the Ainsworth Strange Situation: Linking parental states of mind to infant behavior in a stressful situation. In M. T. Greenberg, D. Cicchetti, & M. Cummings

(Eds.), *Attachment in the preschool years: Theory, research and intervention* (pp. 339–426). Chicago: University of Chicago Press.

Main, M., & Hesse, E. (1992). Disorganized/disoriented infant behaviour in the Strange Situation, lapses in the monitoring of reasoning and discourse during the parent's Adult Attachment Interview, and dissociative states. In M. Ammaniti & D. Stern (Eds.), *Attachment and psychoanalysis* (pp. 94–120). Rome: Gius, Latereza & Figli.

Main, M., Kaplan, N., & Cassidy, J. (1985). Security in infancy, childhood and adulthood: A move to the level of representation. In I. Bretherton & E. Waters (Eds.), Growing points of attachment theory and research. *Monographs of the Society for Research in Child Development, 50*(1–2, Serial No. 209), 66–104.

Malatesta, C. Z., Grigoryev, P., Lamb, C., Albin, M., & Culver, C. (1986). Emotion socialization and expressive development in preterm and full-term infants. *Child Development, 57*, 316–330.

Marks, M. N., & Kumar, R. (1993). Infanticide in England and Wales. *Journal of Medical Sciences and the Law, 33*, 239–339.

Martin, J. (1981). A longitudinal study of the consequences of early mother–infant interaction: A microanalytic approach. *Monographs of the Society for Research in Child Development, 46*(3), 1–58.

Maslin, C. A., & Bates, J. E. (1983, April). *Precursors of anxious and secure attachments: A multivariant model at age 6 months.* Paper presented at the biennial meeting of the Society for Research in Child Development. Detroit, MI.

McCord, J. (1980). Patterns of deviance. In S. B. Sells, R. Crandall, M. Roff, J. S. Strauss, & W. Pollin (Eds.), *Human functioning in longitudinal perspective* (pp. 157–165). Baltimore: Williams & Wilkins.

McGee, R., Partridge, F., Williams, S., & Silva, P. A. (1991). A twelve-year follow-up of preschool hyperactive children. *Journal of the American Academy of Child and Adolescent Psychiatry, 30*, 224–232.

McMahon, R. J., & Forehand, R. (1988). Conduct disorders. In E. J. Mash & L. G. Terdal (Eds.), *Behavioral assessment of childhood disorders* (pp. 105–153). New York: Guilford Press.

Meloy, J. R. (1988a). *The psychopathic mind: Origins, dynamics, and treatment.* Northvale, NJ: Jason Aronson.

Meloy, J. R. (1988b). Violent homicidal behavior in primitive mental states. *Journal of the American Academy of Psychoanalysis, 16*, 381–394.

Meloy, R. J. (1992). *Violent attachments.* Northvale, NJ: Jason Aronson.

Moffitt, T. E. (1990). Juvenile delinquency and attention deficit disorder: Boys' developmental trajectories from age 3 to age 15. *Child Development, 61*, 893–910.

Moffitt, T. E. (1993). The neuropsychology of conduct disorder. *Development and Psychopathology, 5*, 135–151.

Monkkonen, E. H. (1981). A disorderly people? Urban order in the nineteenth and twentieth centuries. *Journal of American History, 68*, 536–559.

O'Connor, M., Sigman, M., & Kasasi, C. (1992). Attachment behavior of infants exposed prenatally to alcohol. *Development and Psychopathology, 4*, 243–256.

Olweus, D. (1979). Stability of aggressive reaction patterns in males: A review. *Psychological Bulletin, 86*, 852–875.

Olweus, D. (1984). Development of stable aggressive reaction patterns in males. In R. J. Blanchard & D. C. Blanchard (Eds.), *Advances in the study of aggression* (pp. 103–137). New York: Academic Press.

Patterson, G. R. (1982). *A social learning approach to family intervention: III. Coercive family process*. Eugene, OR: Castalia.

Patterson, G. R. (1986). Performance models for antisocial boys. *American Psychologist, 41*, 432–444.

Patterson, G. R., & Stouthamer-Loeber, M. (1984). The correlation of family management practices and delinquency. *Child Development, 55*, 1299–1307.

Pettit, G. S., & Bates, J. E. (1989). Family interaction patterns and children's behavior problems from infancy to 4 years. *Developmental Psychology, 25*, 413–420.

Pieterse, J. J., & Van Urk, H. (1989). Maltreatment of children in the Netherlands: An update after ten years. *Child Abuse and Neglect, 13*, 263–269.

Popenoe, D. (1987). Beyond the nuclear family: A statistical portrait of the changing family in Sweden. *Journal of Marriage and the Family, 49*, 173–183.

Reiss, A. J., & Roth, J. A. (1993). *Understanding and preventing violence*. Washington, DC: National Academy Press.

Renken, B., Egeland, B., Marvinney, D., Mangelsdorf, S., & Sroufe, L. A. (1989). Early childhood antecedents of aggression and passive-withdrawal in early elementary school. *Journal of Personality, 57*, 257–281.

Richman, N., Stevenson, L., & Graham, P. J. (1982). *Pre-School to School: A Behavioural Study*. London: Academic Press.

Richters, J. E., & Walters, E. (1991). Attachment and socialization: The positive side of social influence. In M. Lewis & S. Feinman (Eds.), *Social influences and socialization in infancy* (pp. 185–213). New York: Plenum Press.

Robins, L. (1991). Conduct disorder. *Journal of Child Psychiatry and Psychology, 32*, 193–212.

Robins, L. N., & Regier, D. A. (Eds.). (1991). *Psychiatric disorders in America: The Epidemiologic Catchment Area Study*. New York: Free Press.

Robinson, E. A. (1985). Coercion theory revisited: Toward a new theoretical perspective on the etiology of conduct disorders. *Clinical Psychology Review, 5*, 577–626.

Roll, J. (1992). *Lone parent families in the European community*. London: European Family and Social Policy Unit.

Rowe, D. C. (1990). Inherited dispositions toward learning delinquent and criminal behavior: New evidence. In L. Ellis & H. Hoffman (Eds.), *Crime in biological, social, and moral contexts* (pp. 121–133). New York: Praeger.

Rubin, K. H., Hymel, S., Mills, S. L., & Rose-Krasnor, L. (1991). Conceptualizing different developmental pathways to and from social isolation in childhood. In D. Cicchetti & S. L. Toth (Eds.), *Rochester Symposium on Developmental Psychopathology: Vol. 2. Internalizing and externalizing expressions of dysfunction* (pp. 91–122). Hillsdale, NJ: Erlbaum.

Rutter, M. (1985a). Family and school influences on behavioral development. *Journal of Child Psychology and Psychiatry, 26*, 349–368.

Rutter, M. (1985b). Resilience in the face of adversity: Protective factors and resistance to psychiatric disorder. *British Journal of Psychiatry, 147*, 598–611.

Rutter, M. (1987). Psychosocial resilience and protective mechanisms. *American Journal of Orthopsychiatry, 57,* 316–331.

Rutter, M. (Ed.). (1988). *Studies of psychosocial risk.* New York: Cambridge University Press.

Sampson, R. J., & Laub, J. H. (1990). Crime and deviance over the life course: The salience of adult social bonds. *American Sociological Review, 55,* 609–627.

Sampson, R. J., & Laub, J. H. (1993). *Crime in the making: Pathways and turning points through life.* Cambridge, MA: Harvard University Press.

Shaw, D. S., & Bell, R. Q. (1993). Chronic family adversity and infant attachment security. *Journal of Child Psychology and Psychiatry, 34,* 1205–1215.

Skuse, D., & Bentovim, A. (1994). Physical and emotional maltreatment. In M. Rutter, E. Taylor, & L. Hersov (Eds.), *Child and adolescent psychiatry: Modern approaches* (pp. 209–229). Oxford: Blackwell Scientific.

Smith, D. J. (1995). Youth crime and conduct disorders: Trends, patterns and causal explanations. In M. Rutter & D. J. Smith (Eds.), *Psychosocial disorders in young people: Time trends and their causes* (pp. 389–489). Chichester, UK: Academia Europea.

Speltz, M. L., Greenberg, M. T., & DeKlyen, M. (1990). Attachment in preschoolers with disruptive behavior: A comparison of clinic-referred and nonproblem children. *Development and Psychopathology, 2,* 31–46.

Spieker, S. J., & Booth, C. L. (1988). Maternal antecedents of attachment quality. In J. Belsky & T. Nezworski (Eds.), *Clinical implications of attachment theory* (pp. 95–135). Hillsdale, NJ: Erlbaum.

Sroufe, L. A. (1983). Infant–caregiver attachment and patterns of adaptation in the preschool: The roots of maladaptation and competence. *Minnesota Symposium in Child Psychology, 16,* 41–83.

Sroufe, L. A., Egeland, B., & Kreutzer, T. (1990). The fate of early experience following developmental change: Longitudinal approaches to individual adaptation in childhood. *Child Development, 61,* 1363–1373.

Steele, H., Steele, M., & Fonagy, P. (1996). Associations among attachment classifications of mothers, fathers, and their infants. *Child Development, 67,* 541–555.

Strayhorn, J. M., & Weidman, C. S. (1991). Follow-up one year after parent–child interaction training: Effects on behavior of preschool children. *Journal of the American Academy of Child and Adolescent Psychiatry, 30,* 138–143.

Sutherland, E. H., & Cressy, D. R. (1978). *Principles of criminology.* Philadelphia: Lippincott.

Tomasello, M., Kruger, A., & Ratner, H. H. (1993). Cultural learning. *Behavioral and Brain Sciences, 16,* 495–552.

Tonry, M., Ohlin, L. E., Farrington, D. P., Adams, K., Earls, F., Rowe, D. C., Sampson, R. J., & Tremblay, R. E. (1991). *Human development and criminal behavior: New ways of advancing knowledge.* New York: Springer-Verlag.

Troy, M., & Sroufe, L. A. (1987). Victimizaion among preschoolers: Role of attachment relationship history. *Journal of the American Academy of Child and Adolescent Psychiatry, 26,* 166–172.

Turner, P. (1991). Relations between attachment, gender, and behavior with peers in the preschool. *Child Development, 62,* 1475–1488.

Urban, J., Carlson, E., Egeland, B., & Sroufe, L. A. (1991). Patterns of individual adaptation across childhood. *Development and Psychopathology, 3,* 445–460.

van den Boom, D. (1994). The influence of temperament and mothering on attachment and exploration: An experimental manipulation of sensitive responsiveness among lower-class mothers with irritable infants. *Child Development, 65,* 1449–1469.

Van IJzendoorn, M.H. (1995). Associations between adult attachment representations and parent–child attachment, parental responsiveness, and clinical status: A meta-analysis on the predictive validity of the Adult Attachment Interview. *Psychological Bulletin, 117,* 387–403.

Voydanoff, P., & Majka, L. C. (1988). *Families and economic distress.* Newbury Park, CA: Sage.

Wallerstein, J. S. (1991). The long-term effects of divorce on children: A review. *Journal of the American Academy of Child and Adolescent Psychiatry, 30,* 349–360.

Weiss, R. S. (1984). The impact of marital dissolution on income and consumption in single-parent households. *Journal of Marriage and the Family, 46,* 115–127.

Weitzman, L. J. (1985). *The divorce revolution.* New York: Free Press.

Werner, E. E., & Smith, R. S. (1982). *Vulnerable but invincible: A longitudinal study of resilient children and youth.* New York: McGraw-Hill.

White, J. L., Moffitt, T. E., Earls, F., Robins, L., & Silva, P. A. (1990). How early can we tell? *Criminology, 28,* 507–533.

White, L. K., & Booth, A. (1985). The quality and stability of remarriages: The role of stepchildren. *American Sociological Review, 50,* 689–698.

Wilson, J. Q., & Hernstein, R. (1985). *Crime and human nature.* New York: Simon & Schuster.

Wyatt, G. A. (1985). The sexual abuse of Afro-American and White-American women in childhood. *Child Abuse and Neglect, 9,* 507–519.

Wyatt, G. A., & Peters, S. D. (1986). Methodological considerations in research on the prevalence of child sexual abuse. *Child Abuse and Neglect, 10,* 241–251.

Zeanah, C., Benoit, D., Barton, M., Rega, C., Hirschberg, L., & Lispitt, L. (1993). Representations of attachment in mothers and their one-year-old infants. *Journal of the American Academy of Child and Adolescent Psychiatry, 32,* 278–286.

II

PREVENTION AND INTERVENTION PROGRAMS FOR CHILDREN AND FAMILIES EXPOSED TO VIOLENCE

I T IS UNREALISTIC TO EXPECT that prevention programs alone can in any way *solve* the youth violence problem in the United States that continues to escalate at an astounding rate, particularly among young males. However, there are excellent precedents in this country for developing very effective multisystem, interdisciplinary strategies to prevent behavior problems as compared with programs and efforts that respond in primarily punitive ways after they have occurred.

Some exemplary prevention and intervention programs addressing the problem of violence prevention and responding to traumatized children and families in cities around the United States, including Boston, Chicago, Los Angeles, New Haven, and New Orleans will be described in this section. All of these programs take a systems approach to the problem, recognizing that the problem of violence prevention is complex, with no simple solutions. Thus, not only are services provided for the children and families, but the programs interface with the police, schools, courts, community programs, health care settings, and others helping children. Efforts are being made to reach children and families earlier—if possible, before the violence or trauma has taken place. Through this work, we are learning about risk factors in homes and environments that may make children more likely to be traumatized, and efforts are being made to prevent the trauma. Clinicians agree that it is crucial to reach children early after the trauma occurs to prevent the most serious effects on the child. In introducing this section, I will describe briefly the intent of the programs that will be presented more fully in the chapters.

In New Haven: The Child Development–Community Policing Program began in the early 1990s as one of the first programs to link the police with the mental health community. This collaborative program facilitates the response of mental health professionals and police to children and families exposed to violence. It attempts to change police officers' orientation in their interactions with children toward optimizing their role as providers of a sense of security and positive authority, and as models to be emulated. The three major components of the program are (1) training of all incoming police recruits about principles of child and adolescent development; (2) clinical fellowships for veteran officers who have field supervisory roles; and (3) a 24-hour consultation service for officers responding to calls in which children are either the direct victims or witnesses of violence. In Chapter 10, Marans and Adelman describe the objectives of their program and provide examples of children's experience of violent trauma in a developmental context.

In Boston: The Massachusetts Attorney General's office has sponsored an initiative in Boston that builds on the city's community policing efforts; the effort is targeted at the community with the second highest level of violence in the city. The collaboration includes police, the district attorney's office, the courts, community business leaders, youth agencies, community health centers, and a hospital. The different agencies and systems can provide a much more comprehensive response to neighborhood crime. This initiative follows the earlier establishment at Boston City Hospital of the Child Witness to Violence Project, which was developed in response to the urgent need to help children and families who witness violence. Groves and Zuckerman urge pediatricians and other health care professionals to be consciously alert, even in regular office visits, to the possibility of exposure to victimization, and to be proactive in providing help. They offer through their program a range of counseling and treatment options, including 24-hour crisis intervention. In Chapter 9, Groves and Zuckerman describe interventions with parents and community caregivers, and provide sensitive clinical examples of their work with these families.

In Los Angeles: In Los Angeles, Robert Pynoos and his team at the Trauma Psychiatry Program at UCLA have done pioneering work in providing an understanding of how children are traumatized by violence, be it through a sniper attack at school, natural disaster, or directly related to the topic of this book, exposure to urban violence. A recent project of his team, which is described in Chapter 11, has been to develop a Community Policing Agency that is somewhat different from their other fine therapeutic programs for traumatized children. Community-based police officers are stationed at an elementary school as a way of promoting a relationship between the officers and neighborhood children, who then become involved in a school-based intervention program. Their interactions build a different type of relationship between children and police officers that can lead to more effective prevention and intervention efforts for children exposed to violence.

In New Orleans: The Violence Intervention Project for Children and Families was designed as a direct response to the crisis of rising violence in New Orleans (paralleling that of other major cities), and the fact that ever-increasing numbers of children were being exposed to violence as victims or witnesses. As the originator of the project in 1992, I was motivated by the frequent reports about both young perpetrators, many not yet in their middle-teen years, and even younger victims. I believed then, and do even more so now, that it is crucial to reach these young people who witness violence and may be traumatized by it long before they reach an age when they might act out their experiences and, learning from their earlier violent world, become either perpetrators or victims. The program, which was initiated in one of the police districts with the highest level of violence in the city, includes several components: (1) education for police officers at all levels who are the first on the scene of most violent incidents about the effects of violence on children, including the frequent occurrence of symptoms of posttraumatic stress disorder; (2) a 24-hour hotline for consultation by police or families and for referral of children who witness violence; (3) therapeutic services for children and families traumatized by violence; (4) in-service education in schools for teachers on the effects of violence on children and what can be done; (5) community-based parent information and support groups. In addition, we have a strong commitment to informing the public about the importance of prevention and interventions that may be helpful to children exposed to violence. In Chapters 12–15, my colleagues and I will describe our project in New Orleans, including perceptions of violence and safety in children, parents, and police officers; children's understanding of their violent environments as shown through drawings; and domestic violence, children, and the interface with community policing.

9

Interventions with Parents and Caregivers of Children Who Are Exposed to Violence

BETSY McALISTER GROVES
BARRY ZUCKERMAN

T HE CRISIS OF VIOLENCE IN this country has left few families untouched. Any description of this nation must include a homicide
rate that leads every other industrial nation, an obsession with
the trial of O. J. Simpson, and national heroes such as Arnold Schwarze-
negger and Sylvester Stallone. Violence bombards children in their homes
via the television. Increasingly, children are witnessing real-life violence
both in their homes and in the community. The prevalence of violence
has been documented elsewhere in this book (see Osofsky, Chapter 1,
this volume). Many of these chapters discuss the impact of this violence
on children, both for children who are direct victims and children who
are bystanders to violence. These chapters attest to the devastating impact
on children of living in violent homes and communities. Whether or not
these children are physically injured by the violence, they carry with
them lasting emotional scars from having been exposed to the chronic
threat and trauma of injury, assault, or killing. This exposure to violence
changes the way children view the world and may change the value they
place on life itself. It affects their ability to learn, to establish relationships
with others, and to cope with stress. This epidemic of violence constitutes
both a public health crisis (Groves, Zuckerman, Marans, & Cohen, 1993;

183

Zuckerman, Augustyn, Groves, & Parker, 1995) and a moral/philosophical crisis (Edelman, 1992; Emde, 1993) in this country.

Nowhere is this crisis felt with more anguish and despair than among the parents, teachers, and other caregivers of children. This chapter will focus on the perspectives of these parents and two other groups of caregivers whose mission is to nurture and raise healthy, productive children: teachers and health care providers. Strategies will be presented for better preparing and supporting these caregivers to do their work. Examples of successful interventions with these groups will also be presented.

The material for this chapter comes from the authors' experiences working with young children who have been the witnesses of violence. These experiences include pediatric and mental health interventions, and consultative experience with parents, teachers, police officers, pediatricians, social workers, judges, lawyers, recreation workers, and others whose job it is to care for or protect children.

As an outgrowth of health care providers' recognition of the particular needs of young children who live with chronic violence, the Child Witness to Violence Project was founded at Boston City Hospital in 1992. This project has provided support services to children and families, and to a large network of teachers, health care providers, and other professionals who work with children. The Child Witness to Violence Project provides therapeutic intervention to young children who witness violence by working with the child, the family, and the network of caregivers who may be involved with the family. A great deal has been learned from this project, not only about how violence affects children, but also about how parents and caregivers are struggling to help children cope with the aftermath of violence (Groves, 1994b). What follows are their stories, presented as case examples. These are both stories of frustration and helplessness and stories of courage and persistence. The Child Witness to Violence Project began as a program that provided therapeutic services to children and families. However, the mission of the project has evolved to include a broader definition of intervention that targets communities. The philosophical premise of this chapter is that providing individual therapeutic intervention for children who are victims or bystanders to violence is insufficient when addressing a problem of this magnitude. One must use an approach that includes the multiple systems that are involved when children witness violence. Perhaps the greatest lesson learned from the work of the Child Witness to Violence Project is that children are helped most effectively by providing therapeutic intervention *and* by mobilizing communities to support them. The facet of mobilization that this chapter will address is supportive work with parents and community caregivers.

PARENTS

In a study conducted in 1991 at Boston City Hospital, it was found that 10% of the children who used outpatient pediatric services had witnessed a knifing or shooting by the age of 6 (Taylor, Zuckerman, Harik, & Groves, 1994). Half of the reported violence occurred in the home, half on the street. In this survey, several major concerns were mentioned by parents when they were asked about how their children were affected by exposure to violence: 51% worried that their children would become habituated to violence; 29% reported that their children were scared or upset; 19% felt exposure to violence would limit their children's personal growth; 24% reported that their freedom was limited as a result of the violence.

Parents whose children have been exposed to violence often mirror the same helplessness as do their children in the face of life-threatening events (Osofsky & Fenichel, 1994). This helplessness is intensified by feelings of guilt about having failed to protect children from the violence. Parents voice both rage and despair about feeling trapped in neighborhoods of high violence. One response of these parents is to limit the movement of their children in the neighborhood. Parents keep their children inside because of uncertainty and danger in the neighborhood. Although this arrangement may work more easily for a young child than for older children, it communicates a set of presumptions that may affect a child's basic desire to move out in the world and explore. Toddlers first experience the world by cautiously moving away from a trusted parent and exploring the larger environment. However, if a toddler receives messages from his or her parent that the world is unsafe and unpredictable, what happens to the child's natural curiosity to explore? Such messages from parents are necessary but come at some expense to a child's budding curiosity about the world.

For parents of older children, the necessity of keeping children at home produces a conflict between the child's developmentally appropriate need for autonomy and the parent's worries about safety. Keeping a child home may interfere with a child's needs to establish a peer group or to pursue outside hobbies. A parent's protectiveness becomes the source of family conflict.

CASE EXAMPLE

A father of a 15-year-old boy who had been the bystander to the murder of his friend described his compulsive worry about the safety of his son. Both father and son had been witness to a drive-by shooting that left one boy dead. The father, who had basic first-aid training, tried unsuccessfully to revive the victim and keep him alive. After the murder, the family sought help because of the father's symptoms of anxiety and the boy's truancy from school. When the father was asked about his worries about his son, he described how he kept very strict curfews and occasionally followed his son when he left the house. If his son was late, even by a few minutes, the father began calling his friends' homes, much to the anger and embarrassment of the 15-year-old boy. His father described his resolute determination to keep his son safe and his haunting worries that something would happen to his son. He felt that if he could track his son's whereabouts at all times, he would be able to protect him from harm. Ironically, his very persistence was a source of anger and defiance in his son. The more the father tried to monitor his son's movements, the more the son evaded his father and began to lie about his whereabouts.

The intensity of parents' feelings about their children's experiences with violence becomes more complicated when the violence the child has witnessed comes from within the home. Approximately two-thirds of the children seen in the Child Witness to Violence Project are referred because they have witnessed domestic violence. The clinical finding from this project is that mothers who are victims of partner violence are often less able to offer emotional support to their children than mothers whose children have witnessed violence outside their homes. These mothers are frequently afraid for their lives. They are preoccupied with basic survival and are unable to attend to their children's psychological needs. If one parent is the terrified victim and the other is the perpetrator of violence, what choice does the child have? For women who live with violent partners, there exists a constant tension and fear about the next violent explosion. Women may focus on making sure things at home are quiet and orderly, in order to avoid another violent outburst from their partner. However, this preoccupation interferes with their ability to be responsive to children's needs and to assess their children's emotional turmoil. There is also a strong correlation between domestic violence and maternal depression (Walker, 1984). Many studies have documented the ways in which maternal depression affects childrearing (Wrate, Rooney, & Thomas, 1985; Zahn-Waxler, Cummings, & Iannoff, 1984; Zuckerman & Beardslee, 1987).

Women who live with domestic violence may suffer from symptoms associated with posttraumatic stress disorder (Carmen, Rieker, & Mills, 1984). One of the manifestations of this syndrome is that women become desensitized to the violence in the home. These parents may have difficulty being emotionally available to their children (Augustyn, Parker, Groves, & Zuckerman, 1995). Mothers' threshold of acceptance of violence is lowered. In the Child Witness to Violence Project it is not uncommon to hear mothers' minimization of violent events or to hear from mothers that their children did not see or hear a violent incident. However, separate interviews with children reveal that they see and hear more than parents think. This desensitization on the part of parents also interferes with their judgment of what is appropriate for children to see and hear. These children are sometimes allowed to watch inappropriate television and movies that are further upsetting to them.

CASE EXAMPLE

> Margaret, a 25-year-old mother of three children, ages 5, 7, and 8, had been a victim of domestic violence since the beginning of her marriage, 10 years ago. The violence grew increasingly frequent and dangerous, culminating in her husband's attempt to murder her by strangulation. This incident was witnessed by the youngest child. The mother escaped and sought refuge in a shelter for battered women. The family sought counseling 1 month after the event. In the first session with her children in the room, the mother began to retell the story of her husband's attempt to kill her. Her account was filled with vivid and upsetting detail. As she told the story, the children became agitated and distressed. However, the mother was so traumatized with her own recall of the events that she was unaware of the effects on others. It was not until the worker intervened and suggested that she stop that she could see how upsetting this account of the incident was for her children. On many occasions after this initial session, this mother began to talk to the therapist about frightening details of her relationship with the father in the presence of the children. She fantasized that she saw him on the street; she freely shared her constant fear that he would get out of jail and come find them. Her own level of trauma destroyed her ability to monitor her children's reactions and impaired her ability to help restore for her children some sense of psychological safety following the trauma.

Parents whose children have witnessed or been victims of violence often do not know how to talk to their children about the violence. Most adults find violent events inexplicable and horrifying (Jackson, 1994). There are no easy explanations for adults or children. Parents are unsure of how to explain the reasons for the violence, or how to explain death or severe injury to their children (Jackson, cited in Osofsky & Fenichel, 1994). In some situations, the entire subject is avoided in families. Although the urge to avoid is understandable, it communicates a powerful message to children: This is an issue that is too big and scary to mention; This is an issue that the adults do not want to talk about. The absence of explanation to children also gives rise to misunderstandings about the causes of the violence. It becomes easier for children to blame themselves or somehow misattribute the causes of the violence.

CASE EXAMPLE

A mother brought her two young sons, ages 5 and 7, in for an assessment of the effects on the children of their witnessing their father's assault on their mother. The father had been arrested over the weekend and was in jail. When asked what explanation had been given to the boys about the father's absence, the mother explained that since the boys had not actually seen the arrest, she had decided to tell them that their father had gone to Virginia. There was a precedent for this explanation: He had left many times before. The mother admitted that she was unsure about how to talk with her sons and thought this explanation would be the least upsetting for them. She then related that the boys had been in court with her several days ago to obtain a restraining order against her husband, and that he was also there. The therapist asked about how the children understood his appearance in court; the mother was unsure, preferring not to talk about it with them.

CASE EXAMPLE

A 3-year-old girl, Sarah, was brought in by her maternal grandmother. Sarah was having nightmares and was clinging and anxious during the day. Her mother had been fatally shot while Sarah was in the room. In the course of the initial evaluation, the grandmother made several references to her daughter, Sarah's mother. At each reference, she would drop her voice to a whisper. Using this whisper, she spelled the word "D-e-a-d." She repeated this dramatic change of tone and affect at every mention of her daughter throughout the session. Sarah mentioned her mother several times during the session; each time the grandmother's emotional response would change; she froze, dropped her voice, and avoided the subject. The grandmother admitted that she had been unable to tell Sarah anything about her mother's death and had simply avoided all mention of the subject. It became apparent to the therapist that the grandmother was also communicating to Sarah that this subject was unmentionable. The child was confused about her grandmother's behavior. The inability to speak about the event made it impossible for the grandmother to respond empathically to Sarah and gave Sarah the message that she should not talk about it.

Counseling Parents to Help Their Children

As mentioned earlier, a hallmark of parents' and children's exposure to trauma is the response of helplessness and hopelessness. All interventions with parents must counter this sense of helplessness that is engendered by violence. Parents need reminders that they are the most important helpers in their children's lives and, as such, are in a strong position to help their children cope with the aftermath. In the Child Witness to Violence Project, parents are explicitly reassured that even though there was little they could have done to prevent their child's exposure to trauma, there is a lot they can do to help their child regain a sense of equilibrium following exposure to violence. The following areas are then explored with parents:

1. *Help reestablish a sense of order and routine.* Children have an additional need for routine and predictability after a traumatic event has shattered their world. It is suggested that parents take particular care at bedtime, that they help children anticipate what will happen each day. Since many children, especially young children, will be anxious about separations from parents, absences should be talked about ahead of time and carefully explained to children.

2. *Children need an explanation of the violent event.* The explanation of the violence event should be appropriate to their developmental stage and should contain only as much information as is necessary. The first goal of the explanation is to help children, who may be egocentric in their thinking, understand that what happened is not their fault. The second goal is to communicate the message that this is a subject that can be talked about. In the case example described earlier, the first intervention by the therapist was to ask the mother if the boys could come in so they could talk together about why they had seen their father in court. With help from the therapist, the mother told the children that their father had become very angry and had hit her. This was wrong and against the law, and the police were called. The boys were then told about the court proceedings. Throughout the discussion, it was stressed that the father had a problem controlling his anger, and that it was their hope that he could get help for this problem. This discussion was obviously relieving for the children. It also freed them to talk about their father. They discussed both their fear of him and their sadness that he was in jail. The therapist then reviewed this discussion with the mother.

3. *Parents need to respond to children's fears and worries honestly and with whatever reassurance is possible.* Part of the helplessness felt by parents is that they are unable to provide safety for their children and guarantees that the violence will not reoccur. This is particularly true for parents who live in chronically dangerous communities. It is our belief that children need to hear that we, as adults, are doing everything we can to make the world safe for our children. This declaration is quite reassuring for young children, who look to their parents as the most important source of protection and comfort. Research (Freud & Burlingham, 1943) and clinical observation have supported the belief that children feel safer

when they maintain physical proximity with their parents in times of war. Sometimes parents use spiritual or religious beliefs to reassure or support children's sense of safety. Research also suggests that families who have a set of religious or spiritual beliefs are more resilient (Garbarino, Kostelny, & Dubrow, 1991). These beliefs provide a coherent and sustaining framework that helps families cope with trauma. In summary, parents who can communicate to their children that they understand their fears and are establishing a plan of action to deal with the problem are the most successful at helping restabilize them.

The following example demonstrates how parental reassurances can be the critical intervention to restabilize children.

CASE EXAMPLE

> Stacey, a 10-year-old girl, was brought to her pediatrician by her mother because of nightmares and school refusal. She had been awakened 2 weeks prior to the visit to see the face of a man in her window. Her mother first thought she was having nightmares; however, the next morning, they found that the screen to her window had been cut in an apparent robbery attempt. Since then, Stacey had refused to sleep in the room and was generally anxious and afraid. The mother initially minimized the incident in an attempt to "help her forget it." However, as Stacey recounted for the pediatrician what had happened and explained her preoccupation with the fear that the man would return, the mother become more agitated. She finally broke in, stating that she thought she knew who did it and would make sure it never happened again. She then explained about some neighborhood rivalries and drug involvement that resulted in the wrong house being broken into. She vowed that she would talk to people and make sure it did not happen again. The pediatrician was concerned that the mother not put herself in danger, but he also noticed that Stacey relaxed visibly as an explanation was given for this scary event, and as her mother vowed that she would protect her. Two weeks later, her mother reported that Stacey was able to sleep and had returned to school.

This forceful and convincing explanation from the mother gave Stacey strong reassurance that she would be safe.

TEACHERS' PERSPECTIVES ON VIOLENCE IN THE LIVES OF YOUNG CHILDREN

CASE EXAMPLE

> The second grade class in a Boston school takes a field trip that includes a lunch stop at the local McDonald's restaurant. As the

children are getting seated at the picnic tables outside, gunfire erupts. There is much screaming and chaos; several minutes later, the children see two young men lying on the ground in the parking lot. Both are bleeding profusely. The teachers have grabbed the children near them and pulled them to the ground. As soon as they can, they gather the children and return to the school. Police officers are trying to get names and information from the children in the hope of finding an eyewitness to the crime.

Increasingly, teachers of young children are being faced with difficult events such as this and must make instant decisions about the best way to help children cope with trauma. In the preceding situation, teachers were in a highly dangerous situation that required instant assessment and critical decision making. This situation also required negotiating with police, parent notification and involvement, and follow-up intervention with children. Teachers typically have not been trained to make such interventions and are unsure about how to help children with such overwhelming life events.

Although this case example may (fortunately) be unusual, it is somewhat more common for teachers to hear children talk in the classroom about violence they have seen: Jimmy, age 3, announces at circle time that he saw someone getting stabbed on his street. Marsha, a pert 4-year-old, says that her Dad hit her Mommy and made her face bleed. Harold, age 5, hears gunshots outside his home and is afraid to go to sleep at night. Particularly in settings in which there are many children who live in chronically violent neighborhoods, stories of violence or danger may permeate the child care center. In addition to talking about it, children may play games that reenact the violence they observe in their environments. Teachers wonder how to respond to these children: "Should children be allowed to talk about these violent incidents in the classroom; or is it too stimulating for the other children?" "Should they be allowed to play out what they have seen or does it scare other children?"

As teachers face these dilemmas, they describe an increasing sense of helplessness about the amount of violence their children live with. They feel inadequate to the task; they resent that they are not able to teach these children because they are too distracted and preoccupied to learn; they receive inadequate support from a system that measures learning only by standardized test scores. It is tragically ironic that the professionals who spend the most time with children are often the least prepared and supported to work with children who live with chronic violence.

Children who live with violence bring many of their concerns and fears into the classroom (Craig, 1992, Groves & Mazur, 1995; Wallach, 1993). These worries are reflected in behavior, in anxiety about being separated from caregivers, and in difficulties with concentration and distractibility. Many of these children show symptoms associated with post-traumatic stress disorder (Drell, Siegel, & Gainsbauer, 1993; Lyons, 1987; Udwin, 1993; Zeanah & Scheeringa, Chapter 6, this volume). Children who live with violence carry with them a fear and distrust of the world. Being the bystander to violence teaches children early and powerful lessons about the outside world. Children learn that the world may be hostile and unpredictable. They may have tremendous difficulty trusting in or being comforted by a teacher. Exposure to violence thus affects the way a child learns and the confidence with which he or she approaches new situations.

Children who grow up with violence have trouble getting along with their peers. They may be aggressive and misread social cues from others. Because they see their world as an unpredictable place, and because they have experienced unanticipated violence in their lives, they expect it from others. An accidental bump while waiting in line for the water fountain is experienced as purposeful aggression. The child responds accordingly by turning around and hitting the child who has jostled him or her.

These children have poor concentration and may be distractible in class. They may be preoccupied with worry about loved ones, or they may be distracted by memories of the violent events. Sometimes this worry translates into chronic anxiety, high activity levels, a general inability to focus on any task for too long, or extreme passivity or listlessness.

When hearing the realities of what some children are asked to cope with, it is no wonder that teachers, too, begin to feel helpless and hopeless about their ability to teach and support children. They begin to question whether they can help the children. A teacher vocalized this helplessness as she learned of the murder of the mother of one of her students: "I cannot deal with this . . . How can I expect to help this child if I can't even think about this horrible event?" In addition, the violence in children's lives may mirror violence in the lives of teachers. Some teachers may live in the same violent communities as their students and struggle with raising their own children in that environment. Also, some teachers may live in violent relationships. Unlike the field of mental health, in which professionals encourage supervision that includes self-reflection and examination, teachers have few opportunities to talk about the personal meanings and experiences in their lives.

Support for Teachers

It is imperative that teachers receive high-quality training and consistent supervisory support in order to adequately help children who live with violence (Garbarino, Dubrow, Kostelny, & Pardo, 1992; Levin, 1994). Specific training about the impact of violence in children's lives should be woven into preservice training and should be focused on, again, as a part of in-service training for teachers. College-level teacher training curricula should include material about working with children who are affected by violence.

Training for teachers may be divided into three content areas. The first component should cover specific information about general child development and the effects on children at differing ages of exposure to violence. This information should include a discussion of behavioral, cognitive, and developmental regressions or interferences that are consequences of exposure to violence. This training may include a discussion of posttraumatic stress disorder and how it affects children's classroom performance. It should contain specific information on domestic violence and its impact on children. Teachers should be exposed to this training both as a part of preservice education and in-service training. Training should also include information about media violence, the most ubiquitous source of exposure to violence for all children. In the context of training, teachers need practical opportunities to role-play class discussions of violent issues in the classroom and discussion with parents about sensitive issues. These role plays may provide opportunities to discuss domestic violence with parents, file a report of abuse or neglect with the local child welfare agency, or talk to children about a violent incident. Specific information about legal issues, abuse reporting laws, and the intersection of the criminal justice system should be included. There should also be information about conflict resolution skills training and mediation skills.

The second component of training should focus on resilience and coping in children. Research on resilience that emphasizes practical application is presented. It is important for teachers to be reminded that not every child who is exposed to violence is affected in the same way, and that many children make the best out of this adversity. Giving information about resilience and coping counteracts teachers' feelings of hopelessness.

The final component of training should help teachers look at their own reactions to and experiences with violence. This component encourages self-awareness and gives overt permission to teachers to talk about the emotional impact of the work on their lives. This discussion should be followed with a discussion about self-care and support.

The Child Witness to Violence Project has sponsored an intensive summer institute for teachers, in which the preceding topics were covered in a 5-day period. Interspersed with didactic presentations were opportunities for teachers to reflect about the emotional costs of their work and to share with each other classroom strategies that have worked for them. The seminar has been rated highly by teachers, both in terms of gaining new knowledge about the topic and making connections with other professionals in the field. In response to an evaluation conducted 2 months after the training, teachers elaborated that the aspect of the course that was most useful was gaining a greater appreciation of the "whole child." As one teacher stated, "I am now more interested than ever about what this child brings to the classroom, what his experiences have been at home. I realize that I can't teach this child if I don't have some awareness of his life outside of school." The second most appreciated aspect of the course was the opportunity to share experiences with other teachers. Teachers valued the opportunity to share the intense personal feelings that are mobilized when working with such children. Teachers began to see that it is not their personal weakness or failure that gives rise to such negative feelings but the realities of the work. This type of sharing reminds teachers that their reactions are normal and shared by many of their colleagues.

Supervision

It is imperative that teachers have access to ongoing professional supervision/consultation that provides an opportunity to reflect on the emotional difficulty of their work. In the previously mentioned seminars sponsored by the Child Witness to Violence Project for teachers, they recount their anguish at hearing children talk about the violence in their lives. Teachers complain of sleeplessness, nightmares, and somatic symptoms as a response to the stresses of the job. This type of stress leads to desensitization in teachers; it also leads to burnout and, eventually, a departure from the field of teaching.

The ideal supervisory relationship is based on nonjudgmental acceptance from the supervisor and allows for self-reflection and self-revelation. It is not the basis for evaluation of teacher performance or for educational planning or administrative discussion. It may be done individually or in small groups, we hope with a skilled facilitator.

The importance of school climate and administrative support for teachers' growth cannot be overestimated. Schools have an enormous potential for providing emotional support and nurturing for children (Garbarino et al., 1992). Therefore, schools must be recognized as safe havens for students, teachers, and even parents. The potential for schools to help children is maximized when administrators set a climate of respect for students, nonviolence, and positive beliefs in students' abilities. Administrators must be similarly positive about teachers, giving them the training and supervisory support they need. Because most children spend as much waking time at school as at home, this investment in teacher training and support is critical in helping children cope with violence.

HEALTH PROVIDERS' EXPERIENCES WITH CHILDREN WHO WITNESS VIOLENCE

The following case examples highlight issues that medical providers face in caring for children who are impacted by violence.

CASE EXAMPLE

Antonio, a 9-year-old boy, is seen at a neighborhood health clinic for a physical exam for summer camp. He walks into the office and hands his nurse practitioner, whom he knows well, a picture of himself that he has drawn for her. She is astonished to see that he has drawn himself armed with a knife and a machete, and that there is a mutilated victim on the ground. There is no known history of abuse or violence in this family. She is shocked by the picture and unsure about what questions to ask her patient and his family.

CASE EXAMPLE

Dr. Cole, a pediatric resident, saw a teen mother and her daughter in pediatric primary care clinic. The presenting complaint was chronic ear pain in the 3-year-old girl. Dr. Cole noticed that the mother had a bruise under her eye. In response to his query about the injury, the young woman casually mentioned that she and her boyfriend had a fight, but that "Everything is OK now."

Situations such as these are encountered daily by pediatric health providers, who find themselves faced with complex psychosocial problems and severe time constraints with which to explore or solve the problems. In the above-mentioned case examples, practitioners must decide whom to interview in a family, how to ask difficult questions about exposure to violence or domestic violence, whether to report the situations to child protective agencies, and what follow-up is appropriate. All this must be done in the context of a brief office visit. It is no wonder that some medical providers candidly admit that they avoid asking certain questions that pertain to violence, because they have neither the time nor the skills to address the solutions. This avoidance is particularly evident in family situations of domestic violence (Sugg & Inui, 1992; Wissow, Wilson, Roter, Larson, & Berman, 1992).

As is the case with teachers, many medical providers state that their training has not adequately prepared them to face multiproblem families or to handle sensitive issues such as violence in families. Medical providers are trained to make rapid evaluations and diagnoses, and to provide definitive solutions. However, families who live with chronic violence defy speedy evaluations and simple treatment. In the training that the Child Witness to Violence Project has provided for health care professionals, participants (particularly physicians) have voiced both frustration and helplessness in providing helpful interventions to families with violence-related problems. They express a sense of failure, which stems, in part, from the authority that society invests in physicians. Physicians are supposed to have the answers, and there are no easy answers for children who live with chronic violence. This helplessness leads to avoidance of the issue altogether.

Thus, children's experiences with violence may be overlooked by medical professionals (Wolf & Korsch, 1995). Children may be placed at increased risk for physical injury and emotional trauma. (For example, the 3-year-old mentioned earlier is at increased risk for child abuse because she lives with a mother who is a victim of domestic violence (Augustyn et al., 1995).

Training

Training for medical practitioners must include four components. The first component consists of didactic information about the impact of exposure to violence for children, posttraumatic stress syndrome in children, and the dynamics of domestic violence. The second component should include training about how to ask questions sensitively in a pediatric interview (Groves, 1994a). Practitioners can learn how to frame questions to parents that are neither accusatory or condemning. Questions about how conflict is handled at home and neighborhood safety should begin with the first newborn visit and continue with appropriate developmental specificity throughout adolescence.

The third component of training includes information about community resources and the legal system. Medical practitioners may lack knowledge about resources and systems that affect the families with which they work. However, complex problems demand collaborative response. This knowledge is particularly important in evaluating domestic violence situations, in which practitioners must assess the safety of mothers and inform them about resources and legal options.

The final component of training emphasizes the importance of active and empathic listening. Physicians, who may believe that the only useful intervention is one that alleviates the problem, have difficulty believing in the value of empathic listening. They must be reminded of the power they have to validate their patients' emotional experiences. Patients may feel relieved when they are accurately understood.

MULTISYSTEM INVOLVEMENT AT THE COMMUNITY LEVEL: A POTENTIAL SOLUTION

This chapter has targeted parents and groups of caregivers of children for intervention. The inherent risk of approaching the complicated problem of community and family violence in this way is that it implies that the solution lies in working with various professional groups, separately. In fact, the most promising solution lies in a broad, collaborative effort that uses the skills and perspectives from *all* stakeholders in a community. The best community intervention involves parents, teachers, community members, health workers, police officers, court officials, religious leaders, and human service agencies, all working together for the common goal of restoring a sense of stability and safety to a community.

There are innovative collaboratives in major cities across the country that bring together diverse groups of professionals to reduce crime and change the way people feel about their community. In Massachusetts, the Attorney General's office has sponsored an initiative in the city of Boston that builds on the community policing efforts of that city. This initiative is targeted at the community within Boston with the second highest number of murders, violent crime, and domestic violence calls. This collaborative effort includes police, the District Attorney's office, the courts, community business leaders, youth agencies, community health centers, and a hospital. By providing more police and prosecutorial resources, the response to neighborhood crime is more efficient. When arrests are made, the criminals are prosecuted more quickly in court. The increased efficiency gives community residents the feeling that their concerns are being heard. The greater confidence in police and courts engendered by the approach encourages citizens to report crime and cooperate with police in investigations, resulting in more arrests and convictions. Police in this community understand that responding to residents' more "trivial" concerns, such as abandoned cars and graffiti, increases citizens' confidence in them. They also understand that these seemingly "trivial" concerns are important elements in citizens' perceptions of their community.

Another feature of this initiative is the linking of criminal justice professionals with child health and mental health professionals. This linkage has been recognized as important by both mental health providers and police officers. It has been implemented in several ways. First, there are seminars offered for police officers on child development and mental health issues. Officers are selected for this course by the police captains. Typically, sergeants, community service officers, domestic violence detectives, and juvenile officers have been targeted for this training. Instructors for the course include physicians, social workers, victim advocates, and other human service professionals from the community. The goal of the seminar is to increase the skills of police officers in working with children and families. This includes skills at recognizing the impact of violence and crime on children, interviewing children sensitively, and making appropriate referrals to professionals in the community. Officers learn basic concepts of child development and sharpen their observational skills. Evaluations of this seminar have been overwhelmingly positive, with a consistent comment focusing on increased understanding of professionals' roles in the community. Police know how to use mental health services, and perhaps more important, health and mental health professionals know how to use police and the court system for their clients. Police also have additional skills in recognizing the impact of violence on children, especially domestic violence. Their reporting has expanded to include the names of children who have witnessed violence. In one instance, police initiated a community meeting with mental health professionals following a brutal murder that was witnessed by many children. They assumed this leadership, because they saw it as part of their follow-up responsibilities to the community. After participation in this seminar, officers see the connection between exposure to violence and subsequent involvement in violent behavior. They see their role with children, therefore, as connected to prevention of future criminal behavior.

The second feature of this initiative is a closer collaboration between child mental health specialists and court professionals. This collaboration has been especially needed in the area of domestic violence. Judges and court officials have been candid about the difficulty they have in making decisions for children about custody and visitation in domestic violence situations. Because they are faced with two antagonistic adults, their goal is often to create agreements that minimize conflict and risk of further abuse. However, the specific needs of children may be overlooked. There are few guidelines about whether a child should have visitation with an abusive father, and if so, under what circumstances? Training has been instituted for court professionals about the impact of domestic violence on children that includes guidelines about making decisions in visitation and custody matters. In addition, domestic violence advocates at the court now refer children of battered women for support services.

These collaborations between professionals who may not have previously worked together have several important benefits. First, the perception of crime and dangerousness in this community is changing. Residents have increased confidence in the police and believe that their community is improving. This confidence was reflected in a recent neighborhood survey that showed a 10% increase in 1 year in the number of residents who felt comfortable going out at night. Although it has not been measured, this sense of increased stability must help parents in their efforts to reassure children about the neighborhood. Children are getting to know the officers on their streets. They see them as positive models of authority and safety. (The police have greatly increased their popularity with children by handing out "Cop Cards," trading cards with their names and pictures on them. See the accompanying illustration.) Second, rates for violent crime have dropped, and the efficiency of arrest and conviction of criminals has improved. Third, police and court personnel have increased skills at recognizing children who need specialized mental health intervention and are able to make the appropriate referrals. Fourth, social workers and mental health clinicians are more able to work with the criminal justice system.

CASE EXAMPLE

A 7-year-old Vietnamese boy was brought to the police by his mother after disclosing that he had been raped by a man in the community. His mother spoke with the Vietnamese citizen liaison whom she knew and felt comfortable talking with. However, she adamantly refused to file a report directly with the police, believing that such a report would bring disgrace to her family. As a Vietnamese refugee, she had no confidence in the police and believed that sexual crimes were best never mentioned. She was, however, horrified that her son had been raped and worried that this would affect her son's emotional health. The Vietnamese liaison convinced the mother to bring her son to one of the mental health professionals who ran the child development seminar for police officers. Because the police liaison knew this clinician, she was able to reassure the mother that her concerns would be heard, and her needs for privacy would be respected. After two sessions with the mother and child, the mental health clinician, who had also come to know the criminal justice system well, convinced the mother to report the crime. She listened carefully to the mother's humiliation about the event and her concerns about privacy. She reassured the mother that she was doing the best thing for her child by reporting; she promised to accompany her for the interview; and she agreed to provide follow-up services for the family. She was able to tell the mother and son exactly what would happen and provided consultation to the officer and attorney who heard the complaint. The boy was interviewed sensitively and with respect for his culture. The crime was reported, an arrest was made, and the mother and child continued to receive counseling services.

This case is an example of how collaboration resulted in a prompt arrest—in this case, of a man who was wanted for other sexual assaults—and improved services for the family, both from the police and from the mental health system. These services were delivered in a way that acknowledged the family's perceptions and cultural beliefs, and increased their confidence in the judicial system.

SUMMARY

An inherent part of helping children who have been affected by violence is to provide information and support to the network of caregivers in the children's lives. Each of these caregivers has a special role to play. Parents are the first-line buffers and protectors of children. Teachers help children make sense of the world and provide a safe haven for them to learn. Health care providers ensure that children grow to be healthy and productive adults. This chapter has provided strategies for supporting these caregivers in their efforts to help children who are affected by violence. It is only by this united support that communities will succeed in protecting their children against the effects of exposure to violence.

REFERENCES

Augustyn, M., Parker, S., Groves, B., & Zuckerman, B. (1995). Silent victims: Children who witness violence. *Journal of Contemporary Pediatrics, 12*(8), 35–57.

Carmen, E., Rieker, P., & Mills, T. (1984). Victims of violence and psychiatric illness. *American Journal of Psychiatry, 141*(3), 378–383.

Craig, S. (1992, September). The educational needs of young children living with violence. *Phi Delta Kappan*, 67–71.

Drell, M., Siegel, C., & Gaensbauer, T. (1993). Post-traumatic stress disorder. In C. H. Zeanah (Ed.), *Handbook of infant mental health* (pp. 291–304). New York: Guilford Press.

Edelman, M. W. (1992). *The measure of our success.* Boston: Beacon Press.

Emde, R. (1993). The horror! The horror! Reflections on our culture of violence and its implications for early development and morality. *Psychiatry, 56*, 119–123.

Freud, A., & Burlingham, D. (1943). *War and children.* New York: Medical War Books.

Garbarino, J., Dubrow, N., Kostelny, K., & Pardo, C. (1992). *Children in danger: Coping with the consequences of community violence.* San Francisco: Jossey-Bass.

Garbarino, J., Kostelny, K., & Dubrow, N. (1991). What children can tell us about living in danger. *American Psychologist, 46*(4), 376–383.

Groves, B. (1994a). Children who witness violence. In S. Parker & B. Zuckerman (Eds.), *Behavioral and developmental pediatrics: A handbook for primary care* (pp. 334–336). Boston: Little, Brown.

Groves, B. (1994b). The Child Witness to Violence Project. *Discharge Planning Update*, *14*, 14–18.

Groves, B., & Mazur, S. (1995, April). Shelter from the storm: Using the classroom to help children the cope with violence. *Child Care Information Exchange*, *102*, 14–18.

Groves, B., Zuckerman, B., Marans, S., & Cohen, D. (1993). Silent victims: Children who witness violence. *Journal of the American Medical Association*, *269*, 262–264.

Jackson, B. (1994). Three coping strategies for parents living in violent environments. In J. Osofsky & E. Fenichel (Eds.), *Hurt, healing, hope: Caring for infants and toddlers in violent environments* (pp. 12–13). Arlington, VA: Zero-to-Three/National Center for Clinical Infant Programs.

Levin, D. (1994). *Teaching young children in violent times: Building a peaceable classroom*. Cambridge, MA: Educators for Social Responsibility.

Lyons, J. (1987). Posttraumatic stress dieorder in children and adolescents: A review of the literature. In S. Chess & A. Thomas (Eds.), *Annual progress in child psychiatry and development* (pp. 451–467). New York: Brunner/Mazel.

Osofsky, J., & Fenichel, E. (Eds.). (1994). *Hurt, healing, hope: Caring for infants and toddlers in violent environments*. Arlington, VA: Zero-to-Three/National Center for Clinical Infant Programs.

Sugg, K., & Inui, T. (1992). Primary care physicians' response to domestic violence. *Journal of the American Medical Association*, *267*(23), 3157–3160.

Taylor, L., Zuckerman, B., Harik, V., & Groves, B. (1994). Witnessing violence by young children and their mothers. *Journal of Developmental and Behavioral Pediatrics*, *15*, 120–123.

Udwin, O. (1993). Children's reactions to traumatic events. *Journal of Child Psychology and Psychiatry*, *34*, 115–128.

Walker, L. D. (1984). *The battered women's syndrome*. New York: Springer.

Wallach, L. (1993). Helping children cope with violence. *Young Children*, *48*(4), 4–11.

Wissow, L., Wilson, M., Roter, D., Larson, S., & Berman, H. (1992). Family violence and the evaluation of behavioral concerns in a pediatric primary care clinic. *Medical Care*, *30*(5) (Suppl.), MS150–MS165.

Wolf, D., & Korsch, B. (1995). Witnessing domestic violence during childhood and adolescence: Implications for pediatric practice. *Pediatrics*, *94*(4), 594–599.

Wrate, R., Rooney, A., & Thomas, M. (1985). Post-natal depression and child development. *British Journal of Psychiatry*, *146*, 622–627.

Zahn-Waxler, C., Cummings, E., & Iannoff R. (1984). Young offspring of depressed parents: A population at risk for affective problems and childhood depression. In D. Cicchetti & K. Schneider-Rosen (Eds.), *Childhood depression* (pp. 81–105). San Francisco: Jossey-Bass.

Zuckerman, B., Augustyn, M., Groves, B., & Parker, S. (1995). Silent victims revisited: The special case of domestic violence. *Pediatrics*, *96*(3), 511–513.

Zuckerman, B., & Beardslee, W. (1987). Maternal depression: A concern for pediatricians. *Pediatrics*, *79*(1), 110–117.

10

Experiencing Violence in a Developmental Context

STEVEN MARANS
ANNE ADELMAN

BACKGROUND

As the number of children exposed to violence in the United States has increased, so too have concerns about the short- and long-term effects of such exposure (Marans, Berkman, & Cohen, 1996; Pynoos, Steinberg, & Wraith, 1995; Osofsky, 1995; Singer, Anglin, Song, & Lunghofer, 1995; Taylor, Zuckerman, Harick, & Groves, 1992). Rather than viewing violence or its effects as uniform across ages and experiences, it is important to recognize that childhood exposure to violence occurs in the context of shifting modes of adaptation, which reflect the unfolding maturational process and developmental fluctuations in the nature and expression of children's impulses, wishes, and fears. Children's experience of violence is not only determined by the events they witness, but also by their own capacity to mediate both external and internal sources of danger, and to contend with the pressure of conflictual urges and longings that change according to phases of development. These factors are linked to emotional, cognitive, and physical capacities that shape children's responses to internal and external demands, expectations, and impingements. The aggression, for example, that is expressed in the violent acts that children witness also plays a central role in normal development. In this latter context, aggressivity serves as a means of achieving a sense of power and competence; it is also a source of conflict between love and hate. Over the course of development, the more direct enactments of the toddler's hitting, biting, and kicking shift to the pre-schooler's fantasies and play of destructive power, to the competition on the school-age child's sports field, to, finally, the vicissitudes of affection and anger that are a part of adolescent and adult relationships (Marans & Cohen, 1991, 1996; A. Freud & Burlingham, 1973). When the capacity to move from such early, direct displays to more prosocial expressions of aggressivity is undermined by poverty, family dysfunction, overstim-ulation, and threatened or actual physical danger, the basic preconditions for feeling competent—including physical safety, stable relationships, and success in achieving desired goals—are eradicated.

Multiple Experiences of Violence

The Child Development–Community Policing (CD-CP) Program (Marans et al., 1995) and its 24-hour Consultation Service has afforded investigators the opportunity to observe children of varying ages and backgrounds and their families shortly after their exposure to violent incidents that include shootings, stabbings, beatings, maimings, and death. In this work, we have witnessed and investigated the impact of violence on the developmental process of infants and young children. Violence, here, refers to a situation in which individuals' actions carry the intention to injure or to abuse; in which actions become furious, turbulent, and potentially lethal; in which individuals become excited or enraged to a point of loss of control; and in which the essential compo-nents of the sense of psychological safety—regulation of affective states, predictability of the environment, consistency in caregivers' respon-siveness, physical safety and well-being, containment of anxieties and terrors—are shattered. In considering a child's exposure to violence, it is essential to understand the multiplicity of experiences and responses that are determined by an interplay of factors both within the child and in his or her surroundings, which include:

- Characteristics of the violence itself—that is, the child's relation-ship to the perpetrator and victim, proximity to the incident, response of the caregivers.
- The developmental phase of the child who is exposed—that is, the status of emotional and cognitive resources for mediating anxiety associated with objective and fantasized dangers.
- The familial and community context of the violent incident—that is, is the incident isolated and unusual or part of a chronic pattern of experience of daily life?
- Recognition of, and sustained responses to, the possible effects of the child's exposure to violence by family members, school personnel, and community institutions.

Children seen through the CD-CP program have ranged in age from 2 to 17 years. Initial clinical contact has occurred from within minutes of a violent event to several days later. The immediacy of clinical contact has given investigators an unfolding picture of the children's and families' responses from the acute moment to longer term adaptations.

Although there is tremendous variation among children, at the acute moment of a traumatic event, common observations have been reported, including:

- Intense longing for the presence of and concern about the safety of primary caregivers.
- Disbelief and denial of the outcome or occurrence of the event.
- Revival of memories and much talk about previous losses, injuries, fights witnessed.
- Emotional lability that can range from isolation of affects to tearfulness (although not so common) to rage and replaying of events with ideas that might have altered the real outcome (e.g., "If only he had . . . ," "If only I had . . .") and developing intervention fantasies (Pynoos et al., 1995).
- Attribution of blame to those not involved in the violent event (e.g., with social institutions, etc.) and attendant, at times explosive, anger.
- Reveling in the excitement of the action with bravado (e.g., talk of the type of weapons used; who got "capped," "waxed," or "aired").
- Apparent indifference (e.g., "it [violence] happens all the time, it's no big deal")

In both the acute response and longer term adaptation, how the child makes sense of what he or she witnessed and the particular meanings that emerge over time as the child begins to digest and to organize fragments of traumatic memory are embedded in a developmental matrix. A child's responses to traumatic events thus reflect both the unique characteristics of the event, as well as the particular phase-specific concerns, anxieties, and fears that are stimulated and made more complicated by what the child has witnessed. In order to understand both the child's greatest areas of vulnerability to trauma and the phase-specific attempts at restitution and/or symptom formation, it is essential that the clinician consider nodal developmental constellations as they determine the specific experience of each individual child.

Violent Trauma in a Developmental Context

Children's exposure to violence, whether occurring in the home, on the streets, or in the school, may lead to overwhelming levels of stimulation and ego disorganization. Numerous contemporary investigators have contributed to our understanding of childhood trauma, whether elaborating on the traumatic moment and typologies of associated phenomena (Pynoos et al., 1995; van der Kolk, 1994; van der Kolk, Greenberg, Boyd, & Krystal, 1985; Terr, 1989, 1991; Marans, 1994; Marans, Berkman, & Cohen, 1996), the nature of intervention fantasies (Pynoos et al., 1996), rates of children's exposure (Martinez & Richters, 1993; Osofsky, Wewers, Hann, & Fick, 1993; Schwab-Stone, 1996; Garbarino, Dubrown, Kostelny, & Pardo, 1992; Taylor et al., 1992; Singer et al., 1995), or the neurophysiology of mediation/regulation of stress/overstimulation (Southwick et al., 1993; Perry, 1994 and Chapter 7, this volume; van der Kolk, 1994; Yehuda & MacFarlane, 1995).

Perhaps one of the most important elements of earlier conceptualizations of childhood trauma is the notion that internal, or endogenous, dangers change as development progresses, for example, from the threat of loss of the mother as object to loss of bodily integrity, to loss of the mother's love and, ultimately, to loss of the superego's love, and call for alterations in the individual's relationship to the external world (S. Freud, 1926/1974). As Freud suggested, these feelings have their roots in "some situation that has been experienced in the past," and he points out that "in relation to the traumatic situation, in which the subject is helpless, external and internal dangers, real dangers and instinctual demands converge" (p. 168).

Any experience can be traumatically overwhelming for both children and adults. When a situation arises in which the individual's protective and defensive resources are overwhelmed and he or she cannot metabolize an exceptional experience, psychic trauma may ensue. However, what sets childhood trauma apart from adulthood trauma is that, for children, the adaptive capacities, defensive structures, and internal resources—as these are determined by developmental processes—are vastly different than those potentially available to adults. In the throes of the maturational process, children have fewer and more uneven psychological resources at their disposal; their developing defensive organization is acutely vulnerable to traumatic disruptions, derailments, and impingements from the environment. The child's experience of helpless surrender to overwhelming circumstances threatens to undermine newly consolidated and most recently attained developmental capacities. Such regression often leads the child toward earlier configurations of needs, fears, conflicts, and anxieties, as well as earlier modes of mediating them. As children progress through infancy, preschool years, and school-age years into adolescence and adulthood, the nature of their defensive and adaptive capacities is transformed with the unfolding of the developmental processes, becoming more robust, less brittle, and more able to withstand the regressive shifts in functioning at times of extreme stress, whether internally or externally founded. Children whose development is already fragile, and who have not attained the optimal potential of each developmental phase, are at greatest risk. In light of this situation, considering the child's developmental status can help bring us closer to understanding the experience of childhood exposure to violence and trauma.

INFANTS AND TODDLERS

The early development of affective life unfolds within the matrix of the mother–infant relationship, through which the baby comes to know itself, others, and the world in which it lives. The normal developmental tasks of infancy involve the gradual unfolding of a sense of self-consolidation and the emerging capacity to regulate internal states and achieve a state of homeostasis. Neurophysiological development, the ability to engage in and sustain mutually satisfying reciprocal interactions, a sense of orientation to objects and people, and the development of awareness and cognition, flourish at moments when the infant, untroubled by internal distress, interacts with the world with the calm attention of an alert, active state. These tasks are facilitated by two types of experience. One is related to the regular, reliable "good-enough" care the infant receives, including being bathed, held, and rocked, whereas the other arises out of accrued experiences of shifts in internal states and consequent state regulation (Mayes & Cohen, 1993).

Infants must gradually acquire the ability to manage a range of affective state internally and, when they cannot, to develop an ever-increasing array of defensive strategies to protect the self against an onslaught of intolerable emotions. In early infancy, the good-enough mother's empathic sense of her infant's states and her intuitive awareness of its ever-growing affect array enable her to serve as a filter, or auxiliary stimulus barrier. In this way, she allows the child to experience increasingly intense affective states, intervening to provide comfort, and soothing when the tension level threatens to be overwhelming (Krystal, 1988). Gradually, the child internalizes the parent's regulatory function. The caregiver–child matrix thus forms the basis and organization of the baby's earliest affective experiences. Adequate environmental provision permits the infant to develop a cohesive sense of self, which leads to the capacity for purposeful, goal-oriented movement and direction.

A world made unpredictable and hazardous by the intrusion of unanticipated and overwhelming dangers compromises the infant's healthy curiosity and increasing exploration of the environment. Violent events threaten a child's sense of secure attachment, which is an essential, stable base from which the child can venture forth in exploration of the surrounding world. Confronted with adults who harm or fail to protect them, young children may turn inward, no longer expect to find help from adults or others, and attempt to rely on their own (largely inadequate) internal resources.

This unreliability can be particularly devastating to toddlers, whose increased ability to function autonomously rests on the parent's ability to encourage and applaud their strivings toward mastery, while remaining a constant and reassuring source of support and mirroring. Such young children may increasingly doubt their own competency, and may gradually come to avoid contact with potential sources of help, instead of seeking out trusting and helpful relationships (A. Freud & Burlingham, 1943; Hellman, 1962; Laor et al., 1995; Furman, Solnit, & Lang, 1968; Osofsky, 1995).

Conversely, young children who experience violence may evidence their distress by desperately clinging to a parent or caregiver, unable to tolerate the peril of repeated loss. In this case, one may see behaviors that include anxiety, clinginess, inconsolability, sleep disturbances, toileting problems, and temper tantrums related to difficulties in separation. For the young child who is learning to actively master his or her own aggressive impulses—in increasing efforts to conform to parental expectations and, ultimately, internal, or superego, demands—exposure to uncontrolled hostility on the part of others may unleash a wave of regressed, disorganized, and unchecked aggressivity. This, in turn, can produce heightened fearfulness and anxiety for the child, now unsure of either the limits of his or her rageful, destructive urges or the caregiver's capacity to help contain the aggressive behaviors and destructive fantasies.

LARRY

> After his 18-month-old sister was drowned to death in the bathtub while the siblings shared a bath, 2½-year-old Larry became irritable, defiant, and incapable of tolerating even minimal amounts of frustration. Larry was sent to live with his maternal grandparents by the child protective services agency. He was told that his sister was in heaven, where she was happy and well. However, this explanation failed to allay his concern; he repeatedly looked for her and asked to see her. His evident confusion about recent events, including, from his 2-year-old point of view, his sister's mystifying disappearance, his perplexity about why she did not return and why he could not see her, the grief of the adults around him, and his unexplained separation from his mother, left him anxious and insecure. He needed constant reassurance that neither his significant caregivers nor, indeed, he himself would disappear and be gone forever, like his sister. As the weeks progressed, Larry's behaviors became increasingly dis-

ruptive at home, with frequent temper tantrums, demandingness, and clinginess.

There were various ways in which Larry could give expression to his frightening experience of the violent death of his sister. Both Larry's mother and grandmother were frustrated and disappointed by his increased difficulties in separating, which they construed as his "acting like a baby" and "trying to get attention." They had previously viewed him as a precocious youngster and were proud of his independent ways and his saucy manners. Unsure of him now, they alternately indulged him and rebuked him. They were covert in their praise of him and tended to be watchful and to discipline him often, encouraging him to "be a good boy." His family's attempts to make him "grow up" only increased his anxiety and the very behaviors that they found so irritating. Larry became more aggressive, frequently lashing out at his caregivers, kicking and throwing. His preoccupation with themes of aggression, violence, and power were demonstrated in his perseverative play that included dinosaurs that battled, animals that attacked, and baby dolls that were strangled. He was especially worried about his own bodily safety, and was frightened by the intensity of his aggressivity.

What began as play often deteriorated into disorganized, explosive displays in which the line between imagination and reality became frighteningly blurred. The adult caregivers were often unable to recognize when he needed their help in tempering the level of excited, violent activities and the anxiety that often followed. Larry's mother and grandmother began to use the clinical meetings as an opportunity to explore the meanings of his symptomatic behaviors and to respond with increased appreciation for his developmentally appropriate needs. For example, recognizing his anxiety associated with leaving home, they permitted Larry to carry a small toy from home when he went to day care. After a few months, Larry's mother gave him a photograph of his sister and allowed him to keep it in a special place he chose.

PRESCHOOLERS

For preschool children (4–6 years old), normative issues regarding competition with same-sex parents, sibling rivalry, power and size, curiosity, struggles between loving and hating, and concerns about bodily integrity, take the foreground, providing the context in which children experience violent events. Such was the case involving seven children, aged 5 and 6 years, who were sitting on a school bus when their classmate was struck in the head by a bullet that went astray in a gun battle between rival drug dealers (Marans, 1994). The wound was not fatal. The children were seen by CD-CP clinicians within minutes of the shooting. Through drawings and discussion, each of the children initially focused on the wish to see their mothers, and on concerns that something awful might happen to them (e.g., the mothers might be shot themselves, get into a car accident on the way to picking up the children, or get lost). As police officers and clinicians reassured the children that each of their parents had been notified and were on their way, the discussion with the children shifted. As one child asked a clinician to draw a picture of a head, all of the children began discussing their questions about what happens when a head is shot with a bullet. Although there were some questions about what was happening to the friend who had been shot, the majority of questions and comments had to do with curiosity about bodily functions—How much blood does the body have? Can parts of the body fall off?—and quickly turned to a more spirited group discussion about various physical feats each could perform. The discussion was punctuated by the sidelong glances to the door as parents began to arrive to pick up their children (Marans et al., 1995).

Five of the seven children received follow-up psychotherapy because of enduring posttraumatic stress symptoms—disruptions in sleeping and eating; increased separation anxiety; and hypervigilance, generalized anxiety, and avoidant behaviors—that were not part of the premorbid history. Each of these children was in treatment for 4–6 months. The presenting symptoms resolved as the children could be helped to disentangle and clarify what they had witnessed from the age-expectable fantasies and conflicts that were aroused, exacerbated, and complicated by the shooting.

Young children who witness real-life damage to limbs, gunshots to the body, or bloody scenes of violence may worry profoundly about their own bodies being whole and kept together. Similarly, children who witness their parents or caregivers engage in violent fights may be terrified that *one* aspect of their competitive wishes for an exclusive relationship with one of the partners may in fact come true. In addition, preschool children's exposure to interpersonal violence may introduce additional confusion as they are consolidating their sense of right and wrong. In the aftermath of exposure to violence, the unreliability of the developing sense of justice, or conscience, only heightens their anxiety as they attempt to monitor and contain the enactment of their own hostile and destructive urges.

In the face of both external and internal dangers, a range of symptoms may follow, including difficulties in separating from caregivers; difficulties sleeping, eating and toileting; fearful avoidance and phobic reactions; social withdrawal; poor attention; provocative and demanding behavior; regressed or infantile presentation.

When exposure to interpersonal violence breaches the boundary between fantasy and reality, identifications may also be impaired, particularly when caregivers or significant figures in the child's life are violent and/or victimized. For example, a boy's sense of his own masculinity may be complicated if the primary figure for identification demonstrates his manhood through hostile and aggressive behavior. Similarly, for a young girl whose mother is either an overwhelmed, bruised victim or an aggressive attacker, the model for feminine identification is based on frightening images of either helpless submission or destructive power. For both, intimate adult relationships may continue to be viewed in their earliest, infantile forms, dominated by excitement, danger, pain and suffering. This was the case for Dayvon.

DAYVON

Dayvon, a 5-year-old boy who had witnessed his father murder his mother and then shoot himself to death, struggled with what it meant to wish to be like his father—big, powerful, manly—without having to kill his longed-for mother or to receive the fatal punishment that his father inflicted on himself. For this boy, the complication of normative conflicts led to difficulties both in his new home with his grandparents and at school. Dayvon alternated dramatically between, on the one hand, being a hostile, combative, and "tough guy" who was fearless and dangerously powerful, and on the other hand, a fearful infant who could only seek much-needed emotional contact with mother substitutes through clingy, demanding behaviors.

Magical Thinking

Witnessing or being exposed to violence also impacts on the young child's development of reality testing (Marans et al., 1996), making the presence of real experience of death, loss, or bodily injury especially powerful and disruptive. In the aftermath of violence, children's inner lives are affected by their knowledge that things that should reside only within the depths of unarticulable, archaic fantasy, are no longer confined to fantasy. The violent horrors that belong to the world of the child's most primitive fears and terrors are materialized in real-life experiences. In the inner worlds of these children, there is a danger of a blurring of boundaries between fantasy and reality. Individuals who have undergone traumatic events often have difficulty in "maintaining the 'make-believe' quality of fantasy" (Levine, 1982, p. 75). Traumatized children do not have difficulty in drawing the line between what is real and what is unreal, but rather, in distinguishing what is *not* unreal—although it should be—from what is, indeed, the product of their own imagination. A reality infused with terror collides with the world of fantasy and symbolic representation.

A young child's developing representational world permits the child to begin to contain the anxiety associated with forbidden wishes, to give expression, in fantasy, to conflictual urges, and to delay gratification of impulses. Nonetheless, powerful urges press forward, and forbidden wishes that challenge the rudimentary representational capacities rise to the surface. Children who witness or are exposed to violence may evidence confusion about the boundary between the imagined "bad" thoughts they hold inside—the greedy wishes, rageful fantasies, or urges to mess they have attempted to renounce in favor of gaining adult approbation and avoiding censure—and the real-life events that terrify them. Although some children may rely on their magical thinking in an attempt to reassert a sense of control, as a form of restitution in the face of overwhelming helplessness, such thinking may allow them to wrongly conclude that the "evil" thoughts they secretly harbor are indeed dangerous and powerful, and are the root of the "bad" events. The resulting harsh self-evaluation leads to internal confusion, feelings of shame and badness, threatened loss of the real object or loss of love, giving rise to heightened anxiety and attendant symptom formation (Marans, 1994).

Similarly, for the young child whose level of thinking is preoperational, abstract events and concepts such as "death," "heaven," and "God" are confusing and easily misconstrued, with the associated danger of mystification and misapprehensions about the world. A child attempting to make sense of fragmentary knowledge and frightening memories may generate his or her own "explanations," often fantastical and grotesque in nature, that are far scarier or more distressing than what has actually occurred. Such faulty explanations may be accompanied by the onset of behaviors aimed at restoring some sense of order and predictability, which ultimately fail to provide relief, such as perseverative play or ritualistic behaviors. Because young children's thinking can be so concrete, for example, reassuring talk of "heavenly resting places" may also give rise to frightening fantasies of meeting up once again with the victim of violence and attempting to repair the loss, or come to grips with it, while also being terrified by the imagined vengeance that may accompany such a ghostly visit.

SCHOOL-AGE CHILDREN

The next phase of development, latency, occurring between ages 7 and 12, introduces a new context in which the child experiences and organizes his or her exposure to violence. Continued development of intellectual, sensorimotor, and social skills and opportunities offers the school-age child various pathways for less direct expression of the urges and normative conflicts that dominated earlier phases of development. For example, close friendships, involvement with a peer group, and relationships with other admired adults or teenagers support the child's shift away from the exclusive reliance on parents, while introducing an expanded range for the child's exploration of the world outside the family. Optimally, the curiosity about the parents' intimate life, anatomical differences, and the origin of babies that dominated earlier years can now be exercised both in and outside of school. The school-age child is now capable of having a clear sense of right and wrong, of having empathy with the feelings of others, and of "playing by the rules" (Marans et al., 1996). Optimally, the school-age child engages in aspects of daily living such as hygiene, dressing, and looking after possessions with greater autonomy. The capacity for operational thought and problem solving, along with increased frustration tolerance, increases the range of potential activities and sources of satisfaction.

For school-age children, the greatest threat is the reemergence or breakthrough of earlier longings and urges that are now felt to be too babyish, dependent, or intimate, and undermine their emerging sense of competence and autonomy. For that reason, the school-age child's close encounter with violence may be extremely disruptive, requiring various attempts to ward off the associated feelings of fear and helplessness. As with younger children, school-age children may respond to their exposure to violence with circumscribed symptoms, involving sleeping difficulties, nightmares, worries about burglars, bodily injury, and death. In addition, regression to earlier modes of relating to parents may be prominent. For example, increased struggles over food, self-care, schoolwork, or household responsibilities may be some of the behavioral phenomena that accompany children's attempts to defend against and give expression to the anxiety associated with witnessing interpersonal violence.

AMANDA

Eight-year-old Amanda was referred for evaluation after her 14-year-old brother fatally stabbed her mother's boyfriend of 2 months. Amanda reported that she was asleep at the time of the incident, but in the days following, she experienced recurrent nightmares, fearfulness, distractibility, and difficulty separating from her mother. As a young child, Amanda had been exposed to numerous distressing events after her parents' divorce, at which time her father began to stalk and terrorize the family.

Following the murder, Amanda was preoccupied with themes of danger, violence, and lack of protection. In play, pretending to be under assault by a hungry, man-eating dinosaur, she developed elaborate safety devices to secure her hiding spots and built an arsenal of weapons with which to defend herself. She played hide-and-seek games that gradually reached peaks of excitement mingled with foreboding. During this period, she maneuvered to have illicit telephone conversations with her imprisoned father—contact that she knew had been forbidden by the terms of her father's jail sentence. The phone calls gave rise to fantasies of being reunited with her idealized father. As her excitement mounted, so did her fearfulness, dread, and shame. In this instance, the more recent events—the death of her mother's boyfriend, which had transformed her brother into a murderer—had stirred memories of earlier times with a father who was both exciting and beloved, and simultaneously terrifying and dangerous. The intensity of her yearning for her father illustrates her powerful wish to deny and undo the reality of her memories of terror, as well as her inability to relinquish the arousal laden with excitation and dread associated with her father.

When there is no success in helping a child to reorganize and resume progressive development, symptoms may become chronic adaptations to feelings of helplessness and fear. In the wake of exposure to violence, there may be an accretion of secondary disruptions to developmental progression. For example, the child's initial withdrawal into fantasy and inattentiveness at school leads to academic failure, which now serves as an additional source of lowered self-esteem. The response of turning passive into active may move from teasing to bullying, to the child's dominant representation of him- or herself as a strong but bad kid. Similarly, identifying with the aggressor may become a chronic hedge against feeling vulnerable to attack as the child courts recognition and affiliation with the toughest figures on the neighborhood streets and becomes involved in antisocial and violent activities. Whether immediately or long after a violent event, school-age boys in particular may respond primarily with excitement or awe about the technological power of weapons and their effects. These responses may be misconstrued as evidence that they are not upset, disturbed, or affected by what they have seen. Often, it is because of this initial presentation that many of the children who witness violence in the streets of their neighborhoods are not identified as at-risk or in need of greater parental and, perhaps, professional attention.

LEROY

Leroy, an 8-year-old boy, attends a therapy group for children who are HIV-affected. He lives in a violent neighborhood where drug houses and drug lords preside. His mother is HIV-positive, and he has lost several family members to drugs and violence. Leroy was having numerous difficulties both at home and in school. His teachers reported that during classes, Leroy seemed distracted and inattentive, staring out the window and often not responding when addressed. In the past few weeks, he had begun to exhibit increasingly dangerous and reckless behaviors, spoke perseveratively about guns, shootings, and accidents he had witnessed, and expressed vague fears that he himself would come to harm.

On the evening that his mother was hospitalized for a surgical procedure, there was a drug-related shooting behind Leroy's house. Forty shots were fired. The next day in group, Leroy spoke excitedly about holdups and stabbings. He vividly illustrated how he would defend himself if anyone ever tried to get *him*, pantomiming stabbing his assailant in the chest and ripping off his imagined mask. Although the therapist wondered whether Leroy linked these scary ideas to his mother's illness, the boy avoided referring to his mother and instead related in a highly agitated way a series of scary, dangerous events that had taken place in his neighborhood over the last few days. He expressed an admixture of admiration and awe for the drug dealers in his neighborhood and acknowledged that he knew them all and sometimes even worked for them. He gleefully reported that they have lots of money and that he, too, would like to have money to buy things. He referred to their guns, which excited him. He then rapidly spun into a series of frightening episodes, including one younger brother getting hit by a car and another almost choking on a sourball. In his retelling, he leapt up to demonstrate the choking in an exaggerated, wild way, with much excited giggling, and declared that he knew what he would have done if he had been there. A few moments later, he decided to make a get-well card for his mother, which served as a window into the vulnerable and needy feelings so deeply buried beneath bravado. In it he wrote, "Dear Mommy, I hope you get well soon, I love you, you are the best mommy. Love, Leroy."

ADOLESCENTS

Adolescence is one of the most dramatic phases in the course of development, marked by profound changes in biological, psychological, and social functioning. With great intensity, biological processes focus the young adolescent's attention on concerns about bodily changes, sexual sensations, and intimate relationships. These changes are often greeted with a mixture of pleasure and trepidation (Marans et al., 1996; Dahl, 1993; Kestenberg, 1980; Blos, 1970); in the entry into man- and womanhood, the changes can be experienced as happening too quickly or not quickly enough. Increased excitement and anxiety accompany the adolescent's recognition that he or she now possesses the equipment for acting on sexual and aggressive urges in ways that had previously been in the realm of fantasies that accompany earlier phases of development.

One result of increased internal tension may be seen in the adolescent's more tumultuous relationships with parents, involving struggles between the wish to remain dependent and close and the urgency to achieve independence and new relationships. These struggles are often played out around old issues having to do with bodily care and hygiene, cleanliness and orderliness of personal property, insensitivity to the feelings and needs of others, and intense preoccupation with immediate satisfaction of one's own needs (Blos, 1962; A. Freud, 1958; Laufer, 1985; Marans et al., 1996; U.S. Department of Justice, 1995).

Disregard for family rules may at once serve the adolescent's attempts to gain emotional distance while implicitly inviting parents to remain intensely involved. Additionally, the adolescent finds refuge from the claustrophobic pull of family ties in academic, athletic, work/money, musical, and political interests, and potentially in illicit drug use, drinking, and crime as well. Similarly, as the adolescent withdraws from his or her parents, the intensity of the attachment to them is shifted to the peer group and new intimate relationships. The push for mastering anxiety associated with dependency and infantile incompetence provide added push to the adolescent's move toward real independent functioning. Given the enormous demands that are already inherent during this phase of development, exposure to violence places an additional and special burden on the adolescent's attempts to feel competent, autonomous, and safe. As suggested earlier, the individual's response to an acute episode of interpersonal violence will, in large part, be determined by the nature of the violence itself and by the status of the individual's negotiation of past and current developmental tasks. As increasing numbers of adolescents are exposed to violence—particularly in urban, high-crime neighborhoods—the effects may be seen in changes at home, at school, and in perceptions about the world in which they live.

In addition to the posttraumatic symptoms described earlier, adolescent experiences and perceptions of their own vulnerability may lead to increasingly risky reactions that interfere with the tasks and requirements of this phase of development. Reactions may range from staying away from school in order to avoid the potential for violence on the streets and in the classroom, to arming themselves as protection, to involvement in gang or other criminal activities (Appelbone, 1996). As with disturbances of neurovegetative functions, withdrawal into fantasy, social isolation, and regressive symptomatology, these responses serve the adolescent's attempts to guard against and even reverse feelings of helplessness and overwhelming fear.

Adolescents' general experience of feeling unsafe is underlined by the finding of a number of investigators (Harris & Associates, 1996; Schwab-Stone, 1995; Singer et al., 1995; Martinez & Richters, 1993) and by Justice Department reports that teenagers between the ages of 12 and 15 are victims of crime more than any other age group, and that adolescents of all ages are victims at twice the national average (U.S. Department of Justice, 1995). Although the numbers suggest the extent of the real danger of urban violence that confronts all too many teenagers on a regular basis, they do not tell us about the fuller experiences of those who face it. As with younger children, when we are unavailable or unable to listen, we are unable to learn about the specific meanings or individual contexts in which exposure to violence occurs, or about the various responses that follow.

CHARISSE

Charisse was 15 years old and living with her mother, father, and two younger brothers when she was robbed of her leather coat at gunpoint and beaten. She suffered minor bruising and was very shaken after the event. She was referred to the CD-CP consultation service by the officer who had responded to the scene, and was seen by a clinician for 3 months following the robbery. For several weeks, she was unable to sleep through the night, refused to go to school and, perhaps most notably, she was unable to go into any of the rooms in her house unaccompanied. After several nights, Charisse insisted that her mother sleep in the same room with her. Although she had been doing well in school and had purchased her leather coat from earnings from a part-time job, Charisse described feeling like a "frightened baby" no longer able to look after herself. As she continued to feel frightened and jumpy, or hypervigilant, both Charisse and her mother reported increased bickering between them that often ended in screaming battles. In the clinical work, a more conscious link could be made between the strength of Charisse's increased feelings of dependence, her repudiation of these feelings, and her fights with her mother. Additionally, helping Charisse's mother recognize the connection between her own anxiety about the event and a resurgence of a wish to overprotect and control Charisse's activities as if she were younger, helped both mother and daughter to disengage from the intensity of the struggles that followed the robbery and assault.

During the course of her treatment, Charisse was also able to confide in the therapist that throughout the robbery she feared that she would be raped. Over time, she made a significant link between this fear and her avoidance of school. She described a budding relationship with a boy at school and the fact that her thoughts about him had become increasingly "romantic." However, since the robbery,

Charisse had felt especially anxious and somehow ashamed every time she thought of this boy. For Charisse, the normative adolescent anxiety associated with burgeoning sexuality had become intertwined with and potentiated by the intense vulnerability she felt following real danger, bodily damage, and loss of control. She came to understand that her school refusal did not simply reflect avoidance of the now dangerous streets she would have to traverse on the way to school. By staying at home, Charisse also attempted to avoid the powerful sexual feelings associated with her ideas about this, potentially, first boyfriend.

Although Charisse experienced disruption in multiple areas of her development following her victimization, her heightened conflicts and symptoms concerning autonomy and sexuality did not continue to dominate her adolescence. She did not forget the robbery/assault or the anger and sense of vulnerability that followed. However, she was also able to disentangle the multiple meanings of what she had experienced and return to school, to important relationships, and to the path of optimal development. For Charisse, this event of close, personal contact with violence was the first. Her healthy development prior to the event, family support, and additional help aided her negotiation of and recovery from her traumatic experience.

However, for many other children the acute episode of violence is experienced in the context of multiple traumatic events and adverse factors that have undermined development from early on.

ANDRE

A clinician from the CD-CP program was called to the hospital to consult with medical staff about a 15-year-old boy who had been shot twice in the upper thighs by rival drug dealers. His friend lay in a coma in the ICU with what would prove to be fatal gunshot wounds to the chest and head. The 15-year-old, Andre, was medically stable but was noncooperative with staff, alternating between screaming tirades about the slow food service, rules about visiting hours, checks of vital signs, and so forth, and sullen withdrawal—hours of staring into space, ignoring the attempts of hospital staff to engage him in discussion about his condition or about what had happened to him. When the clinician arrived on the floor, hospital staff described Andre as both a "pain in the ass" and as scary.

After the clinician introduced himself, Andre's deadened stare shifted as he curled his lips and revealed a full set of gold-capped teeth with the initials "RIP" stenciled on the upper caps and his initials in the lower set. When this introduction was followed by angry demands for a second line to his phone so that he could keep up with the incessant beeping from his pager, the staff's description rang true.

What emerged in discussions with his mother and, subsequently, with his public defender was the story of a boy who had multiple contacts with social services, the police, and the courts. He had a long history of developmental difficulties that began with the diagnosis of a malignant tumor at age 2 that was followed by several years of intermittent chemo and radiation therapies. His father, a mainlining heroin addict who seemed to appear in the boy's life only when desperate for a place to sleep, when stealing what meager possessions the family had in order to feed his habit, or when frustrated in those efforts, beat Andre's mother. Andre's mother suffered chronic, untreated depression and had difficulties sustaining any employment. Housing was never permanent, and frequent moves within and between towns contributed to Andre's declining abilities in school and final, persistent truancy. Having lived in another city, it was only in the last 4 months that Andre had begun spending much of his time in New Haven and, with two recent arrests for street-level dealing, Andre was becoming known to the police and to the juvenile courts. In fact, at the time of the shooting, Andre's case was pending, following his failure to stay with an Alternative to Incarceration outpatient drug abuse program. His next court date was to be in 6 weeks.

Andre's threats of seeking violent revenge were intensified with news of his friend's death and by the acute psychotic episode that followed. He was hospitalized on a psychiatric unit for several days until his psychosis cleared and the acute demand for beds led to his discharge. Before appearing in court, 4 weeks after the shooting, Andre was admitted twice to ERs in another town with PCP psychosis and subsequently arrested on another drug dealing and, now, weapons charge prior to his being adjudicated to the state juvenile corrections facility for 18 months. In this case the developmental psychopathology was beyond therapeutic help, and earlier intervention proved too little, too late. Since leaving that institution, Andre has returned to the streets, where he has rejoined the legion of young men who find their sense of potency and effectiveness in the lucrative drug trade and at the business end of a gun.

SUMMARY

In considering the traumatic potential of children's exposure to violence, we have relied on a concept of "trauma" defined as an exceptional experience in which powerful and dangerous stimuli overwhelm the child's capacity to regulate his or her affective state. Initial and subsequent responses can be understood as both restitutive and self-protective in nature. Children's responses to traumatic violence are best understood in light of current developmental attainments and mastery of previous developmental challenges, as each developmental phase brings with it unique developmental demands that simultaneously enrich the children's array of defensive abilities and give rise to particular developmental vulnerabilities.

In the face of a violent episode, children's feelings of insecurity and impotence undermine their normative strivings toward a sense of mastery and competence in the environment.

Younger children, for example, depend on their caregivers to mediate their environment and to titrate and regulate experiences that are distressing. As children learn to mediate the press of normative aggressivity, they enter a developmental period in which acute episodes of danger, loss, and violence can interfere with the age-expectable attainments of school-age children, such as the ability to engage genuinely in academic endeavors, to expand beyond the family into the social world of peers and extrafamilial adults, and to take pleasure in increased autonomy and self-reliance. In adolescence, the experience of violence can give rise to uneasy, dreaded feelings of helplessness or neediness, which threaten to override the developmental thrust toward increasing autonomy, affiliative longings, and burgeoning sexuality.

Without help from the environment or, alternately, without relief from unremitting episodes of violence, specific and circumscribed symptoms may cease to serve a restitutive function and may instead come to reflect a chronic maladaptation that compromises the development of children's more adaptive and progressive developmental attainments, whether in the realm of cognitive, affective, or regulatory capacities. The ways in which children negotiate the consequences of exposure to violence, bodily damage, and loss rely in large part on the environment's capacity to recognize and support the attempts to work through the specific meanings, concerns, and restitutive attempts. When overlooked or misunderstood, children's attempts to ward off feelings of helplessness, guilt, or shame may have an enduring effect on adaptation and may derail the path of optimal development and functioning.

However, a traumatic event may hinder caregivers' abilities to listen or decode children's symptomatic language that signals their distress. The adults' inability to attend to children's needs in the wake of violence may be a natural consequence of their own attempts at restitution and self-protection from the feelings of vulnerability and traumatic disorganization. In the face of traumatic exposure to violence, for example, a mother who is already having difficulties tolerating the demanding advances in her child's development may experience her child's needs especially acutely in the aftermath of violence and overwhelming anxiety. Similarly, a parent who has been exposed to violence may experience a heightened intolerance for the normative aggressivity of young children.

Parents may not readily associate an increase in behaviors such as biting, kicking, or hitting with recent exposure to trauma. Misunderstanding the source of their child's behavior may lead parents to adopt a punitive, detached, or irritable stance, which can frustrate or shame the traumatized child. At these times the child must contend with the dual burden of the caregiver's own experience of anxiety, neediness, and disorganization along with a lowered threshold for the confusing and demanding signals regarding dependence and autonomy. For parents and professionals alike, the nature of a child's traumatization is too often viewed solely in terms of the external circumstances of the violent events. Such assumptions often fail to consider the child's own unique experience and the particular meanings attributed by the child in its aftermath. Thus, an important opportunity may be missed to generate intervention strategies that are based on an appreciation of the interplay between the child's experience, developmental status, and the greater environmental context within which the violence has occurred. If, however, parents are better prepared to appreciate the full range of their child's experience, they can better help him or her to tolerate and work through the feelings, confusion, and uncertainty—neither denying the reality of what the child witnessed with his or her own eyes, nor flooding the child with more detailed and complex information than the child can digest. Exploring the broadest array of the child's unique experience of violent events also has direct implications for developing immediate and follow-up strategies for intervening with those institutions involved in the life of children and their families, and within their community. When there is no one available to listen, children are alone with the distress and disorganization that so often follows their close encounters with interpersonal violence. On their own, attempts to recover from overwhelming fear, uncertainty, and helplessness may be at a very high price to children's developmental potential as well as to the communities that have been unable to protect or support them.

REFERENCES

Appelbone, P. (1996, January 12). Crime fear is seen forcing changes in youth behavior. *New York Times*, p. A6.

Blos, P. (1962). *On adolescence*. New York: Free Press.

Blos, P. (1970). *The young adolescent*. New York: Free Press.

Dahl, G. (1933). The impact of divorce on a preadolescent girl. *Psychoanalytic Study of the Child, 48*, 193–208.

Freud, A. (1958). Adolescence. *Psychoanalytic Study of the Child, 13*, 255–278.

Freud, A., & Burlingham, D. (1973). Infants without families: Reports on the Hampstead nurseries, 1939–1944. In *The Writings of Anna Freud* (Vol. 3, pp. 3–664). New York: International Universities Press.

Freud, S. (1974). Inhibitions, symptoms and anxiety. In J. Strachey (Ed. and Trans.), *The standard edition of the complete psychological works of Sigmund Freud* (Vol. 20, pp. 77–174). London: Hogarth Press. (Original work published 1926)

Furman, E., Solnit, A. J., & Lang, J. L. (1968). Symposium: Child analysis and pediatrics. *International Journal of Psycho-Analysis, 49,* 280–285.

Garbarino, J., Dubrow, N., Kostelny, K., & Pardo, C. (1992). *Children in Danger: Coping with the consequences of community violence.* San Francisco: Jossey-Bass.

Hellman, I. (1962). Hamsted nursery follow-up studies: Effects of sudden separation. *Psychoanalytic Study of the Child, 17,* 159–174.

Kestenberg, J. (1980). Eleven, twelve, thirteen: Years of transition. In G. Pollack & S. Greenspan (Eds.), *The course of life* (Vol. 2). Washington, DC: National Institute of Mental Health.

Krystal, H. (1988). *Integration and self-healing: Affect, trauma, alexithymia.* Hillsdale, NJ: Analytic Press.

Laor, N., Wolmer, L., Mayes, L.C., Gershon, A., Wicznam, R., & Cohen, D. J. (1995). Preschool children under SCUD attacks thirty months later: A developmental perspective on the "protective matrix" as risk-modifying function. *Archives of General Psychiatry, 53,* 416–423.

Laufer, M. (1985). Adolescence and psychosis. *International Journal of Psycho-Analysis, 67,* 367–372.

Levine, H. (1982). Toward a psychoanalytic understanding of children of survivors of the Holocaust. *Psychoanalytic Quarterly, 51,* 70–92.

Marans, S. (1994). Community violence and children's development: Collaborative interventions. In C. Chiland & J. G. Young (Eds.), *Children and violence: Vol. 11. The child in the family* (pp. 109–124). Northvale, NJ: Aronson.

Marans, S., Adnopoz, J., Berkman, M., Esserman, D., MacDonald, D., Nagler, S., Randall, R., Schaefer, M., & Wearing, M. (1995). *Police mental health partnership: A community based response to urban violence.* New Haven, CT: Yale University Press.

Marans, S., Berkman, M., & Cohen, D. (1996). Communal violence: Children's development and their adaptations to catastrophic circumstances. In B. Simon & R. Apfel (Eds.), *Minefields in their hearts: The mental health of children in war and communal violence* (pp. 104–127). New Haven, CT: Yale University Press.

Marans, S., & Cohen, D. (1991). Child psychoanalytic theories of development. In M. Lewis (Ed.), *Child and adolescent psychiatry: A comprehensive textbook* (pp. 129–145). Baltimore, MD: Williams & Wilkins.

Marans, S., & Cohen, D. (1996). Child psychoanalytic theories of development. In M. Lewis (Ed.), *Child and adolescent psychiatry: A comprehensive textbook* (2nd ed., pp. 156–170). Baltimore, MD: Williams & Wilkins.

Martinez, P., & Richters, J. (1993). The NIMH Community Violence Project: II. Children's distress symptoms associated with violence exposure. *Psychiatry, 56,* 22–35.

Mayes, L., & Cohen, D. (1993). Playing and therapeutic action in child analysis. *International Journal of Psycho-Analysis, 74*, 1235–1244.

Osofsky, J. (1995). The effects of exposure to violence on young children. *American Psychologist, 50*, 782–788.

Osofsky, J. D., Wewers, S., Hann, D. M., & Fick, A. C. (1993). Chronic community violence: What is happening to our children? *Psychiatry, 56*, 36–45.

Perry, B. D. (1994). Neurobiologic sequelae of childhood trauma: Post-traumatic stress disorders in children. In M. Murberg (Ed.), *Catecholamine function in post-traumatic stress disorder: Emerging concepts* (pp. 223–225). Washington, DC: American Psychiatric Association Press.

Pynoos, R., Ritzman, R., Steinberg, A., & Goenjian, A., et al. (1996). A behavioral animal model of posttraumatic stress disorder featuring repeated exposure to situational reminders. *Biological Psychiatry, 39*(2), 129–134.

Pynoos, R., Steinberg, A., & Wraith R. (1995). A developmental model of childhood traumatic stress. In D. Ciccetti & D. Cohen (Eds.), *Manual of developmental psychopathology* (pp. 72–90). New York: Wiley.

Schwab-Stone, M. (1996). School consultation. In M. Lewis (Ed.), *Child and adolescent psychiatry: A comprehensive textbook* (2nd ed., pp. 1085–1092). Baltimore: Williams & Wilkins.

Singer, M., Anglin, T., Song, L., & Lunghofer, L. (1995). Adolescent's exposure to violence and associated symptoms of psychological trauma. *Journal of the American Medical Association, 273*, 477–482.

Southwick, S., Krystal, J. H, Morgan, C. A., Johnson, D., Nagy, L. M., Nicolaou, A., Heringer, G. R., & Charney, I. (1933). Abnormal noradrenergic function in posttraumatic stress disorder. *Archives of General Psychiatry, 50*, 266–274.

Taylor, L., Zuckerman, B., Harick, V., & Groves, B. (1992). Exposure to violence among inner-city parents and young children. *American Journal of Diseases of Children, 146*, 487–494.

Terr, L. C. (1989). Family anxiety after traumatic events. *Journal of Clinical Psychiatry, 50*, 15–19.

Terr, L. C. (1991). Childhood traumas: An outline and overview. *American Journal of Psychiatry, 148*, 10–)10.

U.S. Department of Justice. (1995). *Guide for implementing the Comprehensive Strategy for Serious, Violent, and Chronic Juvenile Offenders.* Washington, DC: Author.

van der Kolk, B. (1994). The body keeps the score: Memory and the evolving psychobiology of posttraumatic stress. Boston: Massachusetts General Hospital, Trauma Clinic, Harvard Medical School.

van der Kolk, B., Greenberg, M., Boyd, H., II., &Krystal, J. (1985). Inescapable shock, neurotransmitters, and addiction to trauma: Toward a psychobiology of posttraumatic stress. *Biological Psychiatry, 20*, 314–325.

Yehuda, R., & McFarlane, A. (1995). The conflict between current knowledge about PTSD and its original conceptual basis. *American Journal of Psychiatry, 152*, 1705–1713.

11

The Trauma/Grief-Focused Group Psychotherapy Module of an Elementary School-Based Violence Prevention/Intervention Program

LISA MURPHY
ROBERT S. PYNOOS
C. BOYD JAMES

T HE EPIDEMIC OF VIOLENCE that permeates our society has continued for more than two decades, with a trend toward children of younger ages becoming perpetrators, victims, and witnesses of violence (Bell & Jenkins, 1993; Fitzpatrick & Boldizar, 1993; Groves, Zuckerman, Marans, & Cohen, 1993; Koop & Lundberg, 1992; Osofsky, Wewers, Hann, & Fick, 1993; Pynoos & Eth, 1985; Richters & Martinez, 1993; Schwab-Stone et al., 1995). There is extensive documentation indicating the current high rates of homicide as a cause of death among 15- to 19-year-old African American males (Centers for Disease Control and Prevention, 1994). This information has provoked a public health response that has primarily focused on educational interventions aimed at reducing the escalation of violent behavior within this population. Most notably, this approach has involved teaching strategies to promote nonviolent conflict resolution (Prothrow-Stith, 1991).

At the same time, advances in our understanding of the impact of traumatic stress in children and adolescents has documented the extreme degree of personal distress, the interplay of intra- and extrafamilial violence, the high risk of chronic symptomatology, and the extent of potential developmental disturbance (Pynoos, Steinberg, & Wraith, 1995). This line of investigation has stimulated interest in developing therapeutic approaches to treating children and adolescents after direct exposures to violence (Pynoos & Nader, 1993). In contrast to approaches that narrowly focus on decreasing morbidity and mortality by preventing violent behavior, this chapter describes a public mental health approach that recognizes the importance of addressing the complex personal experience of a child and the need to restore and promote normative cognitive, emotional, and interpersonal functioning adversely affected by trauma and grief.

A developmental approach suggests that it is important to intervene with young children, for whom the consequences of trauma-related psychopathology and interference with the acquisition of developmental competencies may place them at increased risk of future violent perpetration or victimization. It is now routine to offer special mental health services and psychosocial support to occupational groups at high risk for exposures to direct life threat and witnessing of traumatic injuries and deaths (Ursano, McCaughy, & Fullerton, 1994). It is only of late that comparable, school-based services are beginning to be made available to the thousands of children with similar exposures at home and in their communities.

We are beginning to appreciate the powerful influence of violent exposures on the child's developing sense of the social contract. This includes the child's understanding and acceptance of the moral rights and responsibilities of self and others, and principles of fairness and social justice. The effects of violence on the intrapsychic life of the child and on an emerging understanding of the social contract influence the child's schematization of safety, security, risk, protection, and intervention (Pynoos, 1993). Whereas trauma-related symptoms may be addressed through psychotherapeutic approaches, addressing concerns about the social contract can benefit from additional strategies, for example, in this intervention, a mentorship program. Such a program provides ongoing relationships with role models and opportunities to interact with representatives of social agencies. Over time, mentorship permits children to discuss their experiences of their community, school, and police, and how these experiences contribute to their developing schematization of the social environment and their expectations for the future.

This chapter describes an elementary school-based violence prevention/intervention therapeutic program for children exposed to intra- and extrafamilial violence. It provides an overview of Project Intervention, a school-based program, including assessment and evaluation tools, and details the goals and session-by-session processes of the group psycho-therapy component. The program staff consists of a unique interdisciplin-ary team that includes expertise on traumatic stress and grief reactions in children, and on the cultural aspects of violence, youth gangs, and the judicial system. A social historical perspective, coupled with a therapeutic one, ensures attention to both the psychological and social adjustment of children exposed to violence.

THE INTERVENTION SETTING

This prevention/intervention program is being conducted in an elemen-tary school located in an inner-city area that has suffered chronically from extremely high rates of crime and gang-related violence to which community members, including many children, are exposed. The ele-mentary school is located on a large campus that also houses a junior high school and high school. Implementation of this type of comprehen-sive school-based therapeutic intervention requires the collaboration, support, and approval of a network of organizations and agencies. Table 11.1 lists the organizations collaborating on this project.

TABLE 11.1. Collaborative Network of Organizations and Agencies

Los Angeles County District Attorney's Victim–Witness Assistance Program
  Gil Garcetti, District Attorney
  Herman Millholland, Program Director

Charles R. Drew University School of Medicine, Center for the Study of Violence and Social Change
  C. Boyd James, Ph.D., Director

UCLA School of Medicine, Trauma Psychiatry Program
  Robert S. Pynoos, M.D., M.P. H., Director
  Lisa M. Murphy, Ph.D., On-site Program Director

Inglewood Unified School District
  McKinley M. Nash, Ed.D., Superintendent
  Hollis Dillon, Jr., Director, Special Services
  Walter Cruz, Assistant to the Director, Special Services

City of Inglewood Police Department
  Oliver M. Thompson, Chief of Police

County of Los Angeles Probation Department
  Barry Nidorf, Chief Probation Officer

An Inglewood Unified School District Elementary School
  Lacey Alexander, Principal

In order for such a program to establish and maintain its integrity and community acceptance, it is imperative that every step of the program be explicitly presented and approved by each appropriate group. This includes open presentations to the Board of Education, to the Principal, school personnel, parents and children, and to the Chief of Police and the individual community-based police officers to be involved. A representative of the Los Angeles County Victim–Witness Assistance Program has attended all of the weekly staff meetings.

DESCRIPTION OF INGLEWOOD UNIFIED SCHOOL DISTRICT

The City of Inglewood is comprised of working-class communities that suffer from economic and political disadvantage, and community disruption. The Inglewood Unified School District is responsible for the education of more than 16,000 students. The district includes 13 elementary schools, 2 junior high schools, 2 high schools, and 1 continuation school. Although the general pattern of school enrollment has grown by 15%, the social needs of the community have grown 100-fold during the same period. Recent trends in this city include a substantial increase in the number of children who are wards of the court, increased frequency and severity of youth violence, increased conflict among ethnic groups, extensive illegal drug activity among teenagers, and one of the lowest high school graduation rates in the Los Angeles area.

Administrators in the Inglewood Unified School District Special Services Department have identified a number of serious problems. These included illegal drug use, adolescent gang activity, truancy and high dropout rates, and violent conduct of juvenile offenders (aged 13–18) who have two or more felonies on their records. In 1994, the Juvenile Justice and Delinquency Prevention Program of the Inglewood Police Department estimated that there are currently over 400 serious, violent juvenile offenders in Inglewood (Weinberg, 1994).

The pattern of violence and crime is evident at the schools: During the 1993–1994 school year, the Inglewood School District reported 2,512 suspensions (47 students were expelled; 676 were referred to the Juvenile Court). Of approximately 1,445 high school students, 682 had been charged or disciplined with minor to serious infractions and felonies. At the same time, the children of Inglewood are exposed to severe losses as well as intra- and extrafamilial violence in their community. During 1993, 54 children lost parents; 399 were physically abused; 27 were raped or sexually abused; 139 were hungry, unclothed, and/or generally neglected; and 7 were murdered. During 1993, over 4,000 truant youngsters were caught roaming the streets and brought to Project Hope—a community social service agency that has subsequently lost its funding.

AN OVERVIEW OF THE ELEMENTARY SCHOOL-BASED INTERVENTION PROGRAM

In contrast to some other efforts at violence prevention, this project maintains a balance between addressing problematic behaviors and the internal mental lives of children who have been exposed to violence. The intervention model has three phases: individual psychotherapy, group psychotherapy, and mentorship. Each phase includes approximately 10–12 weekly sessions constructed around the all-year school schedule. Each phase includes pre- and postintervention assessments. The individual therapy phase centers on identifying and clarifying issues surrounding exposure to violence and traumatic loss, and exploring the meanings of the child's specific reactions and behaviors. There is an effort to fully explore continuing preoccupations with reparative intervention fantasies and to create a therapeutic situation in which the most aggressive and self-blaming components can be expressed and more constructive content can be experienced (Pynoos & Nader, 1993).

A key goal of the individual phase is to increase parental responsiveness to the child. The counselors provide parents with a clearer understanding of the child's experiences and subsequent concerns and reactions. Time is also spent with the parents and/or caretakers to clarify the nature of the interplay between the traumatic experiences of the child and their own, and the impact of these experiences on the parent–child relationship. The individual phase serves as an important preparation for the next phase of group treatment. This two-step process is similar to those employed by successful programs that treat combat veterans and adult victims of crime (Marmar, Foy, Kagan, & Pynoos, 1993).

The goals of group therapy are severalfold. The first goal is to provide a greater acceptance of each child's experiences. A second is to increase affect tolerance and emotional responsiveness of the group participants. A third is to enhance social skills and to help the children speak with genuineness and integrity about their experiences. This sharing is intended to help minimize the incidence of more withdrawn and aggressive behaviors, and improve awareness and tolerance of traumatic reminders or themes. The group then serves as a preparatory phase to the mentorship.

A central presupposition of this prevention/intervention program is that many inner-city children in the course of their experiences evolve a social schema of being "excluded" from the general social contract of the society in which they live. The mentorship intervention component has the primary goal of enhancing children's conception of, and sense of participation in, the social contract. The mentorship incorporates efforts to assist children in accepting fundamental social institutions and maps of meanings which represent avenues to social efficacy and commitment to the common good. The mentors, by having the children discuss and elaborate in play, drawing, and narrative their ideal institutions, seek to refocus the children's perceptions of (1) *home*, as a place of protection, love, and support; (2) *neighborhood*, as a place for play and communion with others; (3) *school*, as a place for study, where teachers reinforce the warmth and reaffirmation of home; and (4) *police officers*, as friends to whom to turn in times of distress and rely on for protection and reassurance.

In addition, the mentors become a window to the world for the children, showing them various career choices as well as social support structures, such as police, firefighters, medical personnel, and librarians. They assist the children in making personal contact with community police officers and firefighters, in order to facilitate an enhanced willingness to rely on them in times of crisis, as well as to instill a sense of trust in the structures they represent. The mentorship is supplemented by a tutoring program, which is staged to take advantage of individual and group gains in alleviating trauma- and loss-related disturbances that interfere with learning.

Differing from other mentorship programs, the mentors are fully informed of the children's traumatic exposures and can respond to children's individual preoccupations regarding their futures and specific concerns as they relate to the social agencies to which they are being introduced. For example, when asked about their career interests, one fifth grade boy volunteered that he wished to become a police officer and to have the authority to kill. The mentor, fully versed about the boy's having experienced extreme ineffectualness while witnessing his mother's murder, recognized that this wish reflected his preoccupations with fantasies of revenge against an assailant that had never been arrested.

The children each have mentors who spend time with them in small group settings and tend to special needs, such as tutoring. We have observed how the mentorship has contributed to the process of trauma recovery. For example, it has been within the mentorship program that the children have begun to demonstrate restored ability for spontaneous play, unencumbered by traumatic themes. This has provided the mentors with more opportunity to address normal developmental themes as these children begin to make the transition to adolescence.

The child program is supplemented by a program for the parents. This program includes home visitations, a parenting skills group, and joint sessions with children. The program specifically offers the parents an opportunity to discuss their histories of traumatic experiences, and how these have affected their lives and parenting. They are also provided with psychoeducational material about the effects of trauma on the lives of their children and specific techniques to improve parental responses to traumatized children. Parents are also assisted to make use of appropriate resources, including other school support services and the Los Angeles County District Attorney Victim–Witness Assistance Program, and in developing confidence and trust in police officers.

The program is designed to be an effective, efficient program that can be instituted within schools throughout the United States. To that end, we have also successfully included the training of school resource specialists, psychologists, counselor-trained teachers, and school-based health clinic personnel to participate in the individual and group treatment components.

INTERFACE WITH A COMMUNITY-BASED POLICING PROGRAM

In keeping with a national trend toward community-based policing, the Inglewood Police Department has established a Community Policing Agency (ICOP). The decision by the Inglewood Chief of Police to station some of the community-based police officers at all the elementary schools, as a way of promoting a relationship between officers and neighborhood children, provides a unique opportunity to involve these officers in this school-based intervention program. As a consequence, the goals of the involvement of police officers in this program differ somewhat from those of model collaborative programs between child mental health professionals and community-based policing. This therapeutic program is uniquely positioned to include the training and participation of a school-based community policing program. Police officers are currently being trained in the psychological effects on children who witnesses violence and about the unique supportive role the police officer can play in their recovery. We are developing guidelines for their participation, for example, how they can complement group leaders in addressing the concerns of children in circumstances in which there has been no arrest for a violent injury or death of a family member or friend. The police officers have already joined constructively with the clinical team in addressing several violent crises, including children exposed in their apartment house to the death of a child by parental abuse, and the shooting death of a gang member on the corner of the school campus. Figure 11.1 provides an overview of the program components.

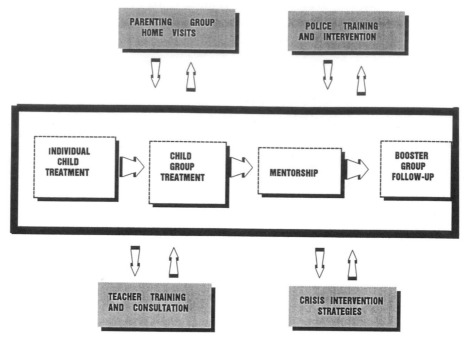

FIGURE 11.1. General program flow chart for safe school program.

ASSESSMENT AND EVALUATION TOOLS

One of the goals of this project has been to develop a battery of selected psychological, behavioral, and academic assessment instruments that could be effectively employed in an elementary school setting. We chose symptom measures with continuous scale ratings because previous findings have suggested that these can provide finer discrimination among children with different degrees of exposure than dichotomous scales (Pynoos et al., 1987; Pynoos et al., 1993) and also permit more sensitive outcome assessments over time.

Rather than relying on an individual case referral system, which may fail to detect students at risk and introduce referral bias, we chose to employ a systematic means of classroom screenings to identify children. We used the Systematic Screening for Behavioral Disorders (SSBD) that has previously proven useful in screening elementary school students within entire school districts (Walker & Severson, 1990). It consists of four components: a ranking of all students in the classroom on externalizing and internalizing behavioral dimensions; a critical life event checklist; adaptive and maladaptive frequency of behaviors scales; and a direct observational rating of classroom and playground behavior. We were specifically interested in using a teacher rating scale that forced teachers to identify children with severe internalizing as well as externalizing behaviors, because our current work has suggested that children with severe posttraumatic stress disorder (PTSD) secondary to violent exposures may predominantly manifest either of these dimensions, or both. Children who were ranked in comparison with their classmates at the top of either list were then screened by clinicians for their exposures to violence, using a modified form of the Richters Exposure to Community Violence Scale (Richters & Saltzman, 1990) and through clinical interviews with child and parent. Finally, the teachers also completed a temperament assessment scale that has been field tested among war-exposed children in the former Yugoslavia region (Petrovic, 1994). The teacher–child rating scale used in this program is an abbreviated version of the Child Behavior Profile (Achenbach & Edelbrock, 1986).

Our prior studies have indicated high rates of comorbid depression with chronic PTSD among children and adolescents (Goenjian et al., 1995). Recent studies have reported on depression correlates among urban school-aged children exposed to violence (Freeman, Mokros, & Pozanski, 1993). We have presented additional data that acute exposure to violence can also be associated with attention deficit symptoms (Pynoos & Nader, 1990). Therefore, three specific symptom checklists are being used: the Likert-scale Child Posttraumatic Stress Disorder Reaction Index (Pynoos et al., 1993), a modified version of the Birleson Depression Scale (Asarnow & Carlson, 1985); and the Conners Abbreviated Teacher Rating Scale for symptoms associated with attention deficit disorder (Conners, 1969; Atkins & Pelham, 1991). The first two are completed by self-report with clinician assistance, and the latter is completed by the child's teacher.

Information about the child's current and prior academic functioning is obtained from school records, as well as a narrative report from the teacher and parents. The children's California Achievement Test (CAT), their class standing, as well as their academic progress shown on their report cards are recorded. Whether the child had been given an Individualized Education Program evaluation or referral is also noted. Delinquency history is gathered from the principal and the children's cumulative files. Data from other agencies, such as the Department of Children's Services, are also recorded at the beginning of treatment.

The data also include the following: (1) a family assessment form, which outlines the history of violence for the caretaker, family, and child, and psychosocial, psychiatric, infant, and medical histories; (2) progress notes on the individual, group, mentorship, and parenting sessions; (3) records of teacher–counselor interactions, which reflect teacher observations on the child's progress; (4) notes concerning informal interactions between staff members and children, for example, on the playground or in the classrooms, that were of clinical import; (5) consent and release of information documents; (6) notes of referrals and contacts with outside agencies; (7) termination summaries.

The children are reevaluated after their group treatment. Teachers rerank the children in their classroom on the SSBD, and again complete the behavioral and temperament scales. At the end of their participation in the mentorship component, the children's class standing, as well as their CAT scores are again recorded. All of the clinical scales are readministered. In addition, the children's delinquency history during the time of participation is reviewed. Figure 11.2 illustrates the entire evaluation process.

GROUP TREATMENT COMPONENT

The specific goals of the group psychotherapy treatment component are (1) to promote peer understanding of each group member's experiences; (2) to increase emotional regulation while with peers and group tolerance of more extreme negative emotions associated with their exposures; (3) to foster empathy and emotional responsiveness of the group participants; (4) to enhance social skills, especially in regard to speaking with genuineness and integrity about their experiences and their personal meaning; (5) to encourage the use of help-seeking behaviors, especially at times of renewed reactivity to traumatic reminders or losses; (6) to enhance an understanding of the links between traumatic experiences and specific posttrauma behavior with peers; and (7) to facilitate a supportive, holding environment to address the consequences and meanings of loss of family members and friends. This group therapeutic approach is intended to reduce the children's future engagement in withdrawn or aggressive behaviors.

Groups consist of 5 to 8 children who have completed the individual therapy component and are conducted in 1¹/₂-hour weekly sessions over one quarter of the school year (approximately 12 sessions). As with other components, parents are notified when their children are about to enter the group phase. Parents are informed of the goals and are asked to attend one session during the midphase so that the children can share the work of the group with them. The scheduling of the group is completed with the cooperation of the teachers. A written schedule is posted in each of the children's classrooms, and, for the first session, each child is accompanied to the group therapy office by the group therapist. The

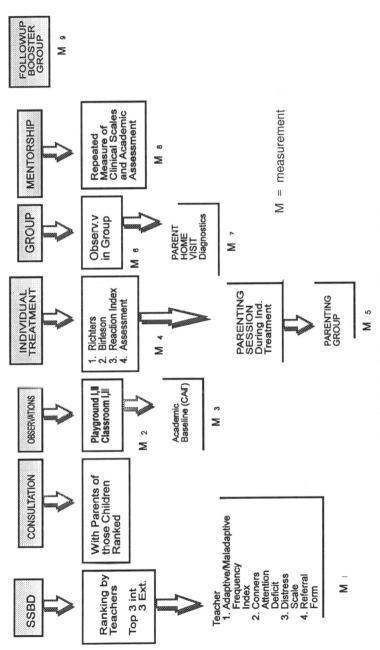

FIGURE 11.2 Evaluation process for safe school program.

233

following is an overview of the opening, middle, working-through, and termination phases of a 3-month course of group psychotherapy.

Opening Phase

The opening phase is directed at forging a therapeutic ambience that promotes the sharing of traumatic narratives. This phase includes specific therapeutic exercises during each session that are designed simultaneously to enhance group cohesion while introducing important traumatic concepts. The therapist frames the explanation of goals to the children in terms that recognize their emerging, developmental awareness of a dichotomy between a private inner world and a public arena (e.g., to bring what has been on the inside, privately talked about with the therapist and family, to the outside with the rest of the group members). Anticipating children's distress in sharing particularly frightening and painful material, the therapist acknowledges a prominent developmental fear over the somatic and physiological reactivity that may accompany the relating of traumatic narratives. At the same time, respect is given to their individual autonomy to decide when, if at all, to speak about traumatic moments (e.g., "You don't have to say anything that feels like it would be too much for your body to handle"). The therapist sets up an expectation of mutual support that will increase affective tolerance of trauma-related emotions ("But I hope as a group we will learn that other people can help us carry these feelings that sometimes feel too big").

It can be expected that school-aged children typically will be reluctant to speak in the group about their referent trauma(s) or other current difficulties. Common to this age group, they fear some form of peer rejection and being overwhelmed by negative emotions (including shame, guilt, rage, sadness, etc.) in front of others. In the first exercise, children are invited to play a game designed to increase their personal comfort with each other and their confidence in the ability to express and regulate emotions, and to introduce the traumatic concepts of helplessness and compensatory responses. They are asked to say their name, identify a favorite animal, and become that animal by making its characteristic sound. For example, "My name is John, my favorite animal is a leopard, and leopards go 'roar'!" Each time, the other children repeat together the child's name, his or her favorite animal, and the sound. With the help of the other group members, each child then names all the other children, their animals, and sounds. The therapist concludes that they now know something about each other and have helped each other out, and suggests that sometimes feelings about a favorite animal can help one not to feel so alone or afraid, and, like the roar of a leopard, can help one not to feel so small or helpless.

The therapist returns the focus to their own trauma/loss experiences by wondering, "Does anyone know what 'helpless' means?" Our experience is that, as a group, the children will begin to talk about their own ideas about why they are in the group, referring to trauma, injury, or loss. The task of the therapist is to relate the material introduced to concepts that underlie the subjective nature of traumatic experiences, posttraumatic reactions, and concerns about group participation. Groups will vary. For example, one group of children began by describing minor physical scars. The therapist extended the group discussion of physical scars by drawing the analogy with "inside feelings from what happened that have not gone away" and experiences that have left a "mark on your life."

We have observed the following about how children first listen to the brief, often emotionally constricted traumatic narratives of other group members: (1) Typically, they do not ask the children to discuss more fully their experience; (2) they may respond competitively in revealing traumatic experiences and, (3) they are likely to become anxious at the material, often manifested through increased motoric activity. In terms of the latter, the clinician must repeatedly clarify how they may wish to divert attention away from upsetting material by physically distracting themselves or disrupting the group.

For this age group, we purposely include motoric activities, designed, in part, to subtly address issues of traumatic avoidance. For example, after a brief sharing of referent traumas, members are invited to get up, search, and locate from among posters on the wall of the room one that depicts the feeling associated with this experience. After reforming the group, each child shares the connection between the affect he or she located and the experience related. For example, a boy who had been intentionally burned spoke of his anger toward the person accountable.

Toward the end of the first session, the clinician invites the children to review their contributions, to reflect on the experiences they related, and to continue to think about what they would like to share with each other in the sessions to follow. Finally, to enhance the sense of group identity, the clinician asks the children to select a name for the group, which often tends to reflect a therapeutic theme; for example, one group choose to call themselves "The Feeling Group."

Even after the first session, we have observed an emergence of a sense of affiliation among group members outside the group, for example, on the playground, when one group member said to his therapist, "Oh, there is the guy who loves the hairy lion." During the remainder of the opening phase, a major goal is to facilitate a transition from a journalistic recounting of trauma and loss to a sharing of genuine expression of subjective experiences. The exercises and therapeutic interventions are intended to enhance children's listening skills and increase empathy and mutual trust, while confirming the legitimacy and seriousness of each other's experiences.

In one exercise, each child in turn is blindfolded and led around by an assigned partner. During this exercise, some children will be extremely vigilant to harm, frequently peeking out, whereas others may get angry with their partner if they trip or bump into something. This exercise leads to a discussion of additional trauma-related concepts, including lack of trust in a safe outcome or failure of adequate protection, hypervigilance in response to threat, intervention fantasies of a protective lookout, or the need to be self-sufficient when it comes to danger, and a sense of estrangement from another if protection fails. The therapist builds on this exercise by commenting, "I wonder if there are times in your life when you felt blind like that, unable to foresee what was about to happen or how bad a situation may become, or wishing you or someone else would stop something bad from happening and not having a way to do so." We have observed that at this point there is a beginning group transference to the therapist as a third-person intervenor to guarantee a safe outcome, not just to the exercise, but primarily to the security of the group as it refocuses on constructing traumatic narratives.

In a serious manner, one boy responded to the above question, "My brother tried to stab me with a knife." The therapist models a response that is respectful, shows empathy, and reflects back to the child that he is understood. In response to one child laughing as this boy spoke, the therapist, said, "We laugh sometimes when something is very upsetting, because it feels better to laugh than to be sad or troubled," and invited others to suggest to this second boy what they imagine the first boy to have been feeling when he was stabbed. The boy who had initially laughed later said he would have imagined that he would have felt sad if that happened to him, whereas another boy said he would have felt mad. Another child questioned, "Where was your mom or dad?" The clinician used this opportunity to introduce the idea of reliance on a sense of a protective shield against violence, and what it feels like for that to fail. The therapist then sought to legitimize the experience by wondering what the second boy could say that would make the first boy know that he heard the seriousness of this experience. In a genuine voice, he turned to the first boy and said, "I'm really sorry that happened to you." The therapist returned the groups' attention to the experiences described in the first session, inviting each child to describe how he or she was feeling as the events were happening.

Ending exercises help to provide closure to the group sessions. They are designed to instill a sense of the group as a holding environment and repository for traumatic anxieties, while strengthening the children's self-esteem, even in the face of traumatic helplessness. For example, in the second session's final exercise, children form a circle, and each child, in turn, is asked to get into the center and lean back into the linked arms of the other children, relying on them as a net to prevent falling. The clinician explains: "Today, as you shared more of your experiences, each of you has leaned on other group members to catch and hold you, so that you can remain tall, with a good sense of yourself, even as you describe situations in which you were not able to do all you wished to keep something bad from happening."

Middle Phase

The major goals of the middle phase of group psychotherapy are to focus on co-construction of the complexity of traumatic experiences, with special attention to violent elements; to identify intervention fantasies and traumatic expectations that mediate aggressive or withdrawal responses to traumatic cues in peer situations; to create a shared appreciation of how posttraumatic stress and grief reactions interfere with peer relationships, family, and academic functioning; and, to use group dynamics as a source of understanding the link between current behavior and violent exposures.

By the fourth session, children have usually settled down in the group, and there is a shift in therapeutic strategy toward greater reliance on verbal skills. Sessions can begin by the clinician asking if anyone wishes to share thoughts about last week's session or from the intervening days. During this phase, we have observed manifestations of group dynamics that reflect the violent themes in the children's lives. For example, just at the front door of the group therapy office, two boys were play-fighting when a third boy approached, misinterpreted the situation as a real fight, and attempted to intervene and defend one of the boys, who he believed was being hurt. The other boy felt he was being assaulted by the third boy, got angry, and started to retaliate with real physical hitting.

The therapist brought attention to this presession altercation as indicating how violent experiences can set up expectations in us that strongly influence our perceptions and reactions. On the one hand, the therapist suggested that the boy who rushed up to intervene may be telling, in his behavior, how awful it has been for him to feel so powerless at confronting the witnessing of spousal abuse at home, his fear of harm coming to his mother, his strong wish to effectively intervene, even if it required physical force, and his fear that his father would violently retaliate. On the other hand, because of the violence the presumed assailant had witnessed at home, he could not just turn to the intervenor and say, "Hey, we are just playing." Being constantly vigilant to the prospect of a physical attack, he readily retaliated. The therapist suggested that his readiness to intervene told the group something about his experience of violence at home.

The two boys then verbally began to describe some of their most frightening experiences with violence at home. The latter child told about having seen his father threaten his mother with a hammer, of his terror, of his heart racing, of his sense of personal vulnerability, and, of his persistent, exaggerated startle. The therapist linked the children's seemingly reflexive behavior to the formation of traumatic expectations secondary to experiences of violence at home and within their community, and to a rush to aggressive action to counter both their distressing empathic and physiological arousal.

As the enactment behaviors subsided with this type of therapeutic clarification, group members more readily explored different facets of their violent experiences. The therapist introduced different means by which the children could narrate their subjective experiences, through drawings, the use of miniature figures, acting out scenes, letter writing, and murals. With each medium, children were encouraged to share with each other expressions of their physical sensations, their scariest, most threatening or disturbing moments, their intervention fantasies, including revenge and constructive fantasies, and feelings of loss and grief. Using the same narrative media, this stage also included children sharing traumatic symptoms such as intrusive images, nightmares, somatic complaints, "tuning out," and incidents of specific fears, exaggerated startle, sleep disturbances, and difficulties in concentration and learning, connecting these symptoms to aspects of their traumatic narratives.

We have observed that the resultant empathic understanding can resolve long-standing animosities between children. For example, we conducted one group that included three boys who were known to fight with each other. The evaluations revealed that each had suffered dissimilar, but equally serious, traumatic experiences. One had been hit by a truck, another had witnessed his brother's murder by a stranger, and the third had witnessed his mother being violently injured by his father. During this middle phase of the group, as the three appreciated the seriousness of each others' experiences and subsequent reactions, they stopped fighting and began to become good friends outside of the group. In general, we have observed that, with completion of this midphase, the degree of automatic, aggressive response to situational reminders decreases, permitting more prosocial behavior.

Working-Through Phase

During the working-through phase of the group psychotherapy, the therapeutic agenda is expanded to include other life adversities, traumas, and loss that interface with the referent trauma. As these sessions proceed, the children are assisted to identify the most intense negative emotions, including guilt, shame, humiliation, and revenge, to explore the fantasy accompaniment of these self-attributions, to legitimize the underlying concern, and to reframe experiences to ameliorate the excessive self-blame and improve affective regulation.

We have observed that working through of the referent traumas in the preceding phases of therapy often results in spontaneous expressions of grief over major losses, in a shift of attention to the developmental impact of both trauma and losses, and expressions of painful disillusionments over parental failings, which are addressed in this phase. An essential aspect is the inclusion of parents and guardians during one group session. The goals of this session are to enhance mutual understanding and responsiveness, and to encourage parents to foster continuation outside the group of the supportive relationships established by the children.

As a group, the children increasingly interact therapeutically, facilitating and rewarding each others' courageous forays into more difficult, affect-laden material. At this time, the group provides a resource of mutual attachment that permits children to disengage from some serious maladaptive alliances, for example, with older gang members. The therapist is more proactive in having the group formulate more constructive coping strategies that address their developmental needs.

In one group, the therapist noted that two boys who were without fathers had become friends. The first boy had previously addressed trauma-related issues over his efforts to resuscitate his father after waking up to find him unresponsive in a living room chair. The second boy had addressed his witnessing of domestic violence and drug use that led his mother to ask his father to leave the family. The therapist expanded the scope of the therapeutic discussion by remarking, "I have noticed you two have become friends and wonder if you have been drawn to each other because of painful feelings you share about being without your father." The first child immediately responded, "Yea, that's true, he knows what it's like." When asked what he meant, he replied, "Being the oldest, I have had to look after my younger brothers and sisters." The other boy, also an eldest child, nodded in agreement. The therapist then continued, "Sometimes, it feels like you don't get to be just a kid," and, the second boy responded, "I have to look after my mom, too."

Even though the children had been in individual treatment prior to the group phase, on occasion, when the issue of loss came under discussion, a child would describe having witnessed a traumatic death that had not been previously revealed. For example, one boy had been referred to the program because he said to his teacher, "I want to be dead when I grow up." When another boy described his sadness over the traumatic loss of a good friend, who was killed in a hit-and-run accident, this reticent boy dramatically described witnessing the murder of his best friend when he was 7 years old. They had been playing in a lot with toy guns, when his friend, saying "Pow, Pow," pointed it at some gang members in the adjoining lot. One of the gang members turned and without warning shot the child through the head. Although the group member's parents knew of the death of their child's friend, they had never known that he had been there at the time. He had been too afraid to tell them, even though, at the time, he had alerted someone in the neighborhood to call the police. It was quite moving to the therapist to observe how the children helped this withdrawn boy begin to talk about his feelings. This case provides an example of how disclosures in the group setting permit the program staff, teacher, and parents to better understand the child's referent symptoms and behaviors and, in this case, become more responsive to the child's unaddressed traumatic grief.

This case also illustrates how the group extends the individual brief psychotherapy in further addressing the meaning of fantasies of revenge and counterretaliation. The group builds on the children's understanding of the relationship of these fantasies to underlying feelings of traumatic helplessness, and especially helps to reduce children's worries about being different over entertaining these violent fantasies. In addition, the group can address fears over loss of impulse control and introduce more constructive responses, a theme that is elaborated in the mentorship, with its emphasis on the social contract.

In this group, another child remarked, "Guess you want to get back at the guy who killed your friend. What would you like to do?" The first boy responded, "I'm too scared he'll come after me." As a primary witness, he remained afraid of the assailant, a person he had seen kill without compunction, convinced that he could only protect himself by never speaking about it, even to his parents. However, he went on to describe in group that he would want to get back at this person for killing his best friend by shooting him with a gun, too.

The children then mutually examined their respective revenge fantasies and their struggles over human accountability. Another spoke of wanting to beat up an uncle who had so badly beaten him. Another child spoke of wanting to run over the man who had run over his best friend. The group therapist addressed these expressions of two underlying wishes by saying, "I bet you'd like him to feel as bad as you did and to make sure he can never make you feel like that again." In response, one child began to discuss whether putting people in jail might not answer the wish for retribution, punishment, and protection.

Specific exercises related to promoting grief work are also introduced, for example, writing a letter to the deceased or absent parent or sibling. In this age group, the therapist is attentive to protests of unfairness over the loss, without as much self-reflection about the developmental impact on their lives as may be expressed by adolescents. For example, one child addressed his letter to God, protesting that while "I understand people die, why did you have to take my father?" Many of the children in these groups have suffered losses under traumatic circumstances. Special attention is then needed to address the interplay of trauma and grief that complicates childhood bereavement (Pynoos, 1992).

Parental absence or loss is often accompanied by feelings of shame and humiliation. As these feelings arise in the group, children may feel especially vulnerable to the challenging remarks of other children confirming, for example, the presence of their own father. The therapist needs to make a bridging interpretation to the "haves and the have nots," for example, by stating to a boy who is teasing, "For you to have a father is to have something special and important," and to the stigmatized child, "If you don't have a father with you, it feels like you have a hole or something in your life that everyone can see." In this specific situation, the therapist continued by addressing the fatherless boy, who had been referred for skipping school and hanging out with older, known gang members, "Perhaps in hanging out with older boys, you are trying to fill in the missing father piece." This boy then revealed that he was very mad that his father was not around, and, when encouraged to demonstrate how angry, he clenched his fist and started to pound the floor. This exchange appeared to increase the groups support for him and his sense of being understood and accepted. In the weeks following this intervention, the boy stopped skipping school, ceased associating with older boys on the street, and became good friends with the other boys in the group. These gains were consolidated during the mother's participation in a group session by a discussion of ways to increase his opportunities to play with his new friends on weekends and during vacations.

Participation of parents or guardians in a group session has noticeable therapeutic benefit to both parents and child. This is especially true when there had been shared traumatic experiences or when there was traumatic bereavement. For example, one boy spoke up about how he felt his mother began to drink heavily after his oldest brother had died in a car accident. The mother confirmed his observation and shared with the group that she could not handle his death. She was heavily invested in his accomplishing his dream of becoming a minister and her dream of his leading the rest of the children into a better way of life. His death caused in her a crisis of faith. The boy then showed his mother his drawing of her looking sad and commented that he didn't feel it was OK for him to show his sadness if his mother was that sad. Another mother joined the discussion and told about how horribly difficult it had been for her to lose her husband. These types of exchanges led parents and children to become more empathic and responsive to each other.

This phase of treatment broaches other critical circumstances of the children's lives that are often associated with the referent trauma or other intercurrent experiences. In this group of children, a major area of concern is the illicit drug culture within the community and, in particular, involvement of family members. For example, one boy had been referred to the program after he witnessed the police search his house and arrest his mother for possession of illegal drugs. At first, the boy felt terribly guilty at failing to protect his mother, imagining that he could have hidden the drugs so the police would not have found them. Furthermore, he felt it was his job to get revenge on the mother's boyfriend, to whom the drugs belonged, and who had allowed her to be arrested in lieu of him.

The therapist felt the group was far enough along to address the increased risks to the family inherent in there being drugs present. This led to another boy also poignantly describing his intense sense of guilt, because he felt he should have acted on his "bad feeling" and kept his mother from going out of the house on the day she was murdered in a drive-by shooting. He knew that she was supposedly killed by a member of a drug ring and struggled to admit that she had been a drug addict. He spoke vehemently about the real blame belonging to those who killed her. The first boy spontaneously gave him a "high five" for his courage in sharing these intense negative emotions of guilt, shame, and revenge with the group.

Knowing of the boy's previous placement with his grandmother due to his mother's drug use, the therapist remarked that without her drug use, she would have been able to be there more for him. He quickly answered, "Yes, that's true. I wish she could have been my Mom." The children then spoke about how much they did not like drugs and became more receptive to considering the painful, disillusioning awareness of their parents' failings in critical matters of self-care and parenting. The added inner resources from the prior trauma/grief–focused work appear to be essential prerequisites to preparing some of the children to address the harsh realities of family lives that feel as if so much is missing.

Termination Phase

Even though the children will continue in the mentorship component of the program, our experience has confirmed the importance of ensuring proper attention to termination issues during the latter portion of the group sessions. The major goals of termination are to review out the work of the group; to address rekindling of central traumatic themes in the children's lives; to confront reversions to initial or earlier styles of avoidance, aggression, or restricted emotional range; to explore the shared meaning of the loss of the group; to prepare for entry into the mentorship program; and, to take proper leavetaking. We have observed that a dominant termination transference issue is the influence of traumatic expectations of injury, disruption, or loss on attitudes about the impending ending of the group. We find that proper attention to these termination issues can result in children coming to experience the termination as a nontraumatic transition in their lives, with an appreciation that the group experience has promoted their developmental growth.

During the eighth session, the therapist provides the group a timely reminder that there will be four more sessions after they meet that day and gives the exact date of the last meeting. They look at a calendar together to visualize this information. There may be no specific discussion about termination at this point; however, our therapists have observed different forms of behavioral responses that reflect protective reactions against the impending dissolution of the group. For example, some children begin to tell jokes as if to look for ways to lessen the value of the group, and some children can be seen to immediately pair off in play or in joke telling, as if to strengthen an attachment that can outlast the group. As a group, there may be a temporary return to increased motor activity and agitation. Because at this stage of therapy the children understand the significance of these types of behaviors, the therapist makes interpretations; for example, "Here we go with another loss and we're bouncing off our seats. I wonder what that tells us," or "I wonder if you had strong feelings about my speaking about the group finishing. I can see you would like to find a lasting place in a friendship to fill in for losing what we give to each other here in the group." The children clearly hear these interpretations and respond with more considered thought about their own reactions. They take the ending seriously and may stop the therapist on the school playground to remark with concern, "We only have two more times to meet."

During the final group sessions, children often contribute to the interpretative work for each other. For example, when one child began to make jokes as if to laugh off the ending of the group, another child remarked, "Maybe you're laughing 'cause it reminds you of your brother dying." The first child then got mad, exclaiming, "That's not why I am laughing." The therapist commented, "Maybe it feels good to try to be strong and tough about the group ending, even through laughter, and your friend burst the bubble for all of us." At a later point, the therapist added, "Feelings about the group ending can feel like 'weak feelings' inside of you, and you don't want that to happen. You want to feel strong, especially since I brought up the ending of the group." The first boy then said, "Its not fair we can't just keep going on." He followed this protest by continuing, "It wasn't fair when my brother died. I didn't get a chance to say good-bye."

This led to other children talking about premature endings and a general sense of unfairness that this is all the group time that had been allotted. After these exchanges, the therapist suggested that things happen in life that do not feel fair and emphasized, "What can make a difference in the group is that we know together how we are feeling and try to share in understanding it." Underneath some of the protest of unfairness is the incorporation of a traumatic expectation into a self-attribution of being the type of person to whom unfair things happen.

In the tenth session, the two individuals who serve as mentors join the group to be introduced. The time and place of the mentorship program is announced and, at the same time, a notification letter is sent home. The purpose of the mentorship program is discussed, emphasizing its goals of assisting them in respecting one another, in providing a wider discussion of their community and society, and their future expectations. There is an observable change in reaction among the children in response to the mentors. If the work of the group has proceeded well to this point, sufficient group treatment of the traumatizing experiences has resulted in a more self-reflective, private self and a more competent social self. These changes, in combination with diminished personal and group traumatic expectations, allow them more freely to focus on external realities, their emerging beliefs in regard to the social contract, and their developmental transition into adolescence. The therapist must be prepared for the continuing tension of the need to keep children focused on the goals of termination while the children also anticipate, with relief, no longer being confronted by internal explorations and being provided active guidance in their lives beyond the confines of the psychotherapeutic setting.

After the mentors have left, the therapist readdresses the issue of the group's therapeutic identity by introducing a termination exercise that may continue during the remaining sessions. The children are invited to jointly paint a mural that depicts what the group has meant to each of them, as a way of formally initiating an ongoing process of review. The therapist explains that during the last session, they will hang the mural on the office wall to visually preserve the children's group experience. The children readily engage in this activity. Children may write their names or words of gratitude, express sad and grieving feelings in drawings and words, or depict scenes of promise and hope.

The remaining portion of the tenth and eleventh session more thoroughly complete this process of review. The therapist asks each person to tell the other group members "what you really want others to remember and hold onto about what you said in the group." One child said he wanted the group to remember that his mother was killed. The other children said they would remember this having happened to him. This heroic boy insisted on more; he wanted them to remain attentive to the most horrific, personal details of her death. He demanded of the group, "Well, *how* did she die?" The group struggled for a moment, and then a member said that she was shot. "How many times?" the boy inquired. This questioning went on until the boy was satisfied that the group recalled all of the details that he had been struggling to manage within himself.

As has occurred in many similar termination-phase group sessions, children want to ensure a group awareness of the "death imprint" (Lifton, 1979) with which they live. Concomitantly, the wish for others to retain these details surrounding the death may be seen as representing efforts: not to have to explain oneself to others; to internalize the group to help in regulating response to recurring images, nightmares, and fears, even after the group has ended; and, to reconfirm that, even in the face of these horrific traumatic details, their friendships will continue. This use of the group as a repository of images of death appears also to relieve an unspoken sense of stigmatization over the traumatic loss.

During this treatment phase, the intervention fantasies shift from ones that could have changed the traumatic outcome to those that are aimed at easing the unprepared for and abrupt separation brought about by traumatic deaths or separations. For example, in the above-mentioned group, a third child spoke movingly of having held his brother in his arms while he died at the scene of an automobile accident. The therapist then chose an appropriate later moment to interpret that everyone has fantasies of what they wished they could do in order to make it feel a little less painful. The therapist then spoke directly to this boy by saying, "It was important for you to have this thought in your mind." He acknowledged, "Yeah, I knew I was at home when he died." The therapist then distinguished between these traumatic experiences of loss and the loss of the group in terms of the opportunity to talk beforehand and to say good-bye.

It has become our practice to accompany the children from their classrooms to the last session, in recognition of the difficulty many of them feel in attending this final session. The children and therapist form a circle and put all the drawings and other things they have done together in the center. They are then asked to put their hands together and say something they remember about the group. We have observed that most children tend not to speak about themselves, but rather choose to speak empathically of remembrances about sharing their tragic experiences.

The termination phase helps to facilitate a transition from self-preoccupation that is prolonged or exaggerated by violent exposures to a more developmentally appropriate orientation that includes thoughts about the well-being of others. There is a rediscussion of the change in focus that will occur during the mentorship, with an emphasis on the idea of their being part of a school community in which starting this next component does not mean starting over. The children are aware that the group therapists and mentors are part of a larger therapeutic program, and the therapist reminds them of the confidentiality of the material discussed in the group by asking each of them if there is anything that they do not wish the therapist to share with the mentors.

Toward the end of the last session, the children hang their mural on the wall and take a final moment to say something nice about the child sitting next to them. The therapist joins in the emotional exchanges, remembering a significant moment about each child's participation in the group and sharing with them a respect for their courage. The therapist confirms that he or she will continue to be at the school, that they may see each other on the school campus, and that the children should feel free to come by if there is something they wish to talk about, or just to say "hello."

CRISIS INTERVENTION: A BRIEF GROUP THERAPY APPROACH

In addition to the individual–group–mentorship track, we developed a brief group therapy model of crisis intervention that incorporated principles of the overall therapeutic approach to address major intercurrent group exposures to violence experienced by many of the students at this school. We have responded to those violent crises that seemed most salient to the school community or to some group of children. We have included children who had direct exposure at the scene and those who lived in proximity to the event. In order to manage the resources committed to crisis work, we modified our usual procedures to include working with teachers and parents in group settings rather than on an individual basis, and providing additional time for debriefing of project staff engaged in crisis work. This crisis group work has been very important to our recognition and acceptance by the school personnel, especially the teachers.

Within the first year of the program, we had to contend with such events as a major earthquake; the accidental amputation of a kindergarten child's finger while at school; a gang-related murder in which gunfire was audible in the school classrooms and the victim's mutilated body remained visible hanging out of a car at the intersection of the school for more than 6 hours, including at the time of dismissal from the school; the murder of a 3-year-old child by his mother's boyfriend in an apartment building where many school children resided; and the murder of a local merchant, witnessed by many of the school children.

The crisis intervention often includes two phases. First, several staff members conduct a classroom consultation in a class with exposed children. Second, staff members conduct a six- to eight-session group therapy treatment of the most affected children. The classroom consultation follows the format described by Pynoos and Nader (1988, 1993) for psychological first aid following an acute traumatic exposure or death. The format includes an opening discussion, a trauma-focused drawing and storytelling activity, and a summation discussion. During the drawing exercise, children are asked to draw two pictures, one that depicts their feeling about what happened, and another that illustrates how they would have liked things to have been different. During this activity, each child in the classroom is seen individually, with special attention to children who had direct exposure. The discussion centers first on children having different sets of reactions, depending on their degree of exposure, thereby explaining some of the classroom behavior of their peers, and second, on the concerns of most of the children over something like this happening. The affected children are invited to participate in a crisis trauma–focused psychotherapy group. Teachers have described these classroom consultations as helpful in restoring a calmer atmosphere, in which children were able to attend to their studies, by reintegrating affected children with their classmates and teacher.

PARTICIPATION OF COMMUNITY-BASED POLICE OFFICERS IN THE GROUP PSYCHOTHERAPY COMPONENT

There are two main areas in which community-based police officers interface with children in group psychotherapy: during the regular group psychotherapy component, and during the crisis intervention module. Police officers are included in selected group psychotherapy sessions in order to respond to children's conflict over police action or inaction in regard to their traumatic experiences. During these sessions, the children, who through the group have verbalized more of their own internal life, often ask the police officers to share their subjective experience regarding work and relationships. This dialogue has helped to repair the estrangement from the police arising from a specific trauma/loss-related experience. In addition, these exchanges allow the children to appreciate that a police officer can be interested in their experiences and concerned about their welfare. The openness of the police officer in discussing the obligations, limitations, and accountability of police contributes to children's

reframing of traumatic experiences to include more constructive prevention and intervention plans of action.

Two brief case examples illustrate the use of police in the regular
group psychotherapy. A police officer was invited to join a session to
address a child's unremitting distress from having witnessed his older
cousin's arrest more than 6 months before he entered the program. He
felt especially challenged by the police viewing his cousin as a criminal,
whereas he had always experienced him as a protective and caring figure.
Furthermore, he remained extremely upset by the manner of the arrest,
in which he felt the police humiliated his cousin and treated him "like
an animal." They had physically forced him to lie prone on the ground,
handcuffing him in front of neighbors and relatives. At the time, the
child was afraid that the police would also arrest him, thinking he would
be implicated for some unknown crime just because he was a relative.
He ran and hid in the bushes.

During the group session, the child told the police officer that he
felt his cousin was not guilty and had been arrested in an unfair and cruel
fashion. He described how scared he remains of the police, with his
understanding that they were the ones that behaved in a criminal manner.
The community police officer responded nondefensively, first establishing that he was not at the scene, but that police officers sometimes, in
retrospect, may have used more force than necessary in making an arrest.
He added that sometimes this is because police officers are scared themselves for their own safety, and for those in the immediate vicinity of
the arrest. He reassured him that the police officers were not there to
arrest him, and that they are required to obtain a warrant for a particular
individual after diligent investigation. In the aftermath of this exchange,
the boy appeared less burdened by his experience. He also expressed less
conflict over his identification with his cousin, who still cares for him,
and his fear of a sense of betrayal if he views the police as providing
important protective functions in his community.

In another group, a police officer was asked to attend because a child
expressed chronic resentment over the lack of arrest of the person who
hit and killed his best friend with a car. He remained disillusioned over
what he perceived to be police inaction in allowing his friend's death, or
inefficacy in apprehending and punishing the perpetrator. He also struggled with his debilitating rage against the perpetrator. He asked to police
officer, "Are you trying to find the guy?" and, before the police officer
could answer, he added, "What about people who speed. Are you doing
something about people who are reckless drivers?" The police officer
responded first to the latter question, by answering, "We do stop people
who are speeding, but people are responsible for obeying the speed limits,
too, because police cannot be everywhere they would like to be to prevent

people from being hurt or killed." The police officer then addressed the first question. He was not familiar with the case and began by asking the boy what he knew about the incident. The boy described hearing that a man speeding hit his friend and then kept going. The police officer explained what is referred to as a "hit and run," that it is considered a very serious crime, and that any person who commits this crime deserves to be apprehended, tried, and punished according to the law. He explained that this type of case can be very difficult to solve because, without a witness who can describe the car and its license plate, it is difficult to find out who did it. He explained that it is frustrating for the police, because although a case like this remains open for years, without additional information, these types of cases often go unsolved. He added that he understood the horrible sadness the boy felt over the loss of his best friend, and that his rage was made worse by the inability of the police to bring the perpetrator to justice. He concluded by saying how helpless, sad, and angry he feels as a police officer when he is not able to prevent a child from being killed, or to catch the person who did it.

Several children wanted to know how officers feel "if they call your mother names." The male officer answered that it does not bother him, because "I know they do not really mean me, and I know I am a good person and that my mother is a good person." They took his words as an example of how feeling good about oneself can create an inner voice that defuses an impulse to retaliate. They appreciated that good police officers regulate their emotions and think before choosing how to respond.

The children went on to ask the officers about their professional and personal lives. They were looking for ways to bridge estrangements created by tensions in the community over the role of the police, and to assure themselves of the personal interest of the officers in their welfare. They wanted confirmation that police would get up out of bed to respond to emergencies, for example, if a child is in danger, and the police officers answered that they knew in choosing their profession that their responsibilities might interfere with their personal lives. The officers also described how, as community-based police officers, they are being especially trained to be caring and responsive. These exchanges appeared to increase children's trust of the police, without a false idealization, and to generate more hope that the police can be viewed as friends.

Community-based police officers also participate in the brief crisis group therapy module. Two themes often run through children's discussion of the role of the police after an acute violent episode, the first as a protector that physically prevents harm, and the second as a moral gatekeeper that ensures justice, fairness, and obedience to the law. This following brief example illustrates how such a crisis can jeopardize a basic assumption about the value of the police to ensure a wider protective shield beyond that to be expected from parents. From a crisis standpoint, it can be essential to repair an acute rupture in children's expectations about the police. Unrepaired, such an early rupture could potentially have long-term implications for children's readiness to rely on the assistance of the police, or to take actions into their own hands.

Two days after a 3-year-old child had been beaten to death by the mother's boyfriend while she was away, some children who lived in the apartment complex started talking at school about how they had heard screams and pounding on the floor in the middle of the night. Other children talked about missing their dead playmate. A sensitive teacher overheard their conversation and referred them to our project staff. Twelve children who attended the elementary school and lived in this apartment complex were seen in a crisis group psychotherapy. In the second session, the children prepared a list of questions that they wanted to ask, including the following: How did the child die? Why did the police take so long to arrive at the scene? Why did the police let it happen? Were there drugs involved? Why do adults hurt children? Had the police caught the man yet? What are they going to do to him if they do catch him?

In preparing the police officer to join the group, the therapist cautioned her about including unnecessary, gruesome details about the murder, while encouraging her to be open to the children's inquiries. In the third session, the officer and three parents attended. Parents and children first wanted to know the status of the case and were told that the assailant had been arrested and was now in jail. The children asked how the child was killed. The police officer first asked about what they knew or had heard and confirmed that a wooden hanger had been used. This exchange opened up questions about child abuse and the rights of children not to be mistreated. The officer discussed how to call her if they know something like this was occurring. That immediately elicited statements from both children and parents over feeling guilty at not calling when they heard the screams on this and past occasions. A discussion followed about how to distinguish among situations, for example, abuse, boisterous partying, or pounding on the floor from weight lifting.

The police officer, as an authority figure about the social contract, can sometimes directly alleviate children's feelings of guilt and ineffectualness in a manner that supplements clinical efforts. The officer discussed limitations that we all have in knowing what is happening behind a family's closed doors. She confirmed that it can be very difficult to know when to call. She addressed not only the issue of prevention, but also tried to alleviate their guilt by saying, "It's okay and understandable that you feel guilty, yet you didn't really know. We, as police officers, are faced with these types of feelings because of our own limitations."

The children then challenged the police officer as to why it took 6 hours for the police to arrive at the scene. They added, "Why didn't you know he was a criminal and stop him beforehand?" This police officer did not excuse the late arrival, although she did describe the broad responsibilities of the police for other serious emergency calls, including the fact that on that evening there had been a number of very serious calls that they did their best to respond to, and stated that it is not a matter of not caring. At the end of the session, she reiterated that she is specifically assigned to their community and would be available to talk to the children whenever they had a question or were concerned about something happening in their community or where they live.

The crisis program has had to work through issues of confidentiality versus public interest in choosing to include the police in the group work. For example, a group of children had witnessed the murder of a local merchant. These children felt themselves in a dilemma over fearing retaliation as a "snitch" if they provided information to the police, while strongly wishing the police would arrest and imprison the assailant. The clinician experienced a similar dilemma. While trying to accommodate the children's request to discuss the experience with the officer, she, nevertheless, needed to ensure confidentiality and that such confidential material would not be used to involuntarily involve a child in the investigation or prosecution. The officer experienced his own dilemma in reporting to his supervisor, and in the supervisor's wish to interrogate each of the children more fully. The issue was resolved through open discussion with the supervisor, police officer, and the group, and the willingness of the children to inform the police that they thought the suspect was still in the area. The police increased their neighborhood surveillance and eventually captured the suspect. When the police officer returned to the group at a later session to tell them about the arrest, he was rewarded by a genuine and spontaneous expression of thanks from the children, who described relief from their most intense fantasies of revenge and counterretaliation.

CONCLUSION

This chapter describes a school-based prevention/intervention program for elementary school children exposed to intra- and extrafamilial violence and loss. This program emerges from a model that places the child within a complex developmental and social context. The overall strategy gives equal attention to the intrapsychic dimensions of distress and disturbances in expectations regarding the social contract. We have provided an in-depth clinical discussion of the trauma/grief-focused group psychotherapy component of the overall intervention. In the future we intend to provide similar in-depth descriptions of the individual and mentorship components. We hope that these intervention protocols, together with the assessment methodology, will contribute to a more rigorous approach to the evaluation of the efficacy of trauma–grief focused group psychotherapy with children and adolescents (Sugar, 1993).

We would propose that school provides the most accessible, functional, and efficient setting in which to implement a comprehensive mental health program for children exposed to violence, disaster, and loss (Pynoos, Goenjian, & Steinberg, 1995). We hope that the methods described here and the clinical material presented will encourage others to envision the opportunity to further develop and implement this type of integrated school-based mental health–mentorship program. Furthermore, we hope that the examples of the innovative ways in which community police officers have participated in this program will promote others to consider similar police training and the potential therapeutic use of police officers.

We are completing evaluation of this intervention sequence among 65 boys, mostly in the third, fourth, and fifth grades. Preliminary findings indicate that behavioral, educational, and family improvements are evident at the end of the mentorship. Acceptance of the program by school personnel, families, and students has continued to be excellent. Levels of parental participation and teacher satisfaction have increased as the program has progressed.

Specifically, teachers have reported a significant decrease in the most aggressive externalizing behaviors among the students in the program and measurable improvement in their academic performance. They have also reported that those children with the most serious internalizing behaviors have become more prosocial, more communicative, more responsive in the classrooms, and more included by peers in school activities, inside and outside of the classroom. Teachers particularly expressed satisfaction with having been given psychological assistance from the project staff in managing children with behavior and academic difficulties. We have observed a trend for students in the program to refer schoolmates who have had violent exposures and for individual students to approach staff to self-refer.

To date, our experience strongly indicates that a public health approach to the problem of violence should include therapeutic attention to the internal mental life and social ramifications of children's responses to violence and loss. If left untreated, the resultant psychological reactions, impaired acquisition of developmental competencies, and altered sense of the social contract may seriously hamper developmental potential and contribute to the cycle of violence.

Finally, this project has confirmed the necessity and benefit of providing systematic therapeutic intervention with elementary school children for their real-life experiences with violence and loss. The ability of elementary school children to engage in this most difficult therapeutic work should not be underestimated. As a society, we owe it to children throughout the United States to make such services more of a national priority. As we have come to appreciate, there is a need to integrate therapeutic and mentorship programs. The former provides a road to the restoration of personal integrity for children. The latter provides a wider social map by which children can discover a more meaningful vision of "growing up." It has been our hope, and so far our experience, that this psychosocial approach relieves children of traumatic expectations that limit their trust in their own future, in the safety and security of interpersonal life, and in the protection, fairness, and benefit of social institutions.

ACKNOWLEDGMENT

Support for this project was provided by a grant through the Victim–Witness Assistance Delinquency Prevention Program, Los Angeles County District Attorney's Office, and from the Juvenile Justice and Delinquency Prevention Program, Office of Criminal Justice Planning, State of California. Additional support was provided by the Robert Ellis Simon Foundation and the Bing Fund.

REFERENCES

Achenbach, T., & Edelbrock, C. (1983). *Manual for the Teachers' Report Form and Teacher Version of the Child Behavior Profile.* Burlington: University of Vermont, Psychiatry Aassociates.

Asarnow, J. R., & Carlson, G. A. (1985). Depression Self-Rating Scale: Utility with child psychiatric inpatients. *Journal of Consulting and Clinical Psychology, 53,* 491–499.

Atkins, M., & Pelham, W. (1991). School-based assessment of attention deficit-hyperactivity disorder. *Journal of Learning Disabilities, 24,* 187–204.

Bell, C. C., & Jenkins, E. J. (1993). Community violence and children on the Southside of Chicago. *Psychiatry, 56,* 46–54.

Centers for Disease Control and Prevention. (1994). Homicides among 15–19 year-old males—United States, 1963–1991. *Morbidity and Mortality Weekly Report, 43,* 725–727.

Conners, C. K. (1969). A teacher rating scale for use in drug studies with children. *American Journal of Psychiatry, 126,* 884–888.

Fitzpatrick, K., & Boldizar, J. (1993). The prevalence and consequences of exposure to violence among African-American youth. *Journal of the American Academy of Child and Adolescent Psychiatry, 32,* 424–430.

Freeman, L., Mokros, H., & Pozanski, E. (1993). Violent event reported by normal urban school-aged children: Characteristics and depression correlates. *Journal of the American Academy of Child and Adolescent Psychiatry, 32,* 419–423.

Goenjian, A. K., Pynoos, R. S., Steinberg, A. M., Najarian, L. M., Asarnow, J. R., Karayan, I., Ghurabi, M., & Fairbanks, L. A. (1995). Psychiatric comorbidity in children after the 1988 earthquake in Armenia. *Journal of the American Academy of Child and Adolescent Psychiatry, 34,* 1174–1184.

Groves, B. M., Zuckerman, B., Marans, S., & Cohen, D. J. (1993). Silent victims: Children who witness violence. *Journal of the American Medical Association, 269,* 262–264.

Koop, C. E., & Lundberg, G. D. (1992). Violence in America: A public health emergency. *Journal of the American Medical Association, 267,* 3075–3076. Corrections: 1992:*268,* 3074 & 1994:*271,* 1404.

Lifton, R. J. (1979). *The broken connection.* New York: Simon & Schuster.

Marmar, C., Foy, D., Kagan, V., & Pynoos, R. (1993). An Integrated approach for treating posttraumatic Stress. In J. Oldham, M. Riba, & A. Tasman (Eds.), *American Psychiatric Press review of psychiatry* (Vol. 12, pp. 238–272). Washington, DC: American Psychiatric Association Press.

Osofsky, J. D., Wewers, S., Hann, D. M., & Fick, A. C. (1993). Chronic community violence: What is happening to our children? *Psychiatry 56,* 36–45.

Petrovic, V. (1994, September). *Education for conflict resolution and corrective experience for traumatic stress.* Unpublished report submitted to the UNICEF Psychosocial Program in the former Yugoslavia, Sarajevo.

Prothrow-Stith, D. (1991). *Deadly consequences.* New York: HarperCollins.

Pynoos, R. S. (1992). Grief and trauma in children and adolescents. *Bereavement Care, 11,* 2–10.

Pynoos, R. S. (1993). Traumatic stress and developmental psychopathology in children and adolescents. In J. M. Oldham, M. B. Riba, & A. Tasman (Eds.), *American Psychiatric Press review of psychiatry* (Vol. 12, pp. 205–238). Washington, DC: American Psychiatric Association Press.

Pynoos, R. S., & Eth, S. (1985). Children traumatized by witnessing acts of personal violence: Homicide, rape or suicide behavior. In S. Eth & R. S. Pynoos (Eds.), *Post-traumatic stress disorder in children* (pp. 19–23). Washington, DC: American Psychiatric Association Press.

Pynoos, R. S., Frederick, C., Nader, K., Arroyo, W., Steinberg, A., Eth, S., Nunez, F., & Fairbanks, L. (1987). Life threat and posttraumatic stress in school-age children. *Archives of General Psychiatry, 44,* 1057–1063.

Pynoos, R. S., Goenjian, A., & Steinberg, A. M. (1995). Strategies of disaster intervention for children and adolescents. In S. E. Hobfoll & M. deVries (Eds.), *Extreme stress and communities: Impact and interventions* (pp. 445–471). Dordrecht, The Netherlands: M. Kluwer.

Pynoos, R. S., Goenjian, A., Tashjian, M., Karakashian, M., Manjikian, R., Manoukian, G., Steinberg, A., & Fairbanks, L. (1993). Posttraumatic stress reactions in children after the 1988 Armenian earthquake. *British Journal of Psychiatry, 163,* 239–247.

Pynoos, R. S., & Nader, K. (1990, June). *Children's adjustment following a sniper incident in Los Angeles. Community violence and children's development: Research and clinical implications.* Presentation at Conference sponsored by the National Institute of Mental Health, Washington School of Psychiatry, and the Mac-Arthur Foundation, Washington, DC.

Pynoos, R. S., & Nader, K. (1988). Children who witness the sexual assaults of their mothers. *Journal of the American Academy of Child and Adolescent Psychiatry, 27,* 567–572.

Pynoos, R. S., & Nader, R. (1993). Issues in the treatment of post-traumatic stress in children and adolescents. In J. P. Wilson & B. Raphael (Eds.), *The international handbook of traumatic stress syndromes* (pp. 535–549). New York: Plenum Press.

Pynoos, R. S., Steinberg, A. M., & Wraith, R. (1995). A developmental model of childhood traumatic stress. In D. Cicchetti & D. J. Cohen (Eds.), *Manual of developmental psychopathology: Vol. 2. Risk, disorder, and adaptation* (pp. 72–95). New York: Wiley.

Richters, J. E., & Martinez, P. (1993). The NIMH community violence project: I. Children as victims of and witnesses to violence. *Psychiatry 56,* 7–21.

Richters, J. E. & Saltzman, W. (1990). *Survey of children's exposure to community violence.* Bethesda, MD: National Institute of Mental Health.

Schwab-Stone, M. E., Ayers, T. S., Kasprow, W., Voyce, C. Barone, C., Shriver, T., & Weissberg, R. P. (1995). No safe haven: A study of violence exposure in an urban community. *Journal of the American Academy of Child and Adolescent Psychiatry, 34,* 1343–1352.

Sugar, M. (1993). Research in child and adolescent group psychotherapy. *Journal of Child and Adolescent Group Therapy, 4,* 207–226.

Ursano R. J., McCaughey B., & Fullerton, C. S. (Eds.). (1994). Individual and community responses to trauma and disaster: The structure of chaos. London: Cambridge University Press.

Walker, H. M., & Severson, H. H (1990). *Systematic screening for behavior disorders: Technical manual.* Longmont, CO: Sopris West.

Weinberg, M. F. (1994, Fall). *Annual report.* Inglewood, CA: Inglewood Police Department.

12

The Violence Intervention Project for Children and Families

JOY D. OSOFSKY

I N INTRODUCING THE VIOLENCE INTERVENTION PROJECT for Children and Families (VIP), I will share the philosophy that has guided the project and the process of developing this program. In this book, the reader has had the opportunity to review similar and different intervention programs for children and youth who are exposed to and/or witness violence that link mental health services with police training in other cities across the United States, including Boston, Los Angeles, and New Haven. The findings from our project in New Orleans will be presented in subsequent chapters by my colleagues and collaborators on the project: Ana C. Fick, Marva L. Lewis, and Pamela Jenkins.

The VIP was developed as a direct response to the crisis of rising violence in New Orleans (paralleling that in the United States as a whole) and the fact that we found ever-increasing numbers of children being exposed to violence as victims or witnesses. Personally, I became increasingly distressed as reports continued to appear in the press about younger and younger children, those as young as 10 or 11 years of age, having guns in their possession and using them to shoot people. In an effort to learn more about the problem in New Orleans, we carried out a study in 1992 (Osofsky, Wewers, Hann, & Fick, 1993) with 54 parents of fifth graders in an elementary school located in a neighborhood with one of the highest levels of violence. We found that 45% of the children had witnessed a shooting or stabbing and, even more appalling to me, 40% of these 9- to 12-year-old children reported having seen a dead body. In talking to the mothers and children, we learned that children were carrying guns and knives to school in order to feel safe. Mothers taught children to watch television with their heads below the level of the window sills to avoid stray bullets and to dive into the bathtub when they heard shooting. We carried out this study before so much news about children as victims and perpetrators of violence was commonly in the press. Some of the children we interviewed admitted that they did not expect to live beyond their teen years.

As we started to initiate our project in 1993, we joined with an ongoing program that had been in place for about a year called Project LAST (Loss and Survival Team) for children exposed to homicide, which was sponsored by the Children's Bureau, a community agency. We met with many community groups and resident council leaders, presenting our ideas for the project. A problem that we faced from the outset was how to implement such a program and make it work in New Orleans, which is a city with a high level of violence (most of which occurs in inner-city neighborhoods in and around the public housing developments), limited economic resources, diminishing resources for community mental health services, and an overstressed, overburdened, and underpaid police force. At the urging of members of several community groups, we decided to develop a model program in one of the New Orleans Police Districts with the highest level of violence. The program would include education for police officers at all levels on the effects of violence on children, and offer a 24-hour hotline for consultation by police or families for referral of children up to 12 years of age who had been exposed to violence and about whom there was concern. For older children, we would take the calls and refer them to other services. A crucial part of our program, however, was to raise awareness about the importance of prevention and to direct our attention and that of the police toward younger children who witnessed violence.

Before implementing the program, we decided it would be extremely helpful to gather more information from children, parents, and police about their perceptions of violence in the community, their feelings of safety, and for each group, how much they thought children trusted the police. In a neighborhood of New Orleans characterized by a very high rate of violence (hereafter referred to as the sixth Police District), 250 third- and fifth-grade African American children completed an age-appropriate survey regarding issues of trust and safety. Sixty parents from this neighborhood and 335 police officers from the entire city also completed the needs assessment. Seventy-nine percent of the parents had annual incomes below $10,000. The demographics of the sample are presented in Table 12.1. For comparison purposes, only the responses of the 103 police officers in the fifth and sixth Police Districts (areas with comparable high rates of violence) will be discussed (see Figure 12.1).

TABLE 12.1. Demographics: Parents and Police

	Parents ($n = 65$)	Police, 5th and 6th districts ($n = 105$)
Gender		
Male	9%	90%
Female	91%	10%
Ethnicity		
African American	98%	43%
Caucasian	2%	48%
Other	—	9%
Age		
Mean	31.4	35.2
Range	20–52	19–67
Education		
Some high school	34%	—
GED, high school	32%	22%
Some college	24%	54%
College +	10%	23%
Years on the force	N/A	
<4 years		23%
4–17 years		54%
>17 years		23%

Information about perceptions of trust and safety was gathered as background data to be used to develop an educational curriculum for police officers and intervention efforts for children and families exposed to violence. In this chapter, the trust data will be described. Data on other aspects of the survey will be presented in subsequent chapters in this volume—perceptions of safety by Fick, Osofsky, and Lewis (Chapter 13), and attitudes about domestic violence, police procedure, and children by Jenkins, Osofsky, and Fick (Chapter 15). There follows also an analysis of pictures that the children drew of what goes on in their neighborhoods by Lewis and Osofsky (Chapter 14).

The findings from the trust data were very interesting. The majority of these 8- to 12-year-old children (76%) reported trusting the police more than either parents or police officers thought they trusted the police. Although there were no sex differences in children's reported trust of the police, an interesting developmental trend was noted: Third graders reported trusting the police more than fifth graders. Parents reported that they thought children trusted the police more than the police perceived children trusting them. These findings were somewhat unexpected. Based on the amount of violent crime in the neighborhoods where we

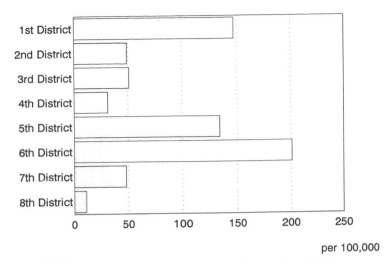

FIGURE 12.1. Estimated 1994 homicide rate by police district.

were working and the general distrust and antagonism that exists between community residents and police, we did not expect to find the majority of the children reporting that they trusted the police. The police were even more surprised by the finding. However, it should be emphasized that it is likely that the police were thinking about older children or adolescents when they answered the question. We used the data from the study to provide an opportunity to learn more about how living in a violent environment may impact on children's development of trust, particularly of the police, and what strategies might be used to increase mutual trust among parents, police, and children.

In developing our program, we worked to find ways to build relationships between the community, police, mental health professionals, and schools to address issues of prevention for referred children who witnessed violence and could not sleep, were disruptive in school, or clung to their mothers. We worked together to develop strategies that police might use when investigating violent incidents, such as homicides, how we could work with parents to find ways that they could protect their children, keep them safe, and away from violent scenes because of the potentially traumatizing impact on both them and their children, and how to build strengths in communities to help parents and children. The police also wanted to find ways that community residents could help them in their crime-fighting work, at the same time as they were trying to become more sensitive to the needs of the children and families.

Our project has continued to evolve and grow. Evaluation of effectiveness has been built into our intervention program from its inception, so that we have been able to learn about what works and what does not and determine the changes that are needed to make the program more effective. We have developed materials to use for training and intervention, including a Police Education Manual, a Children's Safety Booklet, and a quarterly Newsletter about activities of the project. We have recently received corporate and private foundation funding that is allowing us to expand the program to other parts of the city as well as in the schools and community sites. As mentioned, detailed reports of other aspects of the program follow.

REFERENCE

Osofsky, J. D., Wewers, S., Hann, D. M., & Fick, A. C. (1993). Chronic community violence: What is happening to our children? *Psychiatry: Interpersonal and Biological Processes, 56,* 36–45.

13

Perceptions of Violence: Children, Parents, and Police Officers

ANA C. FICK
JOY D. OSOFSKY
MARVA L. LEWIS

COMMUNITY VIOLENCE AS A PUBLIC HEALTH PHENOMENON

In the past few years, interpersonal violence has come to the forefront as a significant public health problem (Rosenberg, 1994; Rosenberg, O'Carroll, & Powell, 1992; Prothrow-Stith & Spivak, 1992) with community violence having reached epidemic proportions (Richters & Martinez, 1993). The United States has the dubious distinction of being the most violent country in the industrialized world (Fingerhut & Kleinman, 1990). It has been well documented in earlier work and in the present book that large numbers of children, even very young children, are exposed to chronic violence as both witnesses and victims (Bell & Jenkins, 1993; Richters & Martinez, 1993; Osofsky, Wewers, Hann, & Fick, 1993; Osofsky, 1995).

The high homicide rates evidenced among young people is often used as an indication of the severity of the problem. For example, the homicide rate has more than doubled since 1950, with the most recently reported rate being 37 per 100,000 people. For African American males ages 15–24, the rate is 158 per 100,000 (Rosenberg, 1994). Yet, the grim homicide statistics do not adequately denote the extent to which violence has infiltrated the lives of many young people. Furthermore, homicide is "only the tip of the iceberg" (Prothrow-Stith & Spivak, 1992, p. 132), with the national rate of nonfatal interpersonal violence being significantly higher; estimates of nonlethal episodes of violence are at least 17 times the lethal rate (Bell, 1987). Not only is homicide the second leading cause of death for adolescents and young adults ages 15–24, but also in 1995, it became the third leading cause of death among elementary school children (Kochanek & Hudson, 1995).

The high rates of exposure to violence for children growing up in some inner-city neighborhoods with pervasive violence have been well documented. In a survey of sixth, eighth, and tenth graders in New Haven in 1992, 40% reported witnessing at least one violent crime in the past year (Marans & Cohen, 1993). Very few inner-city children in New Haven were able to avoid exposure to violence, and almost all eighth graders knew someone who had been killed. Pynoos and Eth (1985) estimated that children witness approximately 10–20% of the homicides committed in Los Angeles. Bell and Jenkins (1991), in a study of African American children living in a Chicago neighborhood with much violence, reported that one-third of all school-age children had witnessed a homicide, and that two-thirds had witnessed a serious assault. Richters and Martinez (1993) carried out an extensive study on elementary school children's exposure to violence by interviewing 165 mothers of children ages 6–10 living in a low-income neighborhood in Washington, DC. Concurrently, Osofsky et al. (1993) gathered similar interview data on 53 African American mothers of children ages 9–12 in a low-income neighborhood of New Orleans characterized by an even higher level of violence, according to police statistics, than the Washington, DC, neighborhood. The data showed that children are victims of and witnesses to significant amounts of violence, with 51% of the New Orleans fifth graders and 32% of the Washington, DC, children reporting being victims of violence. Ninety-one percent of the New Orleans children and 72% of those in Washington, DC, had witnessed some type of violence. Both of these studies also found a significant relationship between children's reported exposure to community violence and intrafamily conflict, as measured by the Conflict Tactics Scale (Straus, 1979). These data emphasize the importance of including measures of family violence in studies of exposure to community violence to determine differential exposure, and to study the separate and combined impact on children of being raised in violent homes and violent neighborhoods.

POVERTY AND VIOLENCE

Violence prevention work makes it clear that violence is a multifaceted problem, one that is closely related to a host of broader social, environmental, and individual conditions and problems. The environment, that is, the social and cultural context in which families live, can help either to promote or buffer violence, and environmental characteristics can either exacerbate or ameliorate its impact on children and families. The American Psychological Association (1993) report. *Violence and Youth: Psychology's Response*, highlighted certain social characteristics as having important effects on the rate of violence in this country. Among these are attitudes toward violence in the larger society, poverty and socioeconomic inequality, and prejudice and discrimination.

Interpersonal violence cuts across racial and socioeconomic lines; nonetheless, some segments of society are more vulnerable and bear a significantly larger share of the problem. For example, the increasing rates in violence have been characterized as a "health problem that takes its greatest toll on young black men" (Prothrow-Stith & Spivak, 1992). Although homicide rates are high for all racial groups, homicide is the leading cause of death for young African American males and females. A young African American male is 11 times more likely to be murdered than a non-African American male, and an African American female is four times more likely to be a victim of homicide than a non-African American female (American Psychological Association, 1993).

In discussing the higher rates of violence documented among ethnic minority groups, it is important to emphasize that a significant risk factor for increased violence exposure and victimization is living in poverty (American Psychological Association, 1993). Poverty and its associated circumstances are recognized as major determinants of violence. The greater violence rates observed among ethnic minority groups may be due to the fact that a significantly greater percentage of these children grow up in poverty: 38% of Hispanic, 44% of Asian and Pacific Islander, 44% of African American, and 90% of Native American children grow up in poverty, compared to 15% of nonminority children. When socioeconomic status is controlled for, few differences in rates of violence among the ethnic groups are found (American Psychological Association, 1993).

The United States is facing a social problem of epidemic proportions—almost one-fourth (23%) of American children live in poverty. According to the *U.S. Kids Count Data Book* (Annie E. Casey Foundation, 1994), the percentage of children living in poverty in the United States increased by 22% over the 1980s. Poverty among U.S. children is getting worse, not better. As previously noted, on a national level, ethnic minority children are disproportionately represented in these numbers. More specifically, in areas of the U.S. with a high percentage of ethnic minorities, such as the city where the study to be reported in this chapter was conducted, 1990 statistics show that over half of African American children live in poverty, compared to 10% of Caucasian children (*Louisiana Kids Count Data Book* [Agenda for Children, 1994]).

The effects of poverty on children are mediated by the environmental and social resources available to them as they grow up (Huston, 1995). These resources include a number of physical and social factors, such as parenting practices, home environment, and neighborhood conditions. Parents living in poverty often report more financial stress and evidence greater depression and psychological distress than more affluent parents (Huston, 1995). In addition to worrying about providing basic needs such as food and housing for their children, these parents must also deal with racial discrimination, dangerous neighborhoods, unemployment, lack of support systems, and lack of status in society.

A large body of research shows that the psychological stresses generated by poverty can affect parents' interactions with their children. Parents from low-income families may be more likely to use harsh discipline and punitiveness, and provide low levels of warmth and support for their children, as well as low levels of supervision and monitoring for older children. Low-income families often have home environments with relatively low levels of social and nonsocial supports for a child's early development and evidence greater incidences of marital or cocaregiver conflict. As noted by Huston (1995), it is important to emphasize that the parenting strategies observed among low-income parents represent a response to the stresses and difficulties of coping with financial stress.

GROWING UP IN URBAN WAR ZONES

Children living in poverty are at significantly higher risk for a number of social and health problems, including living in chronically violent environments and becoming victims of violence (American Psychological Association, 1993; Prothrow-Stith & Spivak, 1992). The escalating rates of violence have led to the labeling of some cities as "inner-city war zones" (Dubrow & Garbarino, 1989; Garbarino, Kostelny, & Dubrow, 1991).

The psychological consequences of growing up and living in such urban "war zones" has only recently garnered attention (Richters, 1993), and relatively little is known about the adjustment and long-term development of children living in these neighborhoods. Even if children in these areas are fortunate enough to avoid becoming victims of violence, they often witness violent events and are affected by living in homes and neighborhoods that are unsafe. As noted by Osofsky (1995) and Cooley-Quille, Turner, and Beidel (1995), although chronic exposure to community violence is believed to have a negative impact on children's development, "psychologists [and other mental health professionals] are just beginning to glimpse the magnitude of the problem" (Osofsky, 1995, p. 782). Indeed, there is a general lack of knowledge and understanding as to how growing up under such unsafe and chaotic conditions affects young children's social, emotional, and cognitive development. Much of the documented research examining the effects of violence on children has addressed children's reactions after a single, acute episode of violence (e.g., sniper attack).

Garbarino (1992) discusses the implications of children exposed to acute versus chronic conditions of danger. Acute episodes of violence often require normal children leading normal lives to make a situational adjustment, and interventions typically consist of reassuring the child that he or she is safe and things are back to normal. Chronic conditions of violence and danger, however, involve a developmental adjustment, and with extreme trauma, a child may exhibit symptoms of posttraumatic stress disorder (PTSD), similar to those seen in war veterans, including alterations of personality and major changes in patterns of behavior (see Zeanah, Chapter 6, this volume, for details). Exposure to chronic violence or danger also causes a change in the children's interpretations of their world as they seek to develop a framework for making sense of the ongoing danger. With children exposed to chronic violence and danger, interventions typically seek to build upon children's primary relationships to create a new positive reality for them, with at least some sense of safety, trustworthiness of adults, and the world.

This strategy is challenging at best, as children are not the only ones affected by violence. When adults are traumatized, as is most likely the case in chronic conditions of violence and danger, it may be harder for them to respond to children in appropriate and sensitive ways. The stress on parents raising families under conditions of poverty, exacerbated by chronically violent and dangerous neighborhoods, is relentless. Parents have to be supported so that they can meet their children's needs (Osofsky & Fenichel, 1994).

Parents' adaptations to dangerous environments may produce child rearing strategies that impede normal development. For example, in order to keep their children safe, parents typically do not allow their children to play outdoors. Although this strategy is a successful one in the short term—keeping their children safe—it has negative long-term consequences, in that it deprives children of important opportunities for exploratory play and physical and social development. The fear experienced by parents living in violent communities may be manifested in a harsh and punitive style of discipline, as they struggle to keep their children safe and away from the negative influences of the neighborhood. This adaptation, however, may result in increased aggression on the children's part and an acceptance of violence as a way to maintain for social control (Garbarino et al., 1991).

Upon reviewing the grim statistics describing these neighborhoods and their expected impact on children and their parents, one cannot help but consider the perceptions of families—parents and their children—and other residents of these areas. Do they indeed perceive their homes and neighborhoods to be so unsafe as to warrant being labeled a "war zone"? How are they adapting to their environment? These and related questions underlie the study presented in this chapter.

VIOLENCE INTERVENTION PROGRAM: AN INTERVENTION FOR CHILDREN AND FAMILIES

In order to address and control this epidemic of violence effectively, prevention and intervention programs must be based on a thorough understanding of safety issues and concerns of families residing in violent neighborhoods, and of individuals involved in facilitating their safety. As researchers and mental health professionals, we are basically on the outside looking in. As such, we can only obtain descriptive measures or indications of certain things that occur inside the community of interest (e.g., crime rates). What is equally important but more difficult to obtain and document is an understanding of how the residents of the affected communities perceive and navigate their environment.

Parents' and Children's Perceptions of Safety and Community Violence

This section presents data from children and parents living in a New Orleans inner-city neighborhood characterized by high rates of violence, as well as from police officers working in this district. These data were collected as part of the VIP for children and parents (see Osofsky, Chapter 12, this volume). As described by Osofsky, a comprehensive needs assessment was conducted prior to implementing the intervention to identify and document issues and concerns of children, parents, and police officers around violence and safety in their neighborhood.

The majority of parents (78%) lived in or within a two-block radius of public housing complexes. These projects, as they are also referred to, have been "historically beset by high crime rates" (Philbin, 1996). In 1994, 25% of the homicides in the city of New Orleans were commited inside public housing projects. Personal communications with police officers (Lewis & Osofsky, Chapter 14, this volume) suggest that, indeed, 70% of the homicides occur in or around public housing developments. To understand issues of violence and safety, it makes sense, therefore, to break down parental responses according to the family's proximity to a housing project.

In order to ascertain parents' and children's perceptions of safety in areas frequented by children, children and parents were asked to indicate how safe they thought children were at school, at home, walking to school, and playing in the neighborhood. Police officers and parents were also asked what they believed should be done to increase the safety of children at home, school, and in the neighborhood. These data will be presented, and implications of the findings will be discussed.

Findings

Is Violence Perceived as a Problem?

In order to determine if residents of communities deemed to be dangerous and plagued by violence, based on homicide and police statistics, perceive their community as "war zones," parents participating in the study were asked, "How violent is your neighborhood?" The overwhelming majority (89%) of the parents felt that violence was either a serious problem or a crisis. A significant difference was found based on proximity to public housing projects. Parents living in or near housing developments were more likely to state that violence was a crisis (43%) than were other parents (21%), and over one-fourth of parents (29%) *not* living near developments felt that violence was not much of a problem ($\chi^2 = 12.6$, $df = 3$, $p < .01$; Table 13.1). Police responses were similar to those of

TABLE 13.1. Is Violence a Problem in Your Neighborhood?

	Parents		
	Live in or near housing development ($n = 51$)	Do not live near housing development ($n = 14$)	Police officers, Sixth District ($n = 52$)
A crisis	43%	21%	54%
A serious problem	53%	43%	42%
Somewhat of a problem	2%	7%	2%
Not much of a problem	2%	29%	2%

the parents living in or near housing developments—54% of the officers stated that violence was a "crisis" in the district in which they worked, and 42% felt that it was a serious problem.

These findings suggest that parents do indeed believe community violence to be a serious issue affecting their lives. The fact that parents living in the more violent and dangerous communities, housing projects, perceive violence to be a crisis as compared to parents living farther away from the most violent communities, suggests they are responding to what they have experienced or have direct knowledge of, as opposed to a "fear" elicited by press reports and media coverage of the violence existing in the city. Similarly, the majority of police officers working in these neighborhoods agree that community violence is a crisis.

Perceived Safety: Issues and Concerns

Table 13.2 shows parents' responses to the questions "How safe is your child at home? At school? Playing in the neighborhood? Walking to school?" Third and fifth grade students were asked similar questions. Their responses are shown in Tables 13.3a and 13.3b. Children and parents perceive similar levels of safety for children at home. The majority of children (75%) and parents (62%) reported that children were

TABLE 13.2. Parents' Perceptions of Child Safety

How safe do you feel your child is:	Live in or near housing development	Do not live near housing development
At home		
Not at all safe	8%	8%
Somewhat safe	38%	—
Very safe	54%	92%
At school		
Not at all safe	9%	15%
Somewhat safe	66%	39%
Very safe	25%	46%
Walking to school		
Not at all safe	37%	25%
Somewhat safe	52%	42%
Very safe	11%	33%
Playing in the neighborhood		
Not at all safe	63%	25%
Somewhat safe	33%	75%
Very safe	4%	—

TABLE 13.3a. Children's Perception of Safety by Gender

How safe do you feel:	Boys	Girls
At home		
Not at all safe	4%	8%
Somewhat safe	20%	17%
Very safe	76%	75%
At school		
Not at all safe	5%	3%
Somewhat safe	31%	34%
Very safe	64%	63%
Walking to school		
Not at all safe	31%	42%
Somewhat safe	41%	47%
Very safe	27%	11%
Playing in the neighborhood		
Not at all safe	21%	30%
Somewhat safe	52%	57%
Very safe	27%	12%

"very safe" at home. Children, however, were more likely than parents to say they were "very safe" at school (64% vs. 31%). These perceptions of safety did not translate to areas outside of home or school, as 37% of the children reported feeling "not at all safe" when walking to school. Similarly, 35% of the parents felt their children were "not at all safe" walking to school. A striking finding is that the majority of parents (54%) felt that their children were "not at all safe" when playing in their neighborhood, compared to only 26% of the children.

Again, significant differences were found on perceived child safety based on parents' proximity to a housing project (Table 13.2). The majority of parents (63%) who lived in or near a housing development felt their children were "not at all safe" playing in the neighborhood compared to 25% of the other parents ($\chi^2 = 7.15$, $p < .05$). An observation of concern is that only 54% of the parents who lived in or near housing development felt that their children were very safe at home ($\chi^2 = 6.8$, $p < .05$).

Gender and grade-related differences were found in children's perceived safety, with boys reporting greater perceptions of safety in the community that girls. Boys were more likely than girls to say they were "very safe" playing in the neighborhood (27% and 12%, respectively; $\chi^2 = 14.99$, $p < .05$) and walking to school (27% and 11%, respectively; $\chi^2 = 12.72$, $p < .05$). Grade and age differences were also found, with the younger children expressing greater belief in their safety at school

TABLE 13.3b. Children's Perception of Safety by Grade

How safe do you feel:	Third graders	Fifth graders
At home		
Not at all safe	7%	6%
Somewhat safe	19%	18%
Very safe	74%	76%
At school		
Not at all safe	5%	3%
Somewhat safe	21%	47%
Very safe	74%	50%
Walking to school		
Not at all safe	33%	43%
Somewhat safe	43%	47%
Very safe	24%	10%
Playing in the neighborhood		
Not at all safe	25%	28%
Somewhat safe	52%	58%
Very safe	23%	14%

and walking to school. Third graders were more likely than fifth graders to say they were "very safe" at school (74% and 49%, respectively; $\chi^2 = 20.7$, $p < .05$) and walking to school (24% and 10%, respectively; $\chi^2 = 8.8$, $p < .05$).

Perceived Impact of Community Violence on Children

In order to ascertain beliefs about the impact of violence on children, parents and police were asked how much they agreed or disagreed (on 5-point Likert scale items) with five attitudinal questions. Table 13.4 shows these items and the responses obtained.

As can be discerned from Table 13.4, an overwhelming majority of parents and police agreed that young children are affected by the violence they witness in their community (85% of parents, 88% of police officers). A slightly greater number of parents living in or near projects did not agree (18% vs. 7%) with this statement. The large majority of parents (78%) and police officers (83%) disagreed with the statement that children are only affected by the violence that occurs within their family (no differences were noted between the groups).

Although the majority of parents agreed that children living in communities with high rates of violence will later have more problems, a

TABLE 13.4. Beliefs about Children and Violence

	Live in or near housing development (n = 51)	Do not live near housing development (n = 14)	Police officers (n = 52)
Young children are affected by the violence they witness in their community.			
Strongly disagree	12%	7%	4%
Disagree	—	—	—
Neither	6%	—	8%
Agree	14%	43%	23%
Strongly agree	69%	50%	65%
Children living in communities with high rates of violent crimes will later have more problems than those living in communities with low rates.			
Strongly disagree	8%	14%	6%
Disagree	26%	—	4%
Neither	8%	—	14%
Agree	28%	57%	29%
Strongly agree	30%	29%	48%
Children are affected only by the violence that occurs within their family.			
Strongly disagree	38%	21%	39%
Disagree	40%	57%	44%
Neither	4%	7%	6%
Agree	12%	—	6%
Strongly agree	6%	14%	6%
It is important that children be present at the crime scene so they can learn what can happen to them.			
Strongly disagree	57%	36%	56%
Disagree	24%	36%	31%
Neither	8%	7%	8%
Agree	4%	14%	4%
Strongly agree	8%	7%	2%
Gang and drug violence is a much more serious problem in my neighborhood than are domestic disputes.			
Strongly disagree	18%	8%	4%
Disagree	12%	15%	14%
Neither	6%	8%	31%
Agree	22%	31%	21%
Strongly agree	41%	38%	

difference was noted based on where parents resided (in or near project vs. other): Over one-third of the parents living in or near housing projects disagreed with this statement, compared to only 14% of the other parents. The majority of police officers agreed with this statement (77%).

The large majority of parents (78%) disagreed with the statement that it is important for children to be present at crime scenes so they can learn from these experiences. This is an important finding, as informal observations and anecdotal evidence, both from police officers and other professionals, suggest that parents frequently bring children to view the bodies of homicide victims in order to "scare them" into staying away from danger.

The majority of parents (65%) and police officers (52%) felt that gang and drug violence is a much more serious problem in their neighborhood than is family violence. More parents strongly believe that gang and drug violence is a more serious problem than are domestic disputes (40% of parents strongly agreed with this, compared to 21% of police officers from the sixth District). A related finding is that a larger proportion of parents living in or near housing developments (34%) felt that the harm done to children by violence among family members was a minor type of violence (compared to 8% of other parents).

What Can Be Done?

Interesting differences were observed between parents' and police officers' responses to the open-ended questions "What can be done to increase the safety of children at home? At school? In the neighborhood?" (Table 13.5). When asked how to increase the safety of their children at home, the response most frequently given by the parents was "more police." In contrast, the most frequent response provided by police was "better parenting." Similarly, parents felt that "more police patrols" were needed to improve the safety of children in the neighborhood, whereas police officers felt that "neighborhood watch" programs were needed. Better security as a means to improve safety of children at school was the top response by both parents and police.

DISCUSSION

At the 1995 meeting of the Society for Research on Child Development, John Richters posed an important question to be addressed: "Do people accurately perceive the 'unsafeness' of their environment?" Findings from these surveys suggest that parents and police officers, and even the young children, living in neighborhoods characterized by high rates of crime

TABLE 13.5. What Things Should Be Done to Increase the Safety of Children?

Parents		Police	
At home			
More police	20%	Better parenting	35%
More supervision	15%	More supervision	15%
Better security	15%	Parents teach safety rules	9%
Stop the violence	10%	Parents take responsibility	8%
At school			
Better security	23%	Better security	41%
Police officer at school	17%	Better discipline, rules	16%
Security guard	11%	Increase awareness, education	15%
More, better teachers	8%	More parental involvement	8%
In the neighborhood			
More police, patrols	40%	Neighborhood watch	22%
Community involvement	8%	Community activities, centers	17%
Neighborhood watch	8%	More police patrols	14%
Better security	8%	Curfew	11%
Remove drugs and dealers	8%		

and violence do indeed perceive the "unsafeness" of their neighborhood. An even more important question to address may be whether it is adaptive to minimize, or to normalize, violence incidence rates and perceive them as less pervasive than they are. Although our data do not give us these answers, a finding of some concern is the fact that almost half of the parents living in high-crime areas felt their children were not even "very safe" at home. This suggests that these parents do not feel that they can fully keep their children out of harm's way, not even in their own homes. How does this perceived lack of a "safe haven" for their children affect a parent's ability to foster and nurture a developing child's view of the world and sense of optimism about the future? How are parents' abilities to parent affected by a diminished sense of self-efficacy about their ability to protect their children?

As Garbarino (1992) indicates, families living in chronically violent and unsafe communities may adapt in ways that are problematic. Families—children and parents—may cope with chronic danger by adopting a worldview that may be problematic in any "normal" situations in which they are expected to participate, such as in schools. Some adaptations to chronic danger, such as emotional withdrawal, may be socially adaptive in the short run but may later interfere with the healthy development of parent–child relationships. In addition, parents may adopt a parenting style similar to those already observed among parents living in poverty—overreliance on harsh and punitive methods of discipline and diminished warmth and nurturance.

Responses to the attitudinal questions also indicate that parents are aware that growing up in violent and unsafe environments can have a negative impact on their children, although a certain degree of "minimization" or "normalization" may be occurring among those parents living in the most dangerous areas. A slightly greater proportion of parents in the most at-risk communities appears to be minimizing or not acknowledging the consequences of growing up in violent communities.

> Children need to be safe and secure at home to develop a positive sense of self necessary to their growing into healthy, productive, caring adults; children need to be safe in their communities to be able to explore and develop relationships with other people; and children need to be safe at school in order to successfully learn. (National Association for the Education of Young Children, 1993, p. 81)

Developmental theory highlights the importance of a safe and nurturing environment for children's social and emotional development. Play is children's work! Yet many children growing up in certain areas of our cities are living under severely constricted conditions, and these children are essentially being robbed of their childhoods. Many children report going home after school and staying indoors, either watching TV or playing games, because their neighborhood is too unsafe to play outside.

Most children are able to cope with dangerous environments and maintain resilience as long as their parents are not stressed beyond their capacity to cope (Osofsky & Fenichel, 1994; Garbarino, 1992). This is especially true for young children, whose immediate caregivers play a central role in addressing their fears and providing them with emotional security. Therefore, it is critical that parents be supported in their efforts to provide as stable a living situation for their children as possible. If families are to allay the anxieties of their children, then they must themselves be provided with support and opportunities to express their fears (Cicchetti & Lynch, 1993). How can parents appease their children's fear, reassure them of their safety, and nurture their development when they themselves do not feel their children are safe, even in their own home?

In neighborhoods characterized by violence, parents are afraid to send their children to school—afraid of what they may encounter on the way. They may see someone trying to sell them drugs; they may have to walk past a dead body; or, tragically, they may become a victim of random shooting. This is a reality in many poor communities, and parents are aware of these dangers, as evidenced in our survey findings.

What can be done? Our data indicate that parents and police perceive better security to be most important to improve children's safety, although differences exist, with police officers seeing the need for "better parenting" and parents stressing the need for "more police." It is time for all people to come together, become involved, and work to change the adverse conditions for many children in our country. Collective responsibility to ensure safety of children is imperative.

REFERENCES

Agenda for Children. (1994). *Louisiana kids count data book*. New Orleans: Author.

American Psychological Association, Commission on Violence and Youth. (1993). *Violence and youth: Psychology's response: Vol. I. Summary report*. Washington, DC: Author.

Annie E. Casey Foundation. (1994). *U.S. kids count data book*. Greenwich, CT: Author.

Bell, C. C. (1987). Clinical care update: Preventive strategies for dealing with violence among blacks. *Community Mental Health Journal, 23*, 217–228.

Bell, C. C., & Jenkins, E. J. (1991). Traumatic stress and children. *Journal of Health Care for the Poor and Underserved, 2*, 175–185.

Bell, C. C., & Jenkins, E. J. (1993). Community violence and children on Chicago's southside. *Journal of Psychiatry, 56*, 46–54.

Cicchetti, D., & Lynch, M. (1993). Toward an ecological/transactionl model of community violence and child maltreatment: Consequences for children's development. *Journal of Psychiatry, 56*, 96–118.

Cooley-Quille, M. R., Turner, S. M., & Beidel, D. C. (1995). Emotional impact of children's exposure to community violence: A preliminary study. *Journal of the American Academy of Child and Adolescent Psychiatry, 34*, 1362–1368.

Dubrow, N. F., & Garbarino, J. (1989). Living in a war zone: Mothers and young children in a public housing development. *Child Welfare League of America, 1*, 3–20.

Fingerhut, L. A., & Kleinman, J. C. (1990). International and interstate comparisons of homicide among young males. *Journal of the American Medical Association, 263*, 3292–3295.

Garbarino, J. (1992). *Children in danger: Coping with the consequences of community violence*. San Francisco: Jossey-Bass.

Garbarino, J., Kostelny, K., & Dubrow, N. (1991). What children can tell us about living in danger. *American Psychologist, 46*, 376–383.

Huston, A. C. (1995, August). *Children in poverty and public policy*. Presidential address to Division 7, Developmental Psychology, of the American Psychological Association, New York City.

Kochanek, K. D., & Hudson, B. L. (1995). Advance report of final mortality statistics, 1992. *Monthly Vital Statistics Report, 43*(6 Suppl.). Hyattsville, MD: National Center for Health Statistics.

Marans, S., & Cohen, D. (1993). Children and inner-city violence: Strategies for intervention. In L. Leavitt & N. Fox (Eds.), *Psychological effects of war and violence in children.* Hillsdale, NJ: Erlbaum.

National Association for the Education of Young Children. (1993). Position statement on violence in the lives of children. *Young Children* (September), 81–84.

Osofsky, J. D. (1995). The effects of exposure to violence on young children. *American Psychologist, 50,* 782–788.

Osofsky, J. D., & Fenichel, E. (Eds.). (1994). *Hurt, healing, and hope: Caring for infants and toddlers in violent environments.* Arlington, VA: Zero-to-Three/ National Center for Clinical Infant Programs.

Osofsky, J. D., Wewers, S., Hann, D. M., & Fick, A. C. (1993). Chronic community violence: What is hapenning to our children? *Psychiatry: Interpersonal and Biological Processes, 56,* 36–45.

Philbin, W. (1996, January 7). Murder rate decreases in housing complexes. *Times Picayune,* pp. A1, A17.

Prothrow-Stith, D., & Spivak, H. (1992). Homicide and violence: Contemporary health problems for America's black community. In R. L. Braithwaite & S. E. Taylor (Eds.), *Health issues in the black community.* San Francisco: Jossey-Bass.

Pynoos, R., & Eth, S. (1985). Developmental perspectives on psychiatric trauma in children. In C. R. Figley (Ed.), *Trauma and its wake.* New York: Brunner/Mazel.

Richters, J. E. (1993). Community violence and children's development: Toward a research agenda for the 1990's. *Journal of Psychiatry, 56,* 3–5.

Richters, J. E. (1995, March). *Research on children raised in violent neighborhoods: Promissary notes and prevailing norms.* Invited address at the biennial meeting of the Society for Research in Child Development. Indianapolis, IN.

Richters, J. E., & Martinez, P. (1993). The NIMH Community Violence Project: I. Children as victims of and witnesses to violence. *Journal of Psychiatry, 56,* 7–21.

Rosenberg, M. L. (1994, January). *Violence prevention: Integrating public health and criminal justice.* Presentation at the U.S. Attorney's Conference, Washington, DC.

Rosenberg, M. L., O'Carroll, P. W., & Powell, K.E. (1992). Let's be clear: Violence is a public health problem. Commentary. *Journal of the American Medical Association, 267,* 3071–3072.

Schwab-Stone, M. E., Ayers, T. S., Kasprow, W., Voyce, C., Barone, C., Shriver, T., & Weissber, R. P. (1995). No safe haven: A study of violence exposure in an urban community. *Journal of the American Academy of Child and Adolescent Psychiatry, 34,* 1343–1352.

Straus, M. A. (1979). Measuring intrafamily conflict and violence: The Conflict Tactics Scale. *Journal of Marriage and the Family, 41,* 75–88.

14

Violent Cities, Violent Streets: Children Draw Their Neighborhoods

MARVA L. LEWIS
JOY D. OSOFSKY
MARY SUE MOORE

T HE PURPOSE OF THIS STUDY was to begin to describe how children perceive their physical neighborhood and the people in that neighborhood when their world is permeated by violence. The context or environment has long been recognized as a critical factor for children's growth and development (Cole & Cole, 1996). Urie Bronfenbrenner (1979) proposed an ecological approach for understanding the crucial role that context contributes to children's development. An ecological framework provides an overall picture of the child's world, gives us a sense of the whole child, and shows the many influences that act on the child. Based on an ecological approach, the neighborhood is part of the microsystem in which children grow and develop and provides a context for the roles children and other people enact, the predicaments they encounter, and the consequences of those encounters. Children play, learn, walk home from school, and interact with nonfamily adults and peers in their neighborhood. It provides an opportunity for exploration, solitude in secret hidden places among buildings, trees, and bushes. The neighborhood context provides fertile ground for young children to nurture the achievement of several important developmental tasks: to feel a sense of autonomy and mastery in walking to and from school and playing alone in the neighborhood; to develop trust in nonfamily members, such as peer play partners, and adults such as storekeepers and neighbors; and to develop a feeling of safety in the larger world outside of the protective environment of their home. There are also opportunities to show off incredible creative feats of physical dexterity such as jump shots on the basketball court and intricate foot patterns in games of double-dutch jump rope.

Sadly, neighborhoods in 1996 are often not the safe, nurturant environments described in the popular children's program "Mister Rogers' Neighborhood." Urban neighborhoods are now the context for another reality of children's lives, exposure to high rates of community violence (Rosenberg, 1994).

The Centers for Disease Control and Prevention and others have declared that children's exposure to community violence is a public health problem (Rosenberg, 1994; Prothrow-Stith, 1991; Bell & Jenkins, 1993). Specifically, young, African American males are a group at greatest risk for death by homicide (Rosenberg, 1994). In studies describing fifth and sixth grade students' exposure in Washington, DC, and New Orleans, 61% and 70%, respectively, reported they had witnessed violence to someone else or seen weapons used (Richters & Martinez, 1993; Osofsky, Wewers, Hann, & Fick, 1993). In a sample of 2,248 students in the sixth, eighth, and tenth grades in a urban inner city, 41.3% of the students reported having seen at least one shooting or stabbing in the past year (Schwab-Stone et al., 1995). Clinical studies of children living in areas with high rates of violence now report that simply witnessing violence or having knowledge of a violent event can have negative implications for children's psychosocial development (Bell & Jenkins, 1993; Garbarino, Dubrow, Kostelny, & Pardo, 1992; Jenkins & Bell, Chapter 2, this volume; McAllister-Groves & Zuckerman, Chapter 9, this volume; Hill, 1992; Osofsky, 1995; Richters & Martinez, 1993). Behaviors of infants and children who have witnessed a violent event may include the same posttraumatic stress disorder (PTSD) symptoms that were originally identified in Vietnam war veterans (Drell, Siegel, & Gaensbauer, 1993; Parson, 1994; Pynoos, 1993; Scheeringa, Zeanah, Drell, & Larrieu, 1995).

Recently there has been an increasing number of clinical studies with small samples of young children, ages 2 to 8. These children have been brought to medical settings by their parents for a variety of behavioral symptoms because of exposure to trauma such as war, or witnessing a violent event, including the murder of their mother or a shooting. They have been diagnosed with PTSD symptoms including night terrors, and play reenactment of the trauma (Drell et al., 1993; Eth & Pynoos, 1994; Groves, Zuckerman, Marans, & Cohen, 1993; Osofsky, Cohen, & Drell,

1995; Nader, Pynoos, Fairbanks, Al-Ajeel, & Al-Asfour, 1993; Parson, 1994).

Many efforts are now underway to study systematically and provide interventions for children living in neighborhoods with high rates of violence (Hill, 1992; McAllister-Groves & Zuckerman, Chapter 9, this volume; Jenkins & Bell, Chapter 2, this volume; Osofsky, Lewis, & Fick, 1993; Parson, 1994). Based on extensive work with children exposed to violence in the Washington, DC, area, Hill (1992) has identified five ways that exposure to violence in the neighborhood may impact children's development: (1) erosion of the sense of personal safety and security; (2) disruption of lifestyle and the major ages of socialization; (3) generalized emotional distress; (4) depersonalization; and (5) a diminished future orientation. Recent empirical studies have shown similar findings of the impact of exposure to violence on children's development.

In a study of 384 elementary school children living in urban neighborhoods, the youngest children and children living in the most disadvantaged neighborhoods experienced more stressful life events (Attar, Guerra, & Tolan, 1994). Stressful life events were significant predictors of higher concurrent levels of aggression and predicted increases in aggressive behaviors 1 year later. In the Schwab-Stone et al. (1995) study of 2,248 elementary school children, 74% reported feeling unsafe in one or more areas of their environment, such as in the neighborhood, on the school bus, or while walking to school. In another study conducted with 250 elementary school children living in an urban neighborhood with a high rate of violence, 68% of the children felt "not at all" or "a little" safe walking home from school, and 56% felt "not at all" or "a little" safe playing in the neighborhood (Fick, Lewis, Osofsky, & Flowers, 1995). Finally, Richters and Martinez (1993) found that a mediating factor for the impact of living in neighborhoods with high rates of violence for elementary school children's adaptational success and failure was if the children also lived in unstable and/ or unsafe homes.

Clinicians have begun empirical studies to describe the emotional impact of children's exposure to community violence using traditional clinical diagnostic criteria (Cooley-Quille, Turner, & Beidel, 1995; Drell et al., 1993; Pynoos & Eth, 1986; Scheeringa et al., 1995; Zeanah, 1994). These studies document parent and teacher reports of clinical symptomatology and the children's reports of fear, hopelessness, and lack of safety. Hill (1992) reports that a majority male adolescents in the study on violence exposure did not expect to reach 25–30 years of age. The finding of a foreshortened future was echoed in a study completed with inner-city elementary school children in the New Haven, Connecticut, area (Schwab-Stone et al., 1995). In contrast, in the New Orleans study conducted with 8- to 9-year-olds, the majority of the children still maintained a sense of hope for the future and trust (Osofsky, Fick, Flowers, & Lewis, 1995). However, young children's perspectives and affective perceptions of the violence that surrounds them in their neighborhood is the missing factor in the discussion of solutions to the problem of children's exposure to violence. How they make sense of, and cognitively process the violence to which they are exposed daily, has not been examined in a systematic manner. One of the primary ways that young children communicate and comprehend frightening and confusing traumatic experiences is through drawing pictures (Coles, 1964; Hammer, 1980; Moore, 1994; Pynoos & Eth, 1986).

CHILDREN'S DRAWINGS

Analysis of drawings has long been used as a method for clinical assessment of children's cognitive and emotional functioning, attitudes toward their families, and traumatic occurrences in their environment (Hammer, 1980; Hibbard & Hartman, 1990; Moore, 1996). Drawings are also an important tool used in clinical treatment of children. Moore (1994), who has done extensive studies of the drawings of traumatized children in a variety of settings, notes that they may be used as an effective means of communication of a child's mental state, quality and accessibility of memories, and likely degree of traumatization in the process. Drawings simultaneously express—graphically and symbolically—multiple levels of self-experience and self-knowledge (Moore, 1994). Drawings encourage the retrieval of experience in the motoric, visual, and auditory recall, as well as the cognitive dimensions represented in the organization, interpersonal patterns, and verbal discussion of the picture (Burgess & Hartman, 1993). For example, Robert Coles (1964) used drawings as a method to assess the impact of the trauma on children of school desegregation in Southern schools. Coles was able to follow the children over several years and described the changes in the feelings of fear and helplessness, as depicted in their drawings.

Drawings have been incorporated into interview formats to evaluate children traumatized through witnessing acts of violence including war, homicide, suicide, rape, aggravated assault, accidental death, kidnapping, and school and community violence (Garbarino et al., 1992; Hill, 1992; Moore & Kramer, 1993; Eth & Pynoos, 1994). The technique of drawing also may serve as an intervention with traumatized children, helping to lessen the emotionally devastating effects of the trauma. In a study of the psychological impact of war on preschool children in South Africa, it was reported that the more a child was able to express emotional trauma through drawings, the less likely he or she would suffer from PTSD (Magwaza, Killian, Petersen, & Pillay, 1993).

To date, no systematic studies using children's drawings as a method of assessment have been conducted to explore the impact that chronic exposure to community violence may have on young children's perceptions of themselves, peers, and adults in the world composed of the neighborhood in which they live. In this chapter, we will describe the presence and frequency of elements related to community violence and its antidote, feelings of hope in drawings done by 248 elementary school children living in neighborhoods with high rates of violence. They were asked, "Draw a picture of your neighborhood" (picture A) and "Draw a picture of what goes on in your neighborhood" (picture B). In the initial analysis comparing groups of picture A to picture B, it was striking that the second stimulus elicited a consistently higher percentage of violent content than did the more benign "Draw a picture of your neighborhood." Whereas only 9% of the children drew one or more acts of violence in the A pictures, over 60% of the children drew acts of violence in their B pictures of "what goes on in your neighborhood."

What follows is a description of the findings from analyses of the second set of drawings of children. What will be reported is the violent content in the pictures, the affect of the people depicted in the drawings, and the hopeful elements portrayed. Finally, a discussion will be presented of the implications of these findings for future research, intervention, and clinical work with children exposed to violence.

METHODOLOGY

Sample

This study of children's drawings was completed as part of a larger study of children's perceptions of violence and feelings of safety and trust when living in communities with high rates of violence. It was conducted as part of the development of a larger intervention program (Osofsky, Lewis, & Fick, 1993; Osofsky, Chapter 12, this volume). The total sample of 248 African American children ranged in age from 8 to 12 years and came from five elementary schools in lower socioeconomic level neighborhoods and four public housing developments with high rates of violence, in a Southern, moderate size city.

The Children and Violence Neighborhood Coding System[1]

A coding system to evaluate the children's drawings was developed in order to describe how children draw what goes on in their neighborhoods. Although there is extensive literature on the clinical interpretation of some of the individual elements contained in this coding system (e.g., of houses, trees and human figures; see Hammer, 1980; Hibbard & Hartman, 1990; Moore, 1994), the current system was not intended for clinical interpretation. The purpose of the coding system was to provide a systematic and standardized method to describe the violent content of children's drawings of their neighborhoods. The coding system was developed by reviewing a sample of the children's pictures and describing the elements present and relevant to the concept of neighborhoods and violence. After establishing conceptually relevant categories, a review was made of all the drawings, and detailed codes were developed to describe the criteria for each element. After extensive revisions and piloting of the coding system for reliability, and both consensual and content validity, a final version of the Child and Violence Neighborhood Coding System (Lewis, Osofsky, & Moore, 1994) was developed. The coding system includes 66 different elements that are conceptually organized into five major categories: (1) community violence depicted; (2) the gender of the victim and aggressor, (3) the affect of the victim, aggressor, and bystanders; (4) the neighborhood context; and (5) the hopeful elements of the drawings. Interrater reliability was achieved on each of the categories with percent agreement ranging from 80% to 98% (kappa = .8).

Procedure

While sitting in their classrooms, the children, as a group, were given a blank sheet of white paper and pencils, and asked to draw two pictures. First they were asked, "Draw a picture of your neighborhood." These pictures will be referred to in the balance of the discussion as "picture A." After completing this picture, they were then asked, "Draw a picture of what goes on in your neighborhood." These pictures will be referred to as "picture B." They then completed age-appropriate questionnaires related to trust, safety in their neighborhoods, and the degree of hopelessness (Kazdin, French, Unis, Esveldt-Dawson, & Sherick, 1983; Osofsky, Lewis, & Fick, 1993).

---

[1] A complete description of the coding system and reliability is available from Marva L. Lewis.

RESULTS

Young African American males are a group at greatest risk for death by homicide (Centers for Disease Control, 1994). Therefore, analyses of picture B drawn were completed and comparisons based on gender of the child.

Types of Community Violence Depicted

Violence was defined for this coding system as "an act or behavior that causes damage or injury, or human figures engaged in verbal threats or activity labeled as fighting, hitting, or someone starting a fire or robbery." This category consists of items that describe the basic characteristics of a typical murder scene in the community; various acts of violence, such as shootings, stabbings, and fights; people in the roles of victims, aggressors, and bystanders; the presence of weapons and dead bodies. Based on the review of the children's pictures, an additional element in this category was added to describe the presence of "inanimate aggressors," which may be the simple depiction of guns pointed at a human figure but with no human figure holding the gun (see Figure 14.1). Three clinically based elements are included in this category in relation to the depiction of humans drawn with no extremities (arms, or legs). Other clinical research on children's drawings of human figures have identified these as indicators of helplessness and powerlessness (Hammer, 1980).

FIGURE 14.1. Illustration of "inanimate aggressor" and "inappropriate effect" in smiling victim (picture B).

Surprisingly, no significant differences were found between boys and girls in their depiction of each of these violent elements. Figures 14.1 and 14.2 illustrate typical drawings by a boy and girl, respectively, depicting violent content.

Gender of the Victim and Aggressor

This category of elements describes the gender of both the victim and aggressor as male (usually wearing pants, or with a "fade" hair cut), female (usually depicted with long or curly hair and wearing a skirt and earrings), or if there are multiple victims or the gender could not be determined. There were five types of aggressors including the rarely occurring "inanimate aggressor" (see Figure 14.1). If human figures were drawn in a stick-like fashion, they were coded as "stick figures." Also if the human figures had no arms or legs, they were coded as a victim, aggressor, or bystander with no extremities.

The pattern of no significant gender differences was found for the portrayal of the gender of the victim and aggressor. Although none of the differences were statistically significant, girls more frequently depicted

FIGURE 14.2. Picture B, "A girl shot a other girl," illustrates elements of violent content, a female aggressor, presence of drugs, and stick figure in car. Drawn by an 8-year-old boy.

female victims and portrayed about the same number of male victims as did the boys. Female aggressors were extremely rare (a total of only three children drew female aggressors; see Figure 14.2).

Inanimate aggressors were also rarely portrayed, but when they were, the weapon typically filled most of the page (see Figure 14.1).

Affect Displays of Victim/Aggressor/Bystander

This category described the affect or emotional expression of the human figures in scenes with violent content. If a human figure was rated as a victim or aggressor in a violent situation, or bystander to a scene of violence, an affect code was assigned. We were primarily interested in the category-inappropriate affect. Affect considered appropriate to the event included, for example, the Victim, Aggressor, or Bystander to a violent event depicted as angry, sad or crying, or neutral facial expression. In other clinical research studies of affect displays with high psychosocial risk populations, inappropriate affect has been reported to be related to depression and dysfunctional parent–child interactions (Osofsky, 1995).

Inappropriate affect is defined in this coding system as a victim or aggressor or bystander smiling in the presence of an act of violence. This definition included human figures in the roles of victim, aggressor, or bystander to a violent event that were portrayed as faceless or displaying their eyes only. A comparison of the percentages of boys versus girls in the depiction of these elements was made for both sets of pictures (A's and B's). In the pictures drawn in response to the first stimulus, "Draw a picture of your neighborhood," there were no significant differences between the boys and girls' depiction of these elements. However, there were significant differences in the affect portrayed in the B pictures that contained violent content.

A significantly higher percentage of girls portrayed victims, aggressors, and bystanders in violent scenes as "smiling" (41%; see Figures 14.3 and 14.4). In contrast, a significantly higher percentage of boys portrayed the victims and aggressors in scenes of violence with "eyes only" (see Figure 14.5). This pattern was most pronounced in the depiction of the affect of the aggressor. Forty-one percent of the girls who drew aggressors in violent scenes drew them with a smile on their face, and 21% of the boys drew aggressors as smiling while committing a violent act. This difference in the depiction of smiling victims, aggressors, and bystanders for girls was consistently statistically significant (see Table 14.1).

Neighborhood Context

This category included 16 different elements that one would expect to find in a child's drawing of a typical neighborhood in an urban commu-

FIGURE 14.3. Picture B, "Killing/Drugs," portrays multiple acts of violence: shooting, drug transactions, victims yelling for help.

nity in the United States. The types of elements ranged from human figures, physical dwellings such as houses and stores, to the physical setting such as the sun, clouds, and trees. Elements that have been identified in other coding schemes of children's drawings that are of clinical interest are also included this category. These items are stick figures, or distorted human figures, a "baseline," which serves to orient the viewer to the other elements in the picture and may be a street or grass or fence around a house. The "special baseline," typically drawn as a jagged or wavy line, is an item recently recognized to be associated with the drawings of children who had been sexually abused (Moore, 1994). Other elements that were considered more atypical of neighborhoods but reflect the reality of children living in areas with high rates of crime included 18 items, such as people smoking cigarettes or drugs, bars, emergency or police cars, drug houses or drug transactions, and clouds/people/sun/moon crying.

In B pictures, a higher percentage of the girls and boys drew both stick figures and cars in their depictions of "what goes on in your neighborhood." There was also a significantly higher percentage of girls' drawings with depictions of clouds and sun.

Other elements that are more atypical of neighborhoods were also analyzed based on gender. Significant differences were found for several of the items (see Table 14.2). A significantly larger percentage of girls drew "drug transactions" than did boys (Figures 14.3 and 14.6; 13% for

FIGURE 14.4. Picture B, "Don't cry run," portrays multiple shootings; crying victims labeled with names; smiling, anonymous aggressors; and presence of police and an ambulance.

girls vs. 2% for boys). A significantly larger percentage of boys drew "police cars" than did girls. Although not significant, a slightly higher percentage of boys drew humans "smoking cigarettes or drugs," "Emergency Medical Service vehicles" such as ambulances, and "steps" to buildings. Figures 14.4, 14.5, 14.6, and 14.7 illustrate the depiction of these elements.

Elements of Hope

The last category of elements, and perhaps the most important, is the depiction of what we are defining as elements of hope in the children's drawings.

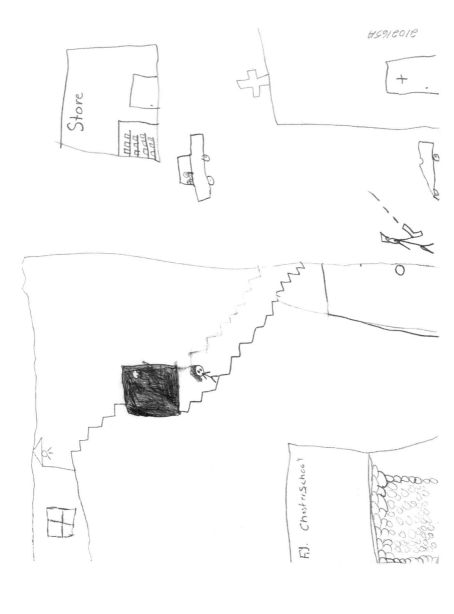

FIGURE 14.5. Picture B, Symbol of hope of church in violent context, drawn by a 10-year-old boy in the third grade.

TABLE 14.1. Comparison of Girls' versus Boys' Depictions of Affect of Victims, Aggressors, and Bystanders: Picture B

Affect	Girls (n = 109)		Boys (n = 85)		Chi-square
	F	%	F	%	
Victim					
Smiling	32	29	6	7	14.21 ($p < .00$)
Faceless	2	2	6	7	ns
Eyes only	1	1	7	8	4.59 ($p < .03$)
Aggressor					
Smiling	45	41	18	21	8.49 ($p < .003$)
Faceless	1	1	4	5	ns
Eyes only	1	1	7	8	4.59 ($p < .032$)
Bystander[a]					
Smiling	23	21	7	8	5.39 ($p < .020$)
Faceless	3	3	6	7	ns

[a] "Eyes only" not coded.

Hope is defined in *Webster's Dictionary* as the following: "To wish for something with expectations or to look forward to with confidence, to expect and desire, a wish or desire accompanied by some confident expectation. Something that is hoped for or desired, a person or a thing that is a source or a reason for hope." These Hopefulness codes were based in part, on the African American concept of Faith or Imani, as described in the literature on African American culture and beliefs (White, 1984). Therefore, this category of elements includes as symbols of Hope the depiction of churches and religious crosses, as well as sunshine, flowers, smiling adults, or children at play (see Figures 14.8–14.11). A comparison will be made of the average number of symbols of Hope drawn by girls versus boys in the B pictures. Finally, the correlation between the number of violent incidents portrayed and the number of symbols of Hope will be reported.

The number of Hopeful elements in picture B ranged from 0 to 10, with the average number 2. Fifty-six percent of the children drew no Hopeful elements. Thirty-nine percent of the pictures had one to three hopeful elements. So, in a context of violence (B pictures) a higher percentage (44% vs. 37%) of all the children drew symbols of Hope than in the first set of A pictures. No significant differences were found between the boys and girls' depiction of mean number of elements of hope in picture B, in contrast to picture A. A one-way analysis of variance was completed to determine if there were gender differences in the mean

TABLE 14.2. Comparison of "Other Neighborhood Elements" for Boys versus Girls

Element	Girls (n = 109)		Boys (n = 87)		Chi-square
	F	%	F	%	
Smoking cigarettes	8	14	14	16	Trend
Drug transactions	14	13	2	2	5.84*
Bars	2	2	0	0	ns
Drug houses	4	4	1	1	ns
Clouds/sun/moon crying	6	6	1	1	ns
People crying	5	5	1	1	ns
Garbage	3	3	2	2	ns
EMS	2	2	7	8	Trend
Police cars	6	6	16	18	6.82*
Steps	10	9	16	18	Trend
Playground equipment	11	10	9	10	ns
Single erasures	25	23	20	23	ns
Multiple erasures	34	31	24	28	ns

* $p < .001$.

number of Hopeful elements drawn by girls versus boys in response to the first stimulus. A main effect was found for gender ($F(1,183) = 5.31$, $p < .02$). Girls had the highest mean number of hopeful elements in this first set of pictures. In the set of A pictures, there were no significant correlations between level of violent content and number of hopeful elements. In sharp contrast, there was a consistent pattern of significant, negative correlations between the number of elements in each violent content category and the number of hopeful elements drawn (see Table 14.3).

As the number of violent incidents increased, the level of hopeful elements decreased. The strongest negative correlations with hopeful elements were with the number of weapons portrayed, number of aggressors, and the number of violent events.

DISCUSSION: IMPLICATIONS FOR CLINICIANS, INTERVENTIONS, AND RESEARCH

The search for solutions to address the issue of children exposed to violence must include an examination of not only the context of the

FIGURE 14.6. "Smoking drugs," the picture of "what goes on in your neighborhood" (picture B), drawn by a 10-year-old girl.

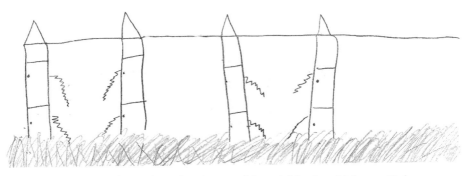

FIGURE 14.7. "The Projects," a picture of the neighborhood (picture A) drawn by the same 10-year-old girl who drew Figure 14.6.

FIGURE 14.8. Picture A, "a picture of my neighborhood," drawn by an 11-year-old, fifth grade girl.

FIGURE 14.9. Picture B, Children at play, contains no violent content; element of hope.

FIGURE 14.10. Picture B, Symbol of hope of large church in violent content, drawn by a 10-year-old boy in the third grade.

violent event, but also their perception of that context. The Children and Violence Neighborhood Coding System provides a method to describe systematically the frequency of specific elements associated with community violence depicted by children living in neighborhoods with high rates of violence. The findings of this study describing the pattern of elements of violence in the drawings of young children's perceptions of the neighborhoods represent only a beginning point. The contrast between the content of the first set of pictures and the second set of pictures in which the children were asked to draw "what goes on in your neighborhood" is startling. Figures 14.6 and 14.7 illustrate the change from a

FIGURE 14.11. Picture B, Symbols of hope, smiling adult and child; no violence depicted; "love" written next to people.

depiction of buildings to the portrayal of humans engaged in violent acts. In the A pictures, the most frequently appearing items were what you expect in a picture of neighborhoods: houses, suns, clouds, trees, and human figures. Yet, in a context of violence, the element most frequently appearing in the B pictures was humans. These human figures were most frequently drawn as stick figures in the roles of victims, aggressors, and bystanders. In other studies of human figures, the use of stick figures for humans is an indicator of clinical distress in children (Hammer, 1980). As noted earlier, this study does not propose to draw clinical interpretations from the findings. The significant presence of stick figures warrants, at minimum, further clinical investigation that explores the meaning of these figures in a context of violence.

In some of the B pictures, the children attempted perhaps to compensate for their bleak surroundings by drawing two suns to frame their depiction of abandoned buildings with garbage-strewn yards and few human figures. Some children appeared to be so overwhelmed with the

TABLE 14.3. Correlations of Number of Elements of Hope with Violent Content in Picture B

Violent content category	Correlation with hopeful elements
Violent acts depicted	$-.31$ ($p < .000$)
Number of victims	$-.23$ ($p < .001$)
Number of victims with no extremities	$-.17$ ($p < .019$)
Number of aggressors	$-.31$ ($p < .000$)
Number of aggressors with no extremities	$-.19$ ($p < .007$)
Bystanders	$-.03$ ns
Bystanders with no extremities	$-.08$ ns
Number of weapons	$-.32$ ($p < .000$)
Number of dead bodies	$-.15$ ($p < .042$)

violent content that they relied heavily on shading, as if to cover up the multiple forms of violence they depicted.

Although the percentage of girls drawing stick figures in picture A was significantly higher than boys, the number of girls drawing stick figures increased 57% in picture B. The increase in the number of boys drawing stick figures from picture A to picture B was also dramatically higher, but still less than that of the girls.

The portrayal of inanimate aggressors, as illustrated in the gun taking up the entire page of one young child's picture, speaks to what may be the preoccupation these children who are living in neighborhoods with high rates of violence may have. This preoccupation with violence may manifest itself in young children in the need to self-protect by whatever means necessary, including taking Daddy's gun to school to settle a fight when threatened, as one 6-year-old kindergartner recently did in the city of New Orleans.

The results of this study provide clinicians with a beginning point to better understand the impact of violence on the inner life of children. In addition, researchers and clinicians are provided with a helpful tool for assessment and intervention with this population. There is a need for future studies using drawings as one method to more accurately assess the impact that chronic exposure to violence has on very young children. More research is needed to better understand the significance of the presence or absence of individual elements of violence, the more dominant use of stick figures, and the striking differences for boys and girls in the depiction of affect in these pictures. In the absence of other clinical supporting data, care should be given to make no single interpretation to these findings (Handler & Habenicht, 1994; Moore, 1994). Even more alarming, the incongruent affect of victims, aggressors, and bystanders depicted by girls more frequently than by boys must be further investigated. More studies are needed to understand the role that gender-based socialization goals for girls to be more submissive and less vocal in their distress as victim will be important clinical topics to systematically explore (Moore, personal communication, March, 1995).

The reality of the general decline of safety in neighborhoods and increase in barriers to children's safe play over the past three generations has been described (Gaster, 1991). The results of these analyses of drawings suggest that hope is still present for some children in these neighborhoods. The finding of a consistent pattern in which the number of hopeful elements increased as the number of violent content elements decreased should serve as a clear mandate to both researchers and clinicians for future studies and interventions based on the findings from these children's drawings. The inclusion of hopeful elements representing churches and crosses in the midst of dead bodies and bloodied victims is also a clarion call to clinicians from these children identifying an existing community strength to build interventions upon. The hopefulness in children must be transformed into a secure and solid, positive connectedness to the neighborhoods and communities (Combrinck-Graham, 1995). It is our role as responsible adults in young children's lives to provide protection as well as nurturing, to help them feel safe as they complete the work of childhood—playing in their neighborhoods.

REFERENCES

Attar, B. K., Guerra, N. G., & Tolan, P.H. (1994). Neighborhood disadvantage, stressful life events, and adjustment in urban elementary-school children. *Journal of Clinical Child Psychology, 23,* 391–400.

Bell, C. C., & Jenkins, E. J. (1993). Community violence and children on Chicago's south side. *Psychiatry, 56,* 46–54.

Bronfenbrenner, U. (1979). *The ecology of human development.* Cambridge: Harvard University Press.

Burgess, A. W., & Hartman, C. R. (1993). Children's drawings: Special Issue: Clinical recognition of sexually abused children. *Child Abuse and Neglect, 17,* 161–168.

Cole, N., & Cole, S. R. (1996). *The development of children* (3rd ed.). New York: Scientific American Books.

Coles, R. (1964). *Children of crisis: Vol. I. A study of courage and fear.* Boston: Little, Brown.

Combrinck-Graham, L. (Ed.). (1995). *Children in families at risk: Maintaining the connections.* New York: Guilford Press.

Cooley-Quille, M. R., Turner, S. M., & Beidel, D. C. (1995). Emotional impact of children's exposure to community violence: A preliminary study. *Journal of the American Academy of Child and Adolescent Psychiatry, 34,* 1362–1368.

Drell, M., Siegel, C., & Gaensbauer, T. (1993). Post-traumatic stress disorder. In C. H. Zeanah (Ed.), *Handbook of infant mental health* (pp. 291–304). New York: Guilford Press.

Eth, S., & Pynoos, R. S. (1994). Children who witness the homicide of a parent. *Psychiatry, 57,* 287–306.

Fick, A. C., Lewis, M. L., Osofsky, J. D., & Flowers, A. (1995, March). *Children's safety issues and concerns: Perceptions of children, parents, and police.* Poster presented at the biennial conference of the Society for Research in Child Development, Indianapolis, IN.

Garbarino, J. Dubrow, N., Kostelny, K., & Pardo, C. (1992). *Children in danger: Coping with the consequence of community violence.* San Francisco: Jossey-Bass.

Gaster, S. (1991). Urban children's access to their neighborhood: Changes over three generations. *Environment and Behavior, 23*(1), 70–85.

Groves, B. Zuckerman, B., Marans, S., & Cohen, D. (1993). Silent victims: Children who witness violence. *Journal of the American Medical Association, 269,* 262–264.

Hammer, E. (1980). *The clinical application of projective drawings.* Springfield, IL: Charles C Thomas.

Handler, L., & Habenicht, D. (1994). The Kinetic Family Drawing Technique: A review of the literature. *Journal of Personality Assessment, 62*(3), 440–464.

Hibbard, R. A., & Hartman, G. (1990). Emotional indicators in human figure drawings of sexually victimized and non-abused children. *Journal of Clinical Psychology, 46*(2), 211–219.

Hill, H. (1992). Social and emotional development. In M. R. Isaacs (Ed.), *Violence: The impact of community violence on African American children and families* (pp. 21–28). Arlington, VA: National Center for Education in Maternal and Child Health.

Kazdin, A., French, N. H., Unis, A. S., Esveldt-Dawson, K., & Sherick, R. B. (1983). The hopelessness, depression, and suicidal intent among psychiatrically disturbed children. *Journal of Consulting and Clinical Psychology, 51,* 504–510.

Lewis, M. L., Osofsky, J. D., & Moore, M. S. (1994). *Coding manual for drawings of children exposed to community violence.* Unpublished manuscript, Louisiana State University Medical Center, New Orleans, LA.

Lewis, M. L. (1995). *Children draw their neighborhood: Drawings as a method of assessment and research for children exposed to chronic community violence.* Poster presented at the biennial conference of the Society for Research in Child Development, March, Indianapolis, IA.

Magwaza, A. S., Killian, B. J., Petersen, I., & Pillay, Y. (1993). The effect of chronic violence on preschool children living in South African townships. *Child Abuse and Neglect, 17*(6), 795–803.

Moore, M. S. (in preparation). *Symbolization and representation in children's drawings: The impact of trauma.*

Moore, M. S. (1994). Common characteristics in the drawings of ritually abused children and adults. In V. Sinason, (Ed.), *Treating survivors of Satanist abuse.* New York: Routledge.

Moore, M., & Kramer, D. (1993). Value reflection in Israeli children's drawings during the Gulf War. *Archivio di Psicologia, Neurologia e Psichiatria, 54,* 3–12.

Nader, K. O, Pynoos, R. S., Fairbanks, L. A., Al-Ajeel, M., & Al-Asfour, A. (1993). A preliminary study of PTSD and grief among the children of Kuwait following the Gulf Crisis. *British Journal of Clinical Psychology, 32,* 407–416.

Osofsky, J. D. (1995). The effects of exposure to violence on young children. *American Psychologist, 50*(9), pp. 782–788.

Osofsky, J. D., Cohen, G., & Drell, M. (1995). The effects of trauma on young children: A case of two-year-old twins. *International Journal of Psycho-Analysis, 76,* 595–608.

Osofsky, J. D., Fick, A. C., Flowers, A. L., & Lewis, M. L. (1995, March 13). *Trust in children living with violence.* Poster presented at the biennial conference of the Society for Research in Child Development, Indianapolis, IN.

Osofsky, J. D., Lewis, M. L., & Fick, A. C. (1993). *The New Orleans Violence and Children Intervention Children's Survey.* Unpublished manuscript, Louisiana State University Medical Center, New Orleans, LA.

Osofsky, J. D., Wewers, S., Hann, D. M., & Fick, A. C. (1993). Chronic community violence: What is happening to our children? *Psychiatry, 56,* 36–45.

Parson, E. R. (1994). Inner city children of trauma: Urban violence traumatic stress response syndrome (U-VTS) and therapists' responses. In J. Wilson & J. Lindy (Eds.), *Countertransference in the treatment of PTSD* (pp. 151–178). New York: Guilford Press.

Prothrow-Stith, D. (1991). *Deadly consequences.* New York: HarperCollins.

Pynoos, R. S. (1993). Traumatic stress and developmental psychopathology in children and adolescents. In J. M. Oldham, M. B. Riba, & A. Tasman (Eds.), *American Psychiatric Press review of psychiatry* (Vol. 12, pp. 205–238). Washington, DC: American Psychiatric Press.

Pynoos, R. S., & Eth, S. (1986). Witness to violence: The child interview. *Journal of the American Academy of Child Psychiatry, 25*(3), 306–319.

Richters, J. E., & Martinez, P. E. (1993). Violent communities, family choices, and children's changes: An algorithm for improving the odds. *Development and Psychopathology, 5*(4), 609–627.

Rosenberg, M. L. (1994, January). *Violence prevention: Integrating public health and criminal justice.* Presentation at the U.S. Attorney's Conference, Washington, DC.

Scheeringa, M. S., Zeanah, C. H. Drell, M. J., & Larrieu, J. A. (1995). Two approaches to the diagnosis of post-traumatic stress disorder in infancy and early childhood. *Journal of the American Academy of Child and Adolescent Psychiatry, 34,* 191–200.

Schwab-Stone, M. E., Ayers, T. S., Wesley, K., Voyce, C., Barone, C., Shriver, T., & Weissberg, R. P. (1995). No safe haven: A study of violence exposure in an urban community. *Journal of the Academy of Child and Adolescent Psychiatry, 34*(10), 1343–1352.

White, J. L. (1984). *The psychology of Black Americans: An Afro-American perspective*. Englewood Cliffs, NJ: Prentice-Hall.

Zeanah, C. H. (1994). The assessment and treatment of infants and toddlers exposed to violence. In J. D. Osofsky & E. Fenichel (Eds.), *Caring for infants and toddlers in violentenvironments: Hurt, healing, and hope* (pp. 29–37). Arlington, VA: Zero-to-Three/National Center for Clinical Infant Programs.

15

Cops and Kids: Issues for Community Policing

PAMELA JENKINS
RUTH SEYDLITZ
JOY D. OSOFSKY
ANA C. FICK

A N OLD CHILDREN'S BOOK shows a picture of a police officer re-
trieving a kitten from tree. A young boy and a young girl look
up at the officer with admiration in their eyes. The unstated
message from this picture is that the young boy usually will want to
emulate his hero and become a police officer, and the young girl can
always count on the police officer.

Law enforcement officers are the moral entrepreneurs of our culture—they are intended to be the heroes. Police are expected to protect
and save people, especially children. In the current era of law enforcement
and crime, how police interact with children is an important area for
research and policy. This chapter focuses on the issues of policing and
the work of police with children. In order to fully explore the issues of
children and policing, several different areas will be discussed.

First, the general role of policing in society is discussed. The police
have several roles to perform as part of their occupation; these roles
are described in terms of children. Second, the situations in which
police encounter children are discussed. Third, data from the Violence
Intervention Project for Children and Families (VIP) (see Osofsky,
Chapter 12, this volume) describe police attitudes toward children.

Finally, these issues are brought together to look at the future role of police with children in light of the national initiative for community policing.

THE ROLE OF LAW ENFORCEMENT

Police are human service workers, unique human service workers. Police work with people everyday—they see the best and worst of the human condition. Police have three basic functions: peacekeeping or maintaining order, crime fighting, and service (Voigt, Thornton, Barrile, & Seaman, 1994). These roles are related, but they are perceived differently by the police and the public. These roles are defined within a particular type of organizational structure, one that is highly bureaucratic and paramilitaristic (Bittner, 1995; Brooks, 1989).

Much of the current crisis in policing has to do with the multiple functions of the police. Police spend most of their time in peacekeeping activities—finding lost children, mediating quarrels, and other activities (Manning, 1995). The diverse and varied activities of peacekeeping are an important part of the police culture. Maintaining order requires a certain set of skills in working with people and involvement of the community. The other type of police work is crime fighting—chasing burglars, solving homicides, issuing traffic tickets, and filling out reports.

The following are controversial issues that police face in areas of law enforcement, order maintenance, and community service.

1. An area of concern in all police work is the use of police discretion. Police discretion is found when officers have some leeway or choice in how they respond to a situation (Brooks, 1989). Even within a bureaucratic, paramilitaristic structure, an officer has a wide range of discretion in both order maintenance and law enforcement activities. Discretion varies according to the organizational style of the police department, the type of neighborhood, situational variables, and the officer (Brooks, 1989).

2. The use of legitimate force is another current issue in policing. Police are placed in the position of having legitimate force as an option for solving problems. This ability is part of what makes police work so different from any other type of occupation. The ability not only to arrest, but also to use deadly force is a critical issue in policing (Fyfe, 1989; Scharf & Binder, 1983).

The use of discretion and the use of deadly force occurs in split-seconds as officers, especially street-level officers, decide the deposition of the call and what level of force is needed.

3. The other context present in police work is the local politics that dominates the perception of police work by the community. Police work is public work in which neighbors, friends, other police, and the media can watch officers' behavior. In this difficult context, the police must do their job.

All of these issues influence an officer's ability and desire to work with the unique problems of children. Again, we return to the image of the police officer helping the kitten down from the tree while the youngster looks on admiringly. Any of the police officers described here would want to be seen as heroes to these young children.

Working with children requires that police engage in activities that maintain order, provide service, and catch the bad guys. In settings involving children, police face challenges to the law and to their own personal beliefs. As officers confront peacekeeping, community service, and crime-fighting scenarios, children can also play a variety of roles to the police. These roles include victim, witness, and perpetrator.

ISSUES OF POLICE AND CHILDREN

The following review shows how difficult and complicated the relations are between police and children. Police facing children must decide within their functions as crime fighters, service providers, and maintainers of order whether the children are victims, perpetrators, or witnesses. Complicating these structural and interactional roles are the attitudes that police have toward children and toward their own work performance.

Children as Victims

There is a growing recognition that children are as victimized as adults, leading to a multitude of serious, long-term problems (Finkelhor & Dziuba–Leatherman, 1994). For example, violence toward children is not limited by a definition of physical harm, but by their life circumstances. Police often are called to the scene in the case of suspected child abuse or neglect. Presently, the nonaccidental physical harm to children by their caretakers ranks as a major part of the violence children experience in our culture today (Tower, 1989).

Also, law enforcement must deal with children who have been victims of sexual assault. As with other forms of family maltreatment, an exact rate for the incidence of child sexual assault is almost impossible to determine. Overwhelmingly, the majority of the perpetrators of sexual assault on both daughters and sons are men (Russell, 1986; Herman,

1981). Russell (1986) found that 1 out of 43 girls (i.e., 2.3%) who lived with their biological fathers had been sexually abused. For girls who lived with their stepfathers, the rate was 1 in 6 (16.7%).

Police Response to Child Victimization

Research has shown that police attitudes toward child victims are basically shaped by the same factors that they use to respond to other matters. It depends on whether they determine these incidents to be peacekeeping or crime fighting events (Gelles & Straus, 1988; Erez & Tonotodanto, 1989). In terms of arrest, it seems that police use the same decision-making strategies for arrests as they do in general. For example, Erez and Tonotodanto (1989) found that of most importance to law enforcement were those incidents that they classify as serious ones, indicating some severe form of physical abuse, including weapon use.

Another way to examine the relationship between police and children is to compare how the police react to child abuse situations as compared to other agencies involved with children. Shireman, Miller, and Brown (1981) found that police were more likely to remove the child from the home than child welfare workers. Shireman et al. stated that children placed in emergency situations tend to remain in placement; children left at home tend to remain at home, without the provision of intensive services. Comparing police response to that of other agency workers (child welfare and community mental health) shows that police favor punishment, whereas child welfare workers and mental health therapists believe that treatment is a better method for handling child abuse perpetrators (Trute, Adkins, & MacDonald, 1992b; Wilk & McCarthy, 1986).

In cases of child abuse and child sexual abuse, police appear to take a position in line with their training and socialization (Shireman, Miller, & Brown, 1981; Trute et al., 1996). Discretion, however, appears to play a part in their determination of whether the child abuse is a crime or merely a domestic dispute. In the Erez and Tontodanto (1989) study, the police classified many of the reports that involved physical force and, in some cases, criminal weapons as domestic disputes. Domestic violence is often the link between order-maintenance functions of the police and the crime-fighting functions. When incidents of domestic violence are considered domestic disputes, they are often viewed by police as order-maintenance rather crime-fighting activities.

Children as Witnesses

When children are not the victims or the perpetrators, they are often the witnesses of violence. Children most commonly witness violence in the home. The number of children, reported in several studies, who are involved in domestic violence situations is staggering. Carlson (1984) states that approximately 3.3 million children witness their parents' interpersonal violence toward each other. Steinman (1989) found that children are present during almost half of all battering incidents. Goodman and Rosenberg (1987) showed that when children are present in the home, they actually witness or are aware of nearly all such violent episodes. Other studies have shown that in homes where domestic violence occurs, the children are aware of the violence (Dobash & Dobash, 1979; Pagelow, 1981, 1990; Geffner & Pagelow, 1990).

Although there is not much literature about how police react to children in domestic violence situations, there has been a growing controversy about the ways in which police react and act in such situations (see Chapter 10 in this volume for further discussion). The effects of proarrest and mandatory arrest policies have not been fully explored. However, one of the consequences of mandatory arrest has been dual arrest, in which both adults involved are arrested. The fate of the children present in the home remains an issue for providing appropriate services, the implementation of public policy, and the need for future research (Osofsky, 1995; Groves, Zuckerman, Marans, & Cohen, 1993).

Children also witness crimes, especially violent crimes, in their neighborhoods and streets. Police know that children may be witnesses to criminal acts—they see someone shot, a store robbed, and sometimes someone dies as they walk home from school or play in their neighborhood. Children witness community violence in many neighborhoods throughout this country (see Osofsky, Wewers, Hann, & Fick, 1993; Garbarino, 1992). Violence in some neighborhoods has reached, in public health terms, epidemic proportions (Prothrow-Stith, 1991; Schubiner, Scott, & Tzelepis, 1993). The rate of homicide, for example, of African American males aged 15–24 is 85 per 100,000; comparable homicide rates exist only in some Third World countries (Reiss & Roth, 1993; Cooley, Turner, & Beidel, 1993). The Bell and Jenkins (1993) study of children in one Chicago neighborhood estimated that one-third of all school-age children in this neighborhood had witnessed a homicide, and two-thirds of all school-age children had witnessed a serious assault.

Children as Perpetrators

Police must respond to children as possible perpetrators of a variety of crimes. Children are not only witnesses and victims of violence, but also perpetrators or alleged perpetrators. One category of children who are sometimes perpetrators and sometimes victims is runaway children. Runaways, as young as age 10, can often be both victims of crime and perpetrators of criminal activity. Maxson, Little, and Klein (1988) classed runaways into four categories of youth, which may help us understand the police role. The four categories are (1) "self-emancipated minors" who leave home (or placement) with a self-image of competence to handle their lives independently; (2) "forced-emancipation minors" who leave home (or placement) with a self-image of competence, but principally because they feel their parents are failing to enact their roles appropriately; (3) "parented children" who acknowledge their need for parenting and the competence of their parents (the runaway episode is a temporary departure from their accepted status); and (4) "victimized children" who acknowledge their need for parenting but find their parents failing their role obligations. Maxson et al. (1988) demonstrated that police view these runaways from a law enforcement perspective. Police classify youth in terms of risk to self and community, community characteristics, and dispositional options available. Runaways and missing children are not all the same; police are often concerned about discerning runaway and missing children as perpetrators or victims.

Some children are involved in criminal activity, and police must arrest them as part of their crime fighting function. Research using both official data and self-reports to measure juvenile delinquency shows that the teenage crime *rate* has remained stable since at least 1975 (Empey & Stafford, 1991; Osgood, O'Malley, Bachman, & Johnston, 1989; Sarri, 1983; Siegel & Senna, 1991). According to Siegel and Senna (1991, p. 32), "The total number of juveniles arrested by police has declined for more than a decade, and the percentage of crimes cleared in which a juvenile was arrested has undergone a similar decline." Of course, the total number of adolescents in the population has also decreased. Thus, the arrest rate for adolescents has remained stable (Cook & Laub, 1986; Siegel & Senna, 1991). In addition, the percentage of youths involved in crimes has been stable (Cook & Laub, 1986). Blumstein (1995), however, notes that this trend may be ending, and future cohorts of youngsters may prove not only more likely to engage in criminal activity, but also in violent activities.

Consequently, when a police officer encounters a young person, he must have the skills to interpret the young person's behavior and to assess his own most effective role. Community policing may provide the most reliable set of skills for working with children and young people.

COMMUNITY POLICING

Working in a community policing framework may be the best way to have the flexibility and creativity to work with children. In the last decade, community policing has emerged as a major style of policing strategy. Yet, community policing is often an ambiguous description of police strategy, and the effects of community policing on reducing the level of crime are uncertain.

The Bureau of Justice Assistance (BJA) Community Policing Framework (1994) outlines the "core components" of community policing as the development of community partnership and problem solving. Community policing demands a relationship with the community that is built on the positive contact between patrol officers and community members. The outcome of this positive interaction is the development of trust between law enforcement and the community. The building stones of this mutual trust are the actions and reactions of law enforcement and the community.

The second core concept to community policing is problem solving, defined as structured policy process designed to reduce crime. "Underlying conditions create problems. These conditions might include the characteristics of the people involved (offenders, potential victims and others), the social setting in which these people interact, the physical environments, and the way the public deals with these conditions" (Eck & Spelman, 1987, p. xvi).

According to the BJA framework (1994), there are as many solutions as there are problems. "The solutions range from simple, inexpensive measures to complex, long-term answers that will require significant investment of staff and resources. Problem solving is limited only by the imagination, creativity, perseverance and enthusiasm of specific concerns of each community" (p. 20).

Community policing also requires that the community become involved in policing and public order in a new way. Goldstein (1993, p. 2) states that "communities must debate the issues in policing that includes the refinement of the authority granted to the police; recognize the discretion exercised by the police and provide a means for its review and control; and provide the police with the resources that will enable them to get their job done." As relationships are built between community and law enforcement, the community must decide which safety and order strategies are to be employed.

POLICE OFFICERS' ATTITUDES AND BELIEFS

Before community policing can be considered as a viable alternative, the attitudes of police toward their present work conditions and their beliefs about the community and the residents they are to serve must be understood. This information was made available through the Violence Intervention Project for Children and Families (VIP; see Osofsky, Chapter 12, and Fick, Osofsky, & Lewis, Chapter 13, this volume).

Needs Assessment

In the survey conducted by VIP, four aspects of police officers' jobs were examined: their perceptions of the degree of violence in the district, their beliefs about their role at a homicide scene, ways in which they believe they can assist children and families in coping with violence, and their suggestions as to how to improve the relationship between police and the community served. This information was obtained via open-ended, objective questions.

To ascertain how serious a problem police officers' perceived community violence to be in the district they served, they were asked, "How much of a problem is violence in your district?" The response categories were: *Not much of a problem, Somewhat of a problem, A serious problem,* and *A crisis.*

The second issue of interest was the officers' beliefs about their roles at a homicide scene. The officers were queried about five aspects of their roles: (1) their key responsibilities; (2) the barriers that prevent them from effectively carrying out these responsibilities; (3) the officers' perceptions of the expectations that homicide victims' friends and family have of police officers at a homicide scene; (4) the officers' perceptions of the expectations that community residents have of police officers at a homicide scene; and (5) the officers' ideas about what they would do if they saw a mother and child looking at the body of a homicide victim.

The third aspect assessed was the officers' ideas about how to assist children and families in dealing with violence in their neighborhoods Specifically, the officers were queried concerning the programs they would like the department to undertake and things they had personally done to assist children and families.

The fourth aspect explored in the present analysis was the police officers' ideas about ways to improve police–community relations. They were questioned about the problems between community residents and police of which they were personally aware, programs they would like the department to implement, and things they had personally done to build better relations with the public.

Background and Work-Related Factors

In order to further our understanding of police officers' ideas about their work, a series of exploratory analyses were conducted to determine if their beliefs and attitudes varied according to (1) the officers' backgrounds (sociodemographic factors); (2) their perceptions of the public's trust (children and community residents); and (3) job satisfaction, including satisfaction with their work and supervisor. Chi-square analyses were conducted examining the relationship between the officers' attitudes and beliefs, and the background and work-related factors delineated in this section.

Sociodemographic factors used to describe the officers' backgrounds included age, marital status, rank, years on the force, education completed, and ethnicity. The second set of variables explored in this analysis concerned the officers' perceptions of the public's trust of police. Two questions were used: "How much do you think children trust the police?" and "How much do you think community residents trust the police?" Responses for these questions ranged from *Not at all* to *A lot* (5-point Likert scale).

The third set of variables dealt with the officers' job satisfaction. To measure their satisfaction with support they receive, the officers were asked how satisfied they were with the support provided by their work in general and by their supervisor specifically. Response options ranged from *Very unsatisfied* to *Very satisfied* (5-point Likert scale). Given the inherent difficulty in thoroughly measuring the officers' working conditions, district assignment was used as a proxy. The districts were divided into three categories: (1) assignment to one of the two districts with extremely high rates of violence; (2) assignment to a "normal" district (i.e., one of the other six districts with lower homicide and violence rates); and (3) special assignments (e.g., SWAT team).

Results

Findings from this exploratory analyses suggest several relationships that have implications for community policing and issues involving children.

First, it was found that district assignment was not done randomly—several background factors were significantly related to the officers' district assignment. Second, the officers' views of the degree of violence in their district differed by objective working conditions (i.e., district assignment), perceptions of trust from the people they protect and serve, and job satisfaction. Third, the officers were apparently well-trained concerning their role at a homicide scene. Despite the use of open-ended items to measure aspects of this role, the officers' answers were quite uniform. Fourth, as occurred with the role at a homicide scene, the officers' replies concerning ways to help children and families cope with violence in their neighborhoods were very consistent. Only two background factors (ethnicity and experience) and two job satisfaction measures were significantly related to the officers' ideas concerning how to assist children and families. Fifth, in contrast with the responses concerning the role at a homicide scene and methods to aid children and families, the results concerning police–community relations showed that several factors affect the officers' answers, including background factors, perceptions of trust, and job satisfaction. Each of these five results will now be discussed in the order presented.

District Assignment

Given the potential importance of the working conditions (as measured by the district in which the officers work) and the officers' experience, it was necessary to determine if the demographics of the officers differed significantly across the three district categories (special district, normal district, or violent district). As Table 15.1 shows, marital status, age, rank, years on the force (experience), and ethnicity differed significantly across the three district groupings. Table 15.2 also shows a significant

TABLE 15.1. Sample Demographics by District

| Demographic characteristics | District type[a] | | | |
	Violent district (*n* = 97–101) %F	Special district (*n* = 36–38) %F	Other (*n* = 177–184) %F	Chi-square
Marital status				16.49
Married, cohabitating	54	74	67	
Divorced, separated	15	18	20	
Never married	31	8	13	
Age				20.60
19–30	45	34	31	
31–38	37	37	25	
39–67	18	29	44	
Rank				15.59
PO I	47	24	36	
PO II–PO IV	41	63	39	
Sergeant and above	11	13	25	
Years on NOPD				22.59
≤4	43	18	27	
5–13	40	47	31	
14–43	18	34	43	
Ethnicity				40.71
African American	69	27	31	
White	25	56	58	
Other	6	14	10	

[a] Ranges for sample sizes (*n*) are included; this range reflects variability in total number of cases available for analysis due to incomplete and missing data.

TABLE 15.2. Officers' Perceptions of Violence, Trust, and Expectations Compared to District

	District type			
	Violent district (*n* = 86–103) %F	Special district (*n* = 26–37) %F	Other (*n* = 155–191) %F	Chi-square
How much do you think community residents trust the police?				16.49
None or low	32	44	34	
Moderate	64	44	51	
High	4	11	15	
How much of a problem is violence in your district?				73.24
Not much of a problem	3	5	9	
Somewhat of a problem	2	5	35	
Serious problem	47	49	41	
Crisis	49	41	15	
What do you believe people directly involved with the victim of a homicide expect of a police officer at the scene of a homicide?				107.17
Collect evidence	2	54	52	
Get ambulance, save victim	49	4	5	
Show compassion	31	23	20	
Other	17	19	23	

difference in perceived trust of community residents. In summary, the findings shown in Tables 15.1 and 15.2 indicate that the youngest, lowest ranking, least experienced officers with the lowest perceptions of trust by residents work in the two most violent districts. In addition, the most violent districts had a significantly higher proportion of African American officers than did the other districts.

A tentative explanation of this finding may be that at the time the survey was conducted, one of the two districts included in the violent grouping was a training district. Reassignment of officers may be needed to place older, more experienced officers who perceive greater trust from residents in the two most violent districts in greater need of community policing. Such a strategy should prove to be beneficial for community policing and working with children. In fact, the police force in this study has undergone significant reorganization.

Degree of Violence

The degree of violence officers perceive in their districts was also significantly related to the district in which they worked (Table 15.2). Almost half of the officers assigned to the two most violent districts considered violence to be a crisis in their district. Although a large proportion of officers in the special assignment district also perceived violence to be a crisis, a larger proportion of these officers perceived it more as a serious problem. Most of the officers in the other districts perceived violence to be a serious problem or somewhat of a problem; only a small proportion of these officers considered violence in their district to be a crisis.

Additional analyses indicate that perceived violence may be related to the police officers' satisfaction with their supervisor, and their perception of the trust residents place in the officers. Regardless of satisfaction, the most frequent answer was that violence is a serious problem; yet the percentage of officers who felt violence was a serious problem or a crisis decreased as satisfaction increased (Table 15.3). In a similar way, as the amount of trust officers felt they received from community residents increased, the perceived degree of violence in their district decreased (Table 15.4).

The results suggest that the officers' perceptions of violence in their districts depended not only on the objective level of violence, but also on their subjective appraisal of resources available to carry out their roles as police officers. These resources included those from the department, as evidenced by satisfaction with supervisor support, and those from the community, particularly the public's trust.

The Role of Police Officers at a Homicide Scene

In general, the officers were quite uniform in their responses to the five questions concerning their roles: (1) key responsibilities, (2) barriers to carrying out their roles, (3) community residents' expectations of officers, (4) expectations that friends and family members of the victim have of

TABLE 15.3. Effects of Satisfaction with Supervisor on Police Officers' Perceptions of Violence

	Satisfaction with supervisor				
	Unsatisfied ($n = 38$) %F	Neither ($n = 49$) %F	Satisfied ($n = 109$) %F	Very satisfied ($n = 92$)	Chi-square
How much of a problem is violence in your district?					18.39
Not much of a problem	0	2	6	13	
Somewhat of a problem	11	22	21	26	
Serious problem	61	51	40	35	
Crisis	29	24	32	26	

TABLE 15.4. Officers' Perceptions of Violence, Barriers in Carrying Out Their Roles, Problems, and Community Residents' Expectations Compared to Perceived Trust from Community Residents

	Perceived trust by residents			
	None/low ($n = 71$) %F	Moderate ($n = 187$) %F	High ($n = 60$) %F	Chi-square
How much of a problem is violence in your district?				15.05
Not much of a problem	5	8	8	
Somewhat of a problem	14	23	39	
Serious problem	45	44	36	
Crisis	37	26	17	
What barriers prevent you from carrying out your responsibilities as a police officer effectively at the scene of a homicide?				20.27
No cooperation	30	28	6	
Spectators at the scene	22	24	24	
Inadequate resources	15	14	9	
Other	29	23	35	
None	4	11	26	
What do community residents expect a police officer to do with children at a homicide scene?				12.29
Keep crowd, children away from scene	41	50	55	
Actively help people (e.g., counsel, comfort)	8	21	18	
None	51	29	27	
What problems do you know about between police and community residents?				24.89
Media image/bad reputation	6	10	13	
Blame residents	25	17	16	
Lack of trust/ community relations	57	56	25	
Other	9	11	31	
None	3	6	16	

police officers, and (5) actions officers should take when mothers and children are on the scene.

Key Responsibilities. The officers' perceptions of their key responsibilities were unrelated to any background or work-related factors. Approximately 46% of the officers responded that their main responsibility was to protect and serve. Other frequent responses included answer calls

(8%), prevent crimes (7%), enforce laws and protect partner and self (7%), and patrol (6%).

Barriers. The officers' perceived that barriers preventing them from carrying out their duties at a homicide scene were significantly related to two factors—ethnicity and perceived trust from residents (Table 15.5). The modal answer for white officers was lack of cooperation from witnesses. The modal answer for African American officers was *other;* the individual responses included the following: interference in the investigation by friends and family, family grief, family and friends wanting revenge, and relationship with the public and the department. Perceived barriers also differed by perceived trust in police by residents. Those officers who perceived lower levels of trust (*None/low* or *Some trust*) most commonly said that lack of cooperation by witnesses was the main barrier, whereas those who perceived a high degree of trust gave other reasons (Table 15.4).

Expectations of Community Residents. The police officers' beliefs about what community residents expected them to do with children at

TABLE 15.5. Barriers and Expectations in Carrying out Role Compared to Officers' Ethnicity

| | Officers' ethnicity | | | |
	African American (n = 101–104) %F	White (n = 134–153) %F	Other (n = 22) %F	Chi-square
What barriers prevent you from carrying out your responsibilities as a police officer effectively at the scene of a homicide?				22.01
No cooperation	19	30	32	
Spectators at the scene	27	23	5	
Inadequate resources	8	16	27	
Other	35	19	36	
None	12	13	9	
What do you believe people directly involved with the victim of a homicide expect of a police officer at the scene of a homicide?				11.09
Collect evidence	31	41		
Get ambulance, save victim	29	12		
Show compassion	21	24		
Other	19	22		

a homicide scene varied significantly depending on perceived trust by residents (see Table 15.4). Officers who perceived little or no trust by residents tended to answer that the community residents have no expectations, whereas those who perceived some or high amounts of trust stated that officers were expected to keep children and crowds away from the scene.

Expectations of Friends and Family. The officers' beliefs about what friends and family members of a homicide victim expected from them varied significantly by four variables: district in which they worked, ethnicity, age, and experience of the officer.

The district in which the officers worked was significantly related to their perceptions of friends' and family members' expectations (Table 15.2). Almost 50% of the officers in the two most violent districts said they were expected to get an ambulance and save the victim's life, whereas approximately 50% of the officers in the special districts and in relatively lower violence districts stated they were expected to collect evidence.

These data suggests that the immediate imperative of officers in the most violent districts may be a reflection of the frequency with which they deal with homicide victims; that is, collecting evidence may take a secondary role.

Ethnicity was also significantly related to perceived expectations of friends and family members (Table 15.5). The most common answer for both African American and white officers was to collect evidence. In addition, two answers were almost equally frequent for African American officers—collect evidence, and get an ambulance and save the victim's life. For the white officers, the second most common answer was to show compassion, which included covering the body and showing respect for the dead.

As Table 15.6 shows, the youngest officers seemed less clear about what friends and families expected from them, in that almost equal numbers said they were expected to show compassion, get an ambulance and save the victim's life, and collect evidence. The older two groups showed more agreement about the expectations—collect evidence was, overwhelmingly, the most common answer, especially among the oldest group of officers.

Experience as an officer was also significantly associated with the officers' perceptions of friends and family members' expectations (Table 15.7). Less experienced officers stated that they were expected to get an ambulance and save the victim's life, whereas more experienced officers said they were expected to collect evidence.

Mother and Child at the Scene. The officers' responses concerning what they should do if they saw a mother and child looking at the body at a homicide scene varied by the age of the officer (Table 15.6). The most common response was the same for all three age groups—move them away/keep them behind the barricade; however, the percentage of officers who said this was lower in the oldest group. A greater proportion of the older officers stated that they would ask them for information, and almost one-third of the youngest officers replied that they would do nothing. In contrast, more of the officers in the middle-aged category stated they would talk with and console the mother and child.

In summary, the police officers' responses concerning their role at a homicide scene did not vary much by the officers' backgrounds, their job satisfaction, or their perceptions of trust. The few significant differences that were found were related to background factors, especially ethnicity and age, and perceptions of trust from residents. These results imply that officers' training concerning their role at a homicide scene produced a consistent view of this role, consistent with the crime fighting nature of their job.

Coping with Interpersonal Violence

Two items tapped the officers' views about ways to assist children and families in coping with violence: (1) programs that they would like to

TABLE 15.6. Actions and Expectations Compared to Age of Officer

	Age of officer			
	19–30 years (n = 91–92)	31–38 years (n = 75–78)	39–67 years (n = 85–88)	Chi-square
You see a mother and child standing around looking at the body at a homicide scene.				
What do you do?				23.40
Ask them for information	5	7	20	
Move them away	52	52	42	
Talk to them/console them	9	16	8	
Other	4	5	8	
None	30	20	22	
What do you wish you could do?				18.54
Collect evidence	28	33	51	
Get ambulance/save victim	25	15	16	
Show compassion	30	22	15	
Be professional	7	15	11	
Other	10	14	7	

see the department implement; and (2) actions the officers themselves had undertaken to assist children and families exposed to violence.

Programs Officers Would Like to See. The officers' replies to the question concerning programs they would like the department to implement were related to two variables, ethnicity and work satisfaction. The most common answer for both African American and white officers was education and counseling programs (40% and 32%, respectively). Almost one-third of African American officers (30%) suggested the need for the police department to implement programs that would improve community relations, such as increasing police–community communication and having community-based centers and activities; only 12% of the white officers gave similar responses. But almost one-third of the white officers (31%) felt that the department was not responsible to assist children and families in coping with violence; only 10% of the African American officers answered similarly.

Actions Officers Have Taken. Initiatives by officers themselves to assist children and families exposed to violence were associated with satisfaction with their supervisor and years of experience. The most frequent answers varied according to satisfaction with supervisor (Table 15.3). In general, officers who were more satisfied with their supervisor reported interacting more with children and families exposed to violence. Very satisfied officers stated that they tried to talk to the children and families, and refer them to counseling agencies; satisfied officers reported that they attempted to console and sympathize with the children and families. But, officers who were dissatisfied or neither satisfied nor dissatisfied claimed they had not undertaken any efforts. Experience was also related to the actions undertaken. A larger proportion of the officers with a moderate amount of experience (5–13 years) reported they had not done anything (Table 15.7).

Very few variables were related to the officers' answers concerning ways to help families and children exposed to violence. Analogous to their replies concerning their role at a homicide scene, the officers' answers about helping families and children cope with violence were uniform. However, the officers' responses to questions about police–community relations varied more than those concerning their role at a homicide scene and helping children and families cope with violence, as will be shown in the next section.

Relationships with the Public

Three questions tapped the officers' beliefs about police–community relations: (1) What problems do you know of that occur between police

TABLE 15.7. Efforts, Expectations, and Actions Reported by Officers Compared to Years on NOPD

	Years on NOPD			
	≥5 years (n = 62–77)	5–13 years (n = 79–93)	Over 13 years (n = 69–88)	Chi-square
What efforts has your department made to build better community relations?				16.92
PALS/athletics/ NOPD band	16	19	29	
Substations/foot patrol/prevent crime	6	13	7	
Community relations programs	13	16	27	
Other	31	18	15	
None	34	35	22	
What do friends and family members of a homicide victim expect of a police officer at the scene of a homicide?				20.44
Collect evidence	22	37	51	
Get ambulance/save victim	27	18	13	
Show compassion	22	28	17	
Be professional	13	11	9	
Other	16	6	10	
Child and mother around a homicide scene, what do you do?				19.37
Counsel/refer to counseling	26	22	10	
Console/show sympathy	29	16	29	
Fulfill role as police officer	21	18	19	
Other	6	10	10	
None	2	8	16	
	16	27	16	

and community residents? (2) What efforts have your department made to build better relations? and (3) How have you tried to build respect for the police among residents in your district?

The majority of officers (54% African American, 52% white) reported lack of trust and poor community relations to be a problem between the police and community residents. Other problems cited varied by ethnicity. A greater percentage of white officers (14%) than African American officers (1%) stated the problems were due to the bad reputation police officers get from the media. However, more African American officers (24%) than white officers (15%) blamed the residents (e.g., "Residents are ungrateful," "They do not understand police procedures," "They have unrealistic expectations," and "They hate police").

Departmental Efforts. Officers' reports of things the police department had done to build better relationships with the community varied significantly across ethnicity, work satisfaction, and experience. Over one-third of the white officers (35%) stated their department had not done anything, compared to 22% of the African American officers. A greater proportion of the African American officers (33%) cited programs such as Drug Abuse Resistance Education (DARE) and increased racial sensitivity training, compared to 12% of the white officers.

Departmental actions reported also varied by work satisfaction. The most satisfied officers (32%) were more likely to identify programs designed to improve community relations, whereas a greater proportion of the least satisfied (47%) reported their department had not done anything. The results by experience were similar; the most experienced officers were more likely to comment on projects that had been tried, whereas the least experienced officers and those with a moderate amount of experience (34% and 35%, respectively) responded that no actions had been taken. A greater proportion of the more experienced officers mentioned programs such as the Police Athletic Leagues (PAL) (29%), and a similar number cited other programs to enhance community relations (27%).

Officers' Efforts. Actions the officers reported they had taken to build respect for police among the residents in their districts were significantly related to rank. The most common answer for the lowest (Police Officer I) and highest (sergeant or higher) ranked officers was treating people with respect, equally and fairly (33% and 39%, respectively). Officers in the middle ranks (Police Officers II through IV) most often said they talk and communicate with citizens (34%).

In summary, the officers' replies concerning police–community relations were diverse. The answers were related to the officers' backgrounds, job satisfaction, and perceptions of trust received from the people they protect and serve.

IMPLICATIONS FOR PROMOTION OF COMMUNITY POLICING EFFORTS WITH CHILDREN

Although the analyses reported in this chapter are exploratory in nature, some of the findings have important implications for community policing and police officers' work with children. Officers with the highest levels of experience, perceived trust, and job satisfaction are more likely to be successful in achieving one of the goals of community policing—to better serve the residents by developing rapport with them and their children. Yet, the results show that at the time of the survey the officers in the two most violent districts were often younger, less experienced, and perceived less trust by the public they serve.

The importance of experience for community policing is highlighted by the following findings. First, more experienced officers showed more confidence about their role—their answers displayed less diversity. Second, experienced officers were more certain about the expectations of police officers held by the victims' friends and family, and they were more likely than other officers to claim that they were expected to collect evidence. Third, more experienced officers were more likely to counsel families and children, and refer them to counseling to help them to deal with violence in their neighborhoods. Fourth, more experienced officers were more likely to mention actions the department had taken to build relationships between the community and the police.

Officers with the highest levels of perceived trust from residents and children should also be recruited for community policing, because these officers showed signs of being less distant from residents and children. First, officers with higher degrees of perceived trust were less likely to view residents as a barrier to performing their role at a homicide scene. Second, these officers were able to name more of the residents' expectations of police at a homicide scene. Third, they were less likely to blame residents for problems between the police and the community. Fourth, they were able to mention more actions taken by the department to build police and community relationships.

Officers with the highest levels of satisfaction are also more desirable for community policing. These officers were more willing to go beyond the obvious requirements of their roles as police officers; they mentioned more actions that they personally had taken and more actions that the department should undertake. Officers with higher degrees of satisfaction mentioned more programs that the department should undertake to assist children and families to cope with violence. In addition, they took more actions to help children and families deal with violence. Finally, they reported more things that the department had done to build the relationship between the community and police.

Both younger and older officers are needed in community policing programs. As the findings suggest, younger officers are desirable, because they may be more compassionate toward community residents. Younger officers were more likely to claim that the friends and family of the homicide victim expected the police to show compassion, and they were more likely to move a mother and child away from a homicide scene. Older officers are important also, because they felt that the friends and family expect officers to collect evidence, and they were more likely to mention programs the department had undertaken to build relationships between the police and the community.

Findings suggest that community policing programs should have teams consisting of both African American and white officers. The data indicate that white officers were less likely to view people as a barrier to completing their job at a homicide scene. In addition, although both white and African American officers claimed that the problems between the police and the community were due to issues of trust, white officers were more likely to blame the media for the problems, whereas African American officers were more likely to blame the residents. African American officers showed the following strengths: First, although both African American and white officers felt that the department should undertake education and counseling to help children and families deal with violence, African American officers were more likely to mention the use of community programs as well, whereas white officers were more likely to claim that the department was not responsible for helping children and families. Second, African American officers mentioned actions the department had taken to build police–community relations more frequently than white officers.

As with any other police problems, children present a unique set of problems and a unique set of solutions. There is not an essential child situation, nor an essential police response to the problems children represent. As this chapter describes, several issues about policing require a new attitude toward children. The national community policing initiative may hold answers for more effective work with children in the future. In order to problem-solve effectively about issues involving children, police need to understand the variety of ways in which they encounter children in their work life, and the potential impact that these encounters may have on the children. Building community partnerships requires that police and neighborhoods work toward creating mutual trust, the other essential ingredient for community policing. Issues of children's safety may, in fact, provide the link between the community and the police.

REFERENCES

Albanese, J. S. (1993). *Dealing with delinquency: The future of juvenile justice* (2nd ed.). Chicago: Nelson-Hall.
Bell, C., & Jenkins, E. (1993). Community violence and children in Chicago. *Psychiatry, 56,* 46–54.

Bittner, E. (1995). The quasi-military organization of the police. In V. E. Kappeler, *The police and society: Touchstone readings* (pp. 173–183). Prospect Heights, IL: Waveland Press.

Blumstein, A. (1995, August). Violence by young people: Why the deadly nexus? *National Institute of Justice Journal, 229,* 2–9.

Brooks, L. (1989). Police discretionary behavior: A study of style. In R. G. Dunham & G. P. Alpert (Eds.), *Critical issues in policing: Contemporary readings* (pp. 146–161). Prospect Heights, IL: Waveland Press.

Bureau of Justice Assistance. (1994, August). *Understanding community policing: A framework for action* [Monograph]. Washington, DC: U.S. Department of Justice.

Carlson, B. E. (1984) Children's observations of interpersonal violence. In A. R. Roberts (Ed.), *Battered women and their families: Intervention strategies and treatment programs* (pp. 147–167). New York: Springer.

Cooley, M. R., Turner, S., & Beidel, D. (1993). Assessing community violence: The children's report of exposure to violence. *Journal of the American Academy of Child Adolescent Psychiatry, 34*(2), 201–207.

Cook, P., & Laub, J. (1986). The (surprising) stability of youth crime. *Journal of Quantitative Criminology, 2,* 256–277.

Dobash, R. E., & Dobash, R. (1979). *Violence against wives: A case against the patriarchy.* New York: Free Press.

Eck, J. E., & Spelman, W. (1987). Who ya gonna call? The police as problem-busters. *Crime and Delinquency, 33,* 31–52.

Empey, L. T., & Stafford, M. C. (1991). *American delinquency: Its meaning and construction* (3rd ed.). Belmont, CA: Wadsworth.

Erez, E., & Tonotodanto, P. (1989). Patterns of reported parent–child abuse and police response. *Journal of Family Violence, 4*(2), 143.

Finkelhor, D., & Dziuba-Leatherman, J. (1994). Victimization of children. *American Psychologist, 49*(3), 173–183.

Fyfe, J. J. (1989). The split-second syndrome and other determinants of police violence. In R. G. Dunham & G. P. Alpert (Eds.), *Critical issues in policing: Contemporary readings* (pp. 465–480). Prospect Heights, IL: Waveland Press.

Garbarino, J. (1992). *Children in danger: Coping with the consequences of community violence.* San Francisco: Jossey-Bass.

Geffner, R., & Pagelow, M. D. (1990). Mediation and child custody issues in abusive relationships. *Behavioral Sciences and the Law, 8,* 151–159.

Gelles, R. J., & Straus, M. (1988). *Intimate violence: Causes and consequences of abuse in the American family.* New York: Simon & Schuster.

Goldstein, H. (1993). The new policing: Confronting complexity. *National Institute of Justice Research-in-Brief* (NCJ 145157). Washington, DC: U.S. Department of Justice.

Goodman, G. S., & Rosenberg M. S. (1987). The child witness to family violence: Clinical and legal considerations. In D. Sonkin (Ed.), *Domestic violence on trial: Psychological and legal dimension of family violence* (pp. 97–126). New York: Springer.

Groves, B., Zuckerman, B., Marans, S., & Cohen, D. (1993). Silent victims: Children who witness violence. *Journal of the American Medical Association, 269,* 262–264.

Herman, J. L. (1981). *Father–daughter incest.* Cambridge, MA: Harvard University Press.

Manning, P. K. (1995). The police: Mandate, strategies, and appearances. In V. E. Kappeler (Ed.), *The police and society: Touchstone readings* (pp. 97–125). Prospect Heights, IL: Waveland Press.

Maxson, C. L., Little, M. A., & Klein, M. W. (1988). Police response to runaway and missing children: A conceptual framework for research and policy. *Crime and Delinquency, 34*(1), 84–102.

Osgood, D. W., O'Malley, P., Bachman, J., & Johnston, L. (1989). Time trends and age trends in arrests and self-reported illegal behavior. *Criminology, 27,* 389–417.

Osofsky, J. D. (1995). The effects of violence exposure on young children. *American Psychologist, 50,* 782–788.

Osofsky, J. D., Wewers, S., Hann, D. M., & Fick, A. C. (1993). Chronic community violence: What is happening to our children? *Psychiatry, 56,* 36–45.

Pagelow, M. D. (1981). *Women battering: Victims and their experience.* Beverly Hills, CA: Sage.

Pagelow, M. D. (1990). Effects of domestic violence on children and their consequences for custody and visitation agreements. *Mediation Quarterly, 7,* 347–363.

Prothrow-Stith, D. (1991). *Deadly consequences.* New York: HarperCollins.

Reiss, A., & Roth, J. A. (Eds.). (1993). *Understanding and preventing violence.* Washington, DC: National Academy Press.

Russell, D. (1986). *The secret trauma: Incest in the lives of girls and women.* New York: Basic Books.

Sarri, R. (1983). Gender issues in juvenile justice. *Crime and Delinquency, 29,* 381–397.

Scharf, P., & Binder, A. (1983). *The badge and the bullet: Police use of deadly force.* Westport, CT: Praeger.

Schubiner, H., Scott, R., & Tzelepis, A. (1993). Exposure to violence among inner-city youth. *Journal of Adolescent Health, 14,* 214–218.

Shireman, J., Miller, B., & Brown, H. F. (1981). Child welfare workers, police, and child placement. *Child Welfare, 60*(6), 413–422.

Siegel, L. J., & Senna, J. J. (1991). *Juvenile delinquency: Theory, practice, and law* (4th ed.). St. Paul: West Publishing.

Steinman, M. (1989). The effects of police responses on spouse abuse. *American Journal of Police, 8,* 1–19.

Tower, C. C. (1989). *Understanding child abuse and neglect.* Needham, MA: Allyn & Bacon.

Trute, B., Adkins, E., & MacDonald, G. (1996). Professional attitudes regarding treatment and punishment of incest: Comparing police, child welfare, and community mental health. *Journal of Family Violence, 11*(3), 237–249.

Voigt, L., Thornton, W. E., Barrile, L., & Seaman, J. (1994) *Criminology and justice.* New York: McGraw-Hill.

Wilk, R. J., & McCarthy, C. R. (1986). Intervention in child sexual abuse. *Social Casework, 67*(1), 20–26.

16

Prevention and Policy: Directions for the Future

JOY D. OSOFSKY

> *Children need to be safe and secure at home to develop a positive sense of self necessary to their growing into healthy productive, caring adults; children need to be safe in their communities to be able to explore and develop relationships with other people; and children need to be safe at school in order to successfully learn.*
>
> —Position Statement on violence in the lives of children (National Association for the Education of Young Children, 1993, p. 81)

THE PROBLEM OF CHILDREN and youth violence is well recognized by the research, criminal justice, clinical, and policy-making communities as a multifaceted problem requiring complex solutions. Most people agree that to address the problem of children and youth violence, both prevention and criminal justice solutions are needed. Following the horrendous killing in 1995 of a 5-year-old child in Chicago at the hands of two children, ages 10 and 11, who dropped him 14 floors out the window of a public housing development, we have seen some increased concern from all sides about the importance of prevention. For example, a February 8, 1996, headline on *The New York Times* Op-Ed page, instead of citing the now well-known African adage, "It Takes a Whole Village to Raise a Child," read instead, "It Takes a Village to Destroy a Child" (Kotlowitz, 1996). David Hawkins, in a recent *National Institute of Justice Journal* (1995), brings to our attention that while the juvenile justice system has traditionally employed sanctions, treatment, and rehabilitation after the fact to change problem behaviors, it may be time for us to start thinking more about how these young people became criminals; that is, what is the environment like that they grew up in, and couldn't something have been done earlier to prevent the youngsters from becoming criminals?

At the same time as discussions are taking place with increased frequency, not only among social service and mental health professionals but also in the law enforcement and criminal justice arenas, there is considerable disagreement about the relative distribution of the precious few resources available to address this enormous problem. Clearly, creative programs designed and implemented from multidisciplinary perspectives are needed. Grassroots, community-designed and-based prevention programs are crucial to the success of this effort.

There have been several strong, clear voices emphasizing the importance of understanding the current epidemic of violence in the United States as a public health problem requiring multidisciplinary solutions (Bell & Jenkins, 1991; Fingerhut & Kleinman, 1990; Prothrow-Stith, 1991; Rosenberg, 1994). One of the most articulate spokespersons for this approach has been Deborah Prothrow-Stith, who has presented her position most comprehensively in her 1991 book, *Deadly Consequences: How Violence Is Destroying Our Teenage Population and a Plan to Begin Solving the Problem.* Unfortunately, since the publication of her landmark book in 1991, the problem has only grown worse and the main "solutions" undertaken in more than a cursory way have been to build more prisons—the idea being that putting more people in prison will deter crime. In fact, just the opposite has occurred; with the increase in the number of prisons and incarcerations, the crime rate continues to grow, particularly among lower socioeconomic status males, ages 14–25.

Although it is unrealistic to expect prevention programs alone to *solve* the violence problem in the United States, there have been some excellent precedents in this country that have worked to prevent unwanted behaviors in the areas of health and injury prevention. Take, for example, the massive campaigns that have been mounted on many fronts to reduce motor-vehicle injuries. Seat belts were only a part of the strategy (see Cristoffel, Chapter 4, this volume, for a more complete discussion). Motor-vehicle injury control was addressed with a multidisciplinary approach, and deaths from automobile accidents dropped significantly. Furthermore, the practical step of using seat belts to keep adults and children safe has become law. How did this happen? Not only were there improvements in automobile construction, changes in driving laws, and increased penalties for those intoxicated, but also much media attention was given to all aspects of motor-vehicle injury within a public health framework. Advocates using the new knowledge provided by research on this problem worked with automobile manufacturers, the media, law enforcement, and criminal justice to change behavior and priorities in decision making and actions. As James Garbarino stated in a public symposium on violence prevention in 1993:

> For a long period of time, we understood injuries to young children in automobiles as being part of random accidents, senseless events that were accidental, not part of anything systematic. Only when we began to see these events in the lives of children as part of systematic phenomena that had to do with the structure, the technology of cars, the regulations of the use of automobiles, the systematic role of alcohol, only when we began to see it as a social phenomenon, did we have the capacity to move on it as a matter of social policy. We are beginning to see that the daily reports of murders, shootings, stabbings and killings are not simply senseless, random acts, but part of a cultural and social phenomenon within our society." (cited in Osofsky & Fenichel, 1993, pp. 38–39)

Although the problem of injuries to children in automobile accidents has not gone away, it has been greatly reduced. Furthermore, the pictures in the media of humorous drunks weaving down the streets have all but disappeared from television and movie screens. Thus, *social tolerance for this dangerous behavior has disappeared.*

Public policy initiatives have been recommended by many different groups, including among them the American Psychological Association (1993), the Children's Defense Fund (1994), the Carnegie Corporation of New York (1994), the National Research Council (1993; 1996), the American Bar Association (1994), and the U.S. Department of Justice, Office of Juvenile Justice and Delinquency Prevention (Hawkins, 1995). It is crucial at this juncture to recognize that *children cannot wait!* First and foremost, commitment to children within our society is needed. Our children deserve to be safe and feel safe at home and in their neighborhoods. What follows is a compilation of public policy recommendations that are needed to focus attention on the issue and guide program development in an effort to find solutions for the enormous problem of children and youth violence.

CHANGE THE IMAGE OF VIOLENCE

A national campaign is needed involving individuals and advocates from health and mental health fields, law enforcement, criminal justice, and the media to *change the image of violence from one that is acceptable, even admired, to something disdained and considered unacceptable.* A media campaign against violence, similar to those developed to encourage and eventually to enforce seatbelt use for car safety and deter individuals from smoking, should be launched. As Murray stated (Chapter 5, this volume) regarding media violence, it is no longer acceptable for media production and distribution companies to assert that they are merely providing what the public wants. They must recognize the social impact of communication—they are also in the business of education.

EDUCATE THE PUBLIC ABOUT THE EFFECTS OF VIOLENCE ON CHILDREN AND HOW TO PROTECT THEM

An educational campaign should be conducted in multiple sites (including schools, churches, businesses, government, corporations, and through the media) to *inform the public about both the many factors that put young people at risk for the development of violent behaviors* and the protective factors that buffer the effects of exposure to risk. There are models in this area to be followed in developing this educational campaign (see Hawkins, 1995, for examples). *To protect children, provide education and support* to parents, caregivers, educators, law enforcement officials, and health and mental health professionals, and those working in the criminal justice system about (1) the damaging effects on children and youth of witnessing violence, and (2) alternative approaches to violence in resolving conflicts.

DEVELOP COMMUNITY-BASED PREVENTION AND INTERVENTION EFFORTS

Prevention and intervention programs must build on family and community strengths. Not only must we adhere to the adage that "It takes a whole village to raise a child" but also that "It takes a whole village to destroy a child." This approach must be used to build programs designed to prevent violence and to treat its consequences. The communities most affected by the violence must play a central role in developing and planning the programs.

ENCOURAGE AND ENFORCE SANE AND SAFE GUN LAWS AND USAGE

"It is impossible to protect the children and guns equally" (Christoffel, Chapter 4, this volume). Limit access of children and youth to guns, with parents

being held responsible for the firearms in their possession and their availability to children. Education is needed for children and adults regarding the dangers of firearms, especially firearms in the home, and ways to reduce both intentional and unintentional injuries resulting from firearm use.

PROVIDE RESOURCES FOR THERAPEUTIC INTERVENTIONS FOR CHILDREN AND FAMILIES IN ACCESSIBLE SETTINGS

"Children should not be shortchanged!" (Murphy, Pynoos, & James, Chapter 11, this volume). Provide resources for early and accessible therapeutic interventions for children and families traumatized by violence—in schools, community settings, churches. Without the availability of such early intervention programs, the developmental potential of the child may be seriously hampered, which can contribute to the cycle of violence. The experience of violence distorts the values of children.

REFERENCES

American Bar Association. (1994). *Report to the President: The impact of domestic violence on children*. Chicago: American Bar Association.

American Psychological Association Commission on Violence and Youth. (1993). *Violence and youth: Psychology's response* (Vol. 1). Washington, DC: American Psychological Association.

Bell, C. C., & Jenkins, E. J. (1991) Traumatic stress and children. *Journal of Health Care for the Poor and Underserved, 2*, 175–185.

Carnegie Corporation of New York. (1994). *Starting points: Meeting the needs of our youngest children*. New York: Author.

Children's Defense Fund. (1994, October). *Children's Defense Fund and religious leaders launch crusade to protect children against violence* (press release). Washington, DC: Author.

Fingerhut, L. A., & Kleinman, J. C. (1990). International and interstate comparisons of homicide among males. *Journal of the American Medical Association, 265*, 3292–3295.

Hawkins, J. D. (1995). Controlling crime before it happens: Risk-focused prevention. *National Institute of Juvenile Justice, 229*, 10–18.

Kotlowitz, A. (1996, February 8). It takes a village to destroy a child. *New York Times*, p. A19.

National Association for the Education of Young Children. (1993). Position Statement on violence in the lives of children. *Young Children* (September), 80–84.

National Research Council. (1993). *Understanding child abuse and neglect*. Washington, DC: National Academy Press.

National Research Council. (in press). *Assessment of family violence interventions*. Washington, DC: National Academy Press.

Osofsky, J. D., & Fenichel, E. (1993). Call for Violence Prevention and Intervention on behalf of very young children. In J. D. Osofsky & E. Fenichel (Eds.), *Hurt, healing and hope: Caring for infants and toddlers in violent environments*. Arlington, VA: Zero to Three/National Center for Clinical Infant Programs.

Prothrow-Stith, D. (1991). *Deadly consequences: How violence is destroying our teenage population and a plan to begin solving the problem*. New York: HarperCollins.

Rosenberg, M. L. (1994, January). *Violence prevention: Integrating public health and criminal justice*. Presentation at the U.S. Attorney's Conference, Washington, DC.

Index

329